LAST

SOUL EATER

SOUL EATER

25

ATSUSHI OHKUBO

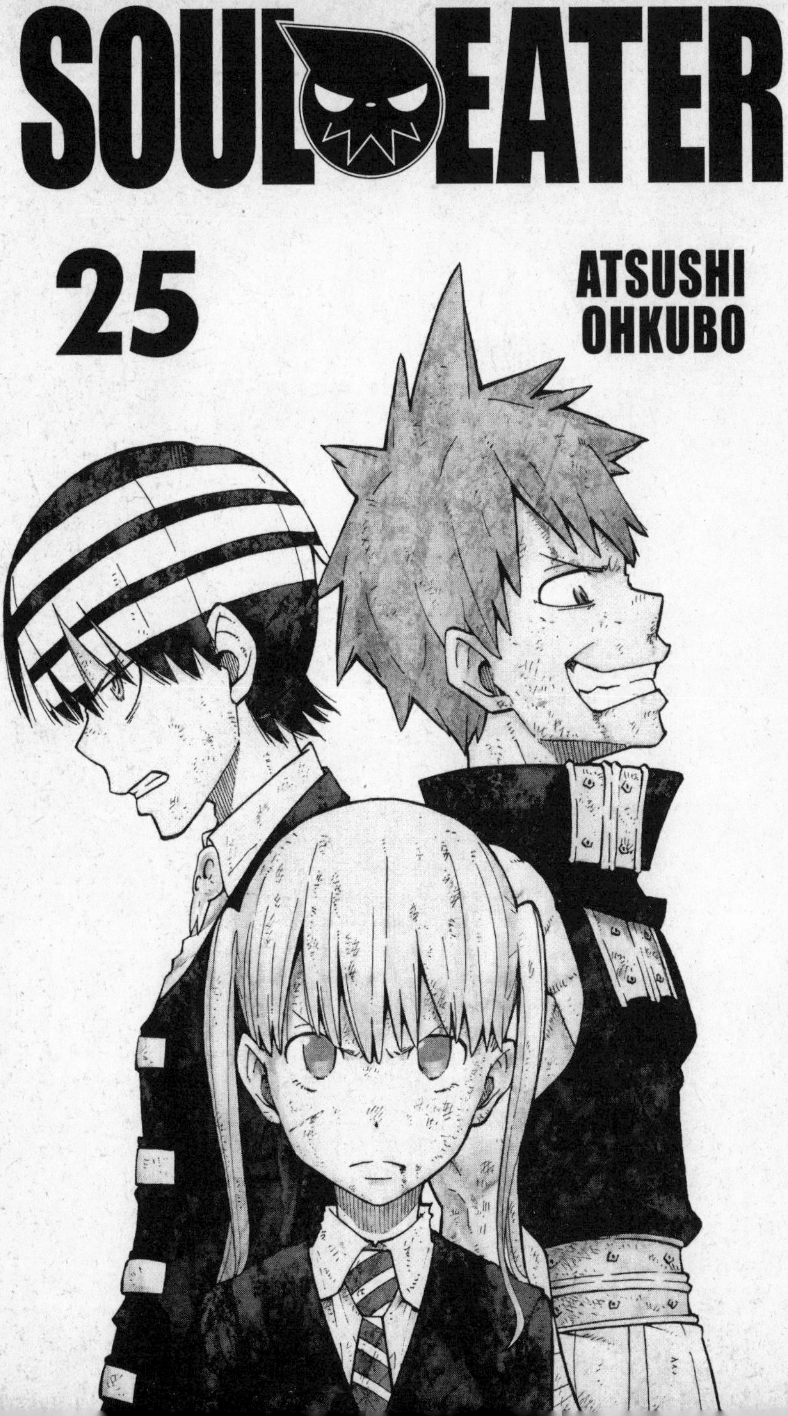

SOUL EATER

vol. 25

by ATSUSHI OHKUBO

The LAST
symphony of
SOUL EATER

SOUL EATER 25

CONTENTS

A SOUND
SOUL...

...DWELLS IN A
SOUND MIND

AND A
SOUND BODY.

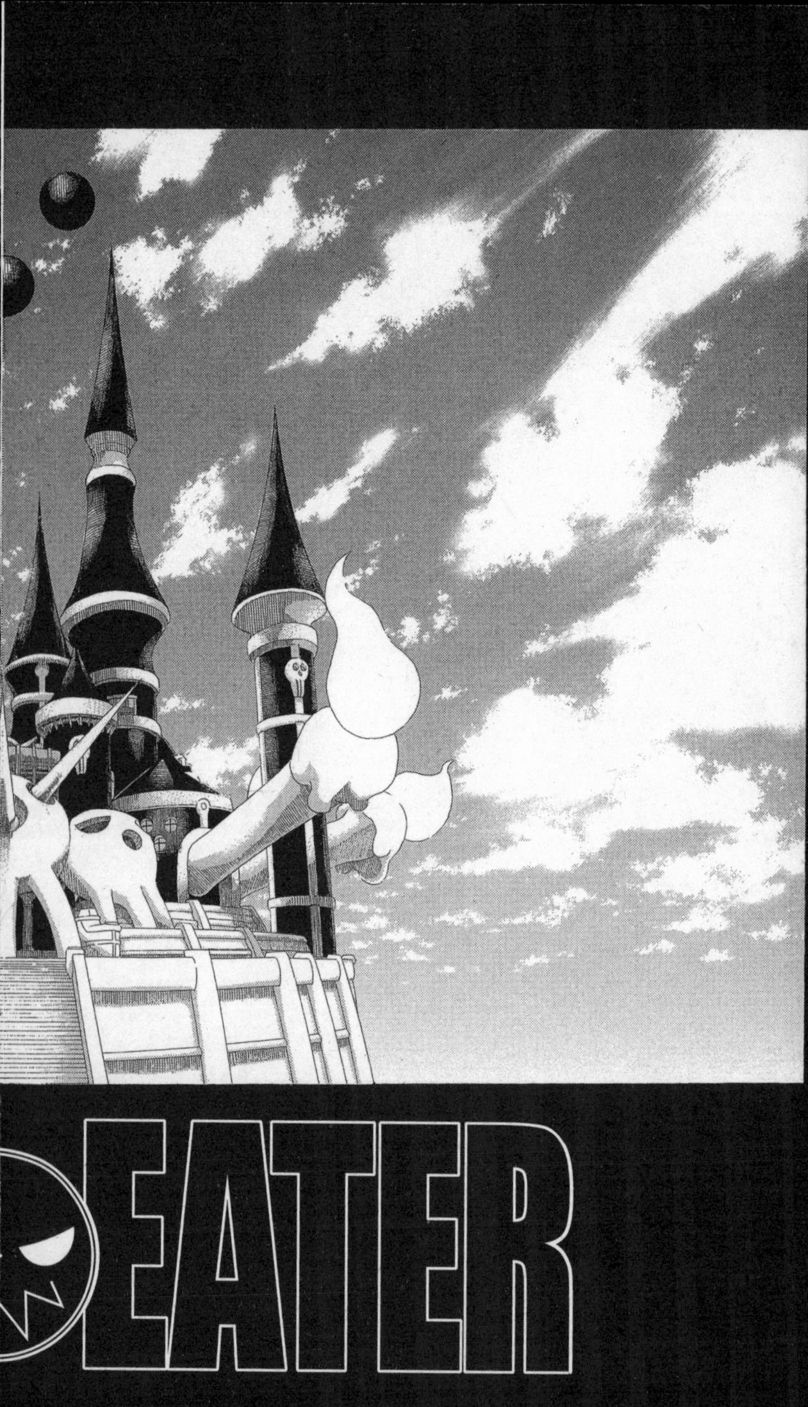
EATER

CHAPTER 108: THE DARK SIDE OF THE MOON V

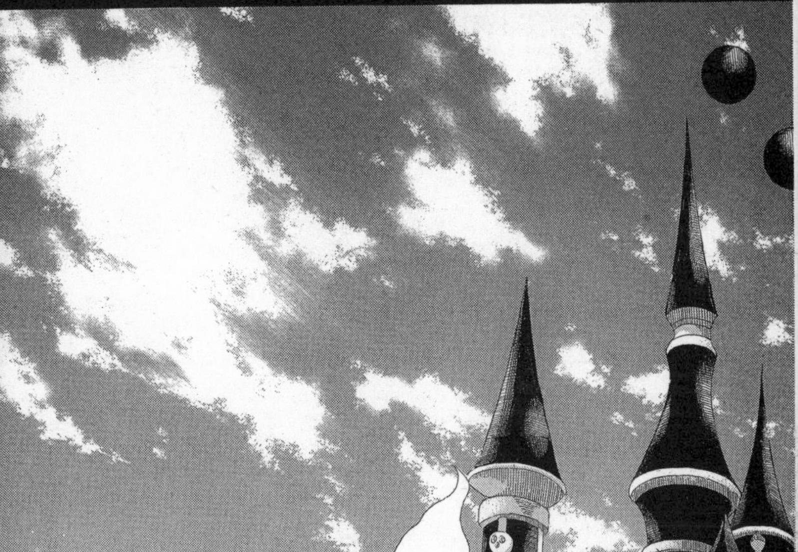

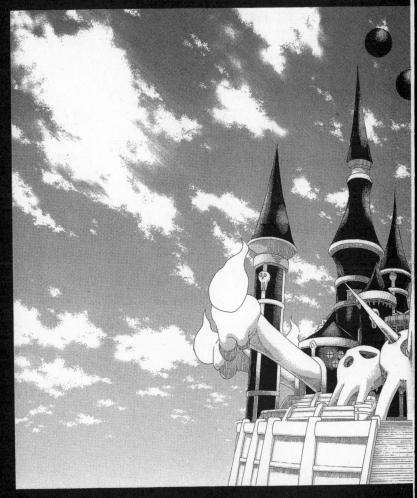

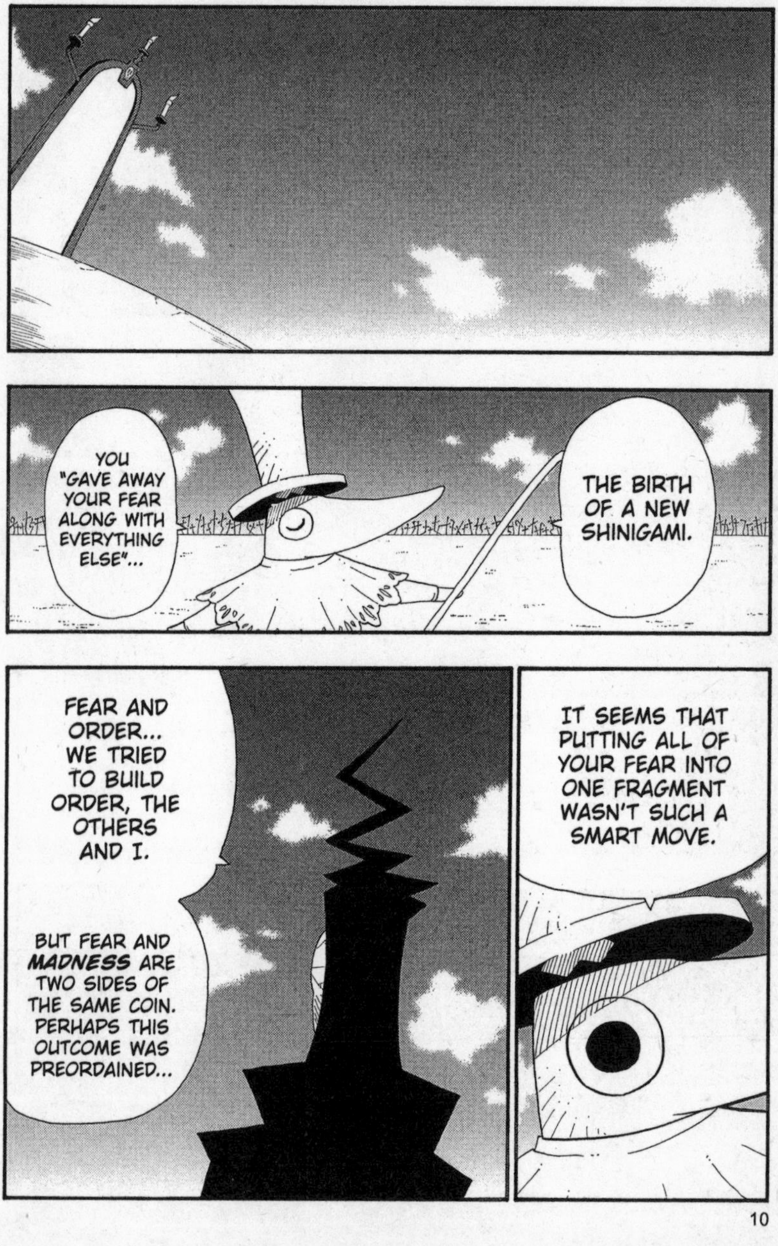
THE BIRTH OF A NEW SHINIGAMI.
YOU "GAVE AWAY YOUR FEAR ALONG WITH EVERYTHING ELSE"...
IT SEEMS THAT PUTTING ALL OF YOUR FEAR INTO ONE FRAGMENT WASN'T SUCH A SMART MOVE.
FEAR AND ORDER... WE TRIED TO BUILD ORDER, THE OTHERS AND I.
BUT FEAR AND *MADNESS* ARE TWO SIDES OF THE SAME COIN. PERHAPS THIS OUTCOME WAS PREORDAINED...

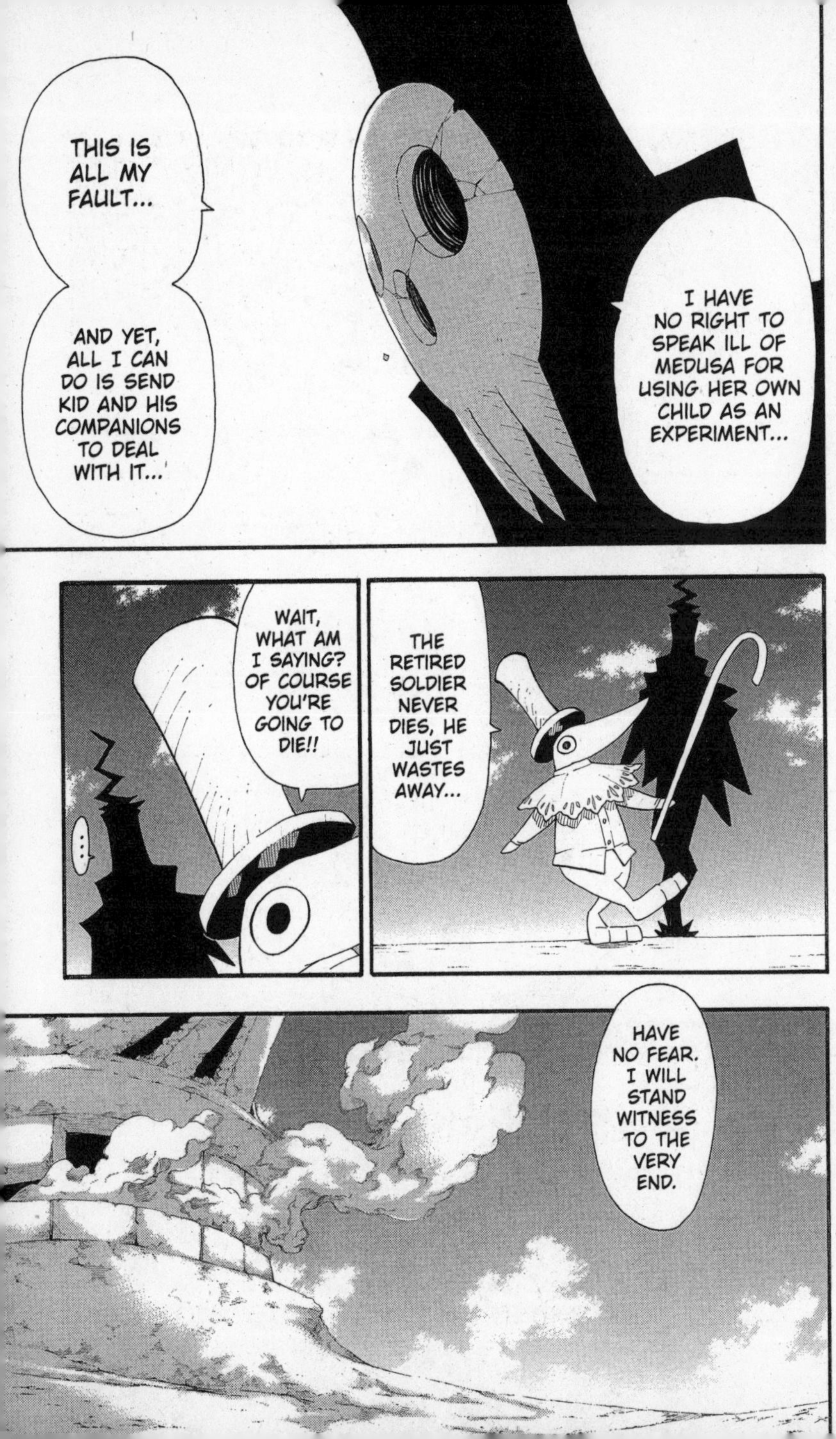
I HAVE NO RIGHT TO SPEAK ILL OF MEDUSA FOR USING HER OWN CHILD AS AN EXPERIMENT...
THIS IS ALL MY FAULT...
AND YET, ALL I CAN DO IS SEND KID AND HIS COMPANIONS TO DEAL WITH IT...
THE RETIRED SOLDIER NEVER DIES, HE JUST WASTES AWAY...
WAIT, WHAT AM I SAYING? OF COURSE YOU'RE GOING TO DIE!!
...
HAVE NO FEAR. I WILL STAND WITNESS TO THE VERY END.

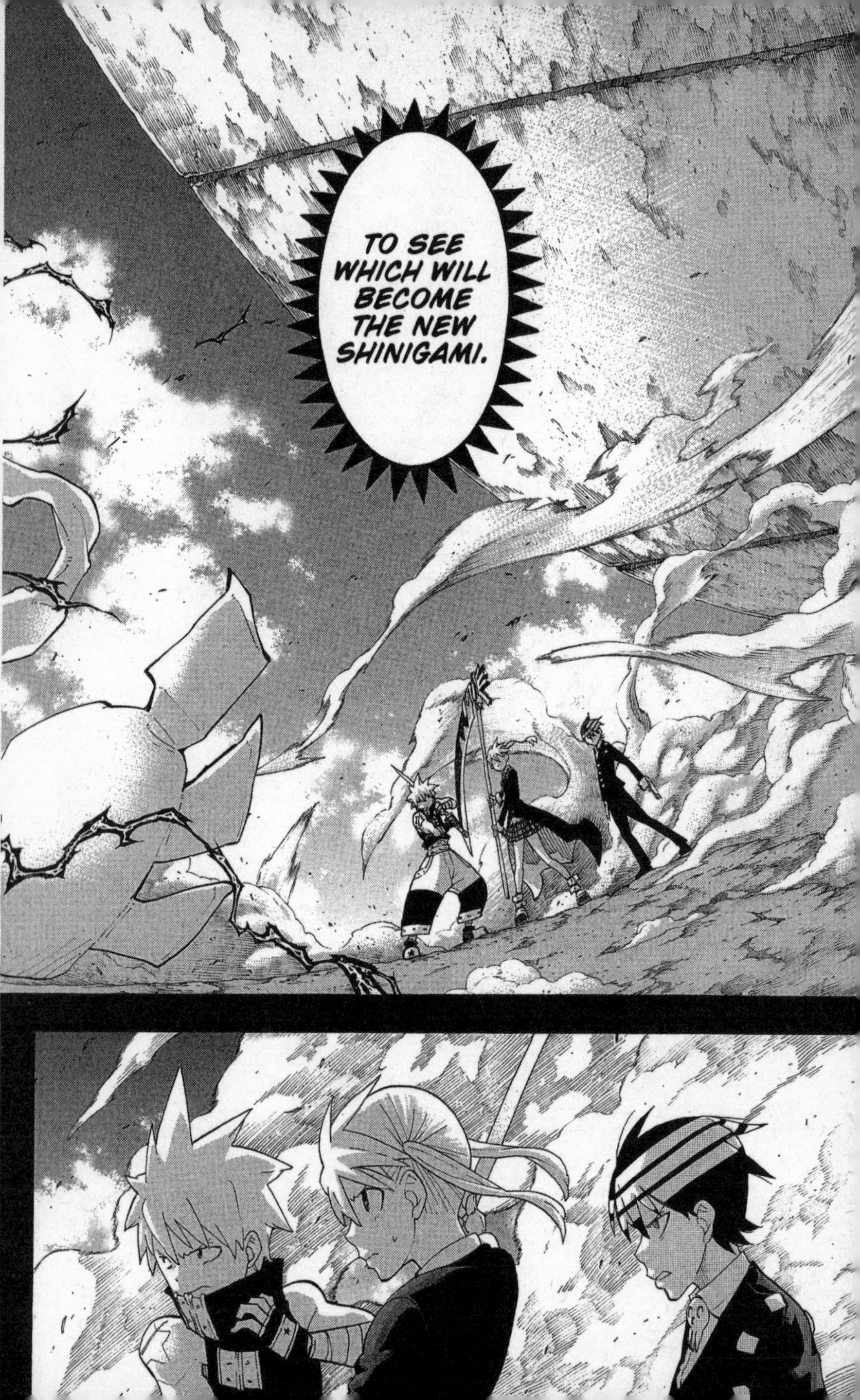
TO SEE WHICH WILL BECOME THE NEW SHINIGAMI.

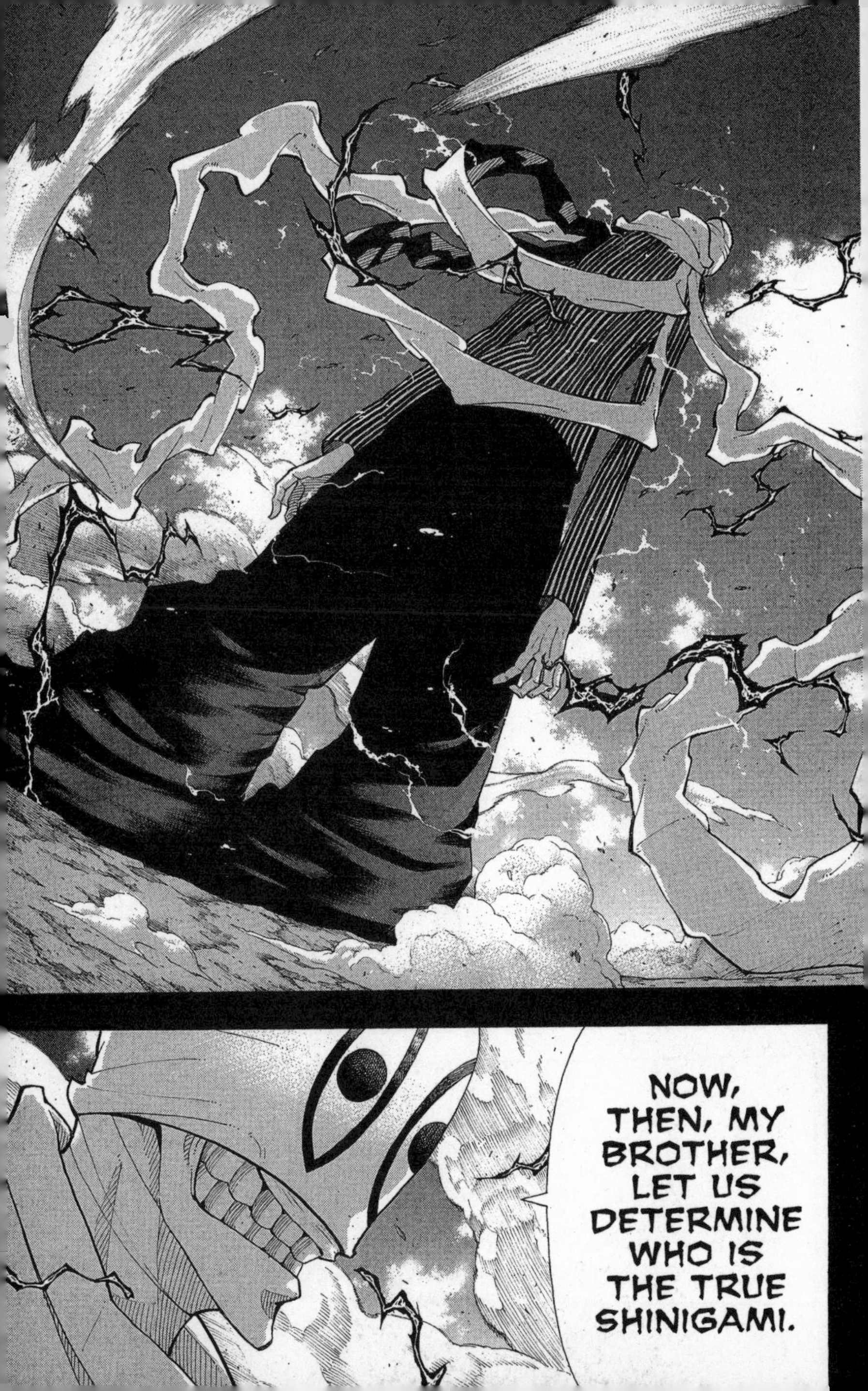
NOW, THEN, MY BROTHER, LET US DETERMINE WHO IS THE TRUE SHINIGAMI.

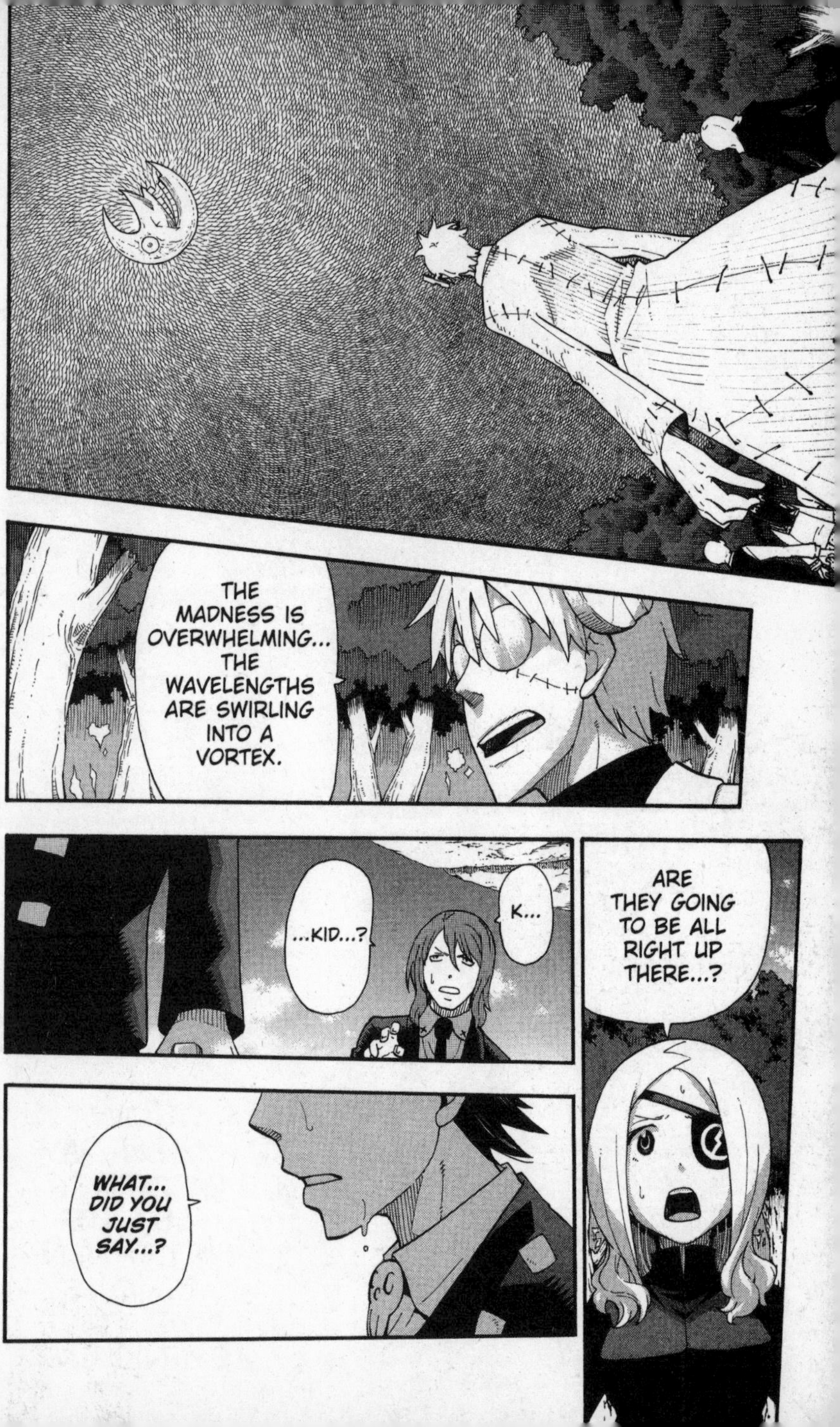
THE MADNESS IS OVERWHELMING... THE WAVELENGTHS ARE SWIRLING INTO A VORTEX.
ARE THEY GOING TO BE ALL RIGHT UP THERE...?
K...
...KID...?
WHAT... DID YOU JUST SAY...?

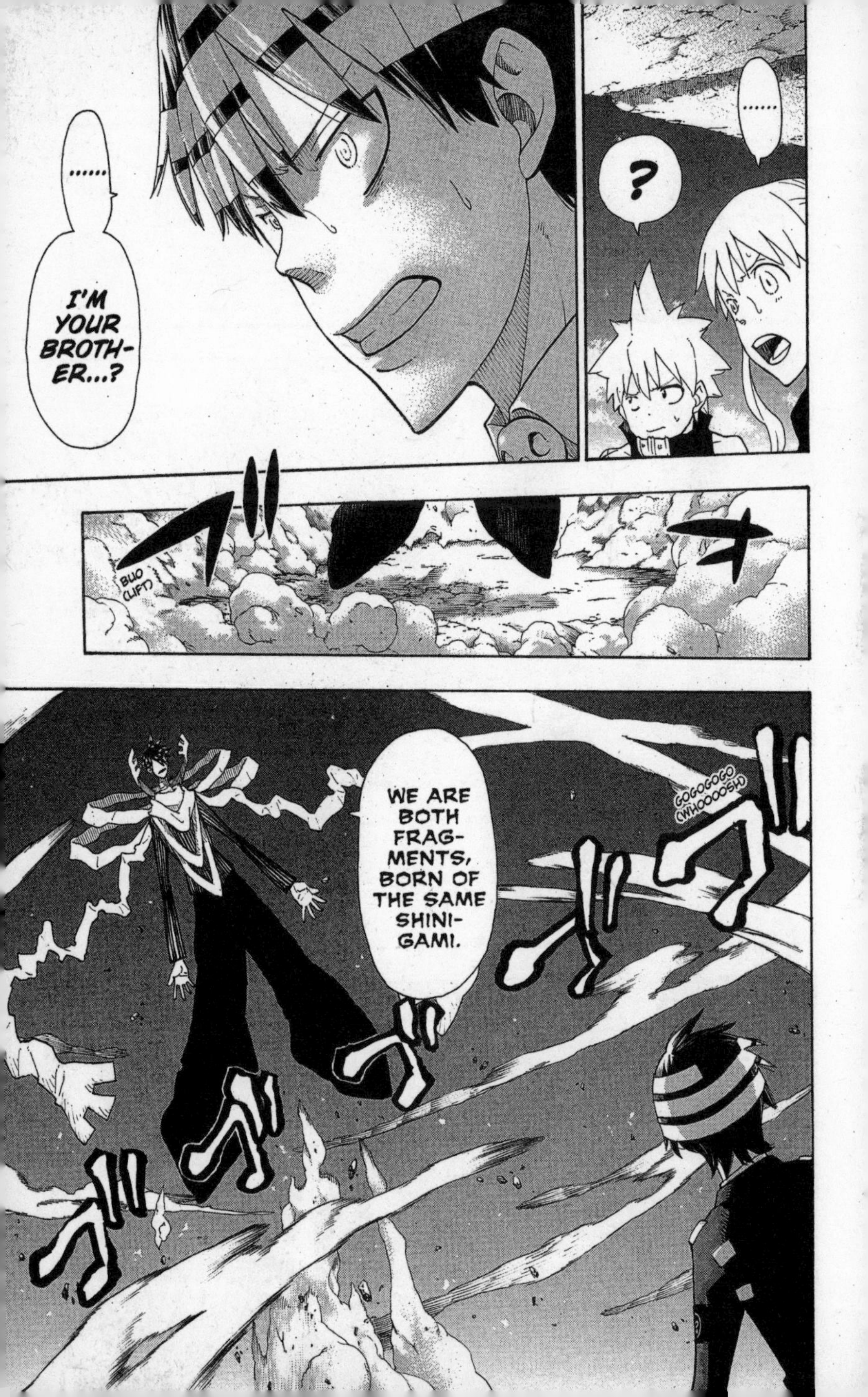
......
?
......
I'M YOUR BROTHER...?
BUO (LIFT)
GOGOGOGO (WHOOOOSH)
WE ARE BOTH FRAGMENTS, BORN OF THE SAME SHINIGAMI.

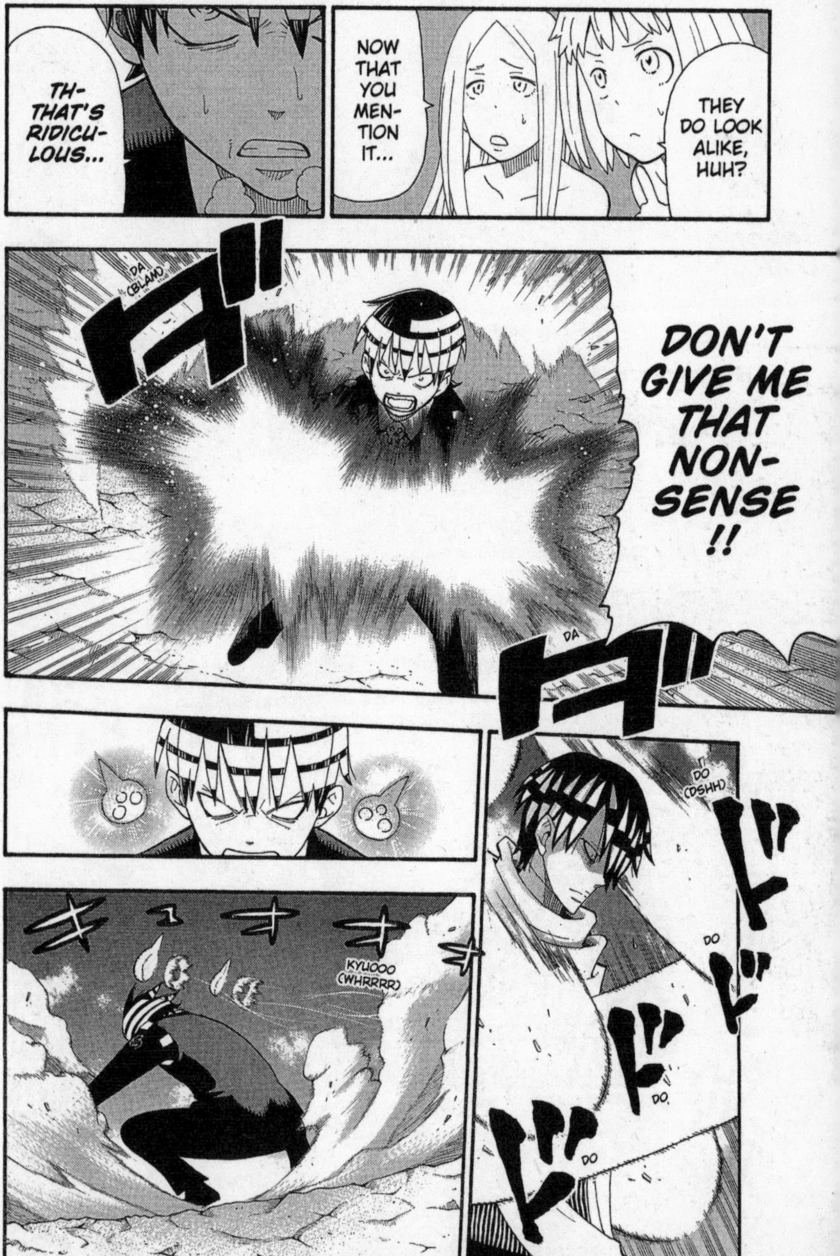
THEY DO LOOK ALIKE, HUH?
NOW THAT YOU MEN-TION IT...
TH-THAT'S RIDICULOUS...
DA (BLAM)
DON'T GIVE ME THAT NON-SENSE!!
DA
DO (DSHH)
DO
DO
DO
KYUOOO (WHRRRR)

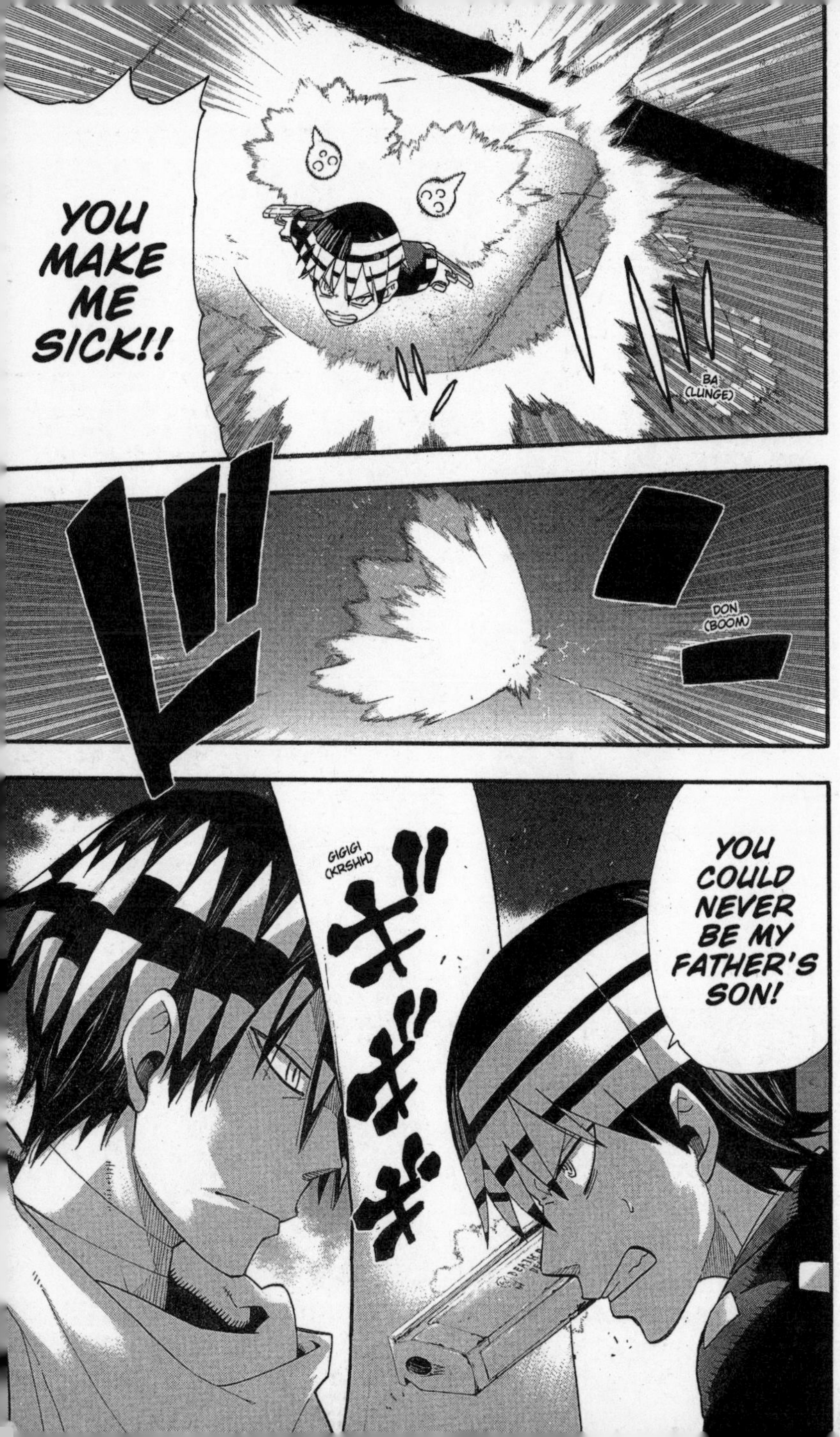

YOU MAKE ME SICK!!
BA (LUNGE)
DON (BOOM)
YOU COULD NEVER BE MY FATHER'S SON!
GIGIGI (KRSHH)

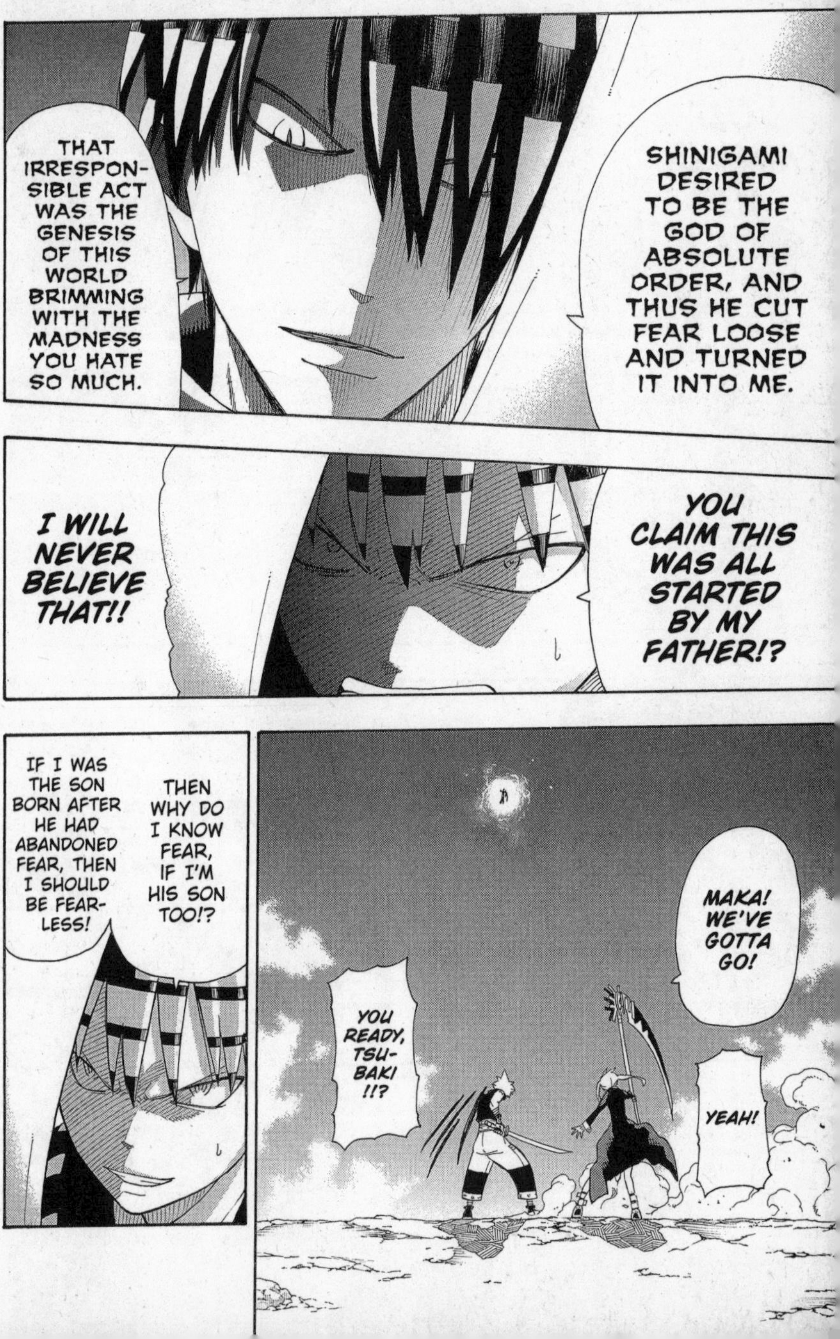
SHINIGAMI DESIRED TO BE THE GOD OF ABSOLUTE ORDER, AND THUS HE CUT FEAR LOOSE AND TURNED IT INTO ME.
THAT IRRESPONSIBLE ACT WAS THE GENESIS OF THIS WORLD BRIMMING WITH THE MADNESS YOU HATE SO MUCH.
YOU CLAIM THIS WAS ALL STARTED BY MY FATHER!?
I WILL NEVER BELIEVE THAT!!
MAKA! WE'VE GOTTA GO!
YEAH!
YOU READY, TSUBAKI!!?
IF I WAS THE SON BORN AFTER HE HAD ABANDONED FEAR, THEN I SHOULD BE FEARLESS!
THEN WHY DO I KNOW FEAR, IF I'M HIS SON TOO!?

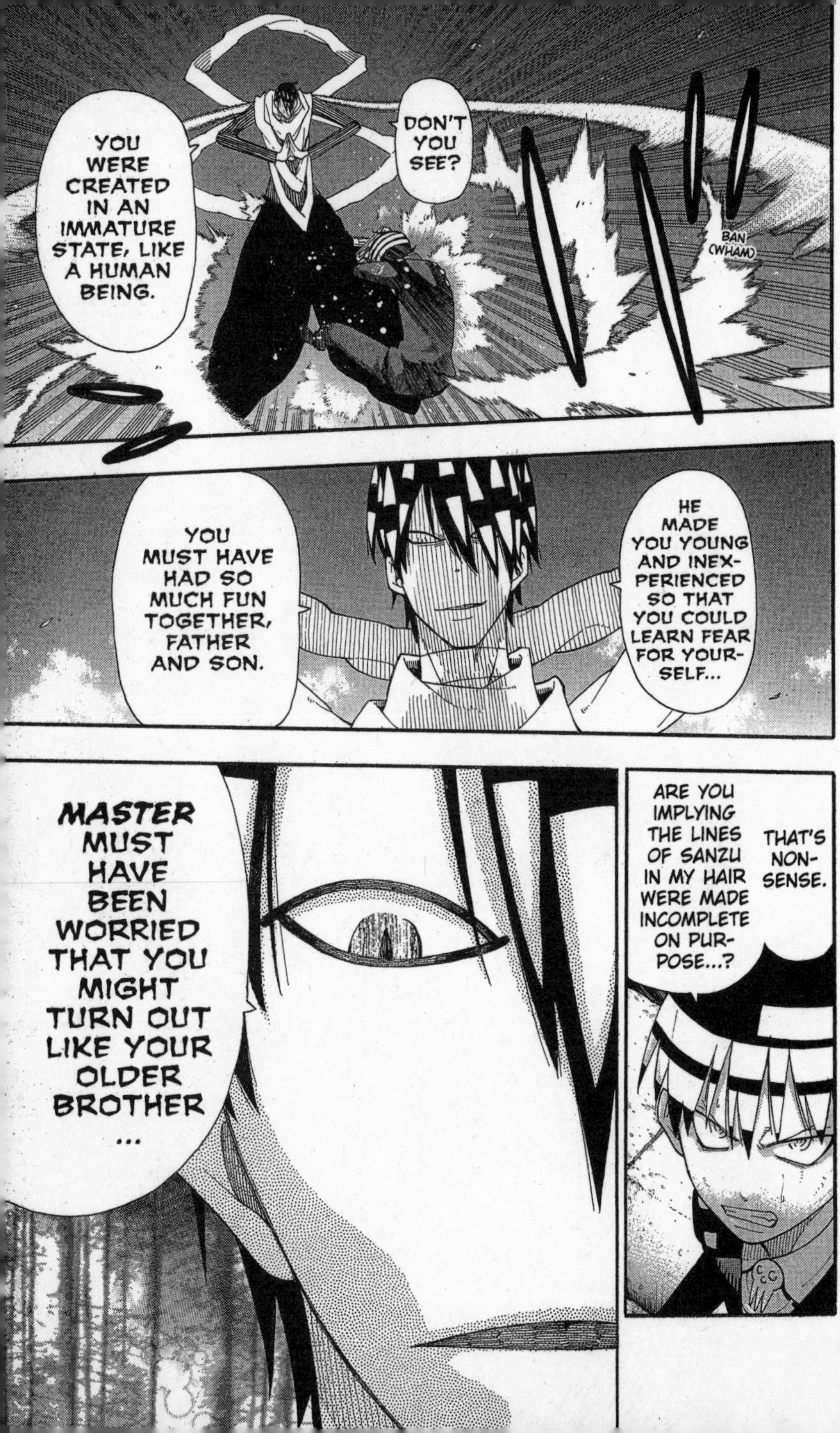
BAN (WHAM)
DON'T YOU SEE?
YOU WERE CREATED IN AN IMMATURE STATE, LIKE A HUMAN BEING.
HE MADE YOU YOUNG AND INEX-PERIENCED SO THAT YOU COULD LEARN FEAR FOR YOUR-SELF...
YOU MUST HAVE HAD SO MUCH FUN TOGETHER, FATHER AND SON.
ARE YOU IMPLYING THE LINES OF SANZU IN MY HAIR WERE MADE INCOMPLETE ON PUR-POSE...?
THAT'S NON-SENSE.
MASTER MUST HAVE BEEN WORRIED THAT YOU MIGHT TURN OUT LIKE YOUR OLDER BROTHER ...

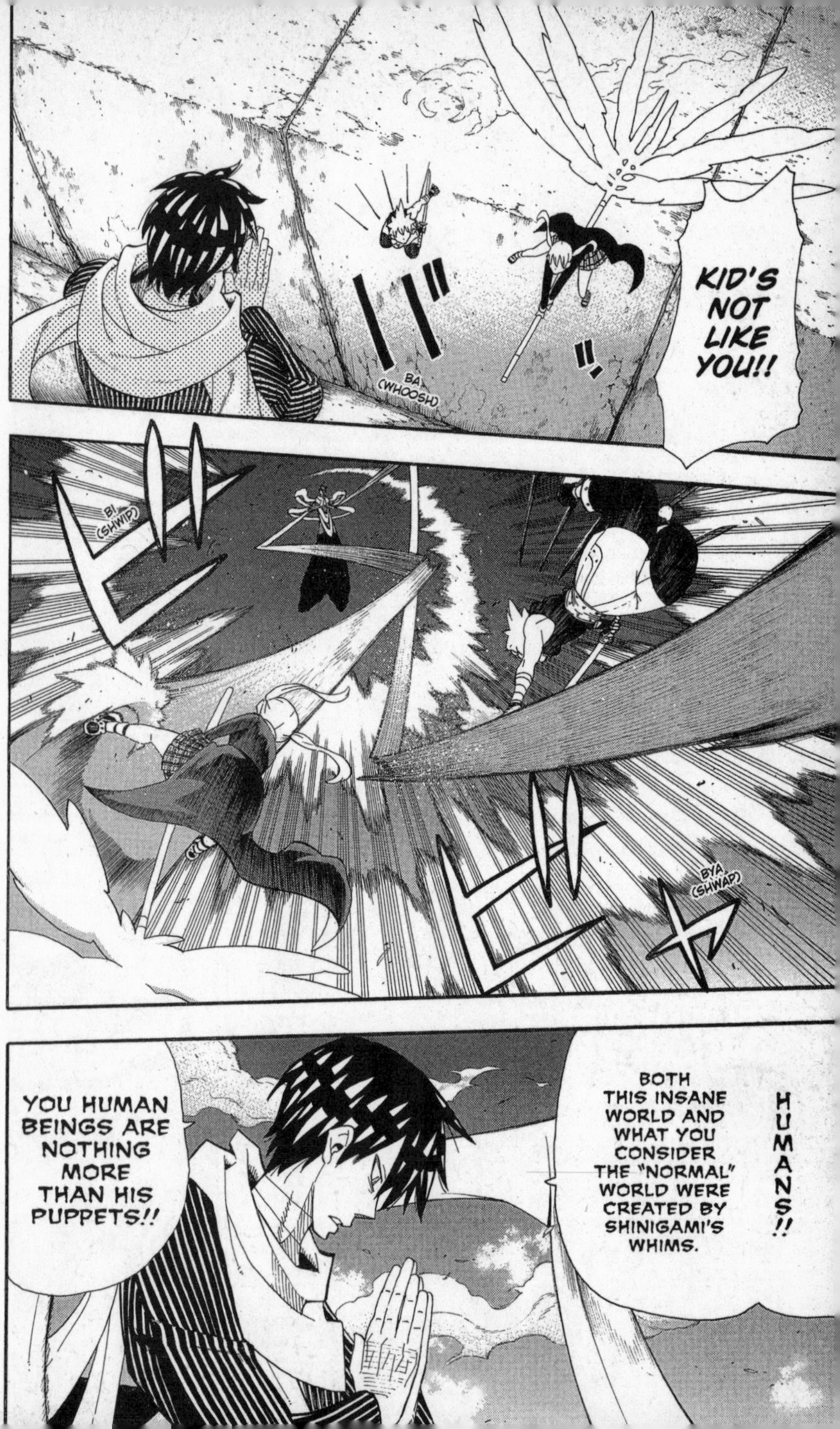
KID'S NOT LIKE YOU!!
BA (WHOOSH)
BI (SHWIP)
BYA (SHWAP)
HUMANS!!
BOTH THIS INSANE WORLD AND WHAT YOU CONSIDER THE "NORMAL" WORLD WERE CREATED BY SHINIGAMI'S WHIMS.
YOU HUMAN BEINGS ARE NOTHING MORE THAN HIS PUPPETS!!

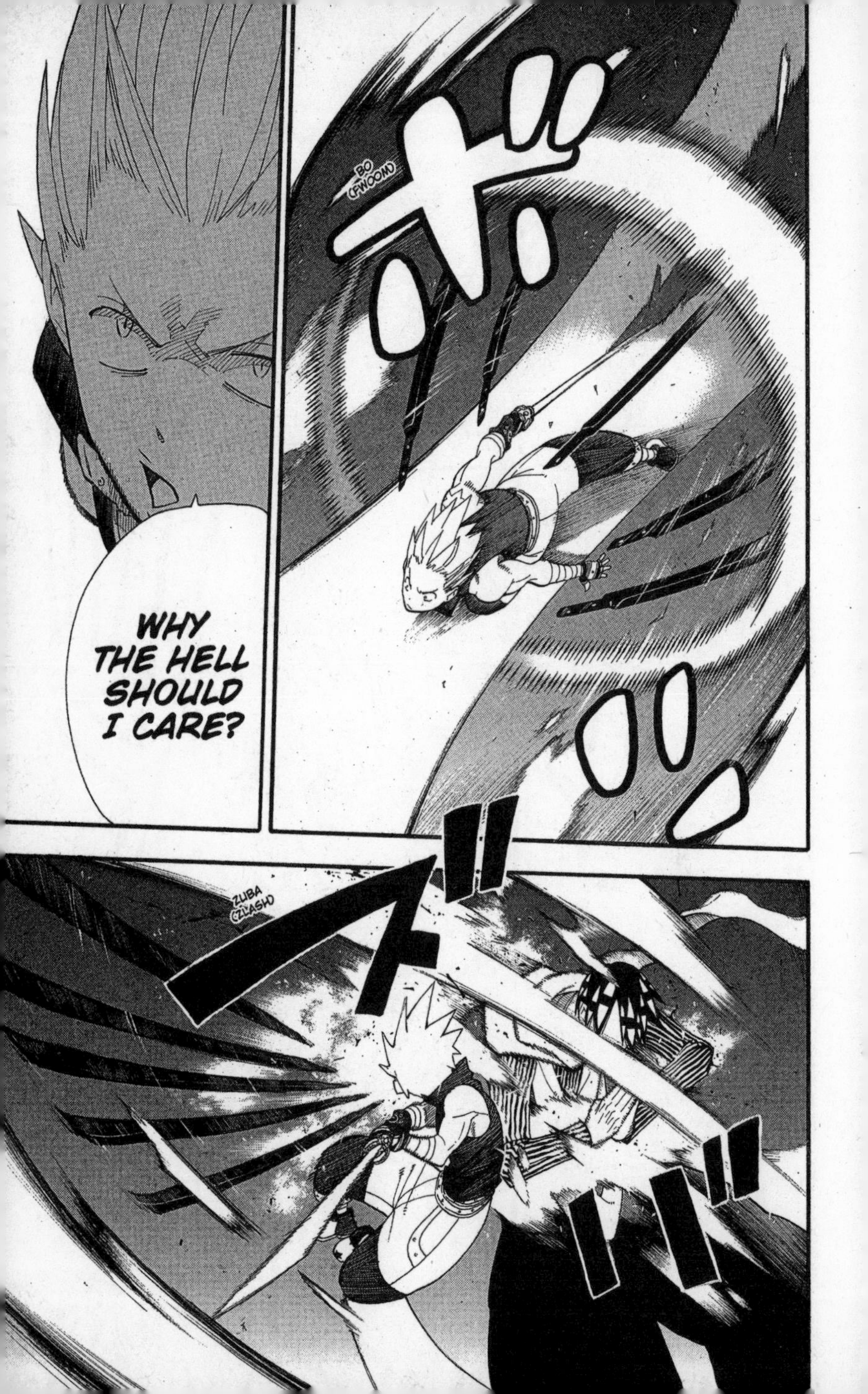
BO (FWOOM)
WHY THE HELL SHOULD I CARE?
ZUBA (ZLASH)

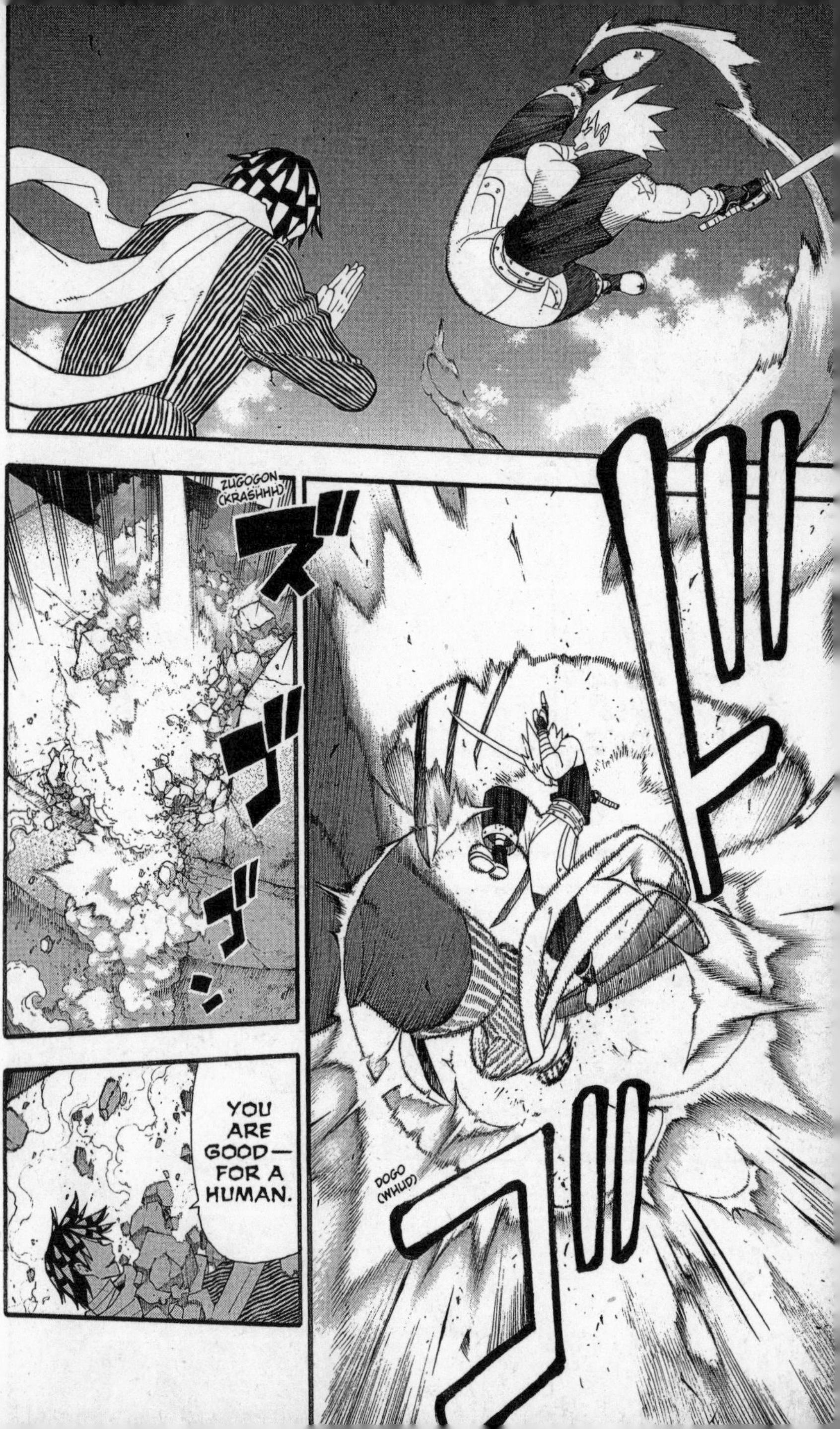
DOGO (WHUD)
ZUGOGON (KRASHHH)
YOU ARE GOOD— FOR A HUMAN.

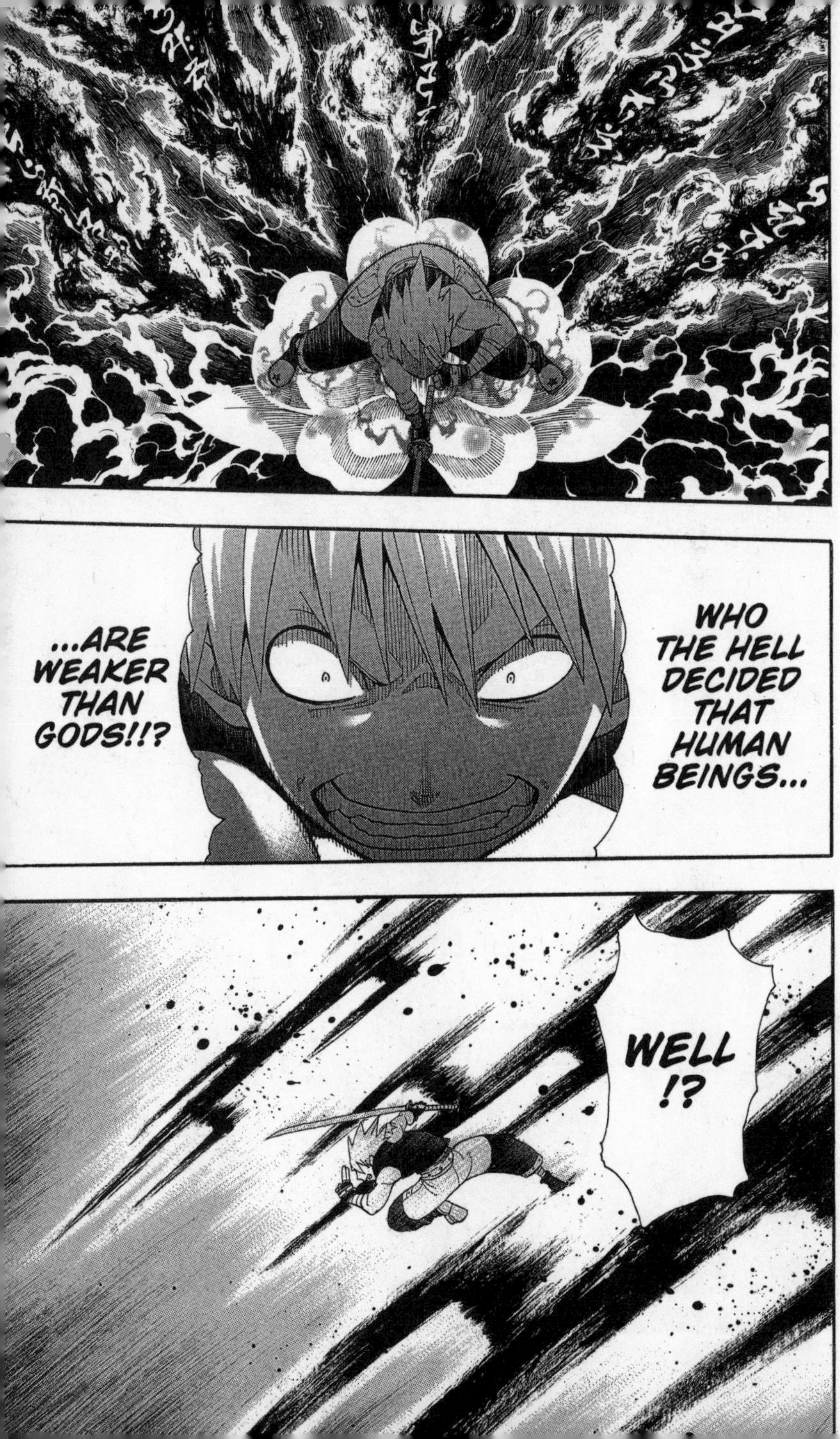
WHO THE HELL DECIDED THAT HUMAN BEINGS...
...ARE WEAKER THAN GODS!!?
WELL !?

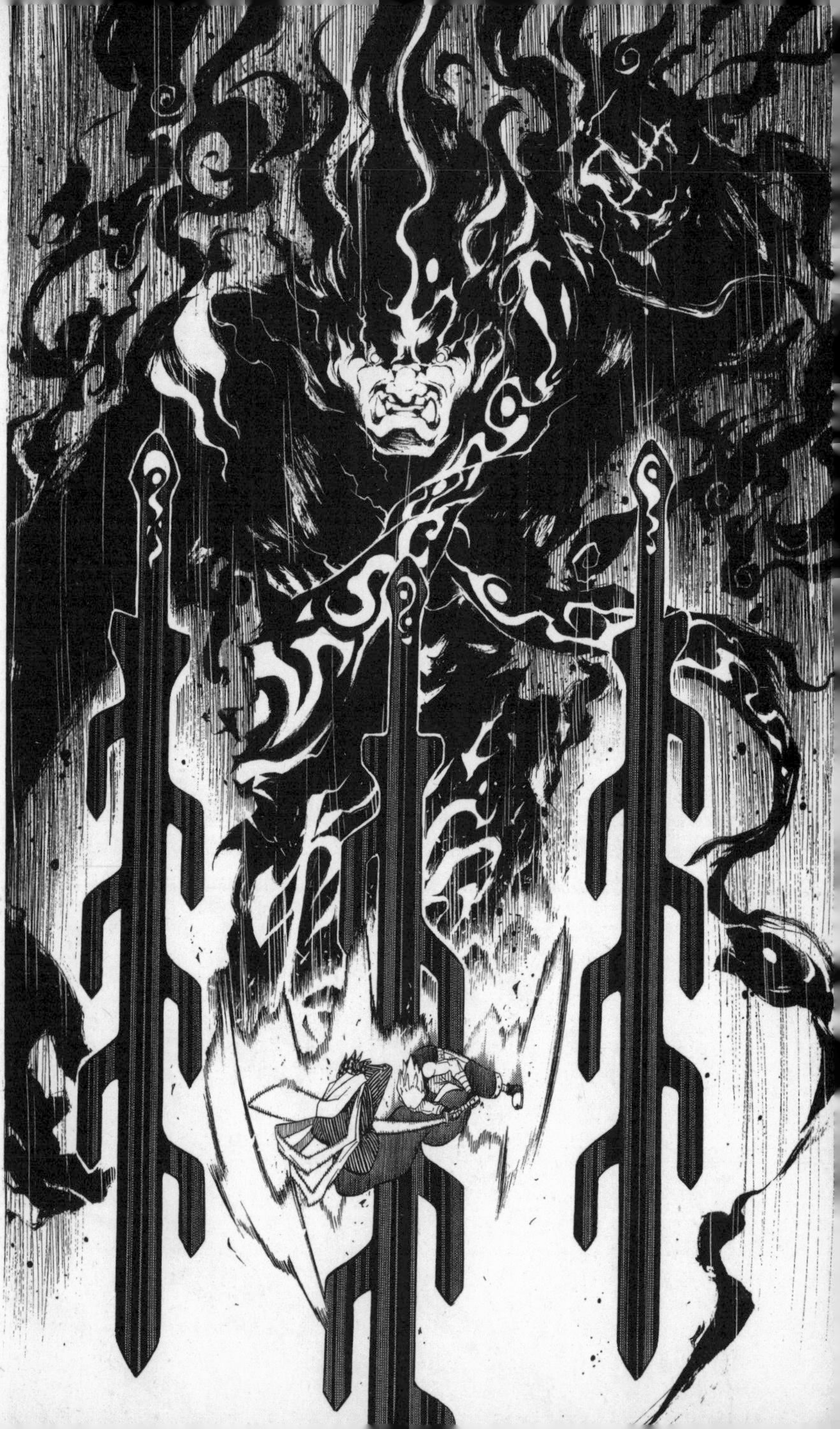

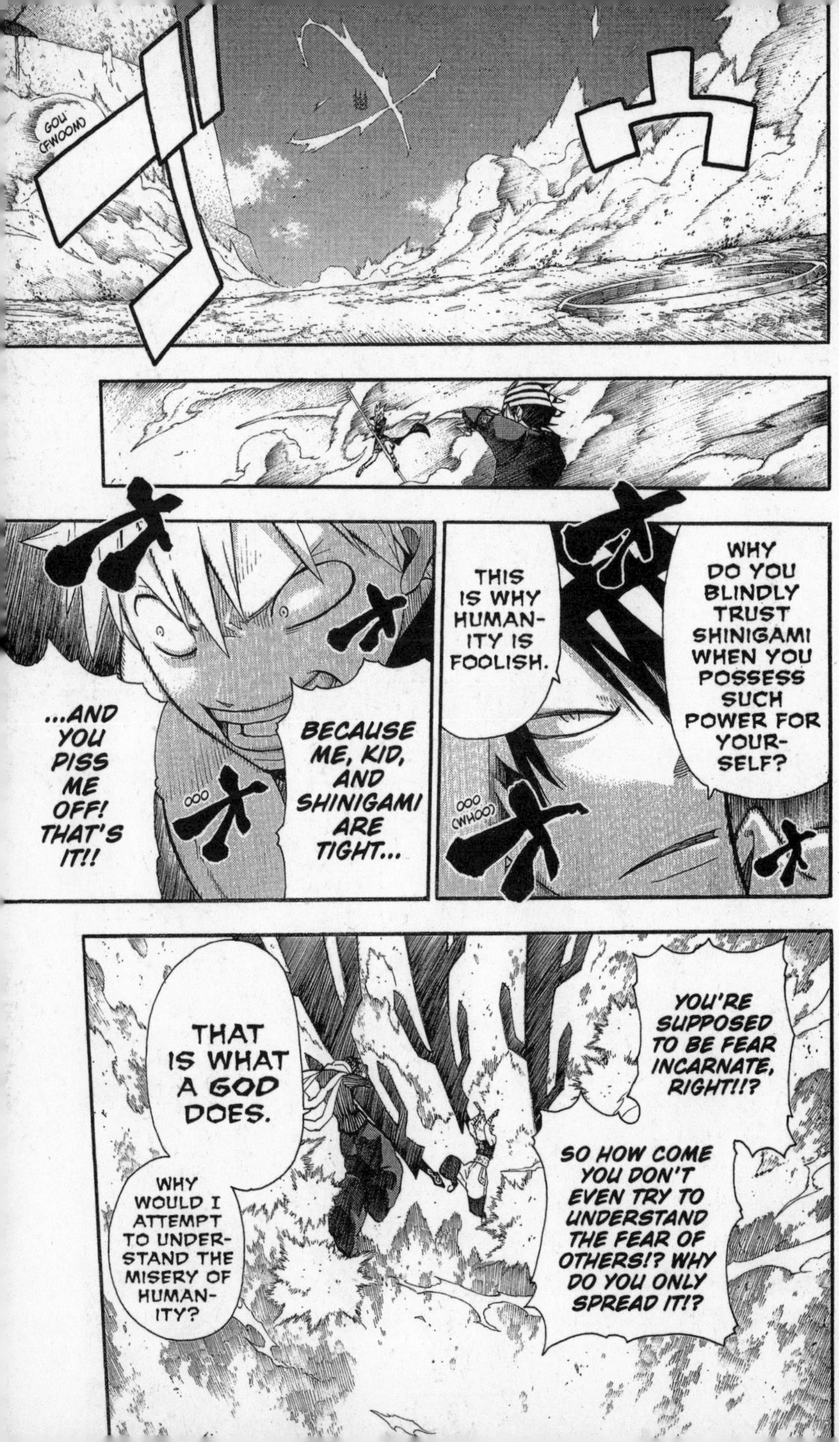
GOU (FWOOM)
WHY DO YOU BLINDLY TRUST SHINIGAMI WHEN YOU POSSESS SUCH POWER FOR YOURSELF?
THIS IS WHY HUMANITY IS FOOLISH.
OOO (WHOO)
BECAUSE ME, KID, AND SHINIGAMI ARE TIGHT...
...AND YOU PISS ME OFF! THAT'S IT!!
OOO
YOU'RE SUPPOSED TO BE FEAR INCARNATE, RIGHT!!?
SO HOW COME YOU DON'T EVEN TRY TO UNDERSTAND THE FEAR OF OTHERS!? WHY DO YOU ONLY SPREAD IT!?
THAT IS WHAT A GOD DOES.
WHY WOULD I ATTEMPT TO UNDERSTAND THE MISERY OF HUMANITY?

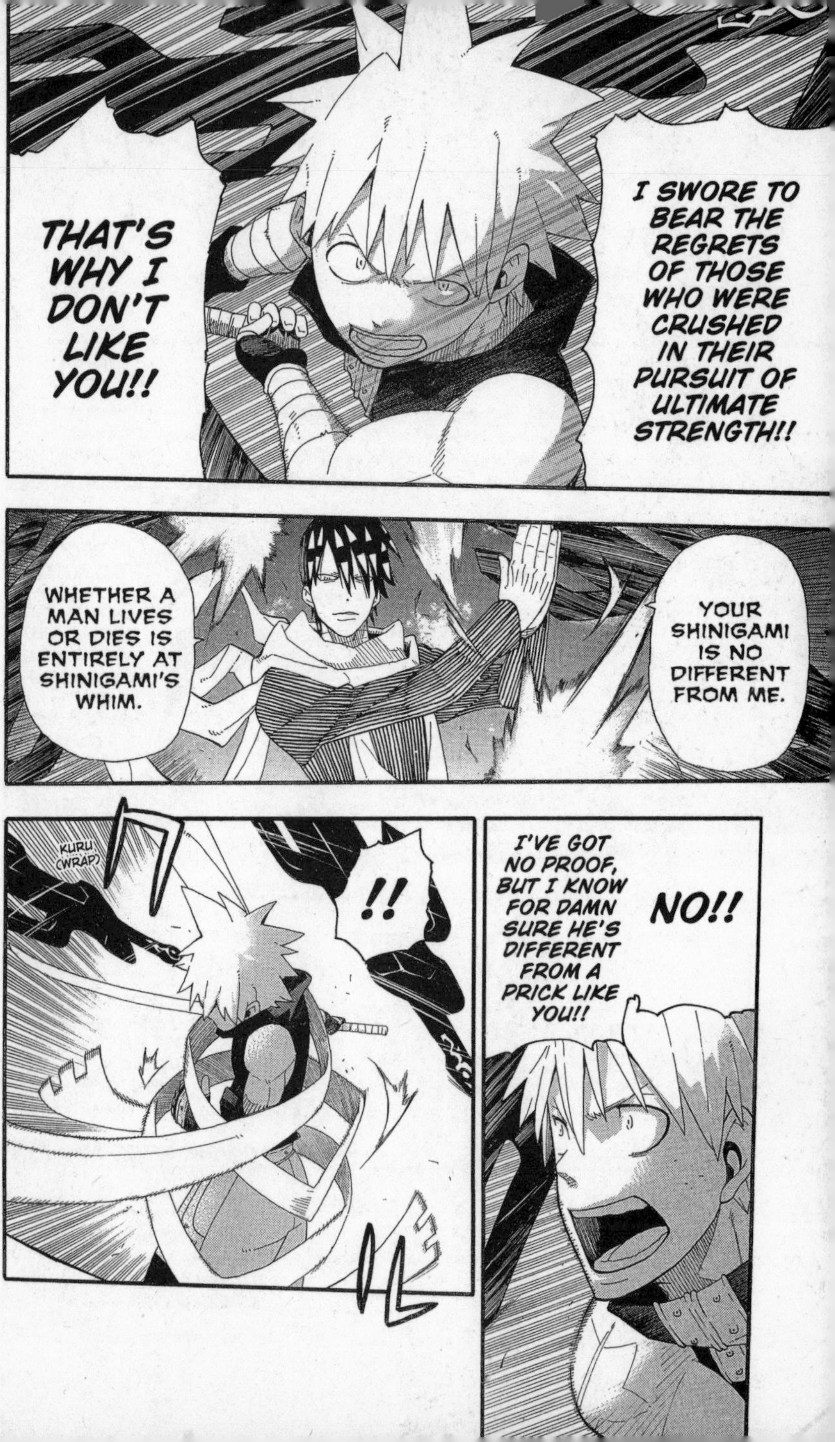
I SWORE TO BEAR THE REGRETS OF THOSE WHO WERE CRUSHED IN THEIR PURSUIT OF ULTIMATE STRENGTH!!
THAT'S WHY I DON'T LIKE YOU!!
YOUR SHINIGAMI IS NO DIFFERENT FROM ME.
WHETHER A MAN LIVES OR DIES IS ENTIRELY AT SHINIGAMI'S WHIM.
NO!!
I'VE GOT NO PROOF, BUT I KNOW FOR DAMN SURE HE'S DIFFERENT FROM A PRICK LIKE YOU!!
!!
KURU (WRAP)

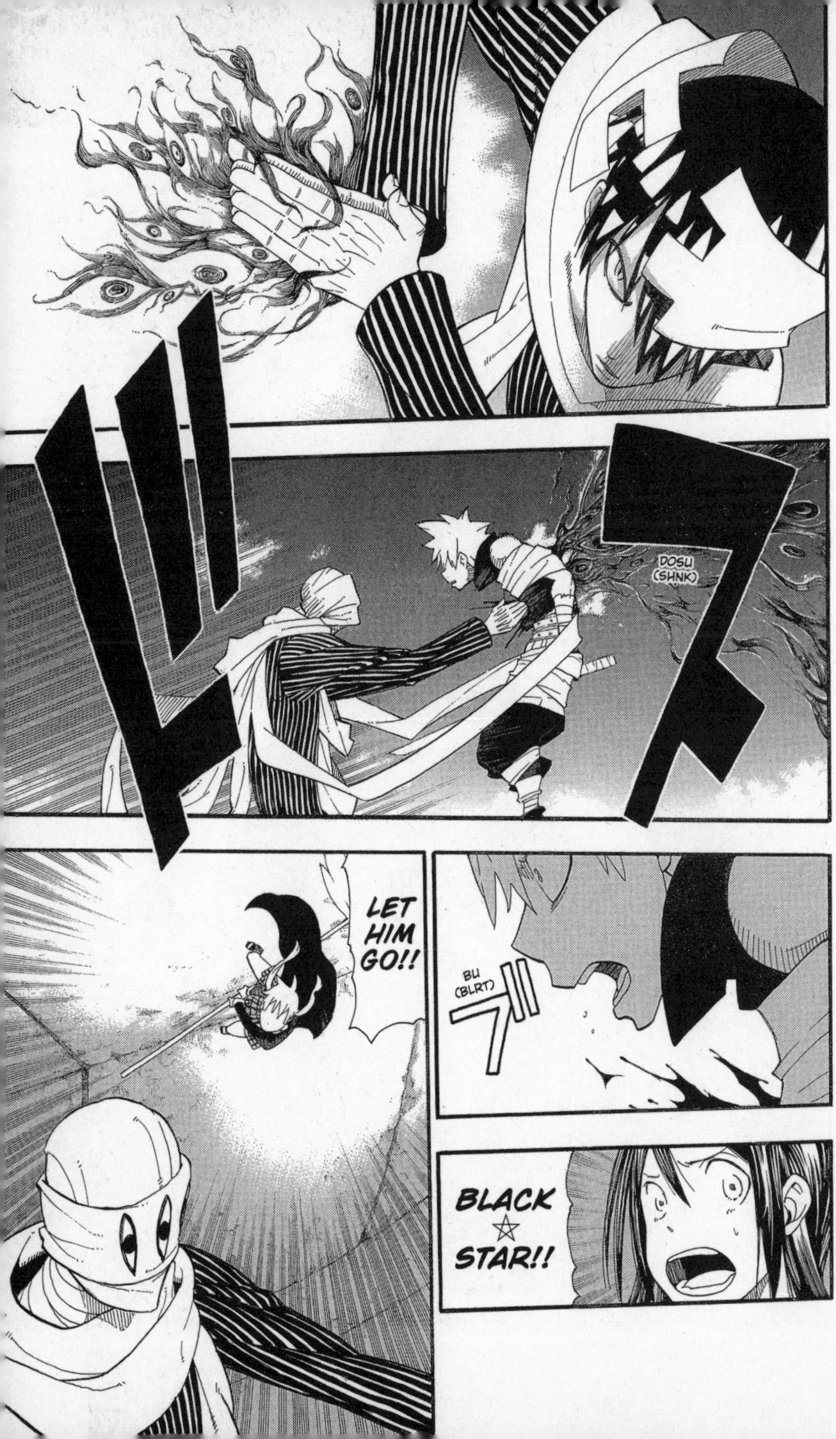
DOSU
(SHNK)
BU
(BLRT)
BLACK☆STAR!!
LET HIM GO!!

AHH HA HA!

SCARY! SO SCARY!

PAN (POW)

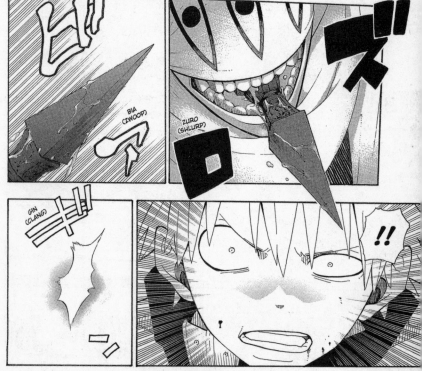

BIA (ZWOOP)

ZURO (SHLURP)

GIN (CLANG)

!!

 GIRIRI (GRIND)

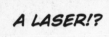 KOOOOO (VWOOO)

IT'S GONNA BLOW!!

A LASER!?

OH NO......!!

VAJRA!!

 GABO (GLRP)

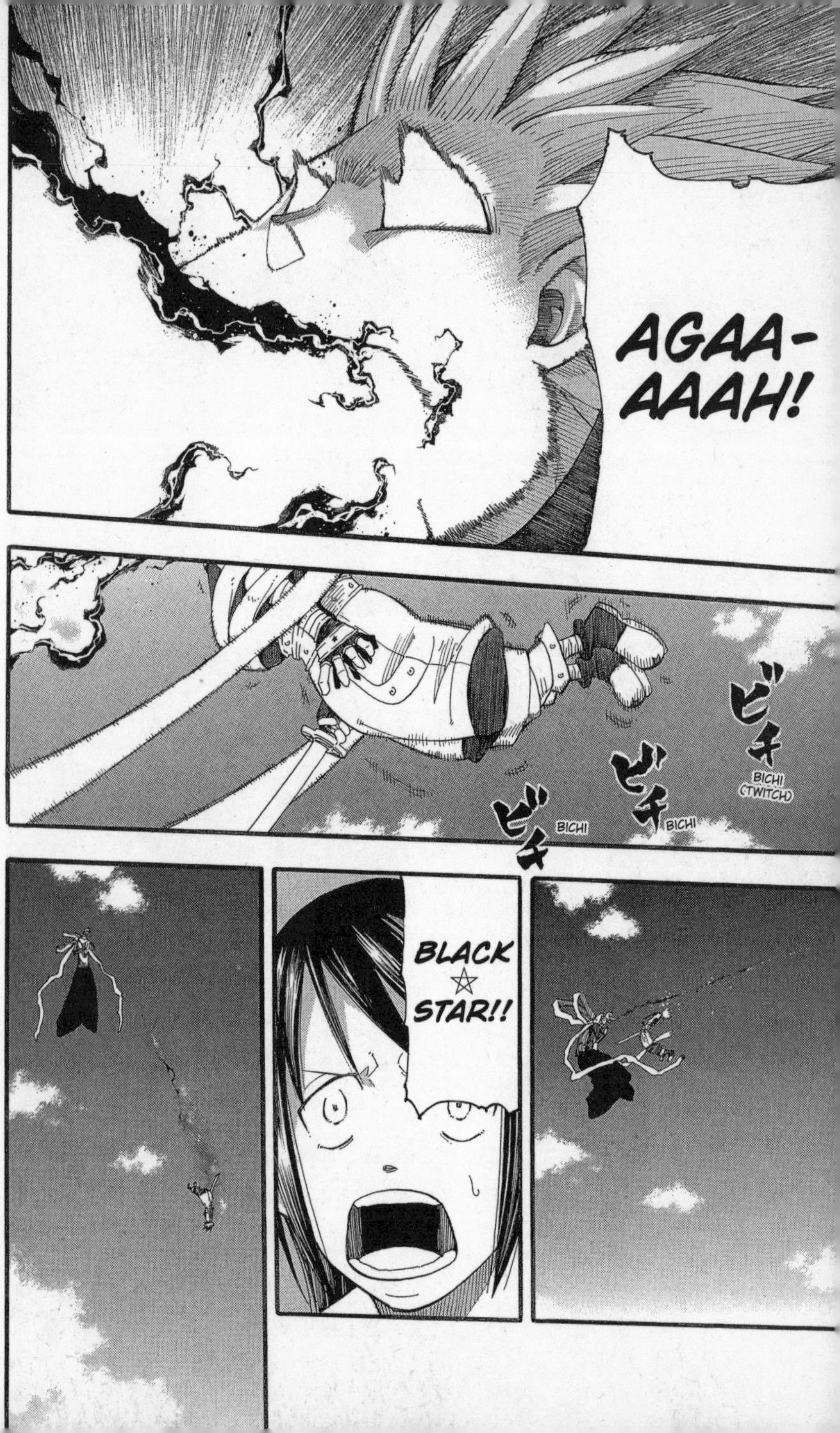
AGAA-AAAH!
ビチ
BICHI (TWITCH)
ビチ
BICHI
ビチ
BICHI
BLACK☆STAR!!

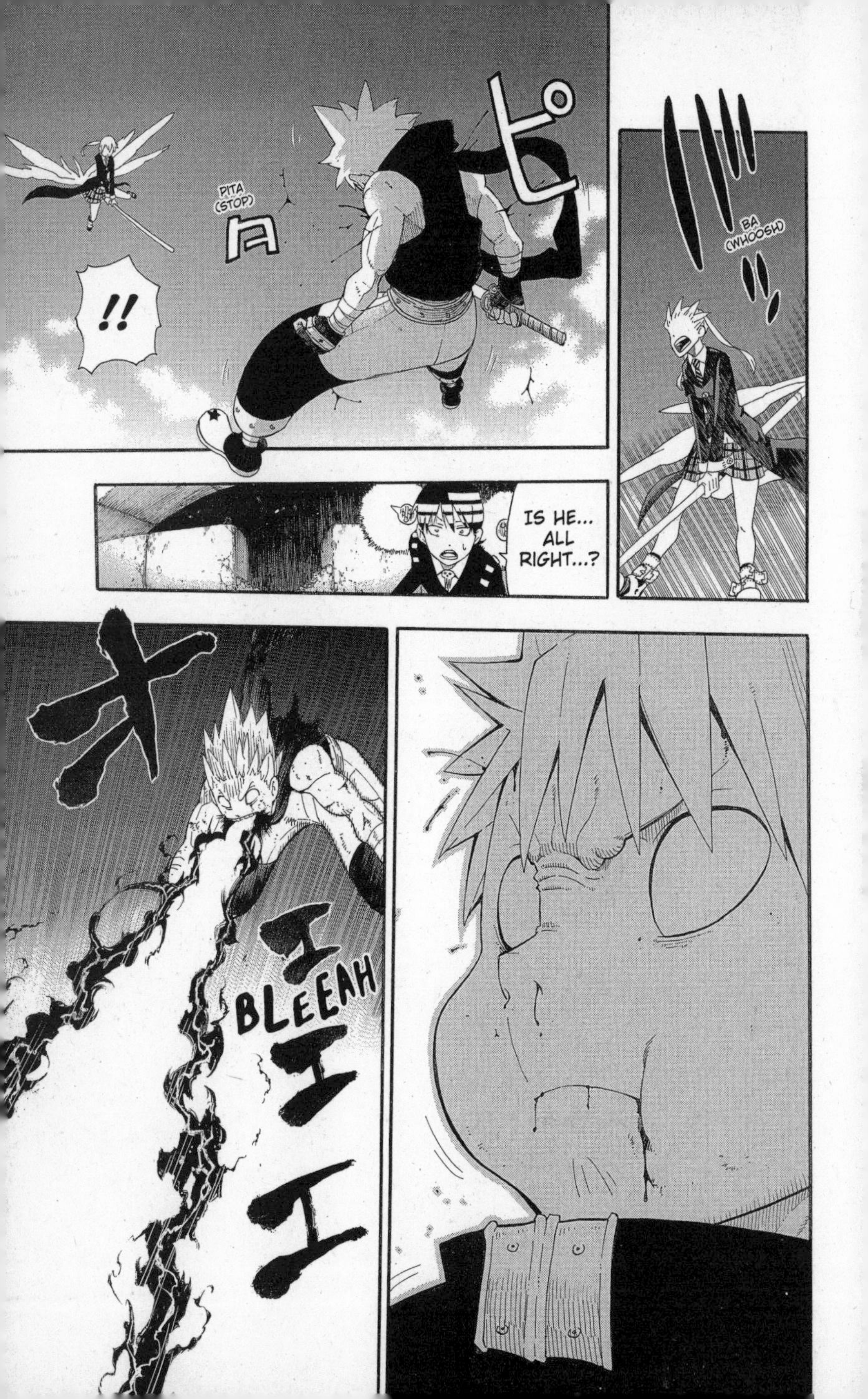
BA (WHOOSH)
PITA (STOP)
!!
IS HE... ALL RIGHT...?
BLEEAH

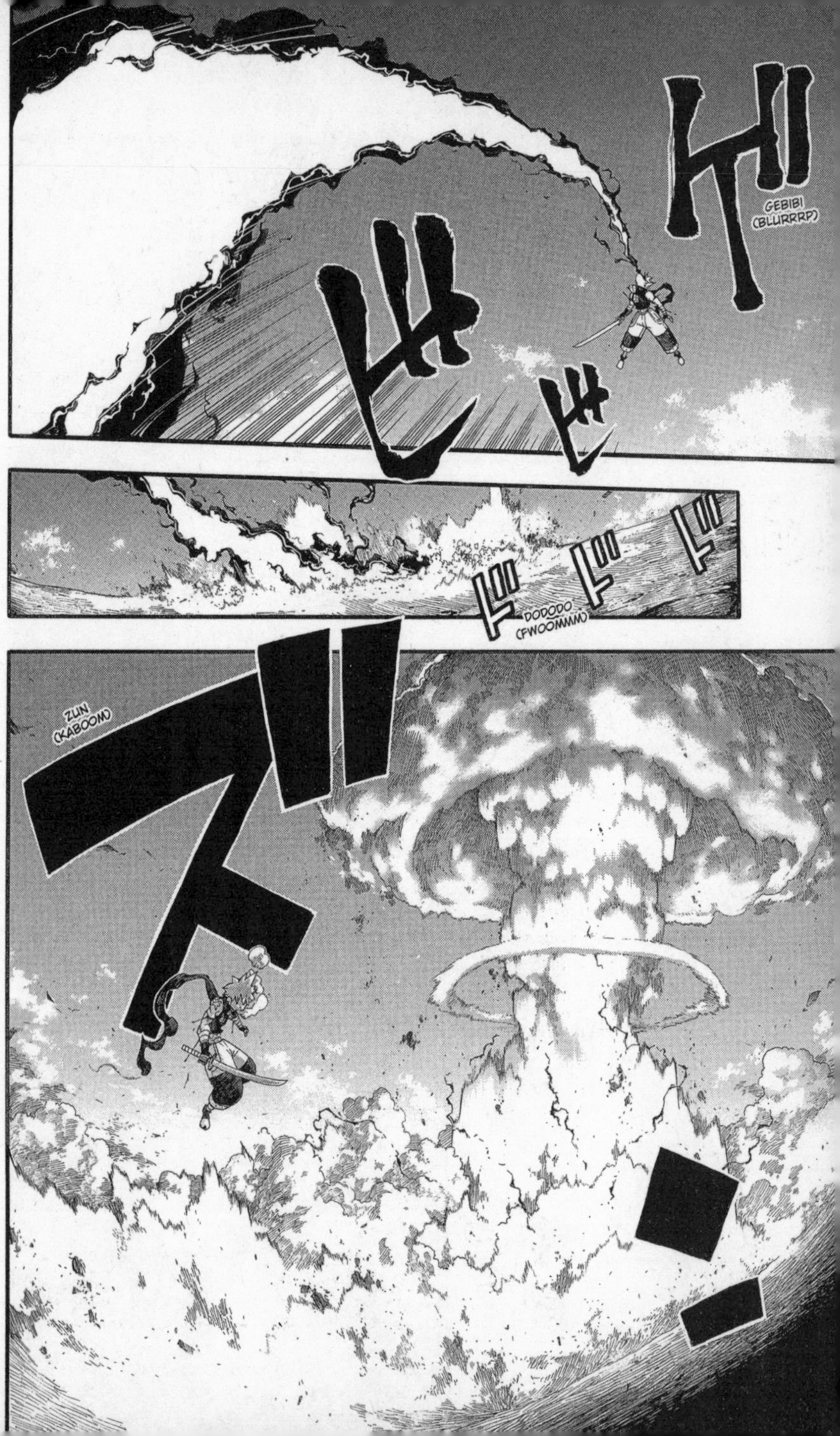
GEBIBI
(BLURRRP)
DODODO
(FWOOMMM)
ZUN
(KABOOM)

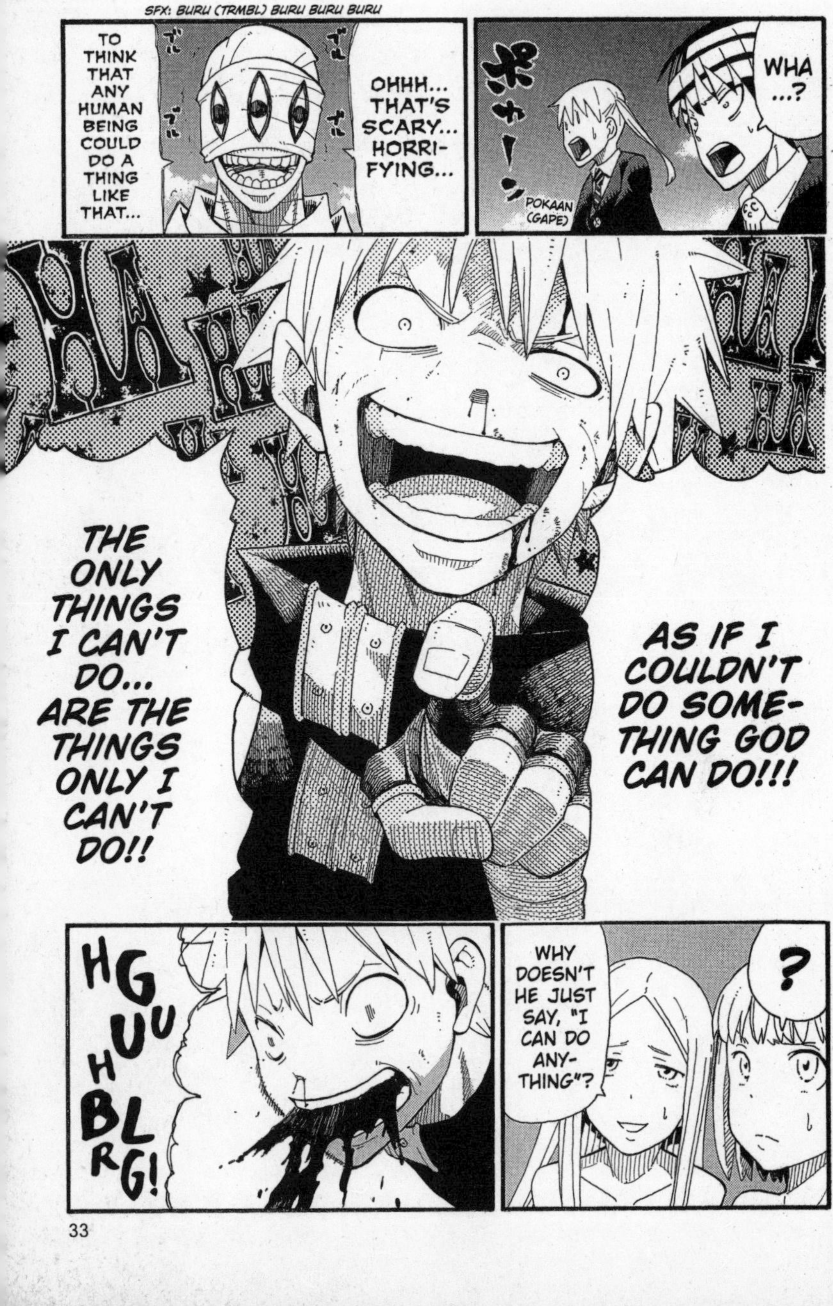
SFX: BURU (TRMBL) BURU BURU BURU
WHA ...?
POKAAN (GAPE)
OHHH... THAT'S SCARY... HORRI-FYING...
TO THINK THAT ANY HUMAN BEING COULD DO A THING LIKE THAT...
AS IF I COULDN'T DO SOME-THING GOD CAN DO!!!
THE ONLY THINGS I CAN'T DO... ARE THE THINGS ONLY I CAN'T DO!!
?
WHY DOESN'T HE JUST SAY, "I CAN DO ANY-THING"?
HGUUHBLRG!

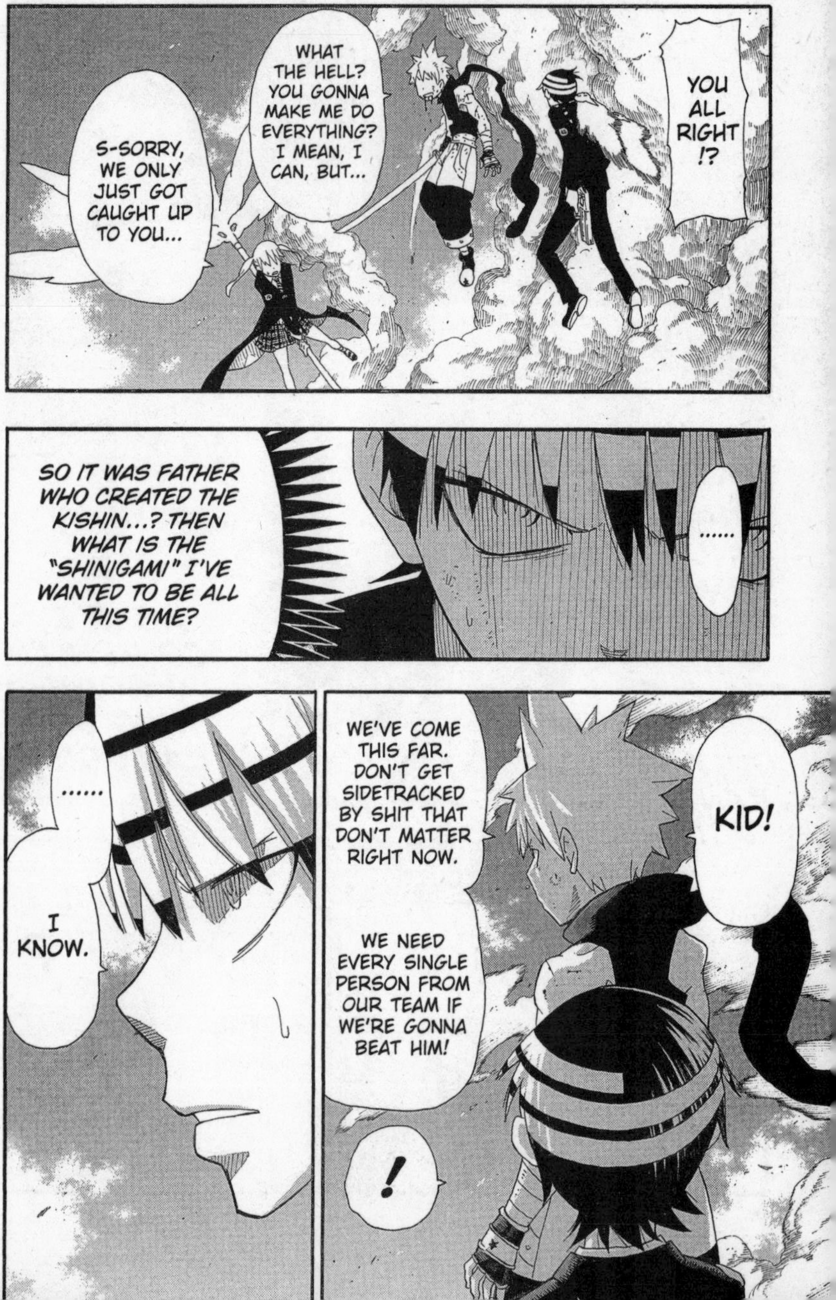
YOU ALL RIGHT!?
WHAT THE HELL? YOU GONNA MAKE ME DO EVERYTHING? I MEAN, I CAN, BUT...
S-SORRY, WE ONLY JUST GOT CAUGHT UP TO YOU...
......
SO IT WAS FATHER WHO CREATED THE KISHIN...? THEN WHAT IS THE "SHINIGAMI" I'VE WANTED TO BE ALL THIS TIME?
KID!
WE'VE COME THIS FAR. DON'T GET SIDETRACKED BY SHIT THAT DON'T MATTER RIGHT NOW.
WE NEED EVERY SINGLE PERSON FROM OUR TEAM IF WE'RE GONNA BEAT HIM!
!
......
I KNOW.

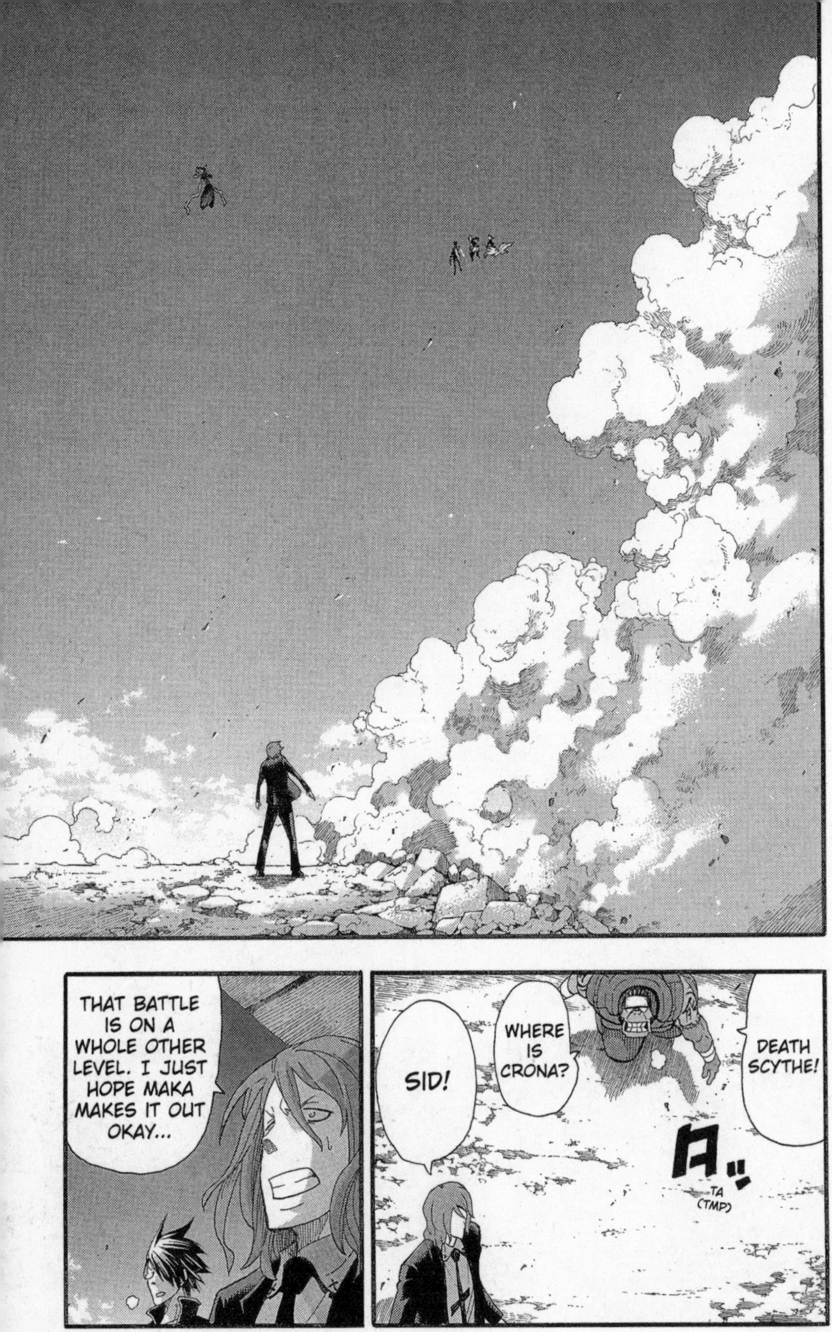
DEATH SCYTHE!
WHERE IS CRONA?
SID!
TA (TMP)
THAT BATTLE IS ON A WHOLE OTHER LEVEL. I JUST HOPE MAKA MAKES IT OUT OKAY...

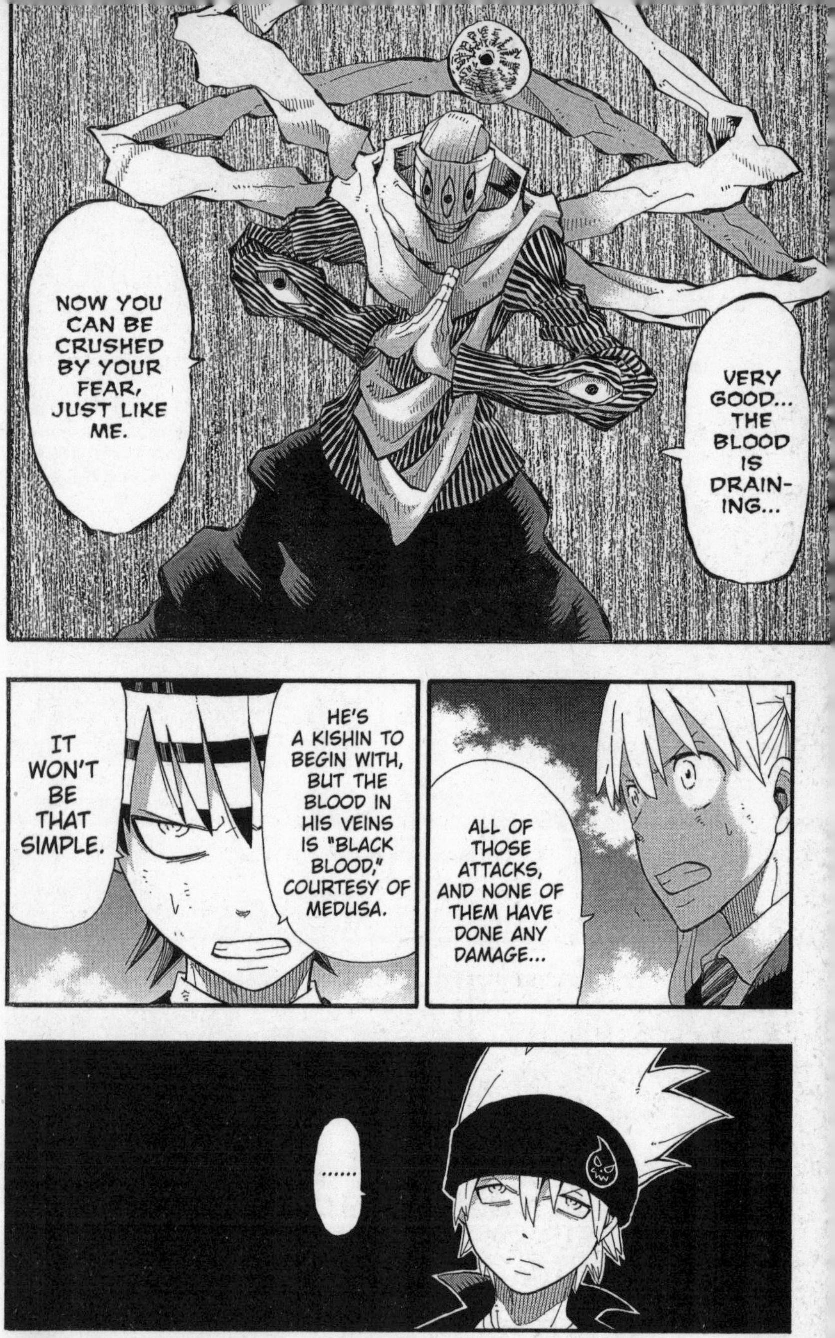
VERY GOOD... THE BLOOD IS DRAIN-ING...
NOW YOU CAN BE CRUSHED BY YOUR FEAR, JUST LIKE ME.
ALL OF THOSE ATTACKS, AND NONE OF THEM HAVE DONE ANY DAMAGE...
HE'S A KISHIN TO BEGIN WITH, BUT THE BLOOD IN HIS VEINS IS "BLACK BLOOD," COURTESY OF MEDUSA.
IT WON'T BE THAT SIMPLE.
......

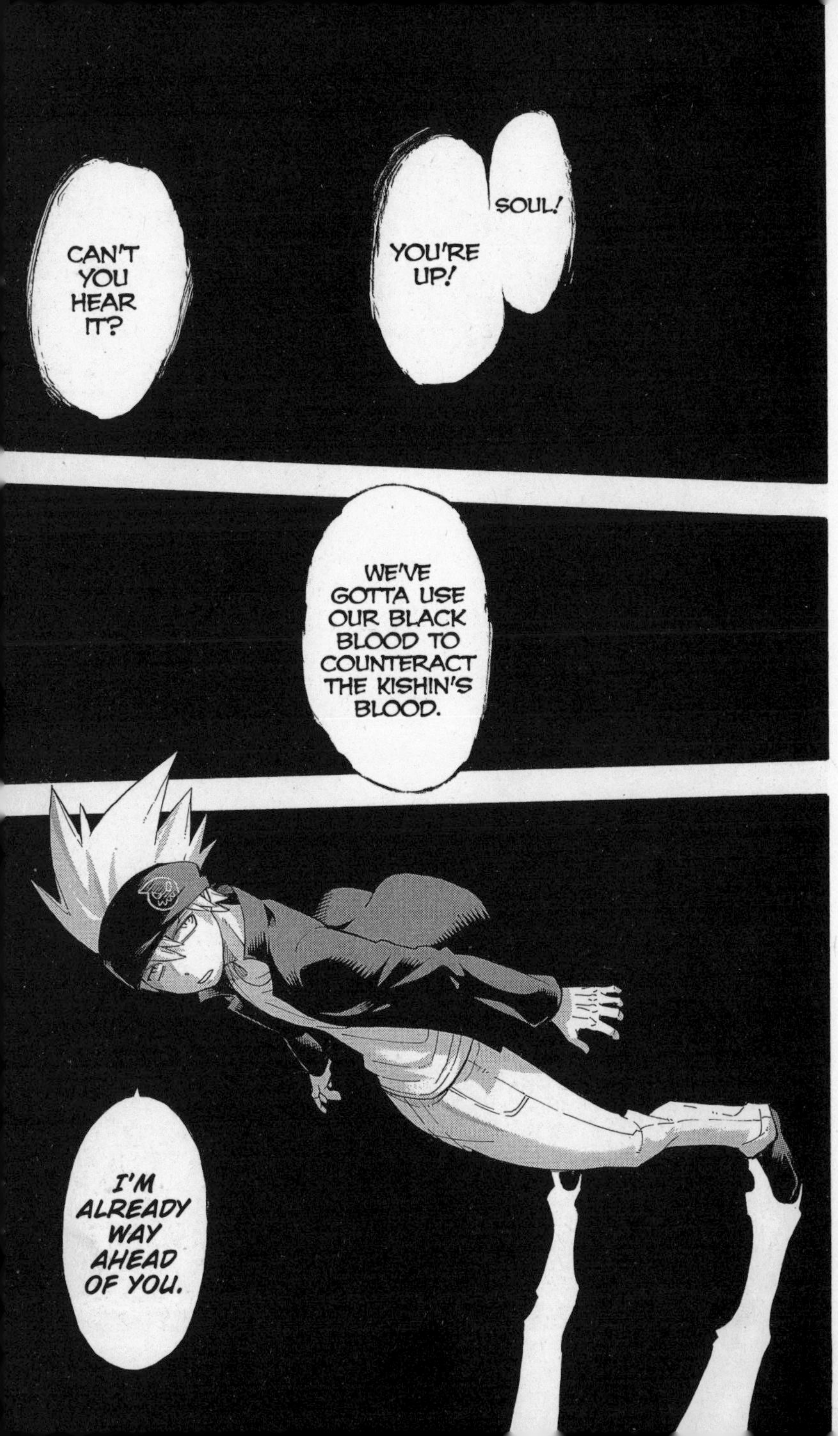
SOUL!
YOU'RE UP!
CAN'T YOU HEAR IT?
WE'VE GOTTA USE OUR BLACK BLOOD TO COUNTERACT THE KISHIN'S BLOOD.
I'M ALREADY WAY AHEAD OF YOU.

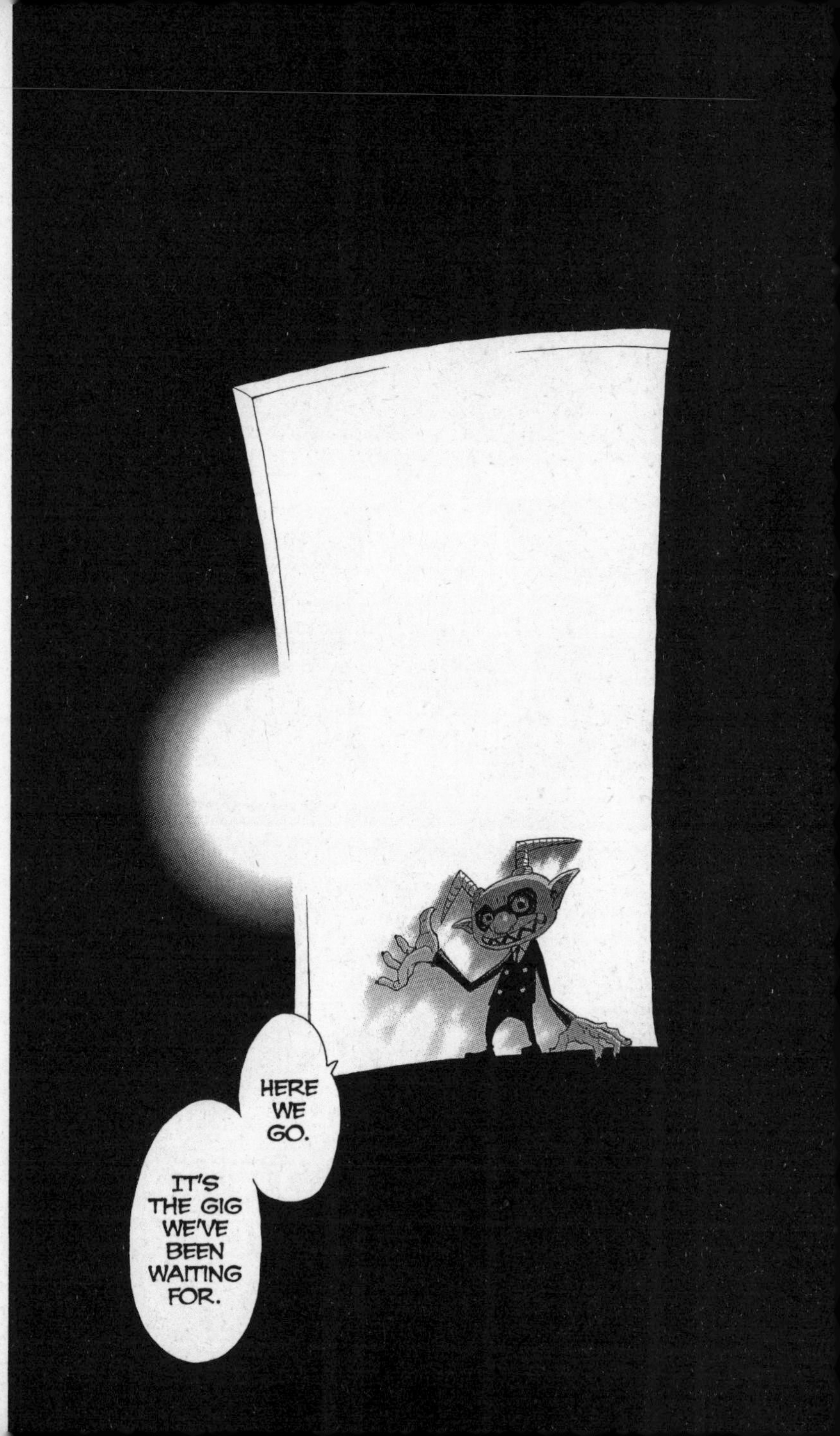
HERE WE GO.
IT'S THE GIG WE'VE BEEN WAITING FOR.

SOUL EATER

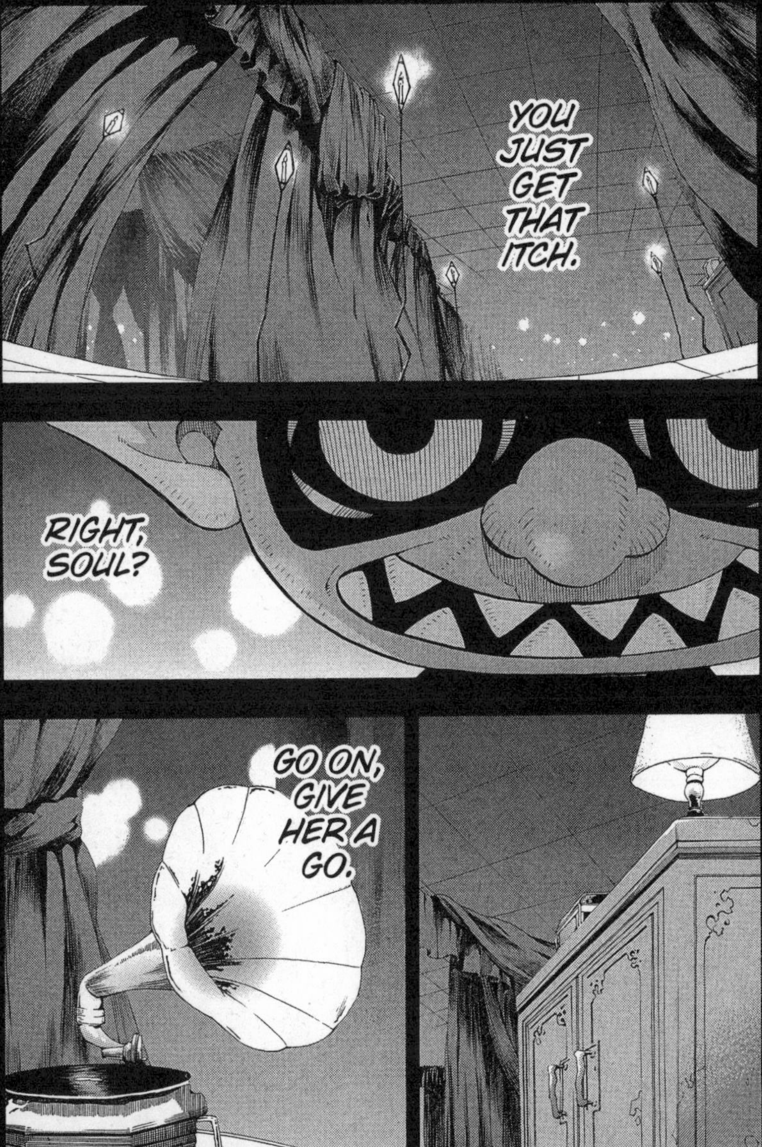
YOU JUST GET THAT ITCH.
RIGHT, SOUL?
GO ON, GIVE HER A GO.

SHE'S BEEN LONELY WITHOUT YOU!

SOUL EATER

CHAPTER 109: THE DARK SIDE OF THE MOON VI

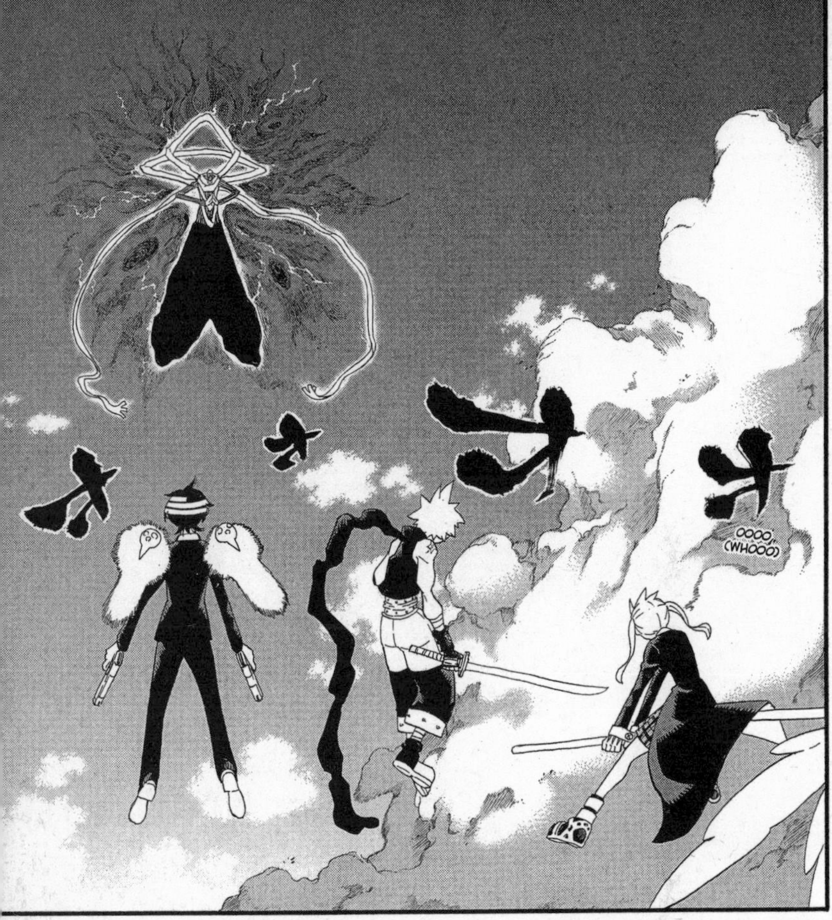
(WHOOO)
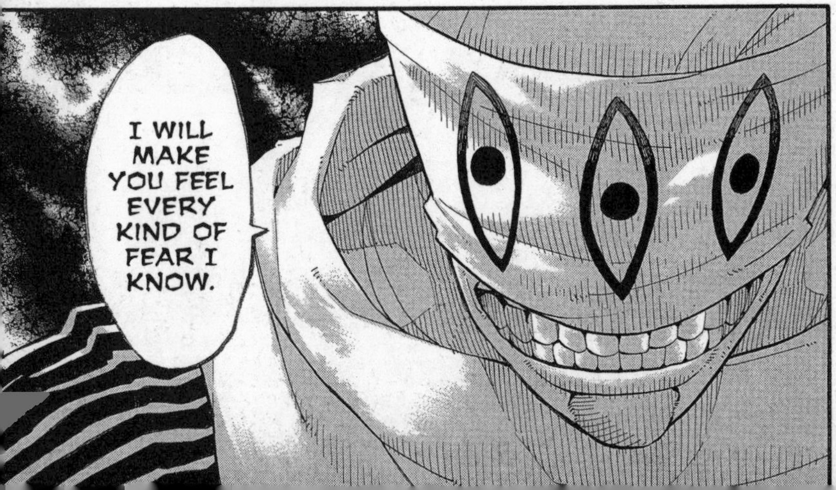
I WILL MAKE YOU FEEL EVERY KIND OF FEAR I KNOW.

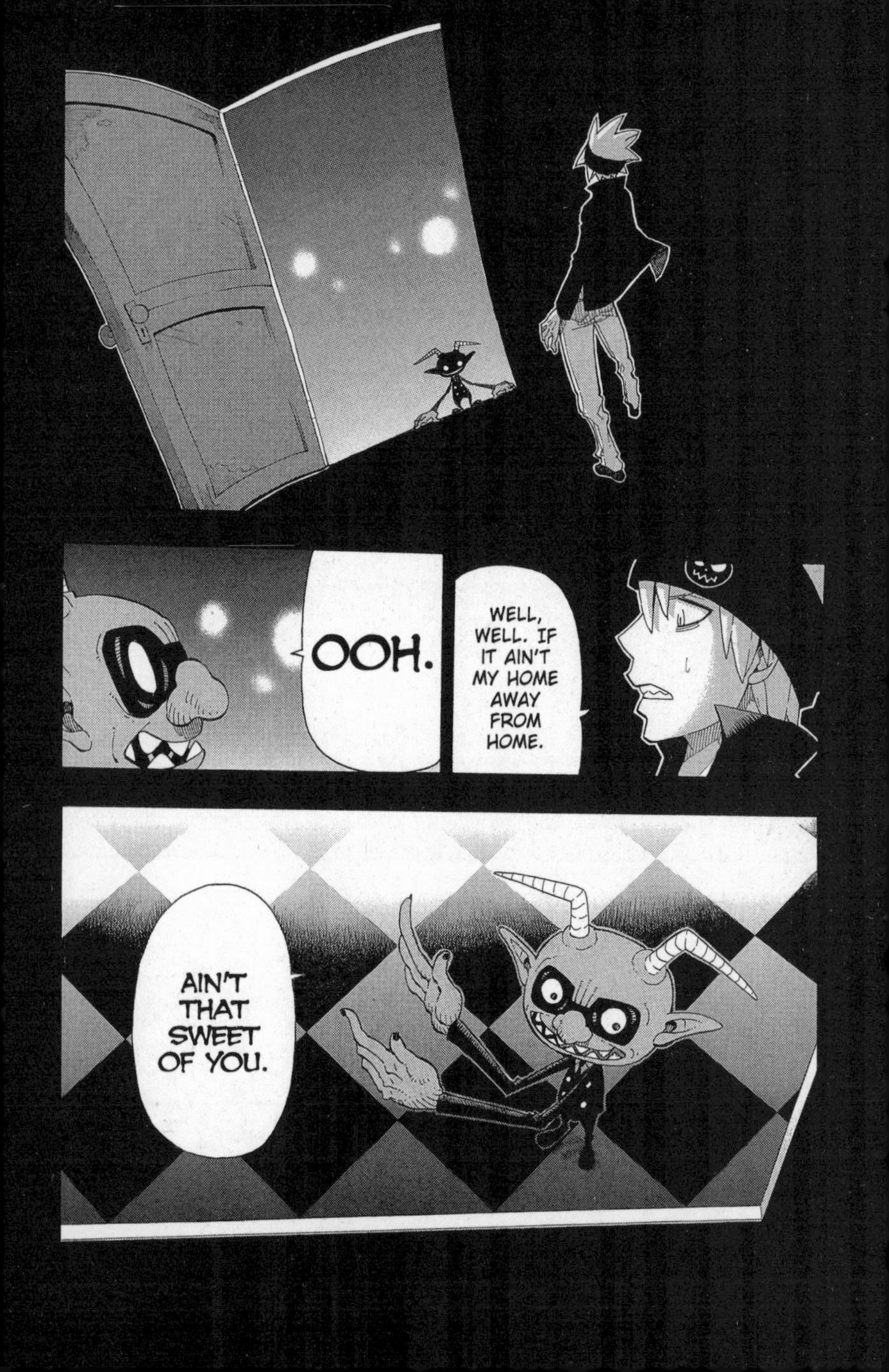
WELL, WELL. IF IT AIN'T MY HOME AWAY FROM HOME.
OOH.
AIN'T THAT SWEET OF YOU.

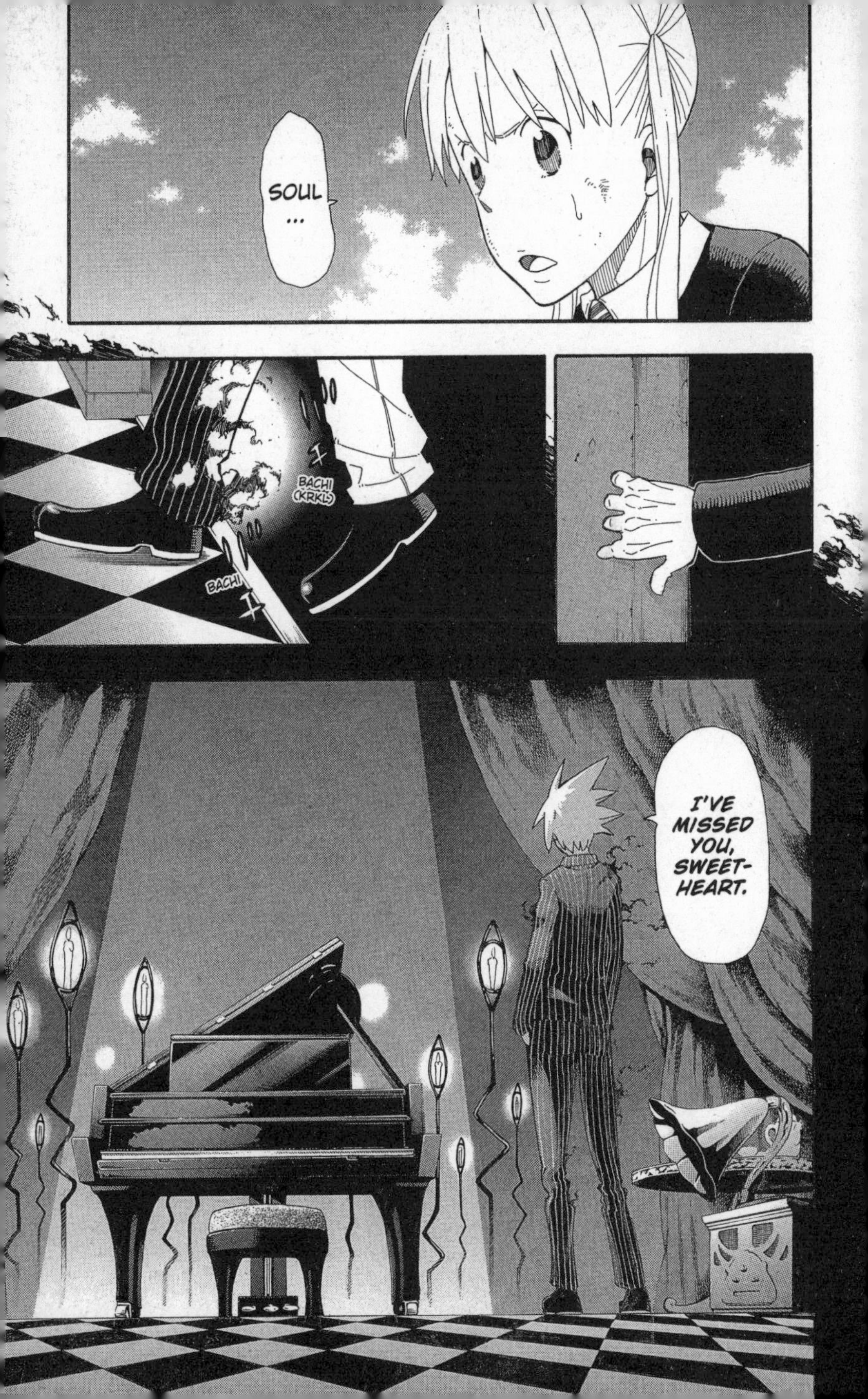
SOUL ...
BACHI (KRKL)
BACHI
I'VE MISSED YOU, SWEET-HEART.

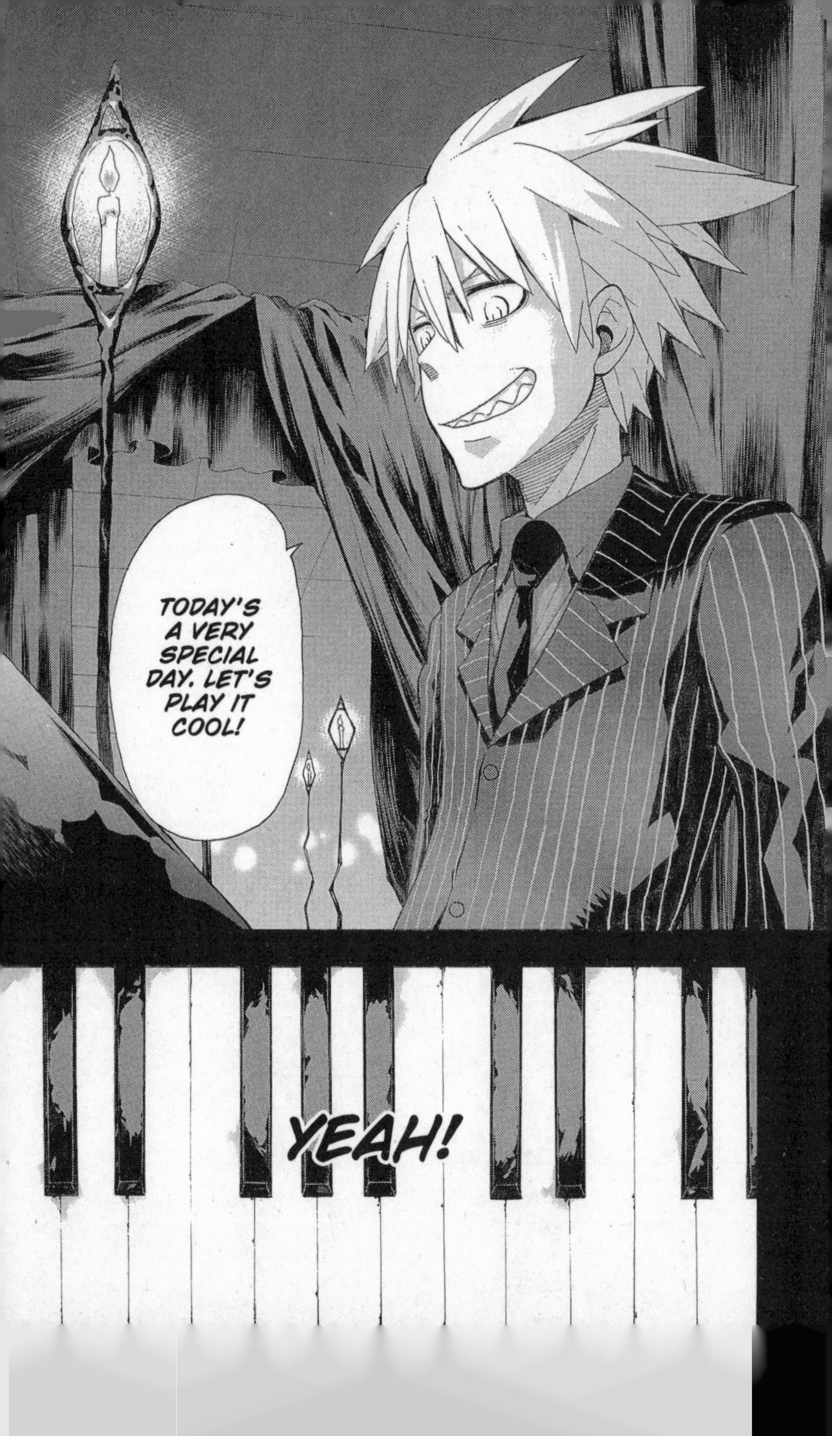
TODAY'S A VERY SPECIAL DAY. LET'S PLAY IT COOL!
YEAH!

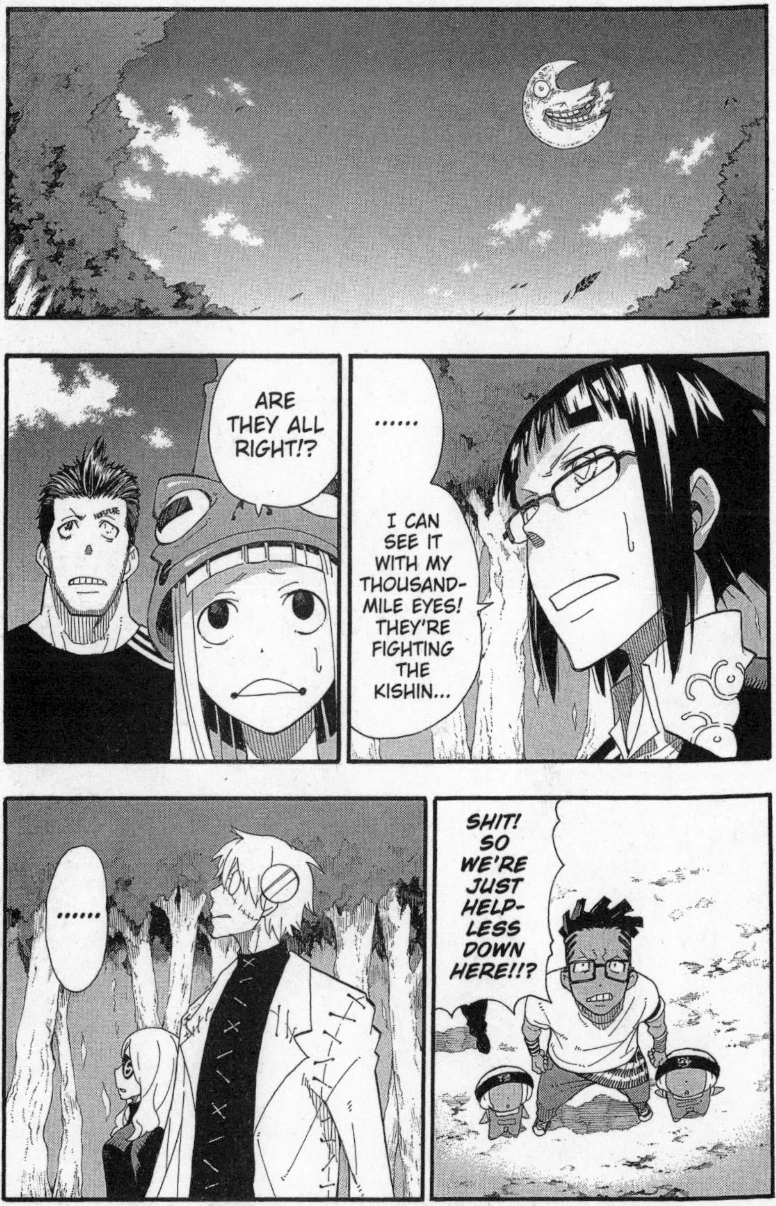
......
I CAN SEE IT WITH MY THOUSAND-MILE EYES! THEY'RE FIGHTING THE KISHIN...
ARE THEY ALL RIGHT!?
SHIT! SO WE'RE JUST HELP-LESS DOWN HERE!!?
......

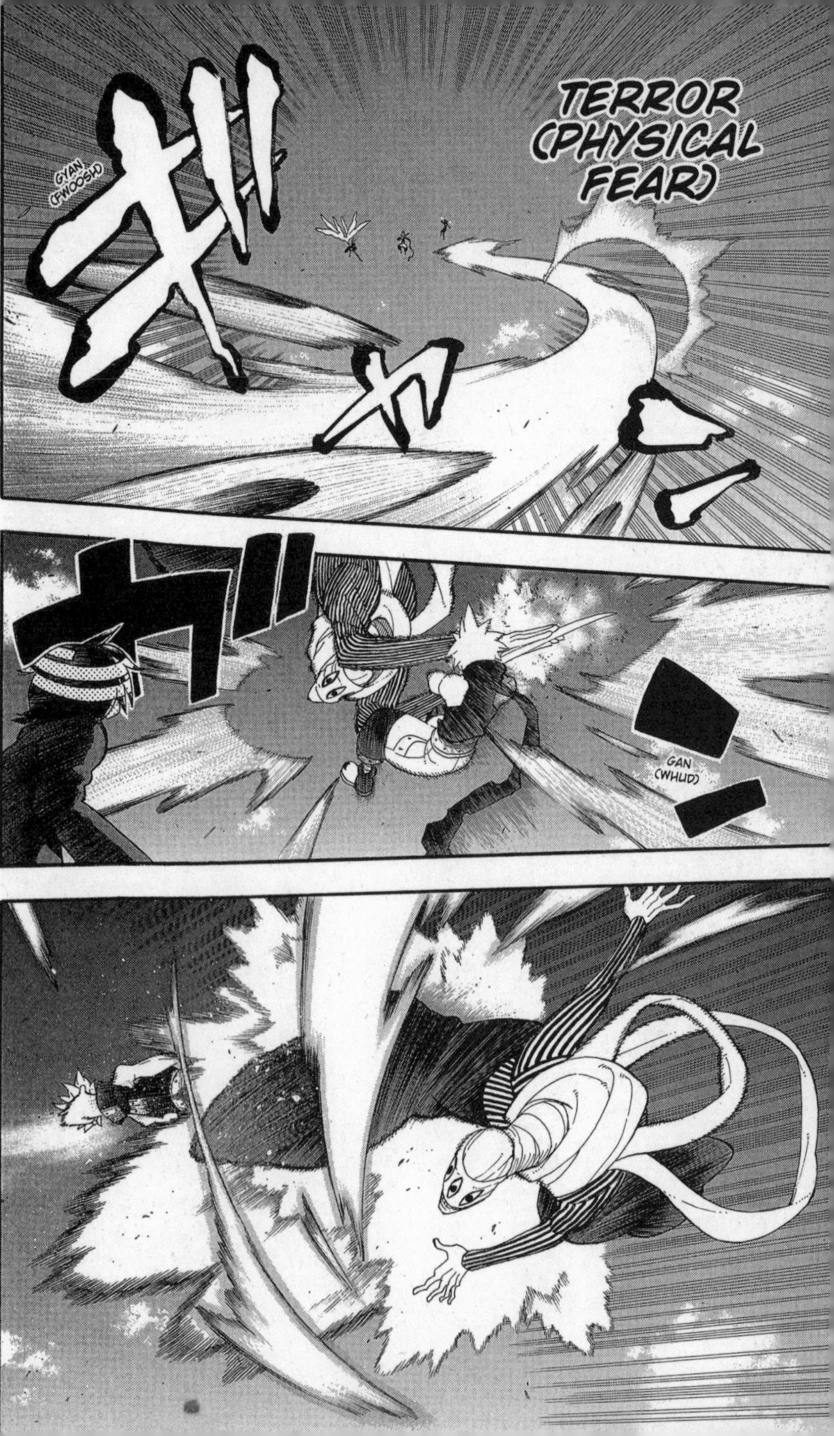
TERROR (PHYSICAL FEAR)
GYAN (FWOOSH)
GAN (WHUD)

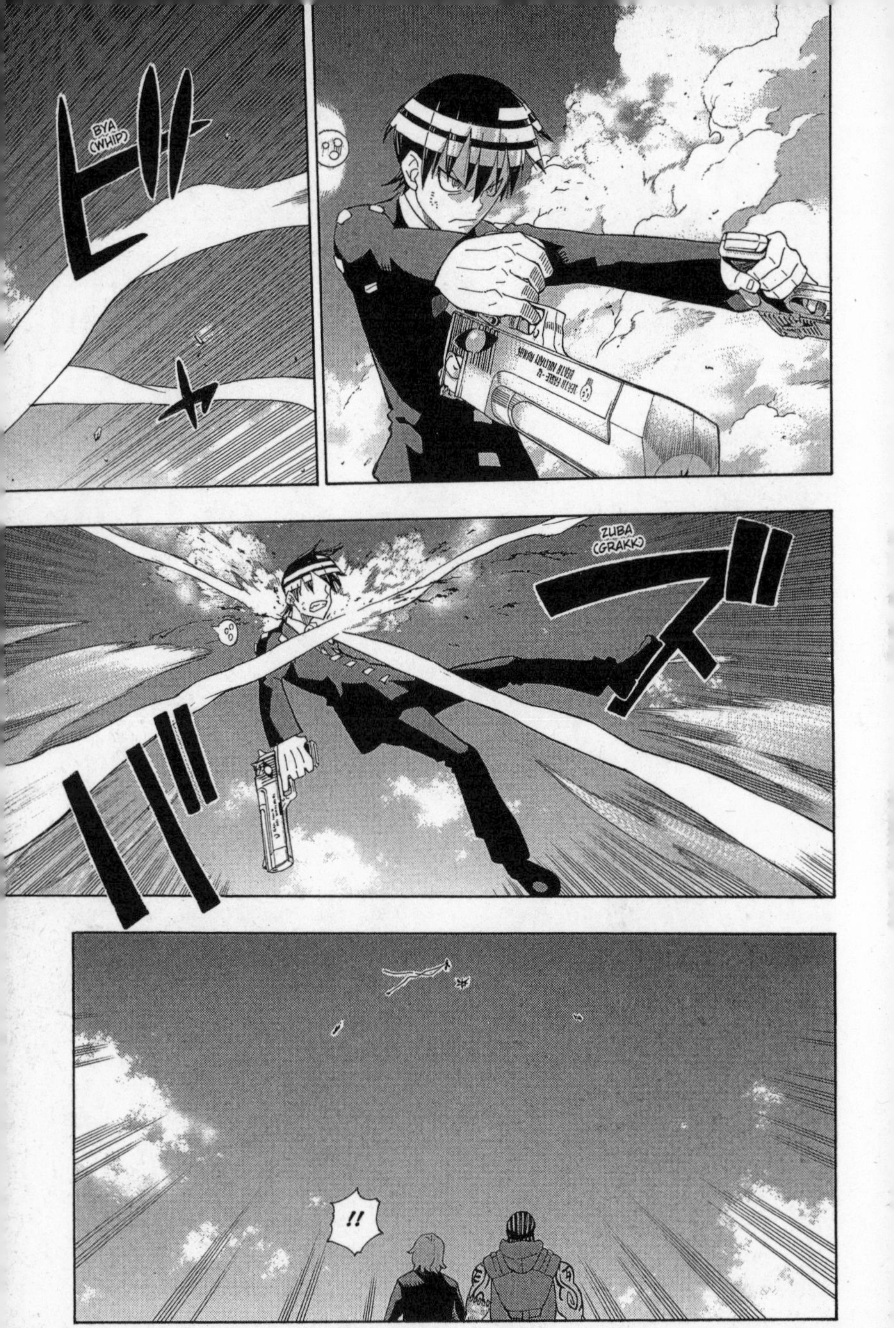
BYA (WHIP)
ZUBA (GRAKK)
!!

BA
(WHOOSH)

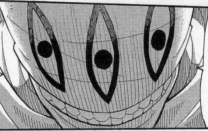

WHAT IS HUMAN SCUM LIKE YOU DOING IN THIS BATTLE?

LEARN YOUR MANNERS!

BUA
(FWOOD)

THIS IS HUMANITY'S BATTLE TOO!

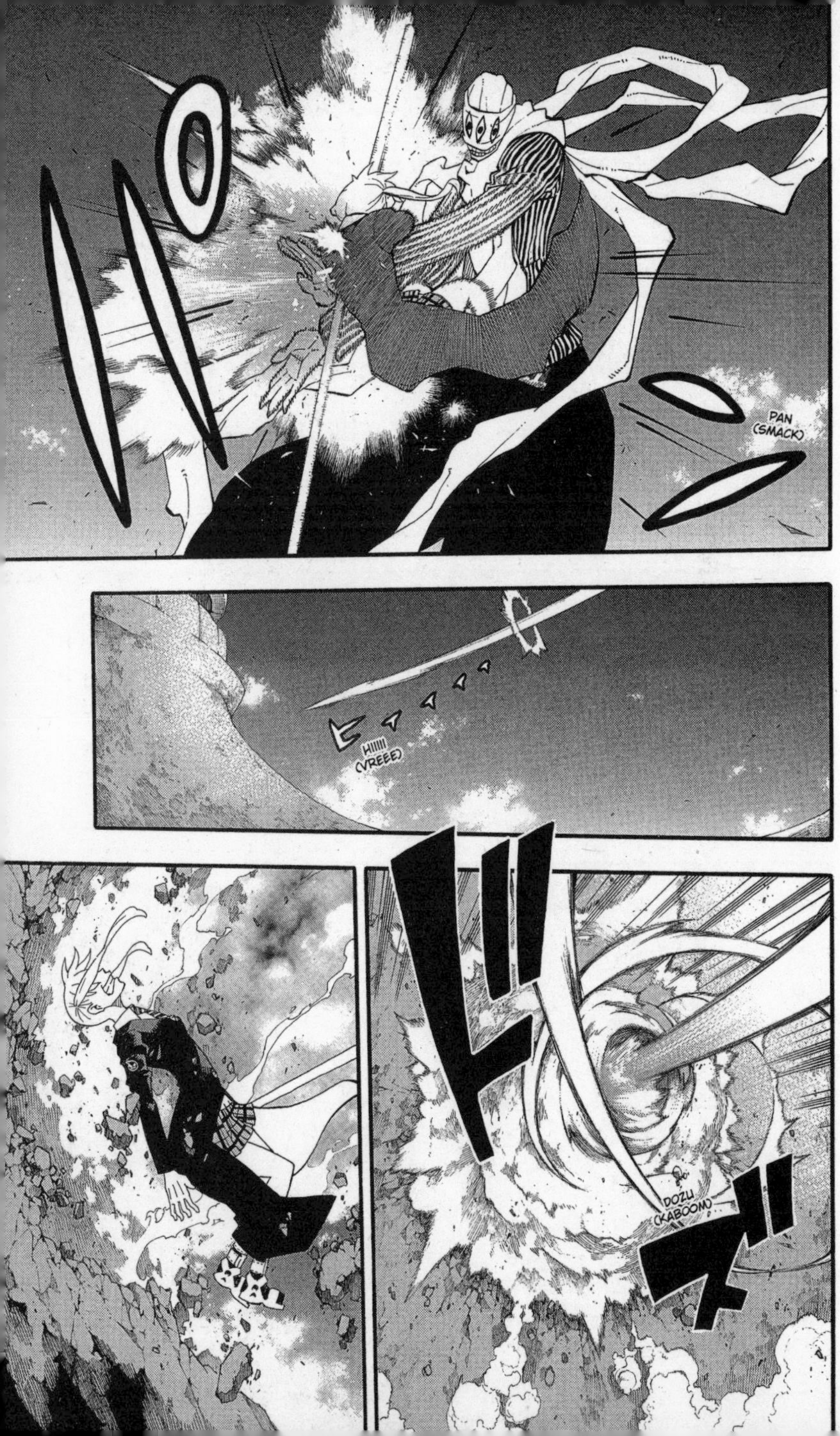
PAN
(SMACK)
HIIIII
(VREEE)
DOZU
(KABOOM)

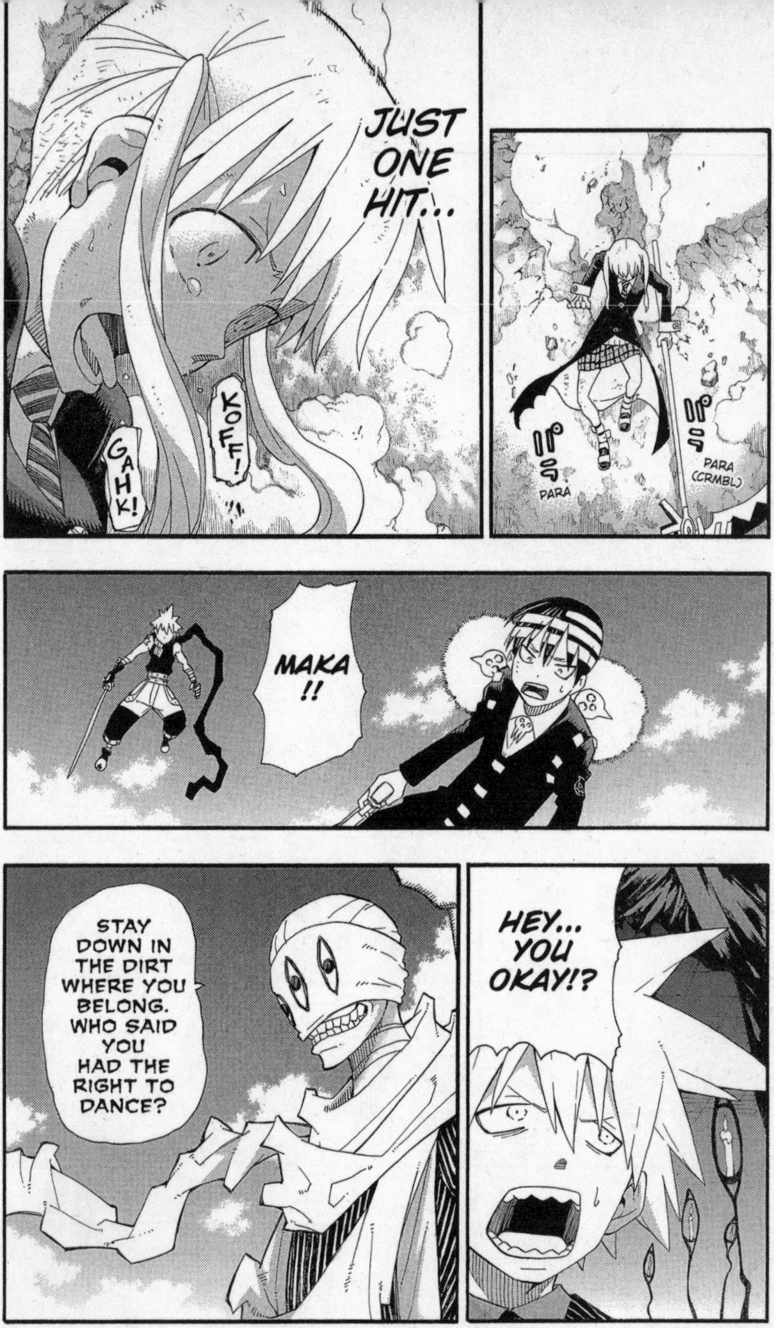

PARA
(CRMBL)
PARA
JUST ONE HIT...
KOFF!
GAHK!
MAKA!!
HEY... YOU OKAY!?
STAY DOWN IN THE DIRT WHERE YOU BELONG. WHO SAID YOU HAD THE RIGHT TO DANCE?

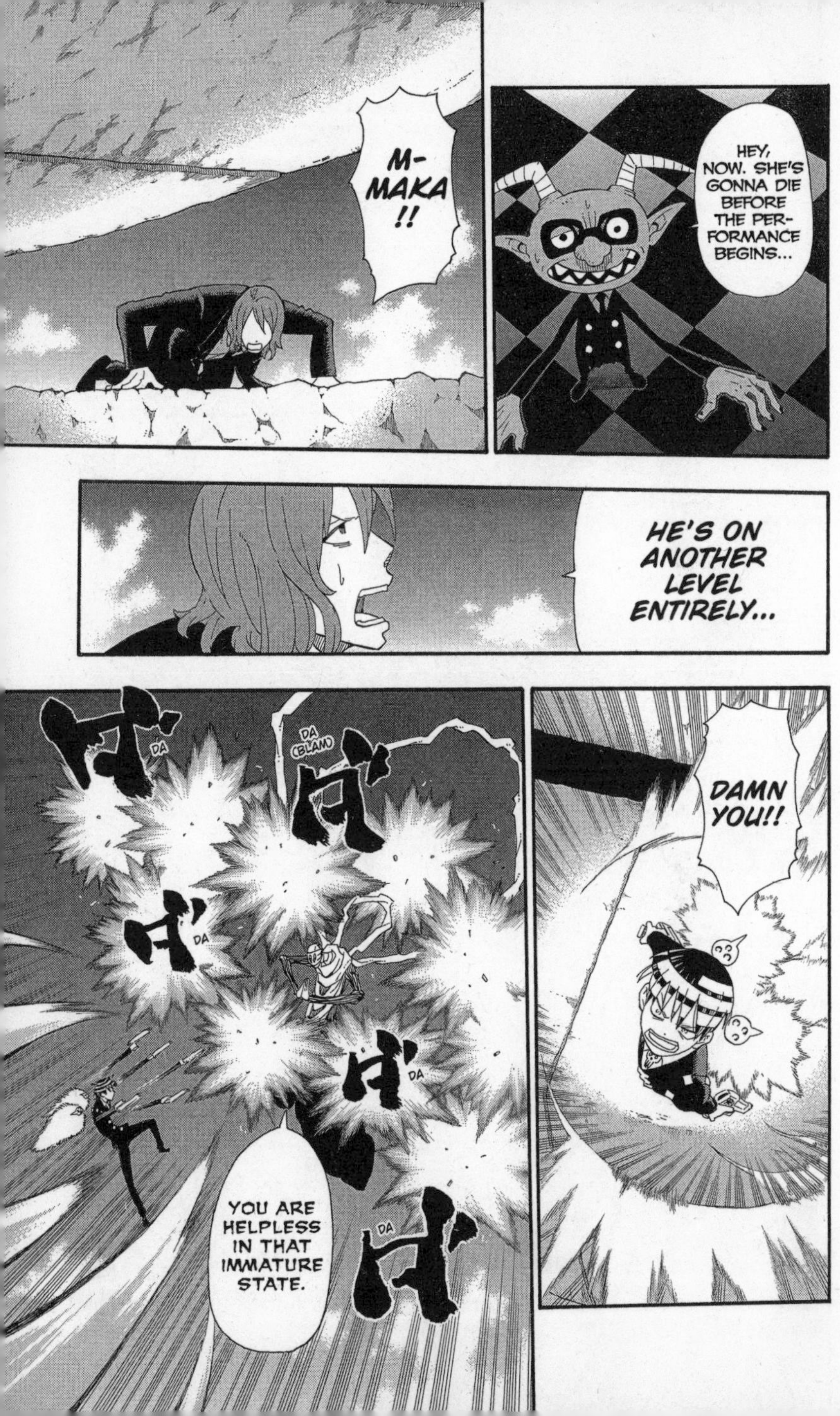
HEY, NOW. SHE'S GONNA DIE BEFORE THE PERFORMANCE BEGINS...
M-MAKA!!
HE'S ON ANOTHER LEVEL ENTIRELY...
DAMN YOU!!
DA
DA (BLAM)
DA
DA
DA
YOU ARE HELPLESS IN THAT IMMATURE STATE.

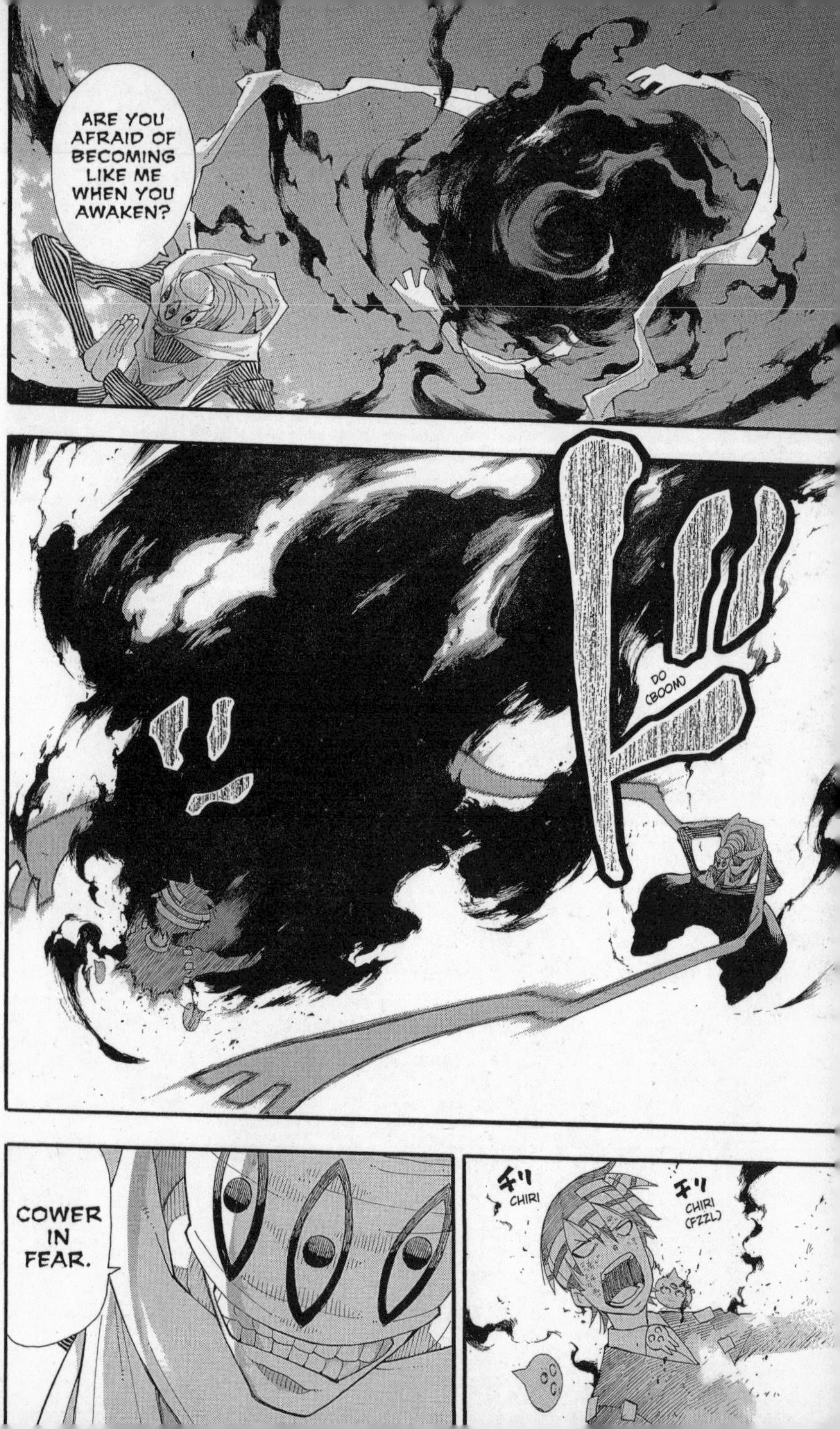
ARE YOU AFRAID OF BECOMING LIKE ME WHEN YOU AWAKEN?
DO (BOOM)
チリ CHIRI
チリ CHIRI (FZZL)
COWER IN FEAR.

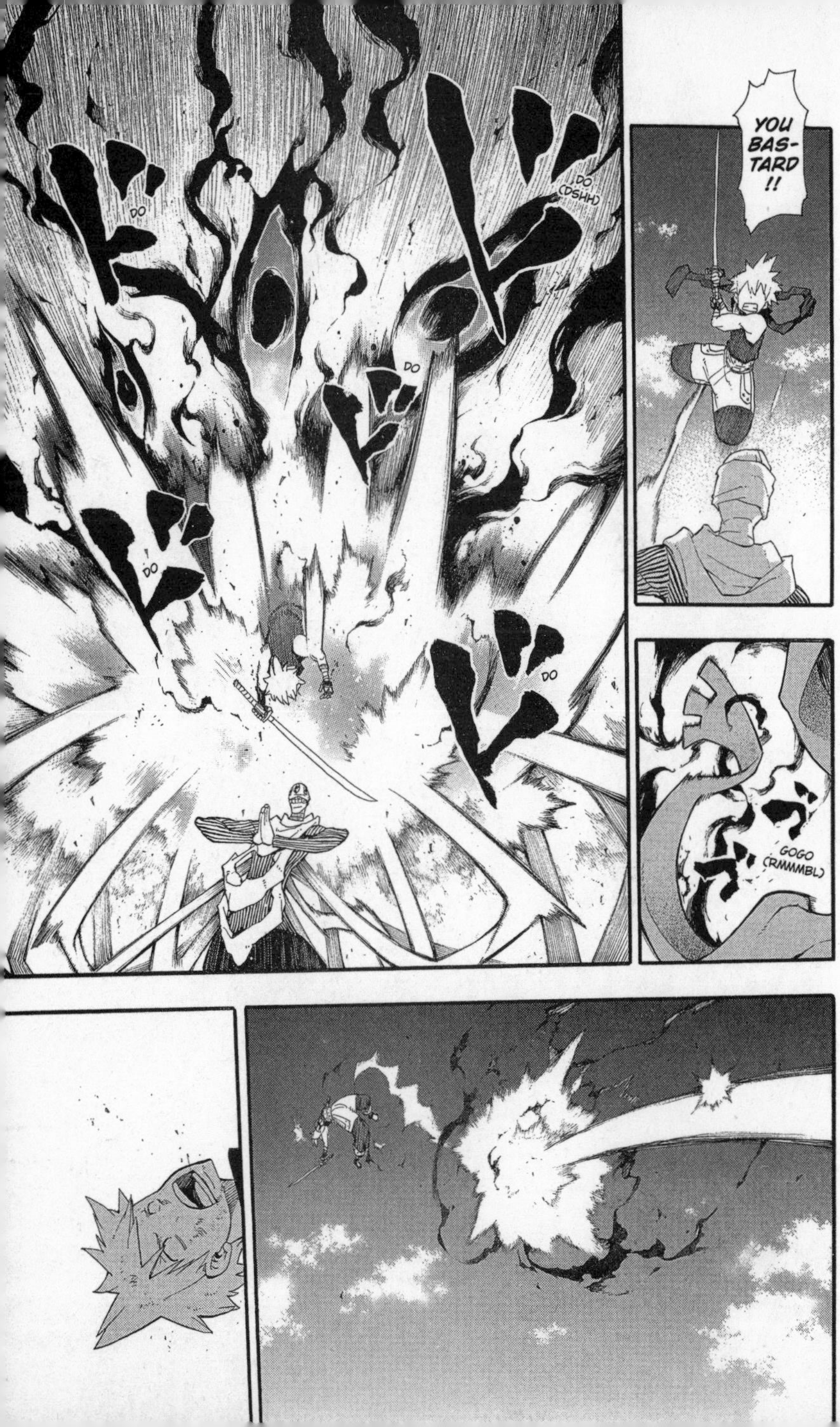
YOU BAS-TARD!!
GOGO (RMMMBL)
DO (DSHH)
DO
DO
DO
DO

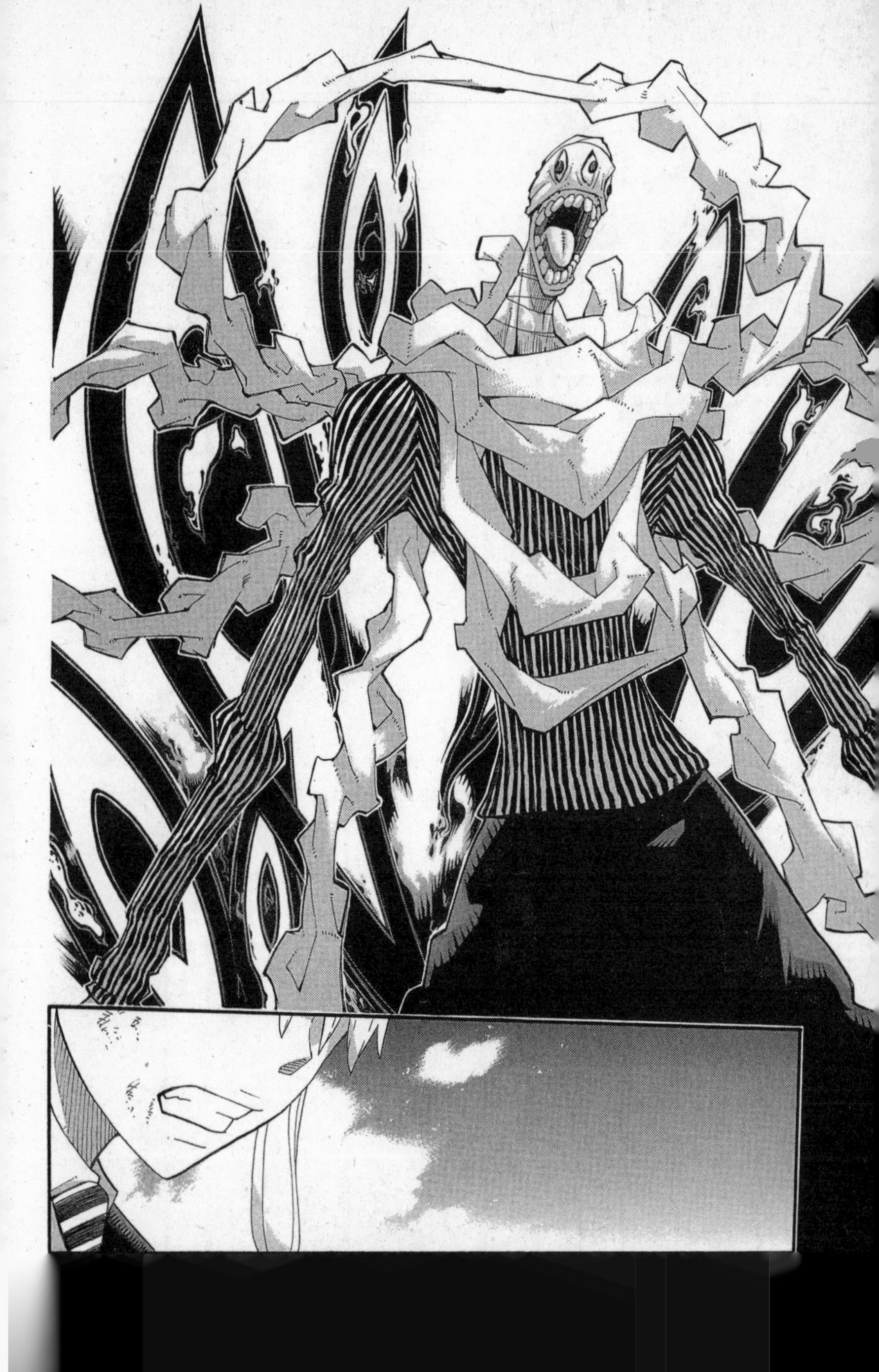

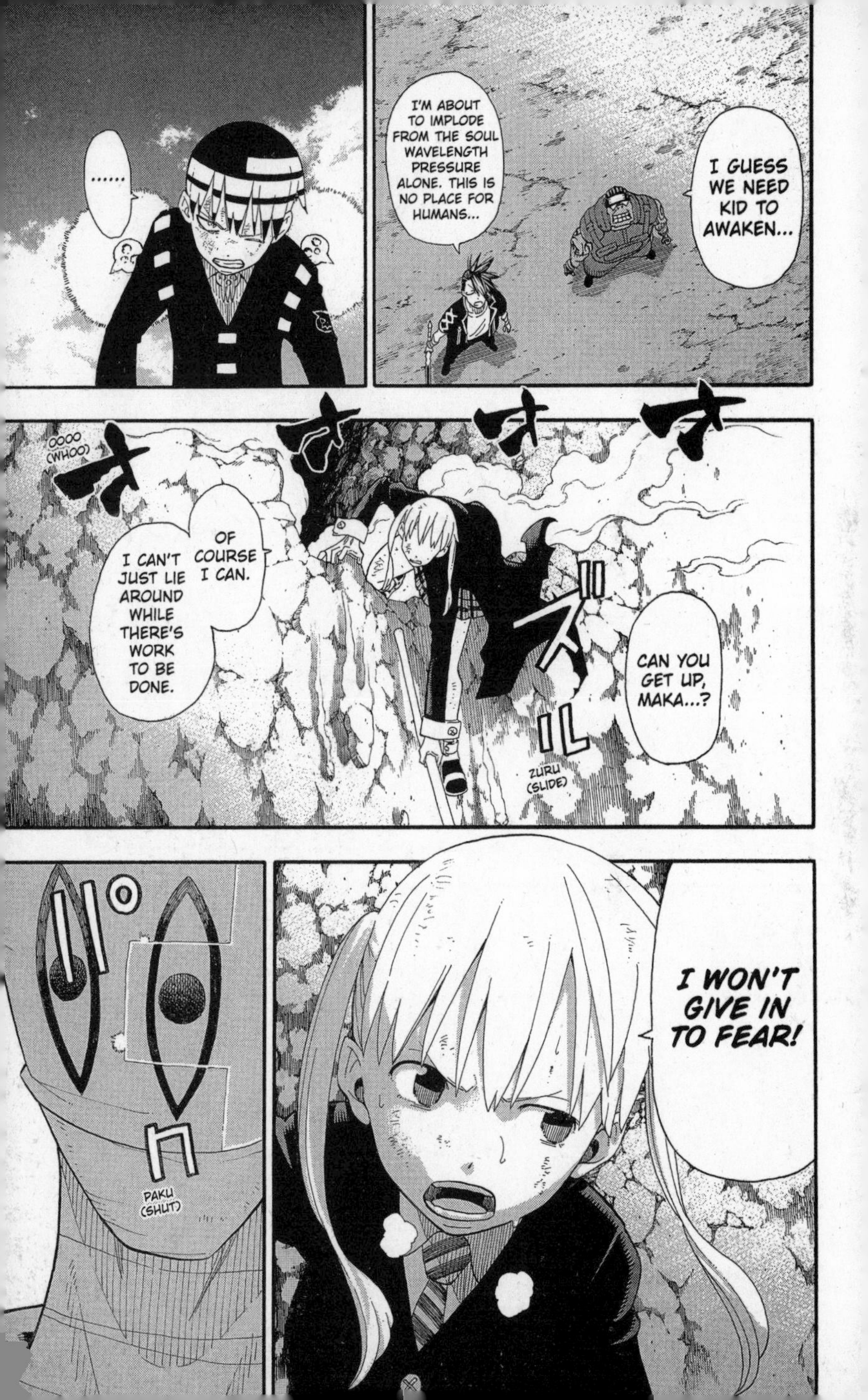
I GUESS WE NEED KID TO AWAKEN...
I'M ABOUT TO IMPLODE FROM THE SOUL WAVELENGTH PRESSURE ALONE. THIS IS NO PLACE FOR HUMANS...
......
OOOO (WHOO)
CAN YOU GET UP, MAKA...?
ZURU (SLIDE)
OF COURSE I CAN.
I CAN'T JUST LIE AROUND WHILE THERE'S WORK TO BE DONE.
I WON'T GIVE IN TO FEAR!
PAKU (SHUT)

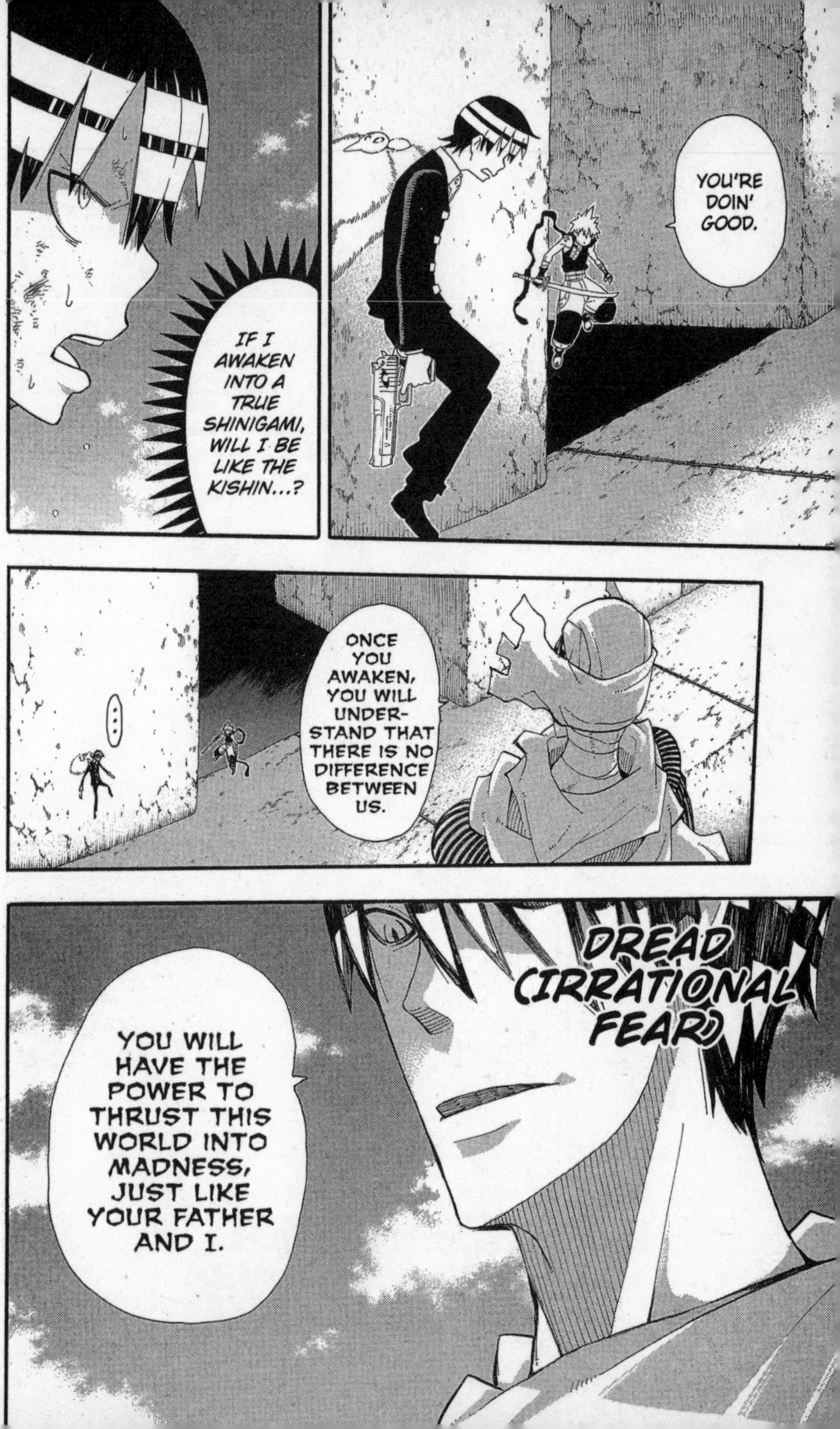
YOU'RE DOIN' GOOD.
IF I AWAKEN INTO A TRUE SHINIGAMI, WILL I BE LIKE THE KISHIN...?
ONCE YOU AWAKEN, YOU WILL UNDER-STAND THAT THERE IS NO DIFFERENCE BETWEEN US.
...
DREAD (IRRATIONAL FEAR)
YOU WILL HAVE THE POWER TO THRUST THIS WORLD INTO MADNESS, JUST LIKE YOUR FATHER AND I.

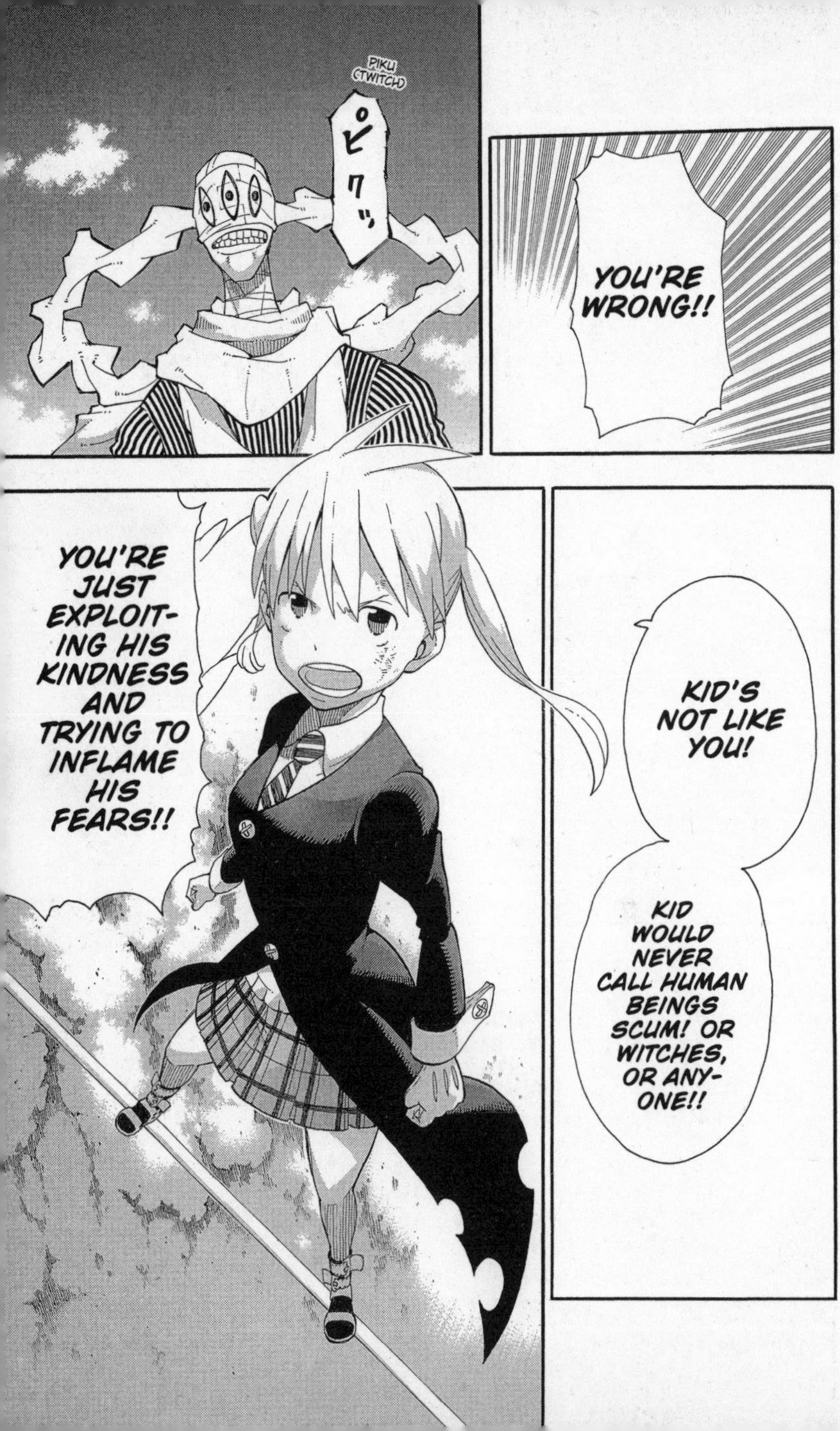
YOU'RE WRONG!!
ピクッ
PIKU (TWITCH)
KID'S NOT LIKE YOU!
KID WOULD NEVER CALL HUMAN BEINGS SCUM! OR WITCHES, OR ANY-ONE!!
YOU'RE JUST EXPLOIT-ING HIS KINDNESS AND TRYING TO INFLAME HIS FEARS!!

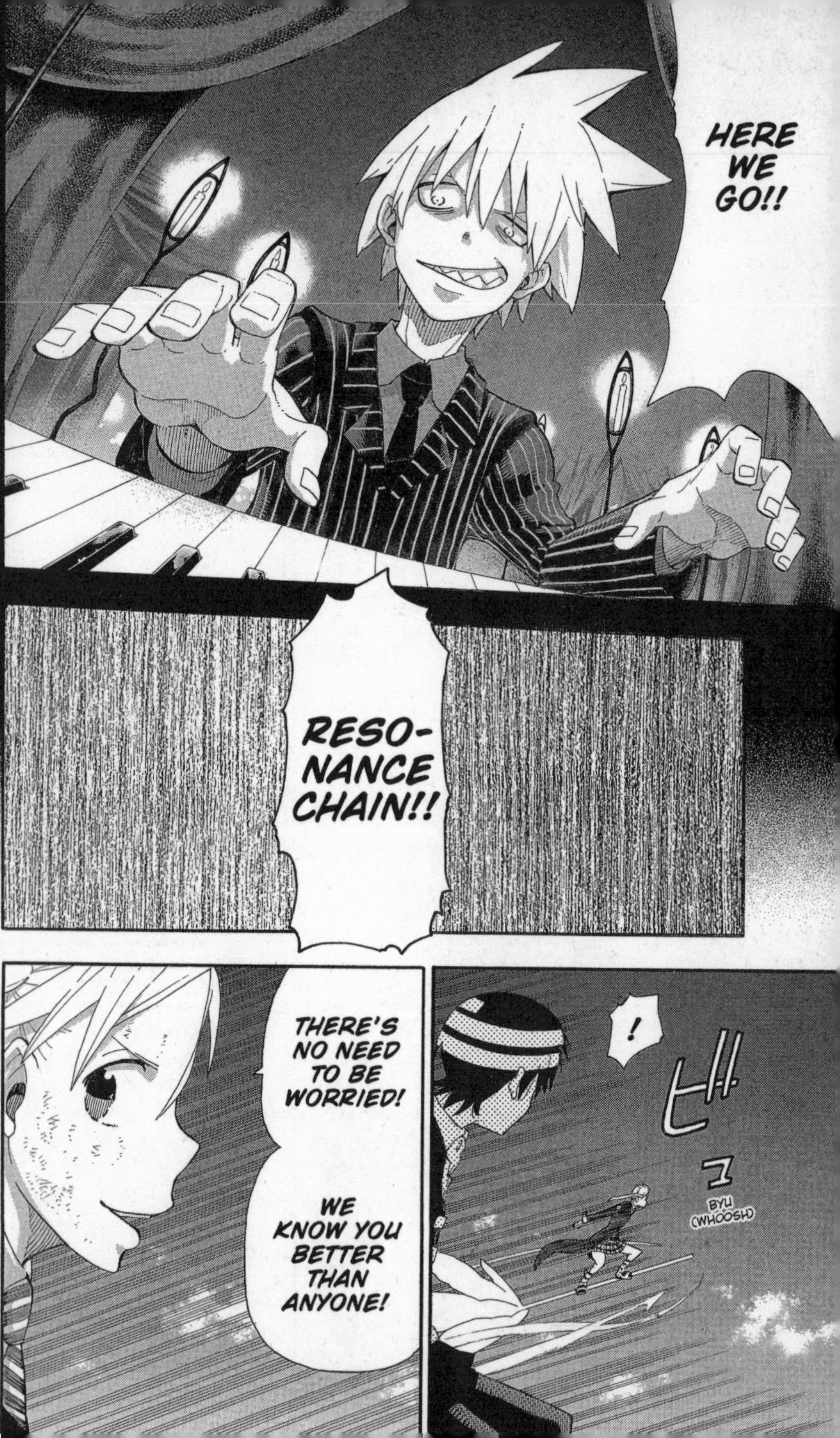
HERE WE GO!!
RESO-NANCE CHAIN!!
!
BYU (WHOOSH)
THERE'S NO NEED TO BE WORRIED!
WE KNOW YOU BETTER THAN ANYONE!

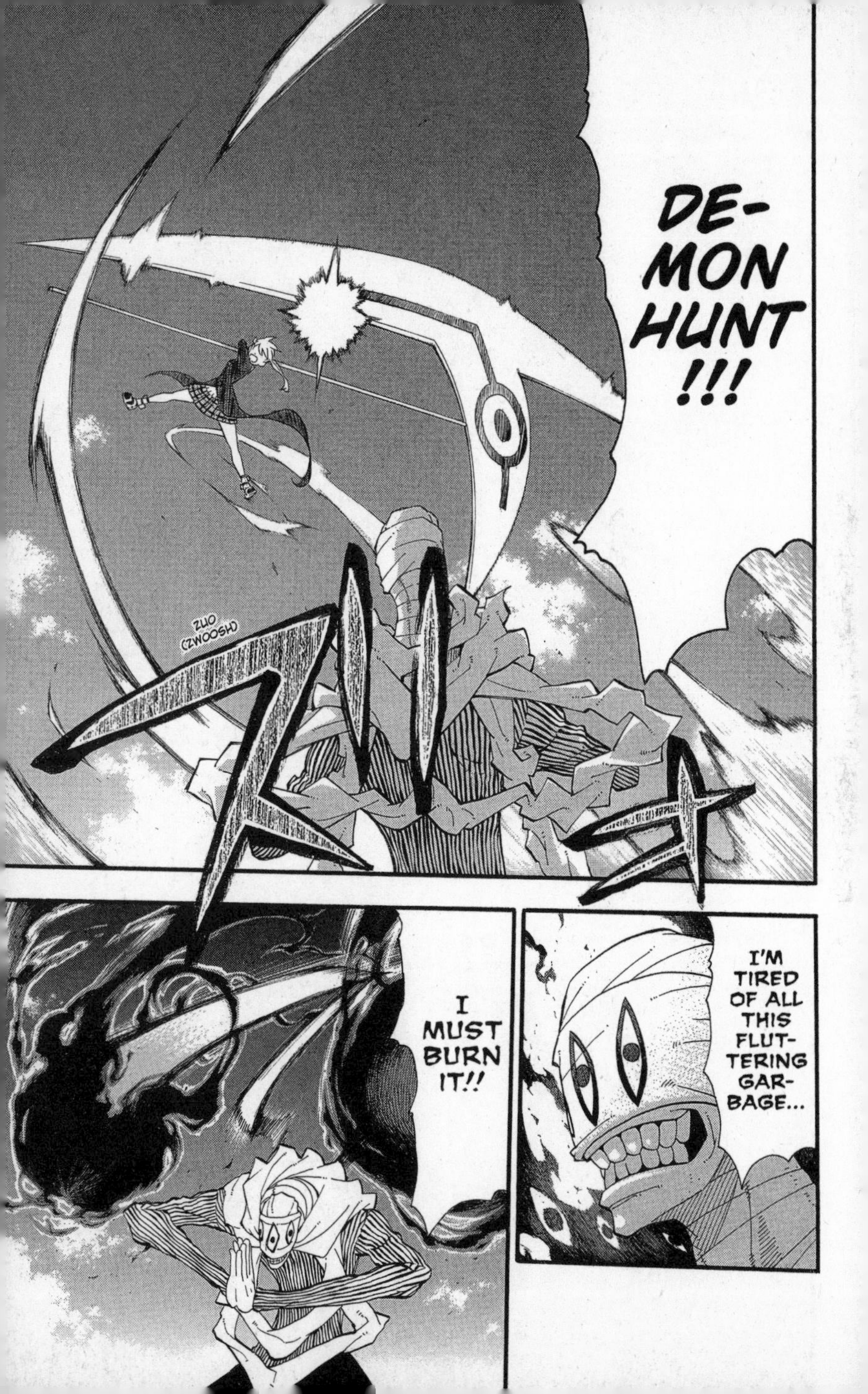
DE-MON HUNT!!!
ZUO (ZWOOSH)
I'M TIRED OF ALL THIS FLUT-TERING GAR-BAGE...
I MUST BURN IT!!

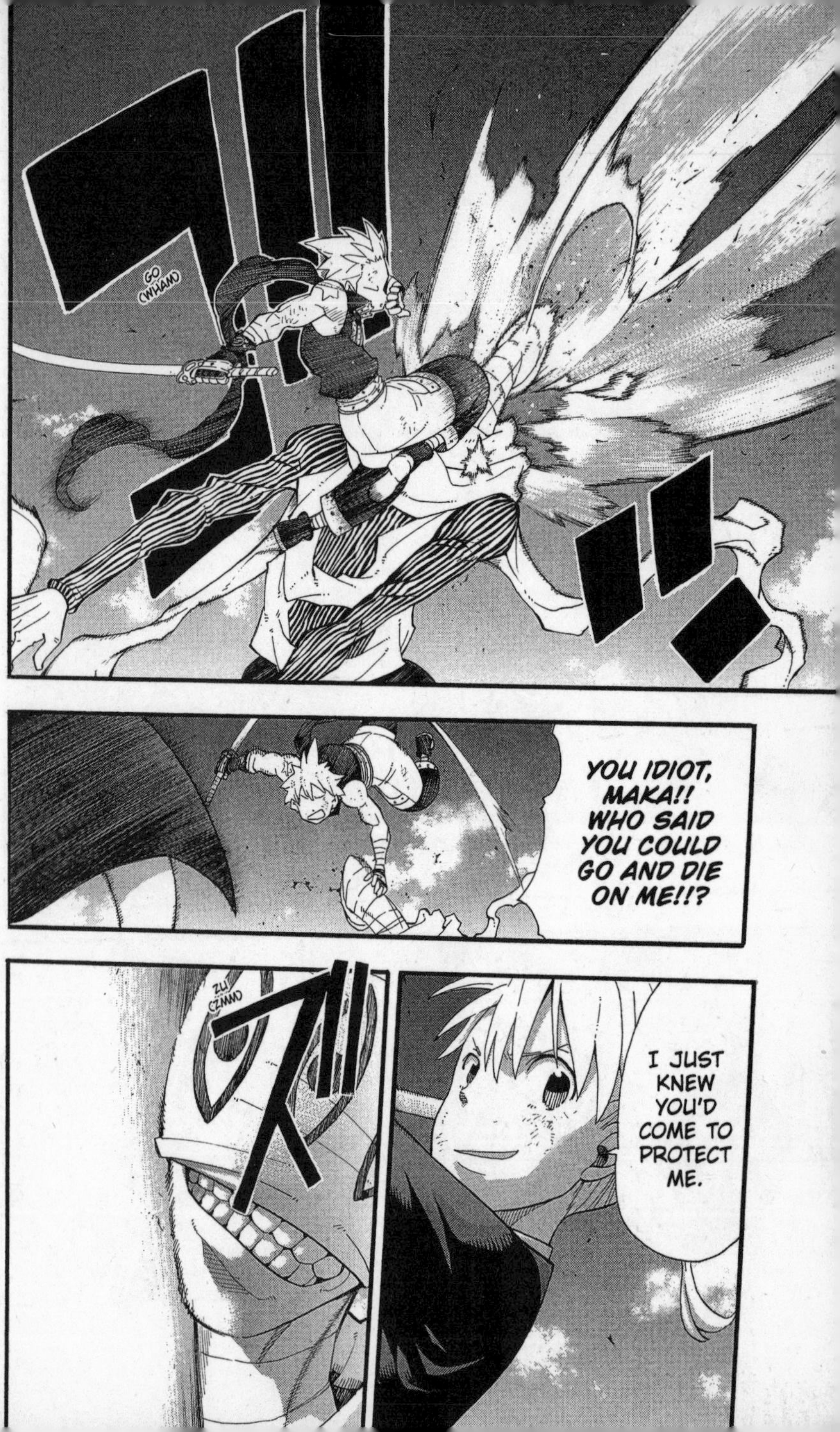
GO
(WHAM)
YOU IDIOT, MAKA!! WHO SAID YOU COULD GO AND DIE ON ME!!?
ZU
(ZMM)
I JUST KNEW YOU'D COME TO PROTECT ME.

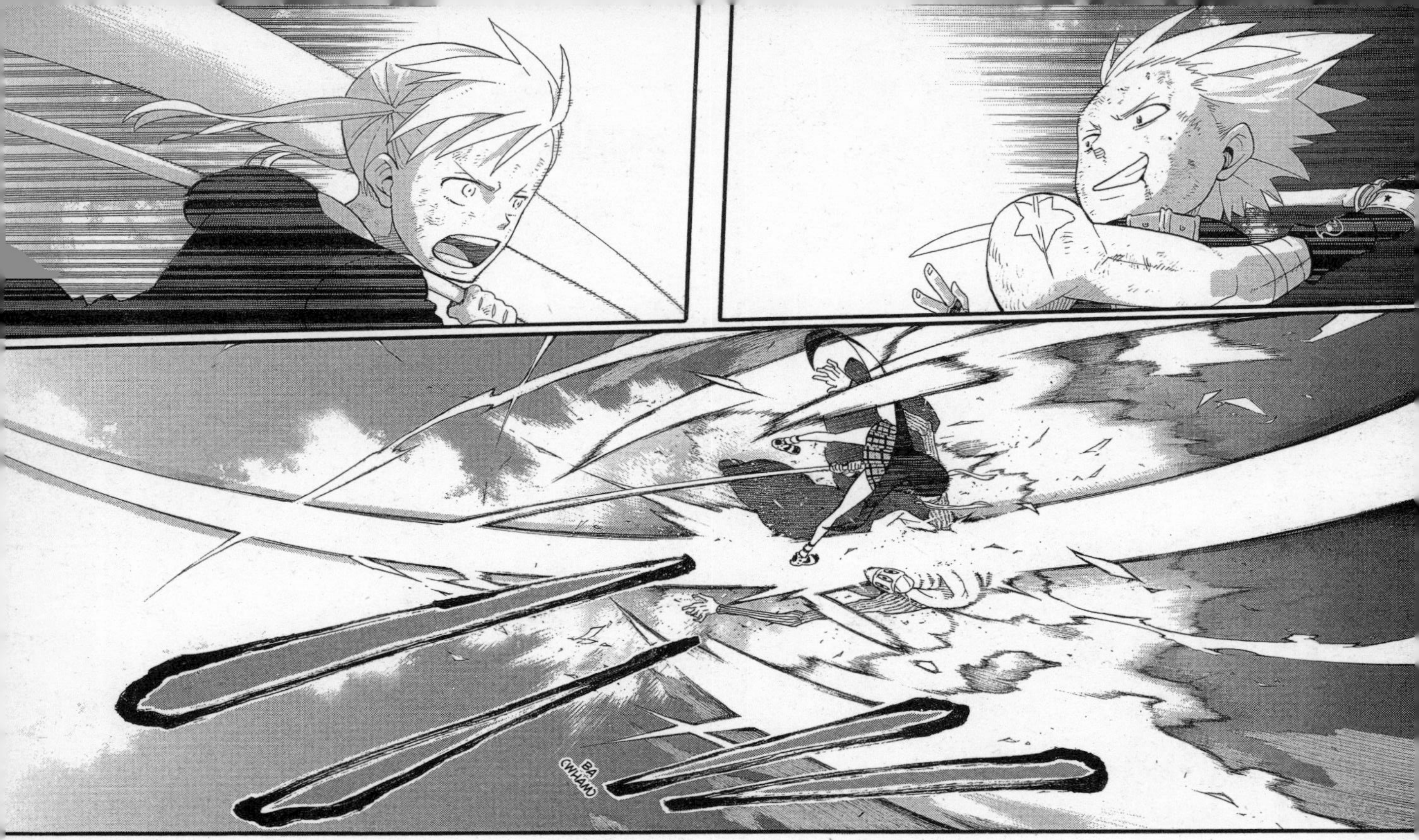
BA
(WHAM)

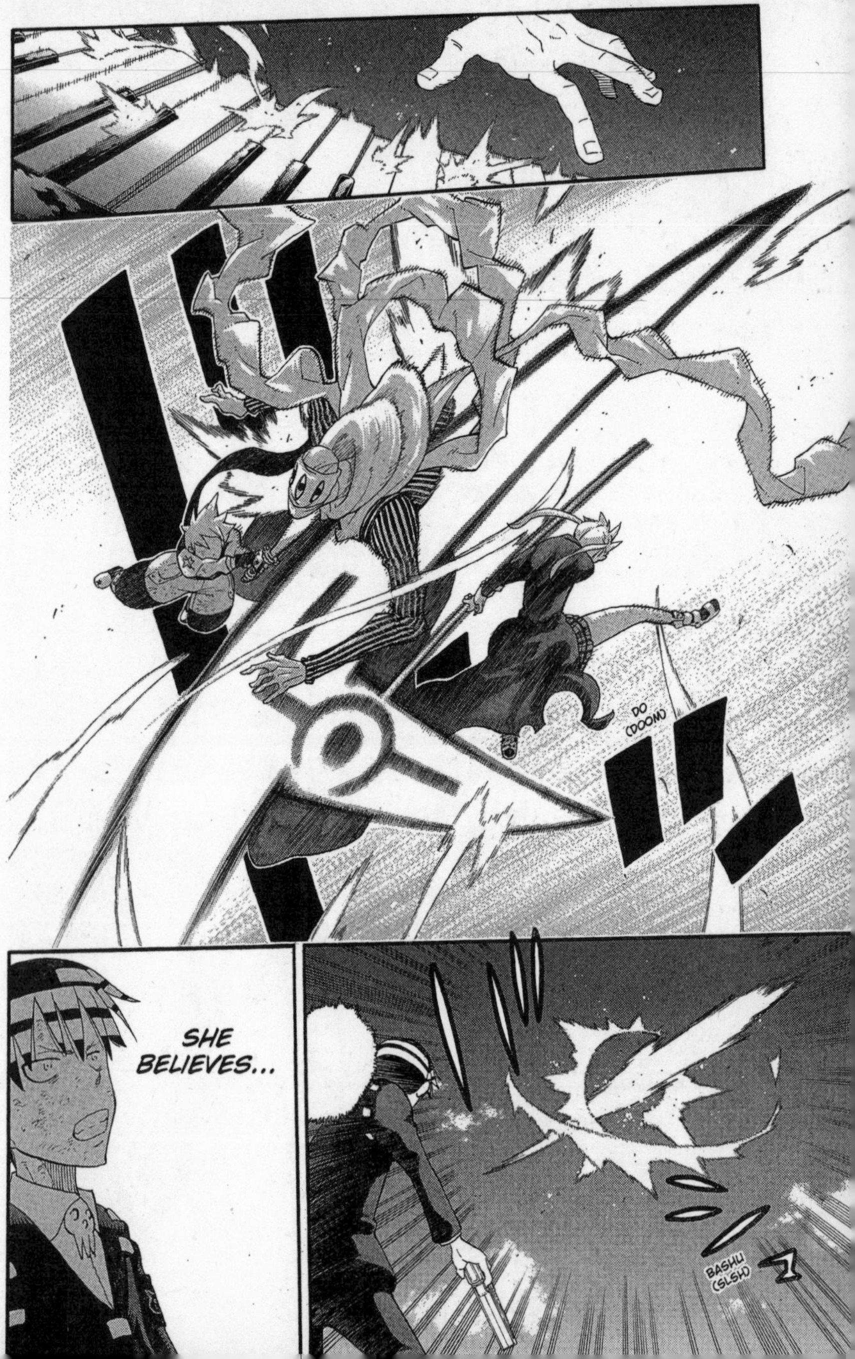
DO
(DOOM)
SHE BELIEVES...
BASHU
(SLSH)

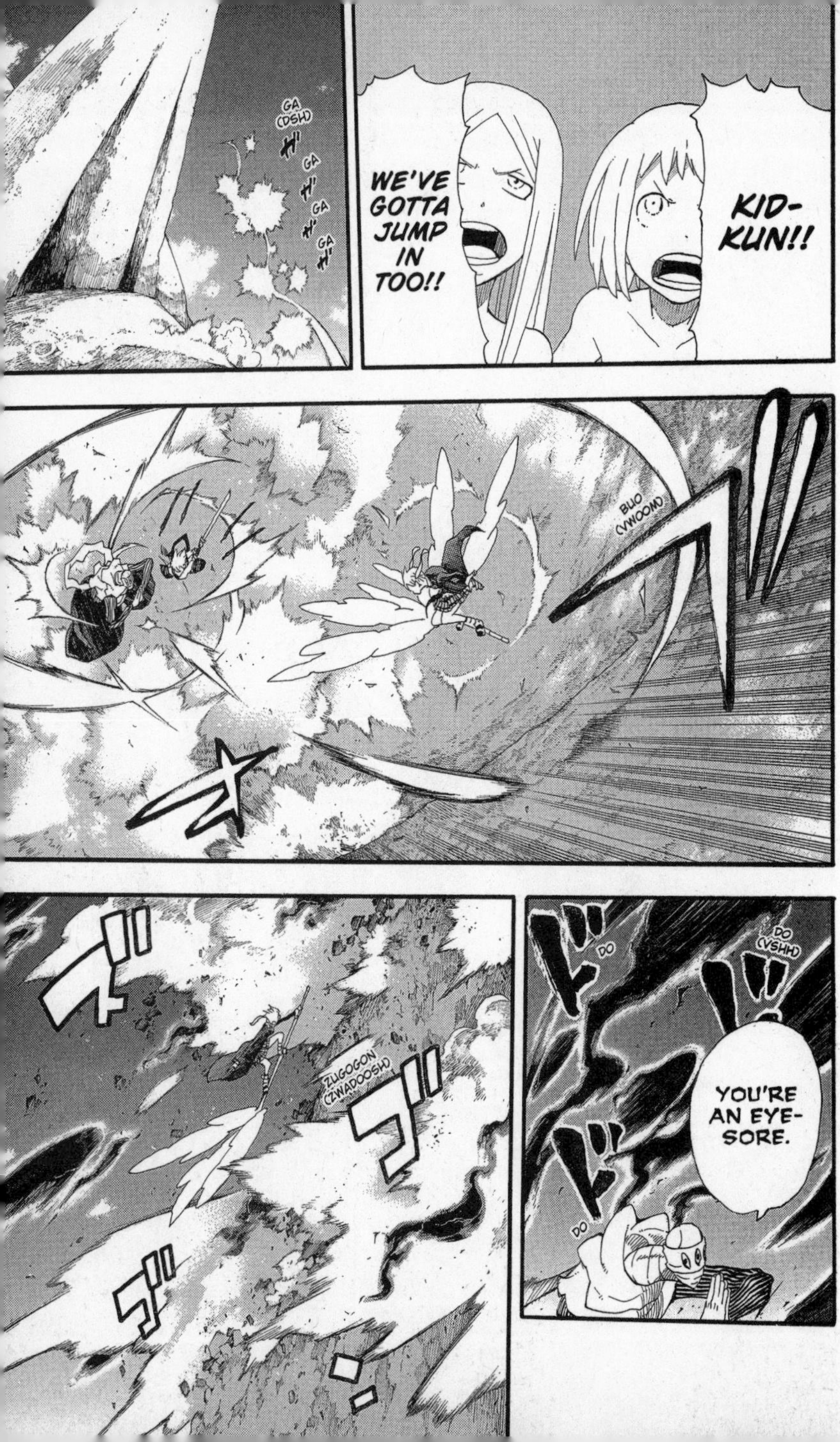
KID-KUN!!
WE'VE GOTTA JUMP IN TOO!!
GA (DSH)
GA
GA
GA
BUO (VWOOM)
DO (VSHH)
DO
YOU'RE AN EYE-SORE.
DO
ZUGOGON (ZWADOOSH)

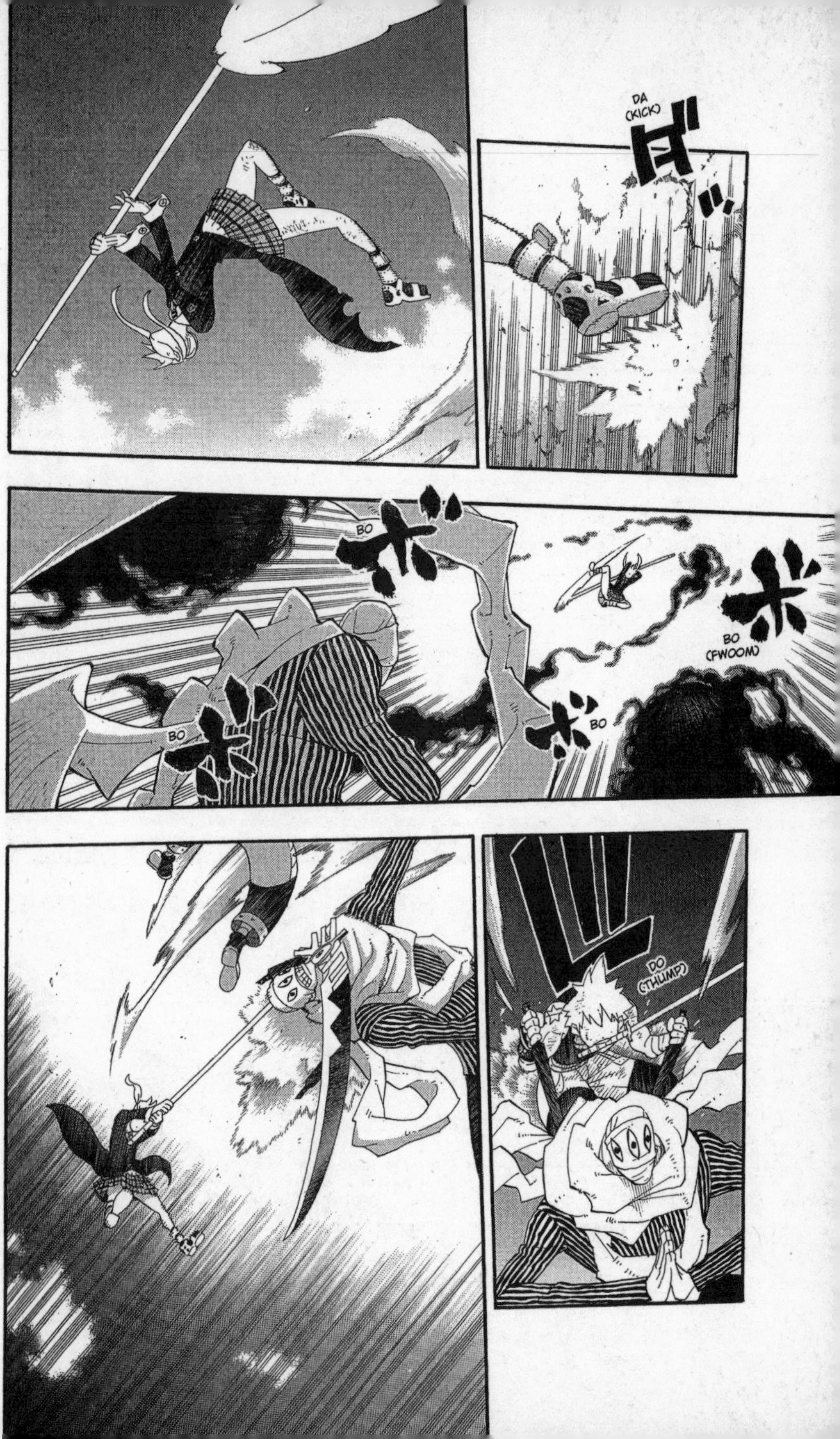
DA
(KICK)
BO
(FWOOM)
BO
BO
BO
DO
(THUMP)

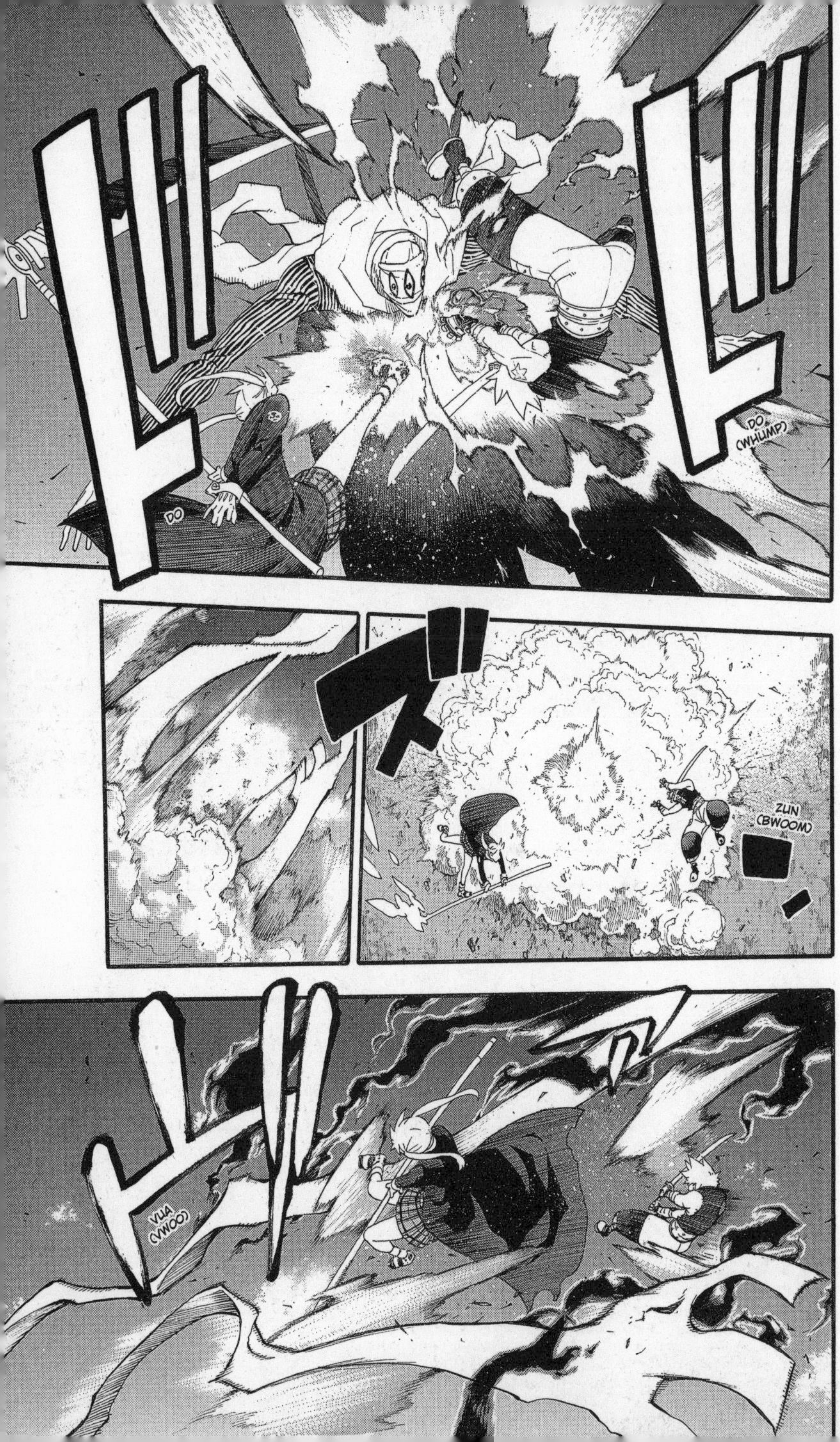
DO (WHUMP)
DO
ZUN (BWOOM)
VUA (VWOO)

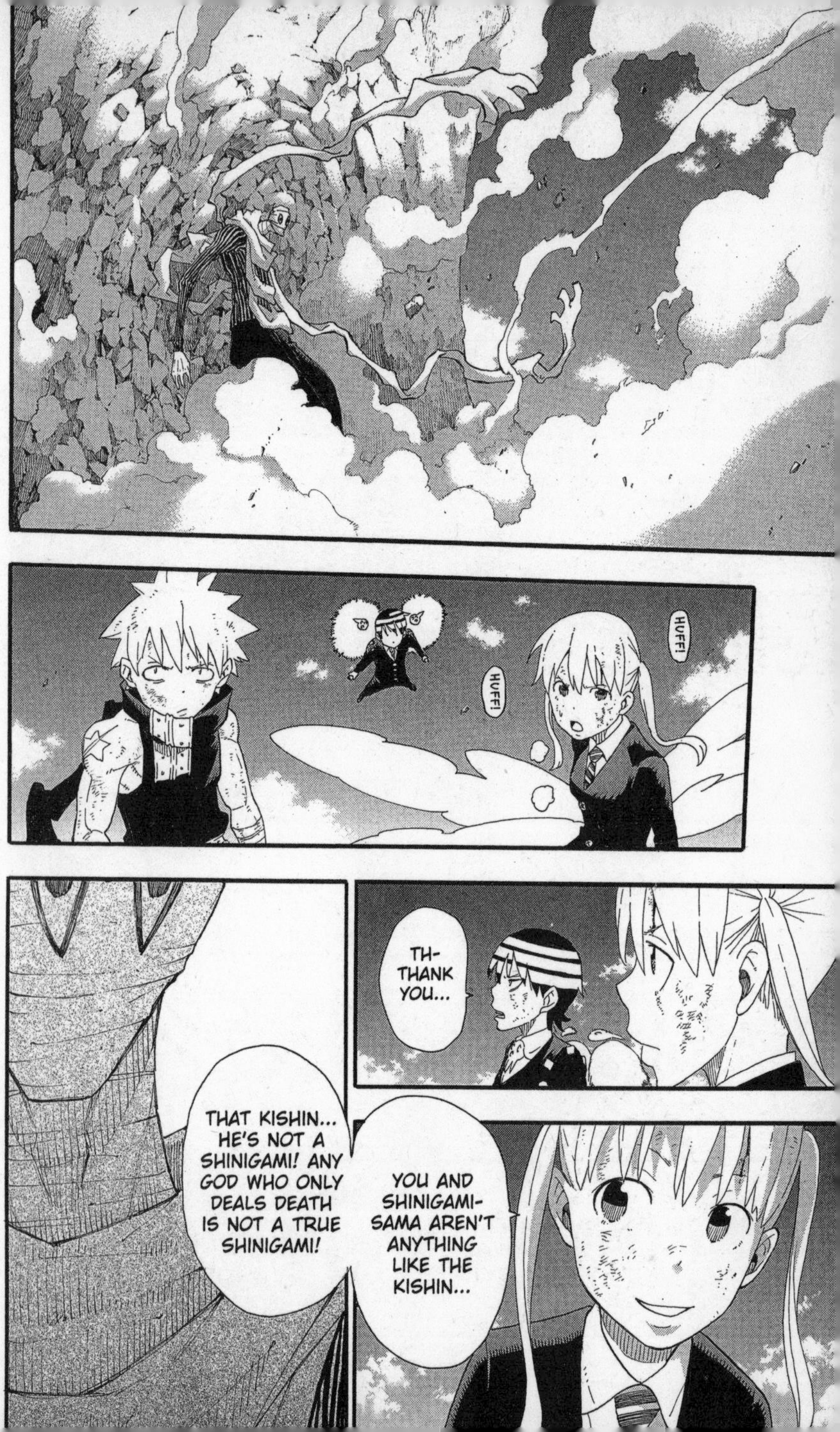
HUFF!
HUFF!
TH- THANK YOU...
YOU AND SHINIGAMI-SAMA AREN'T ANYTHING LIKE THE KISHIN...
THAT KISHIN... HE'S NOT A SHINIGAMI! ANY GOD WHO ONLY DEALS DEATH IS NOT A TRUE SHINIGAMI!

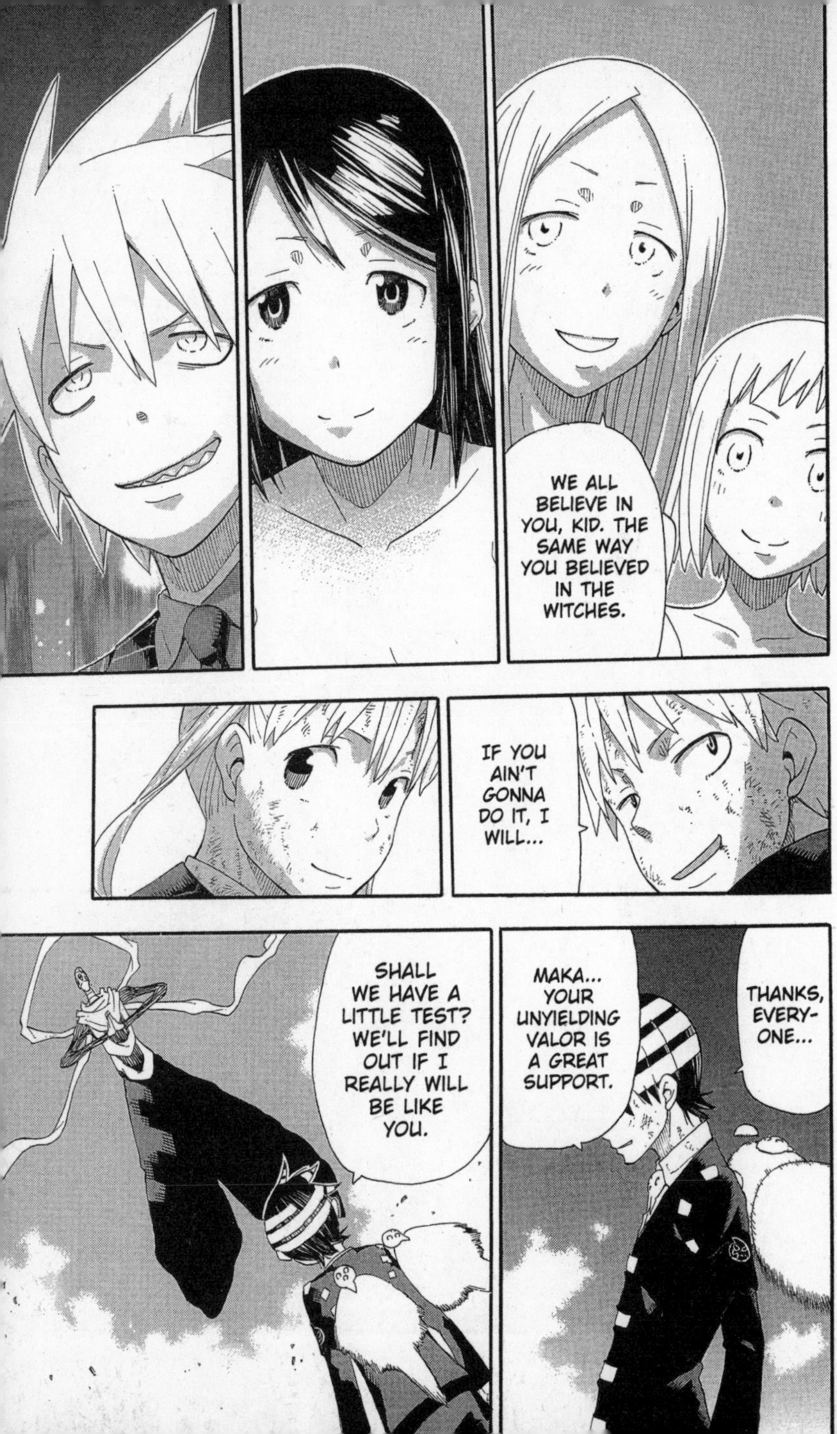
WE ALL BELIEVE IN YOU, KID. THE SAME WAY YOU BELIEVED IN THE WITCHES.
IF YOU AIN'T GONNA DO IT, I WILL...
THANKS, EVERY-ONE...
MAKA... YOUR UNYIELDING VALOR IS A GREAT SUPPORT.
SHALL WE HAVE A LITTLE TEST? WE'LL FIND OUT IF I REALLY WILL BE LIKE YOU.

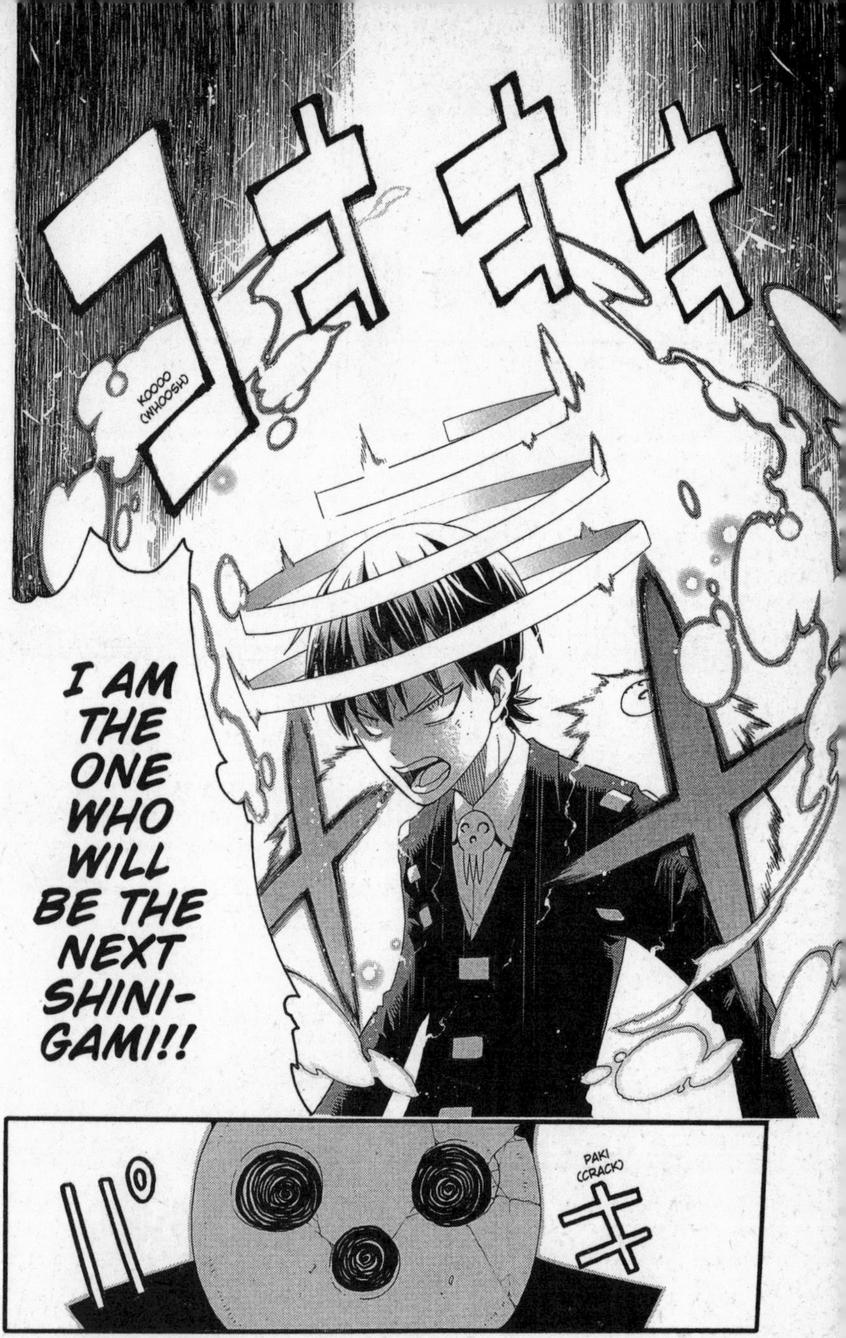
コォォォ
KOOOO (WHOOSH)
I AM THE ONE WHO WILL BE THE NEXT SHINI-GAMI!!
パキ
PAKI (CRACK)

CHAPTER 110: THE DARK SIDE OF THE MOON VII

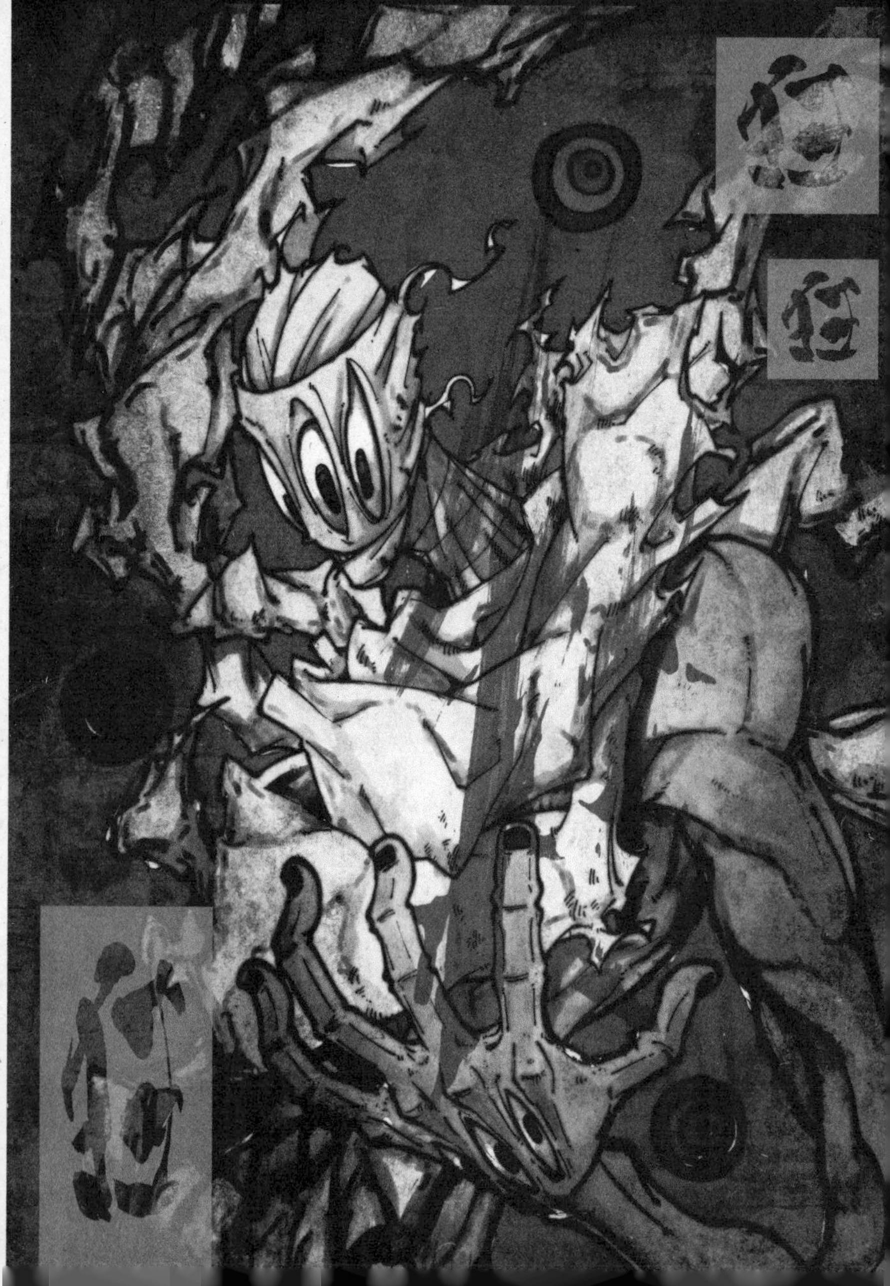

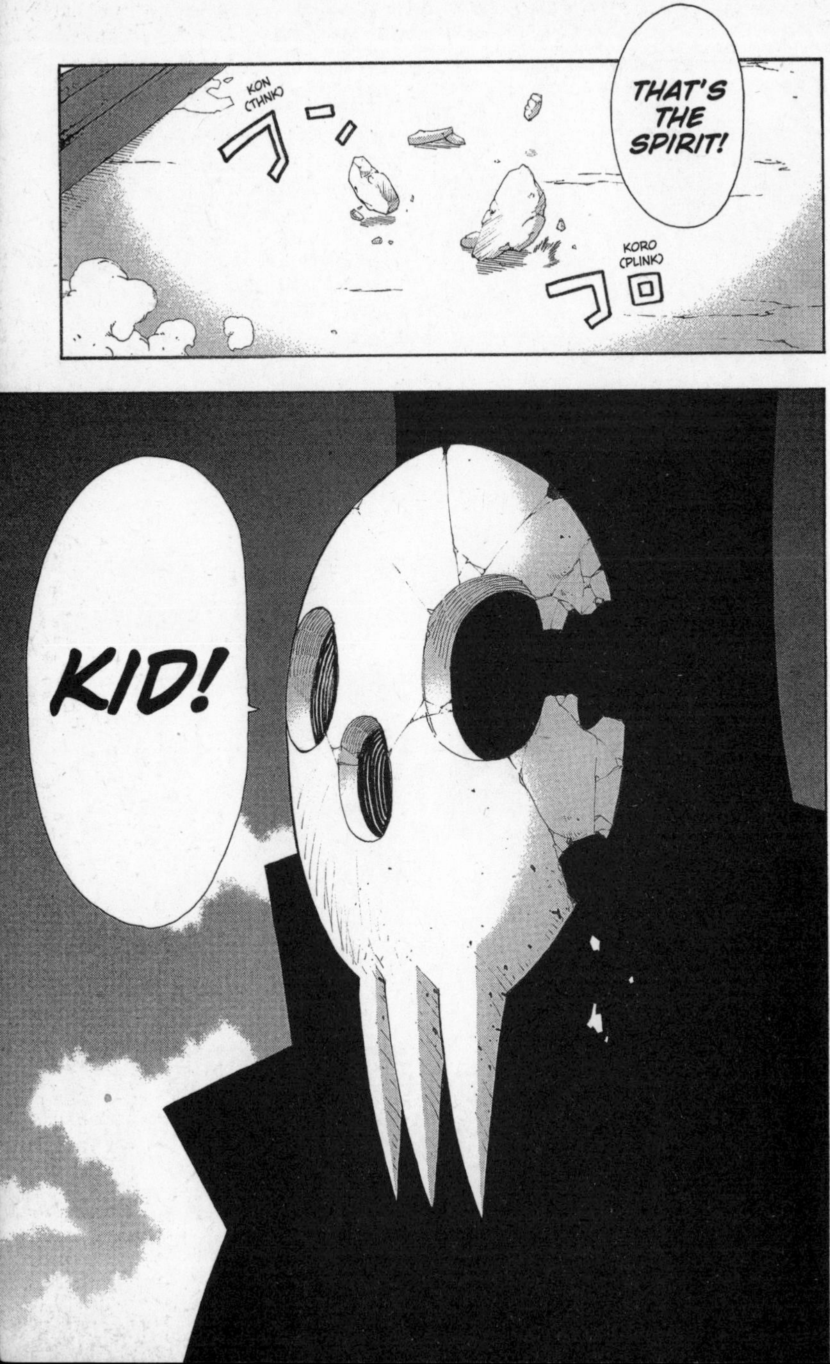
THAT'S THE SPIRIT!
KON (THNK)
KORO (PLINK)
KID!

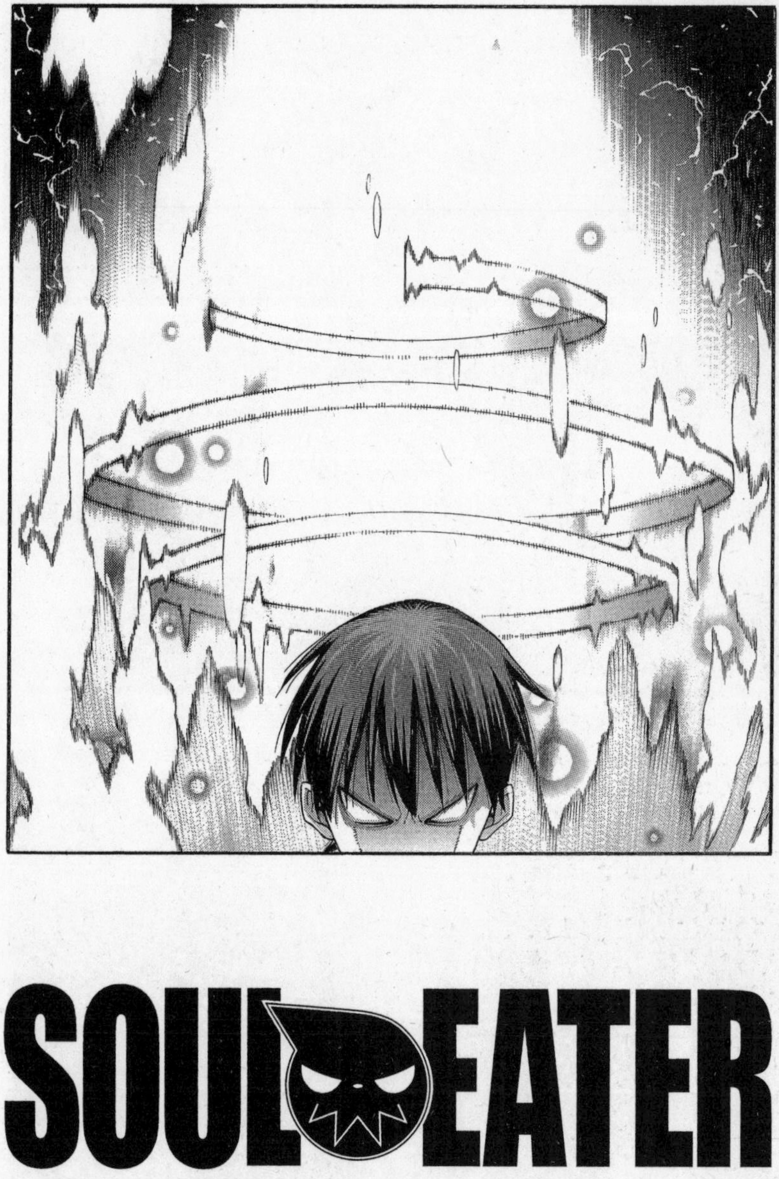

SOUL EATER

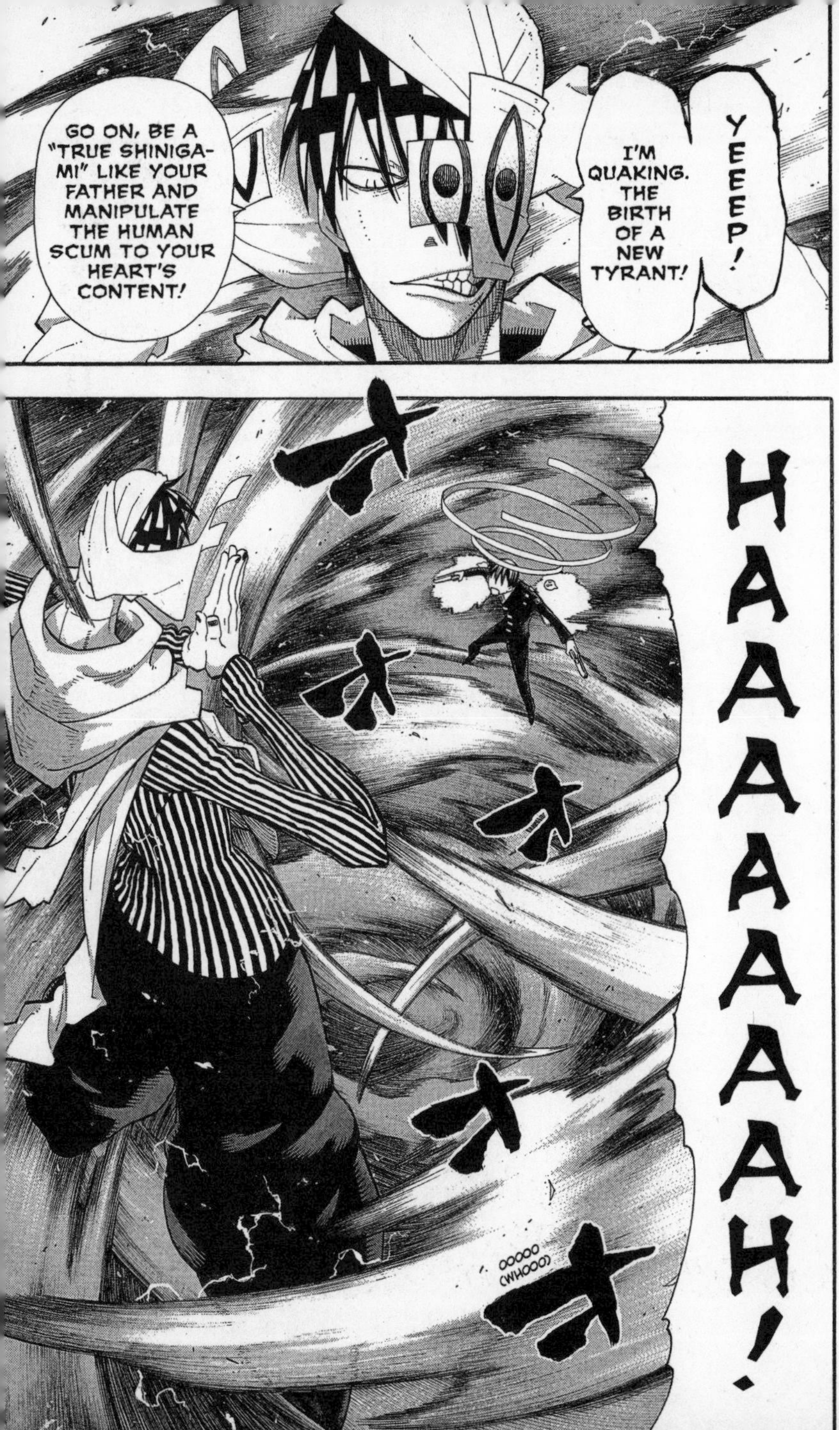
YEEEP!
I'M QUAKING. THE BIRTH OF A NEW TYRANT!
GO ON, BE A "TRUE SHINIGAMI" LIKE YOUR FATHER AND MANIPULATE THE HUMAN SCUM TO YOUR HEART'S CONTENT!
HAAAAAAAH!
OOOOO (WHOOO)

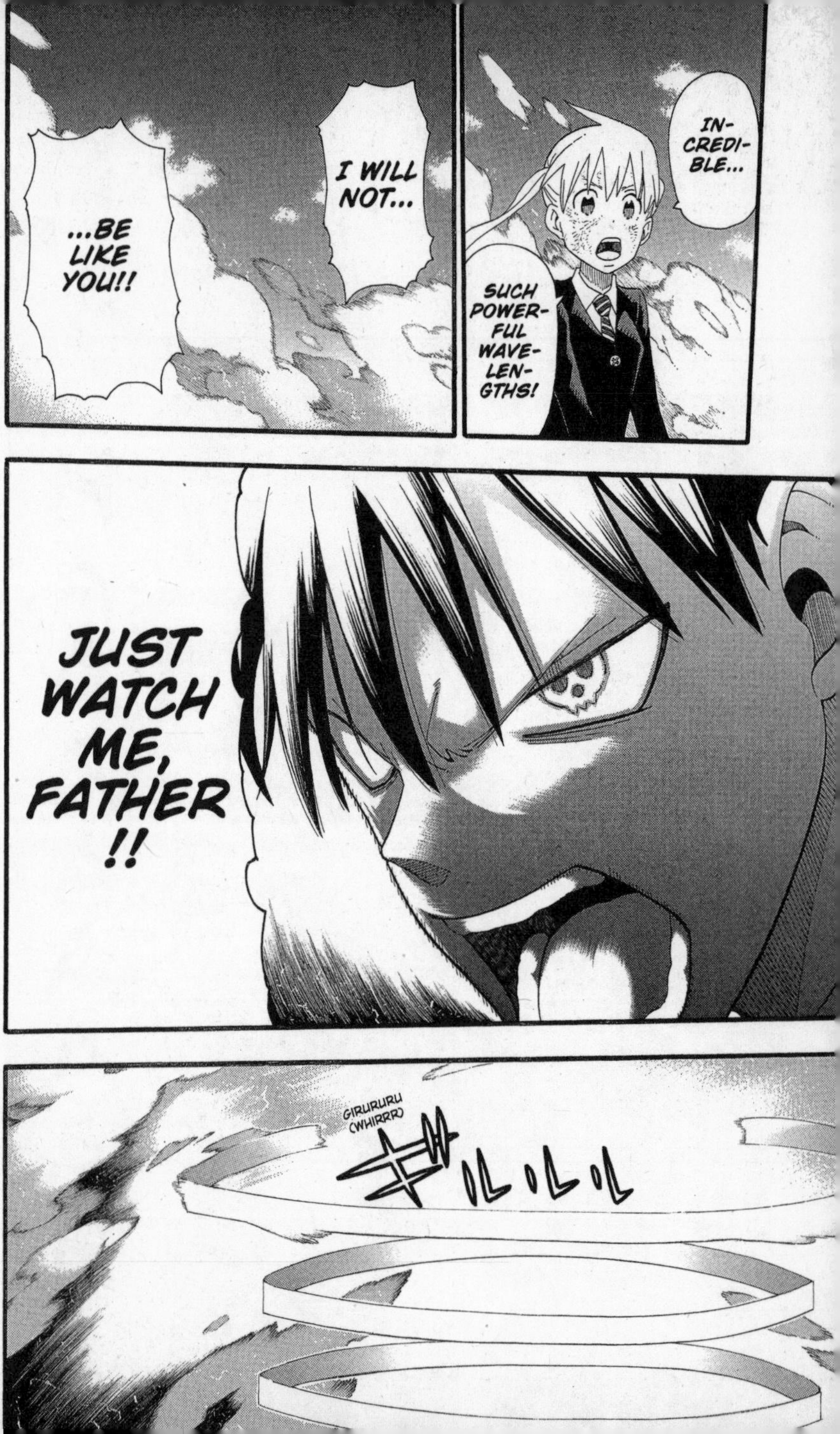
INCREDIBLE...
SUCH POWERFUL WAVELENGTHS!
I WILL NOT...
...BE LIKE YOU!!
JUST WATCH ME, FATHER!!
GIRURURU (WHIRRR)

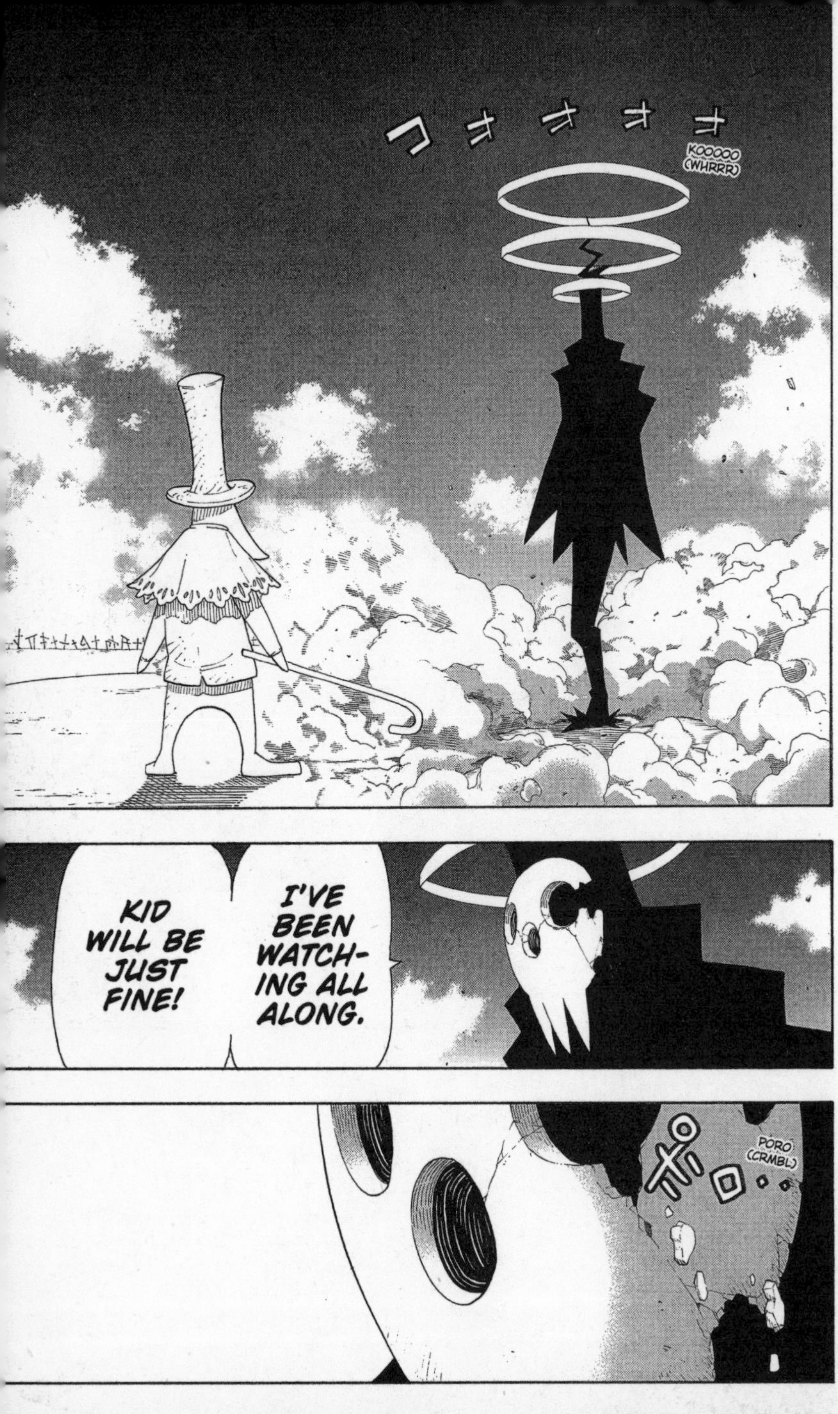
コォォォォ
KOOOOO (WHRRR)
I'VE BEEN WATCHING ALL ALONG.
KID WILL BE JUST FINE!
ポロ
PORO (CRMBL)

GO, KID!!

KOOOOO (WHRRRR)

NOT A KISHIN!!

I AM MY FATHER'S SON!! A SHINI-GAMI!!

I WILL BECOME A SHINIGAMI JUST LIKE THE FATHER I BELIEVED IN!!

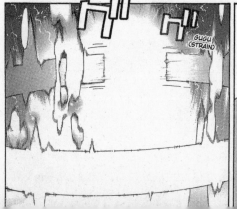

GUGU (STRAIN)

HIS THIRD LINE IS GOING TO CONNECT!!

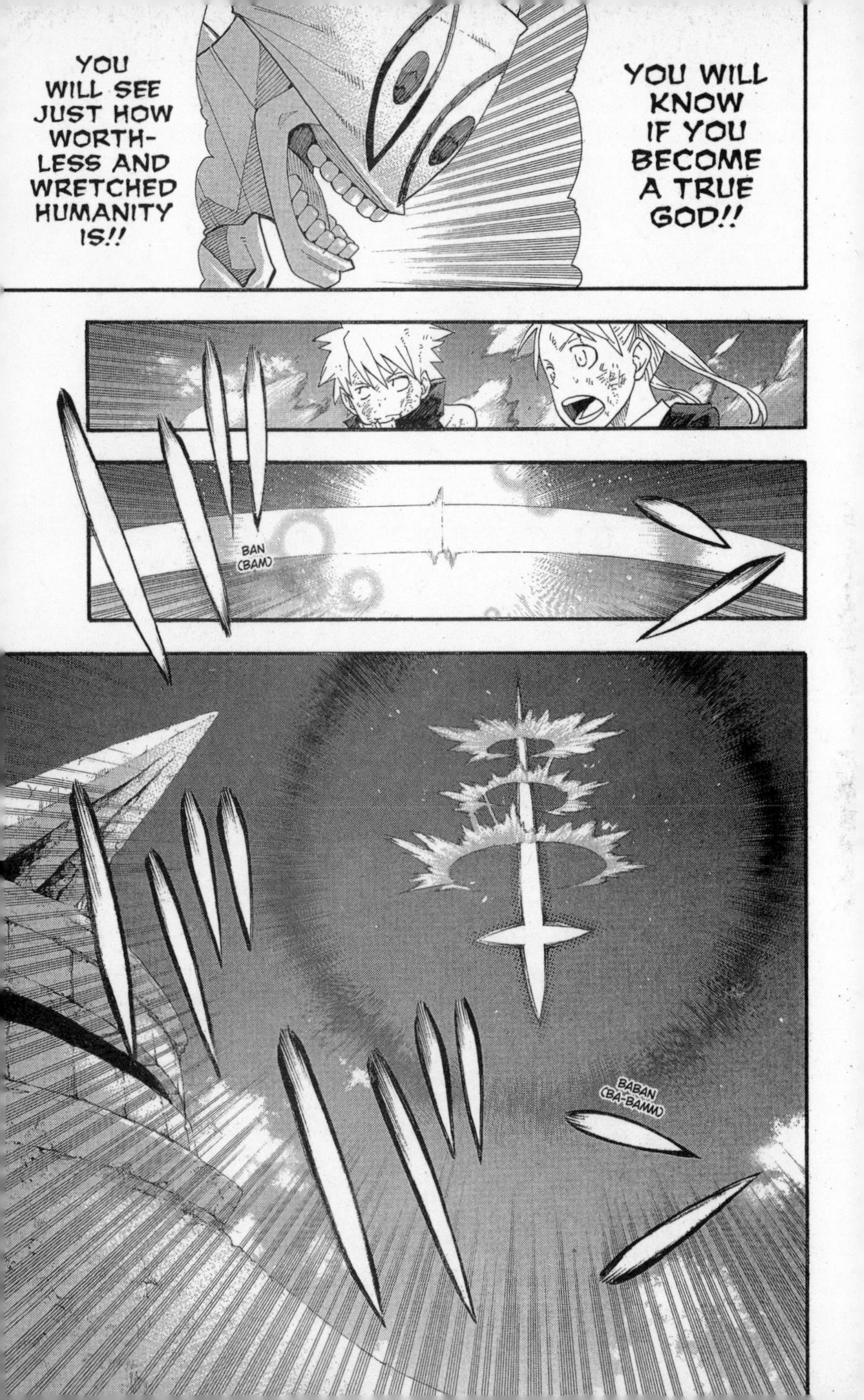
YOU WILL KNOW IF YOU BECOME A TRUE GOD!!
YOU WILL SEE JUST HOW WORTH-LESS AND WRETCHED HUMANITY IS!!
BAN (BAM)
BABAN (BA-BAMM)

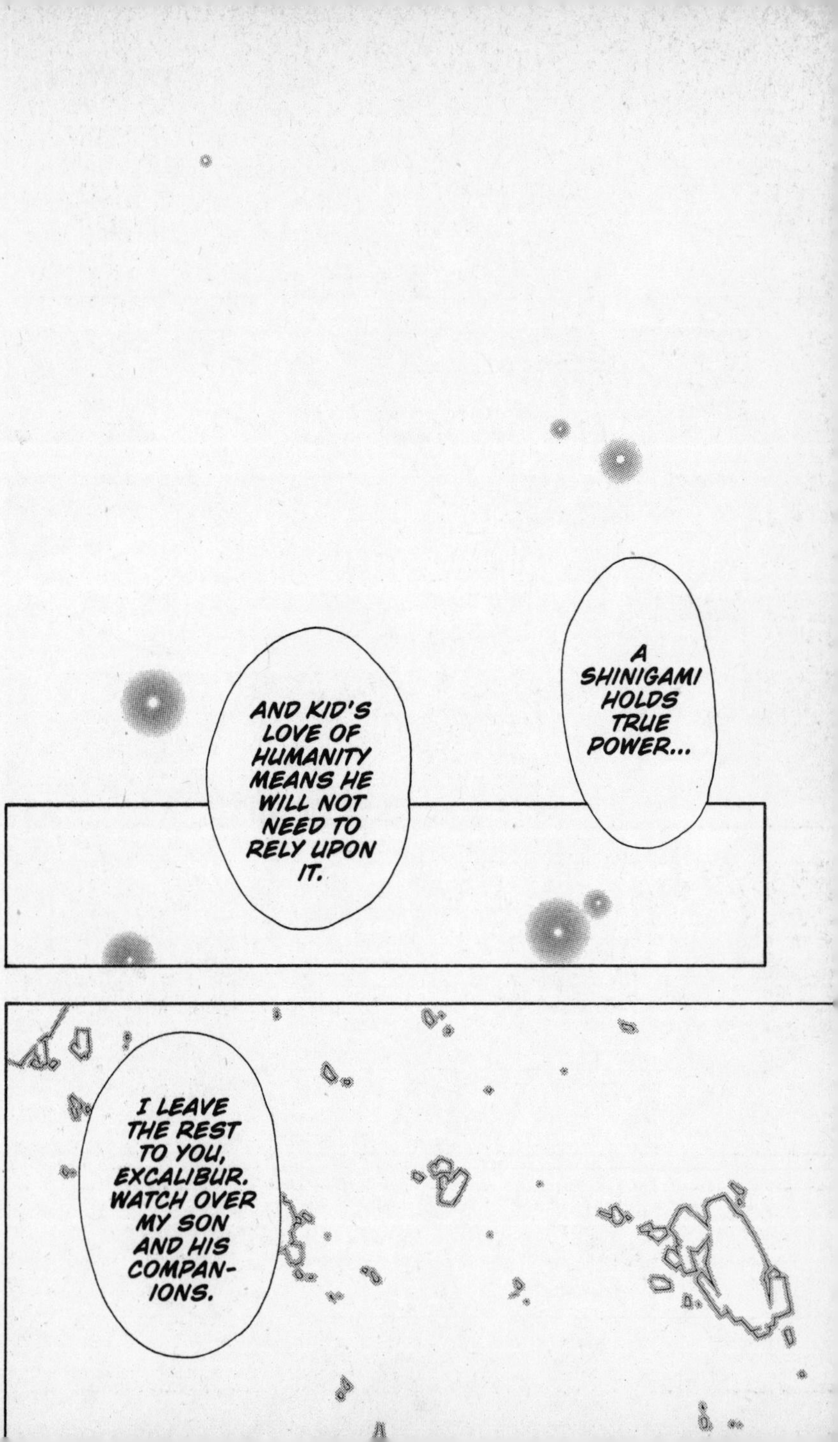
A SHINIGAMI HOLDS TRUE POWER...
AND KID'S LOVE OF HUMANITY MEANS HE WILL NOT NEED TO RELY UPON IT.
I LEAVE THE REST TO YOU, EXCALIBUR. WATCH OVER MY SON AND HIS COMPAN-IONS.

WELL,
BYE-
BYE.

UNDER-
STOOD...

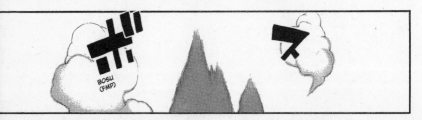

BOSU
(FMP)

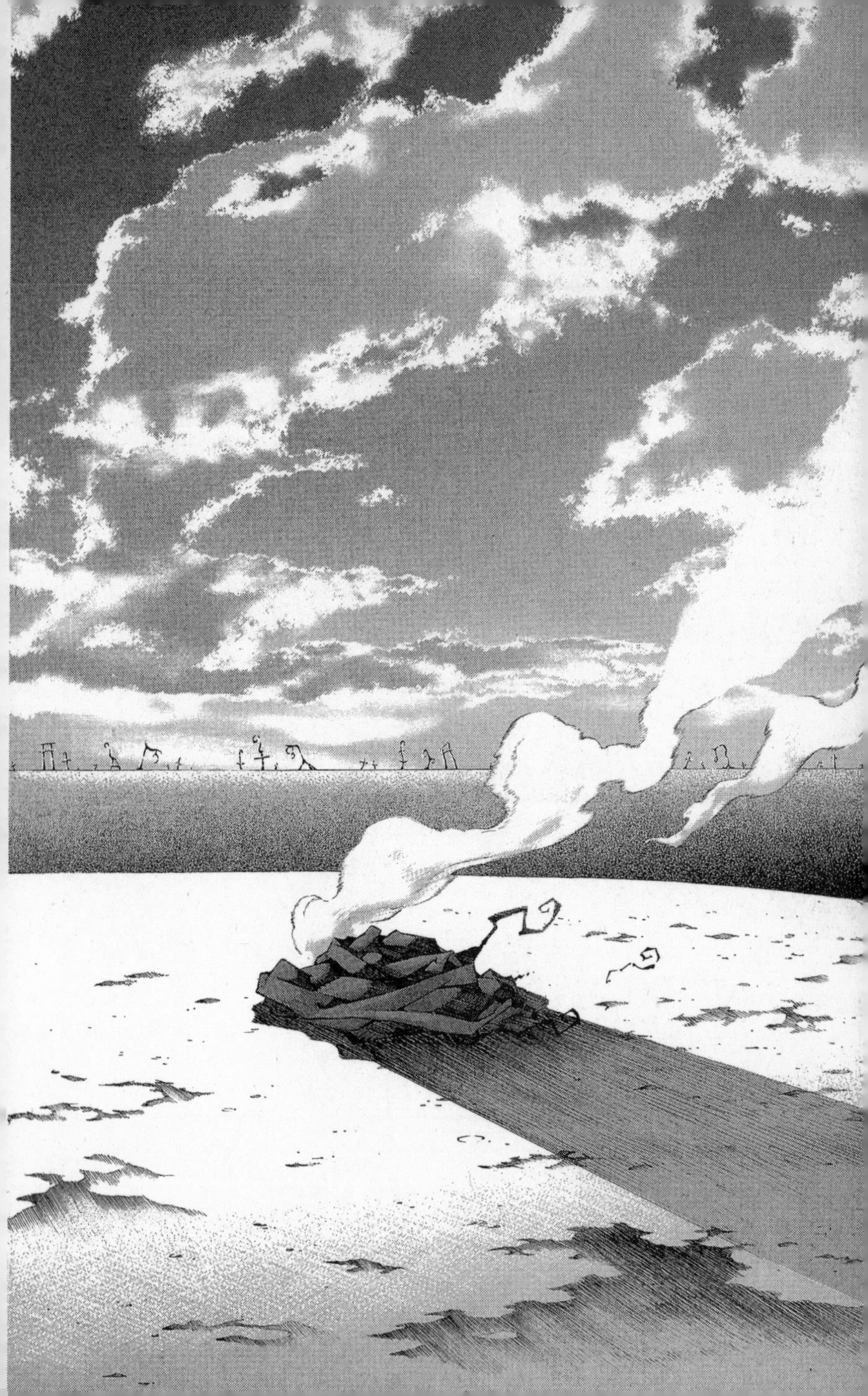

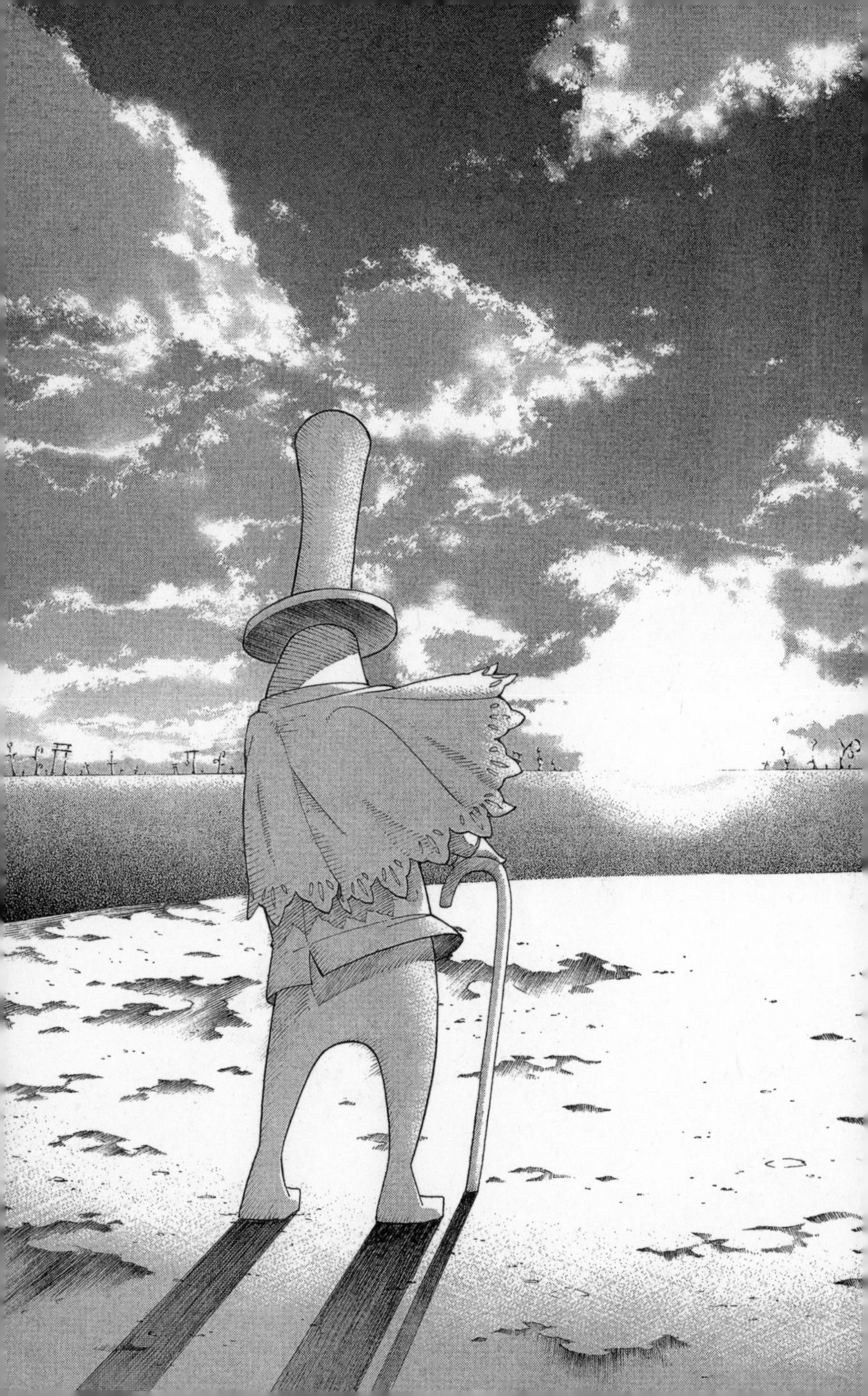

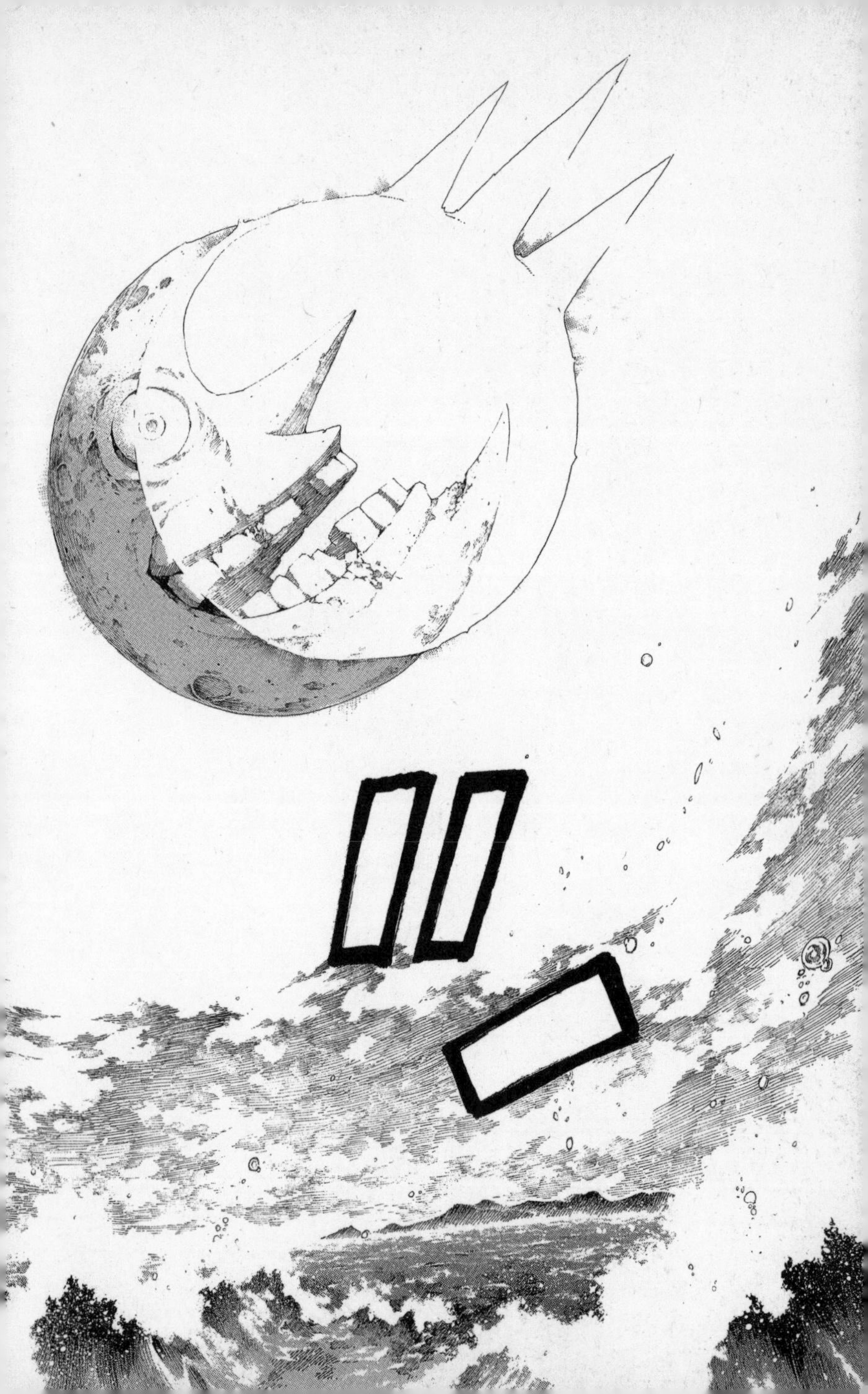

DO
COMMMO

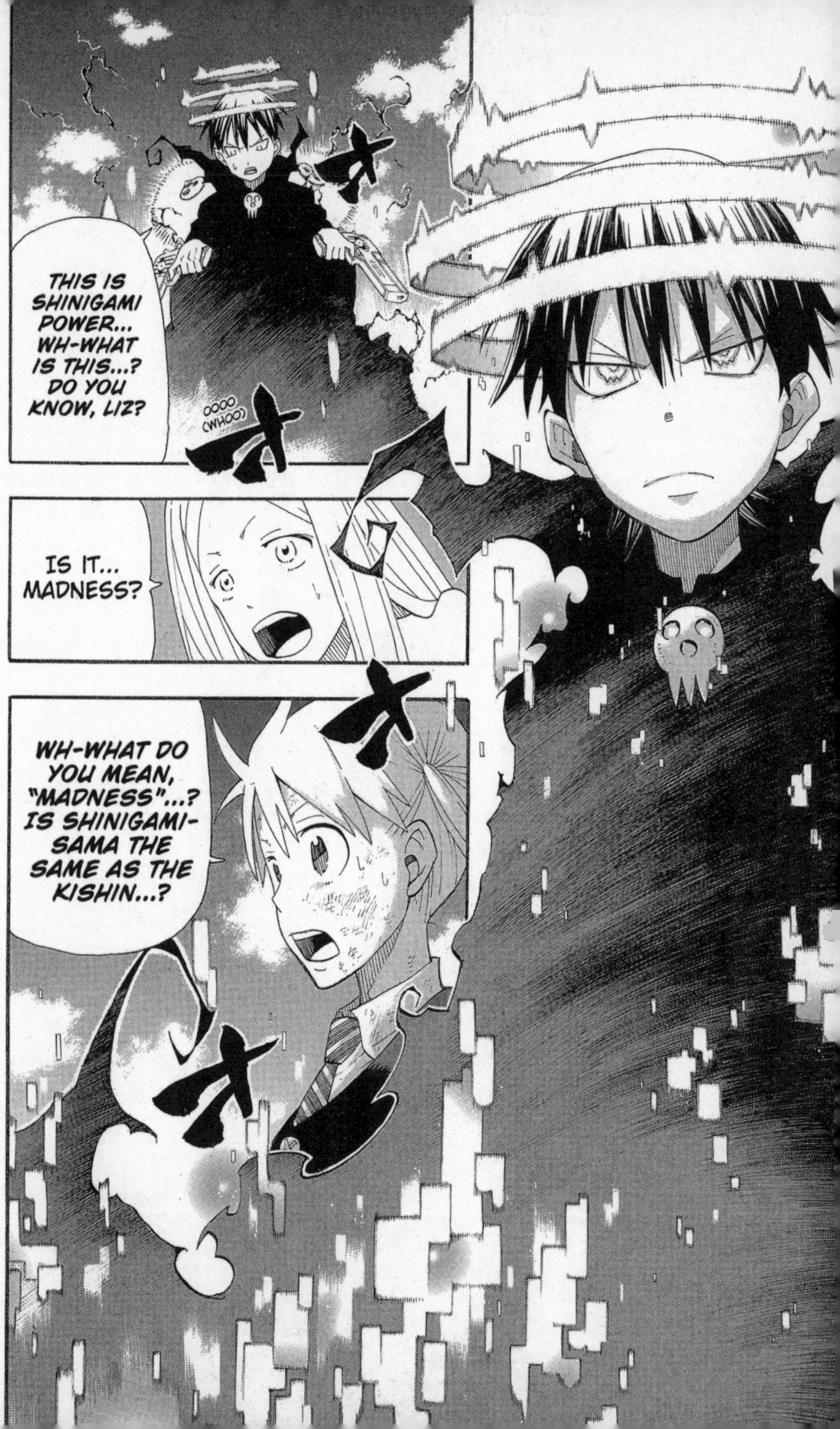
THIS IS SHINIGAMI POWER... WH-WHAT IS THIS...? DO YOU KNOW, LIZ?
OOOO (WHOO)
IS IT... MADNESS?
WH-WHAT DO YOU MEAN, "MADNESS"...? IS SHINIGAMI-SAMA THE SAME AS THE KISHIN...?

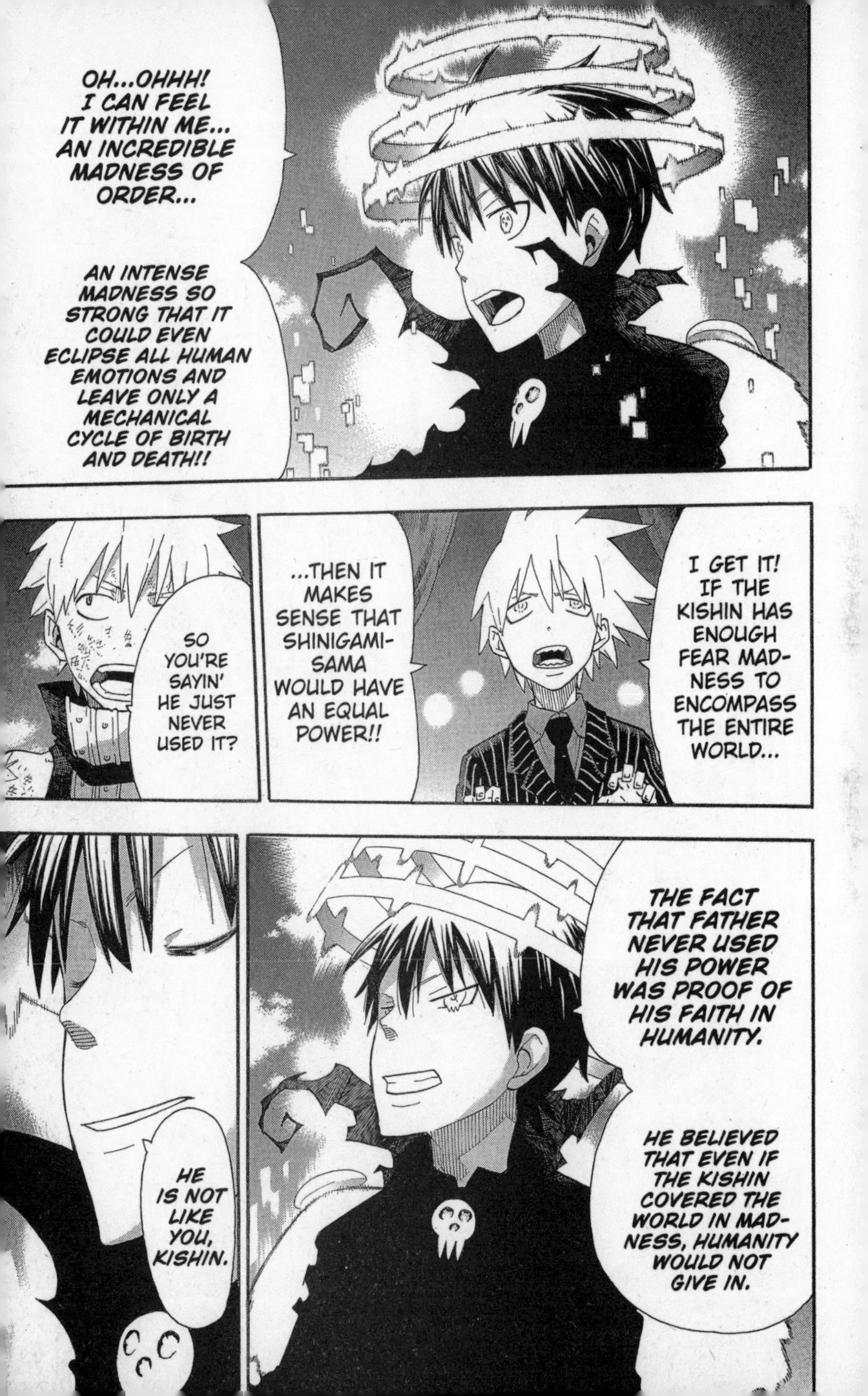
OH...OHHH! I CAN FEEL IT WITHIN ME... AN INCREDIBLE MADNESS OF ORDER...
AN INTENSE MADNESS SO STRONG THAT IT COULD EVEN ECLIPSE ALL HUMAN EMOTIONS AND LEAVE ONLY A MECHANICAL CYCLE OF BIRTH AND DEATH!!
I GET IT! IF THE KISHIN HAS ENOUGH FEAR MADNESS TO ENCOMPASS THE ENTIRE WORLD...
...THEN IT MAKES SENSE THAT SHINIGAMI-SAMA WOULD HAVE AN EQUAL POWER!!
SO YOU'RE SAYIN' HE JUST NEVER USED IT?
THE FACT THAT FATHER NEVER USED HIS POWER WAS PROOF OF HIS FAITH IN HUMANITY.
HE BELIEVED THAT EVEN IF THE KISHIN COVERED THE WORLD IN MADNESS, HUMANITY WOULD NOT GIVE IN.
HE IS NOT LIKE YOU, KISHIN.

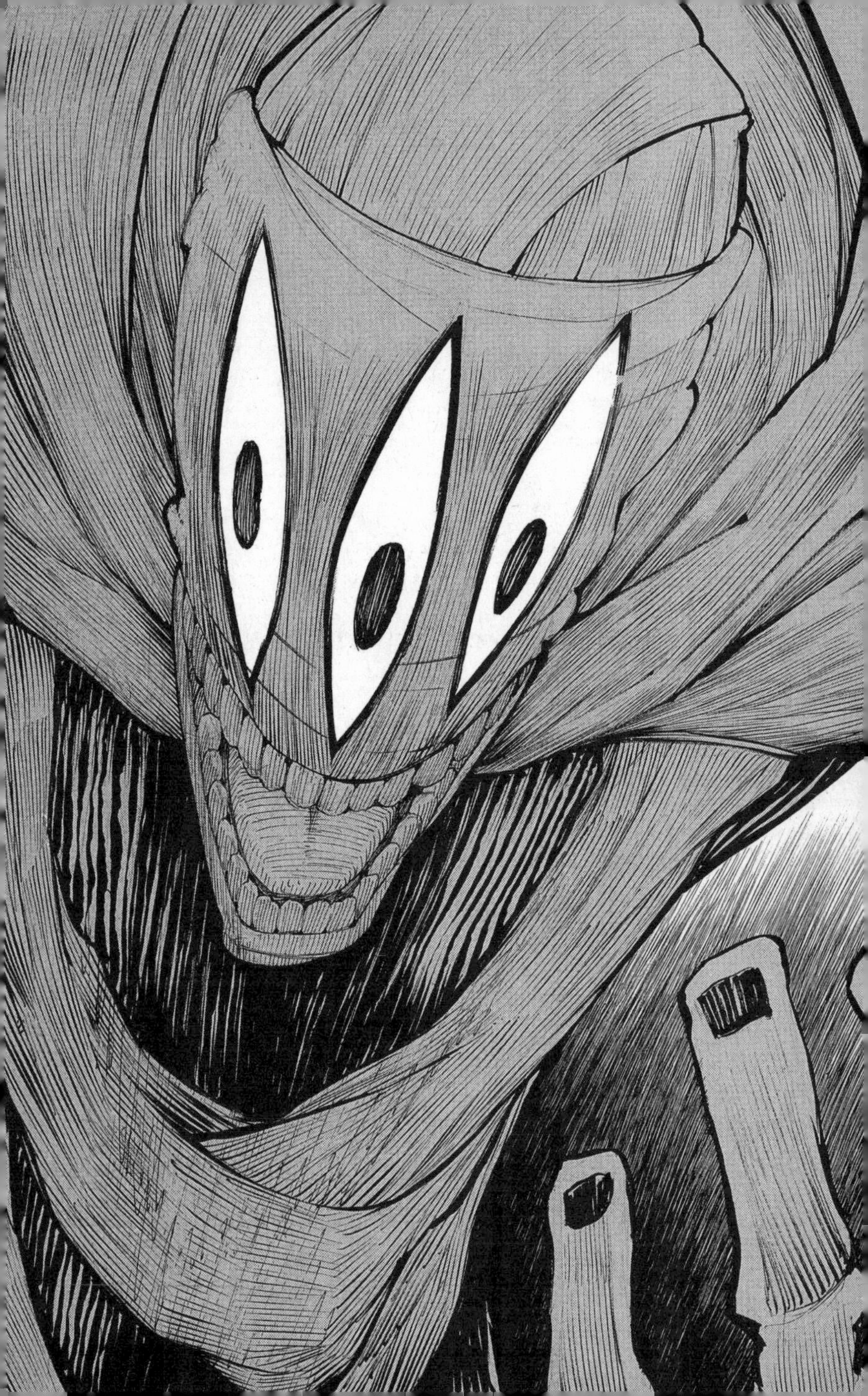

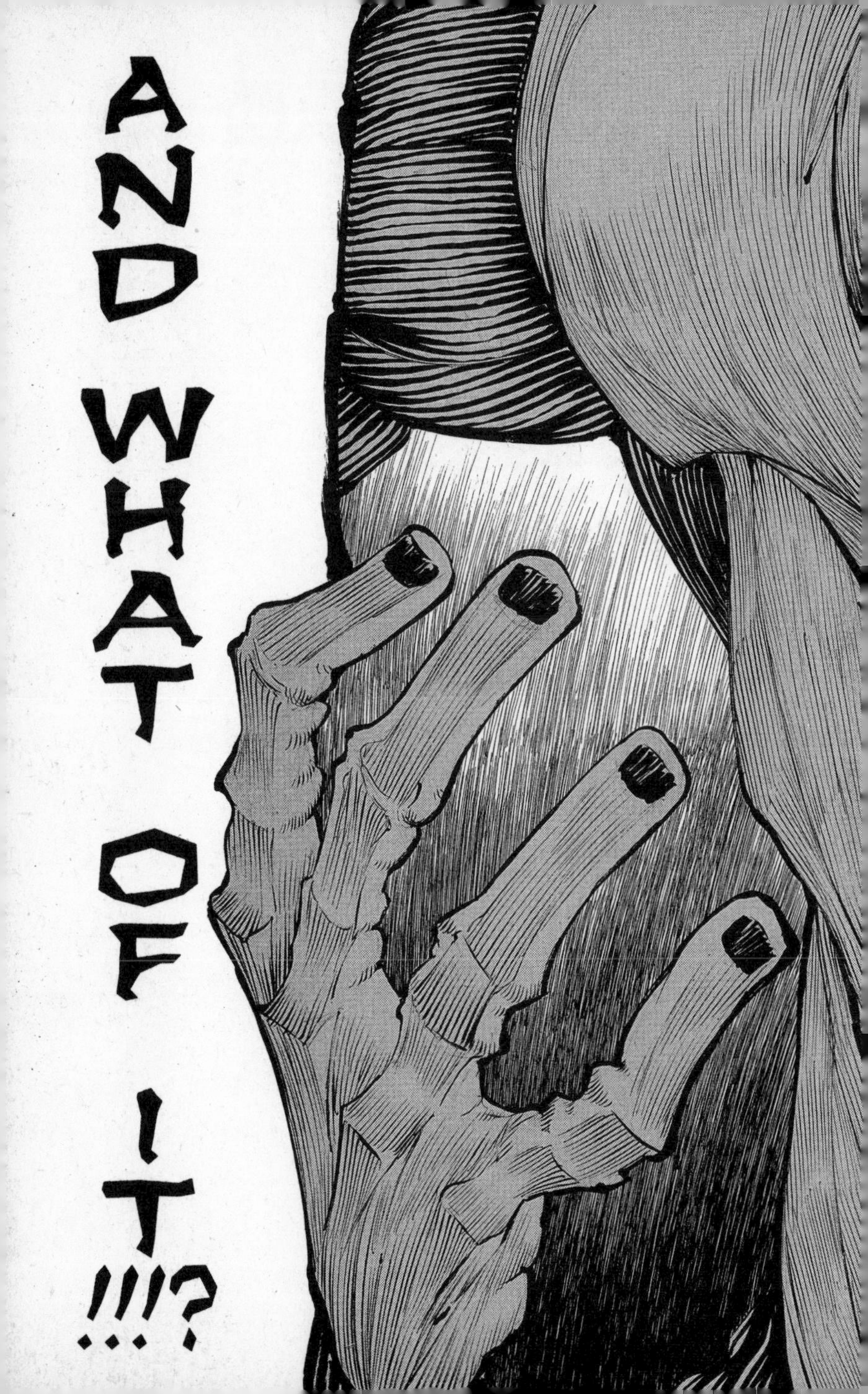
AND WHAT OF IT!!!?

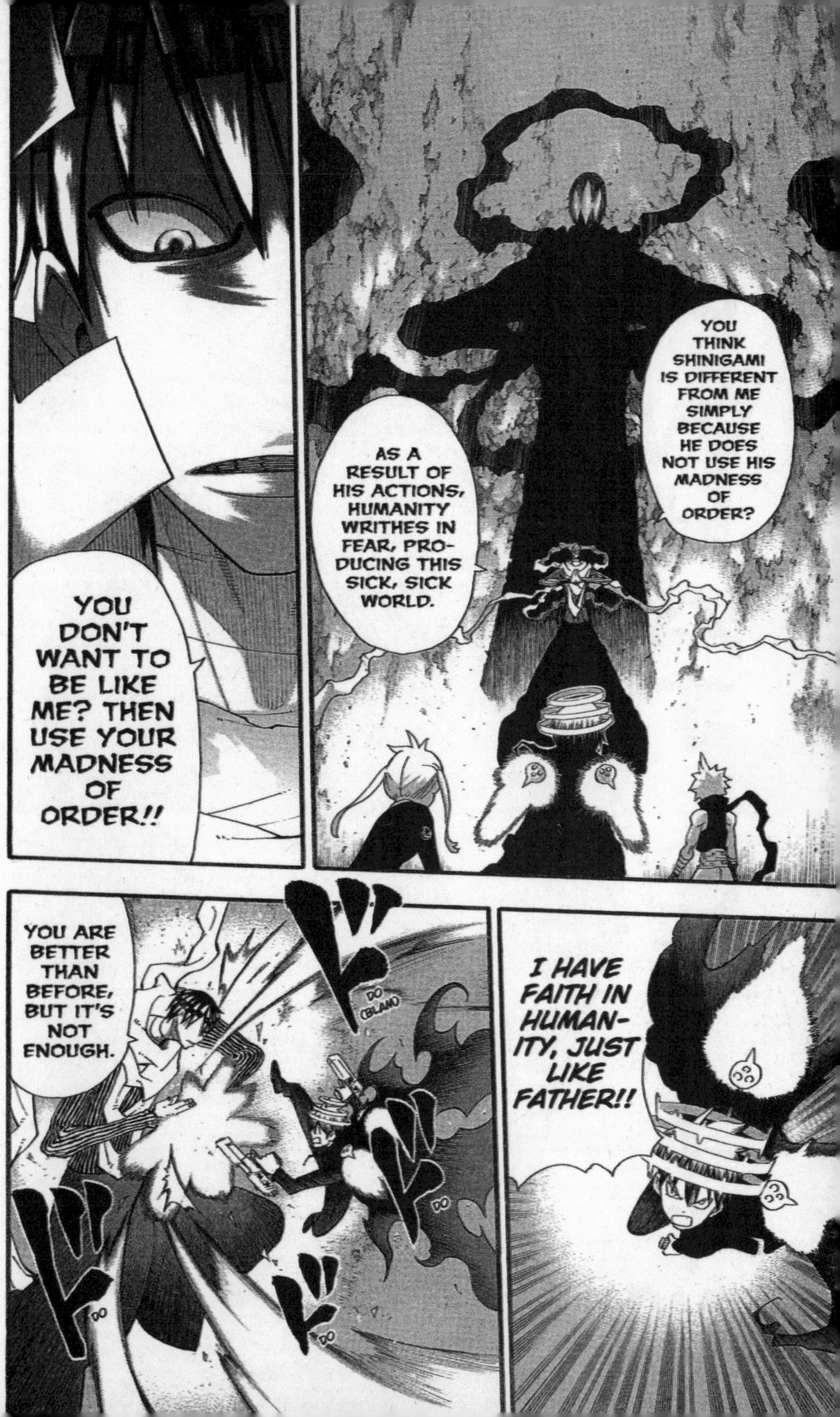
YOU THINK SHINIGAMI IS DIFFERENT FROM ME SIMPLY BECAUSE HE DOES NOT USE HIS MADNESS OF ORDER?
AS A RESULT OF HIS ACTIONS, HUMANITY WRITHES IN FEAR, PRODUCING THIS SICK, SICK WORLD.
YOU DON'T WANT TO BE LIKE ME? THEN USE YOUR MADNESS OF ORDER!!
I HAVE FAITH IN HUMANITY, JUST LIKE FATHER!!
YOU ARE BETTER THAN BEFORE, BUT IT'S NOT ENOUGH.
DO (BLAM)
DO
DO
DO

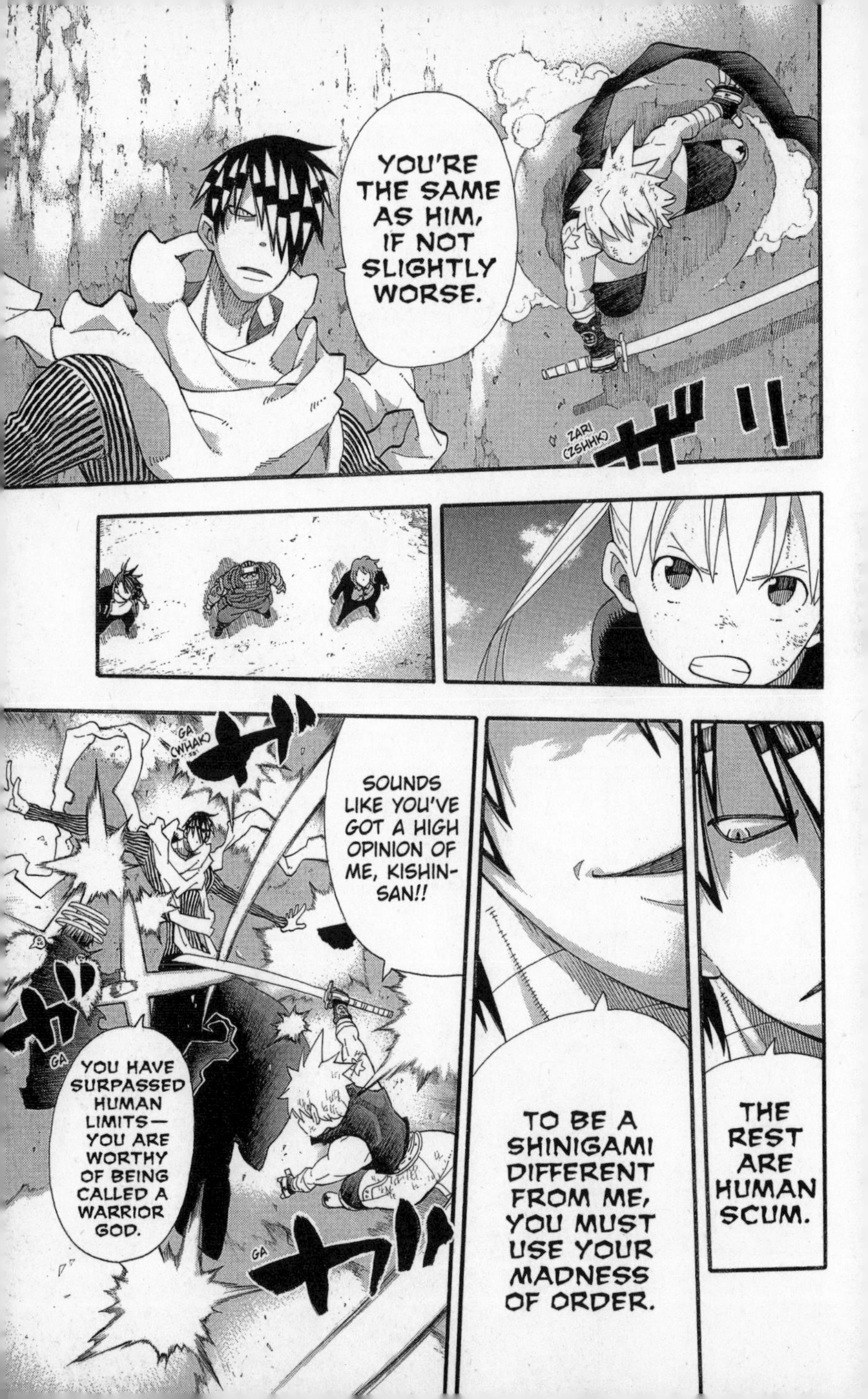

YOU'RE THE SAME AS HIM, IF NOT SLIGHTLY WORSE.
ZARI (ZSHHK)
THE REST ARE HUMAN SCUM.
TO BE A SHINIGAMI DIFFERENT FROM ME, YOU MUST USE YOUR MADNESS OF ORDER.
SOUNDS LIKE YOU'VE GOT A HIGH OPINION OF ME, KISHIN-SAN!!
GA (WHAK)
GA
YOU HAVE SURPASSED HUMAN LIMITS— YOU ARE WORTHY OF BEING CALLED A WARRIOR GOD.
GA

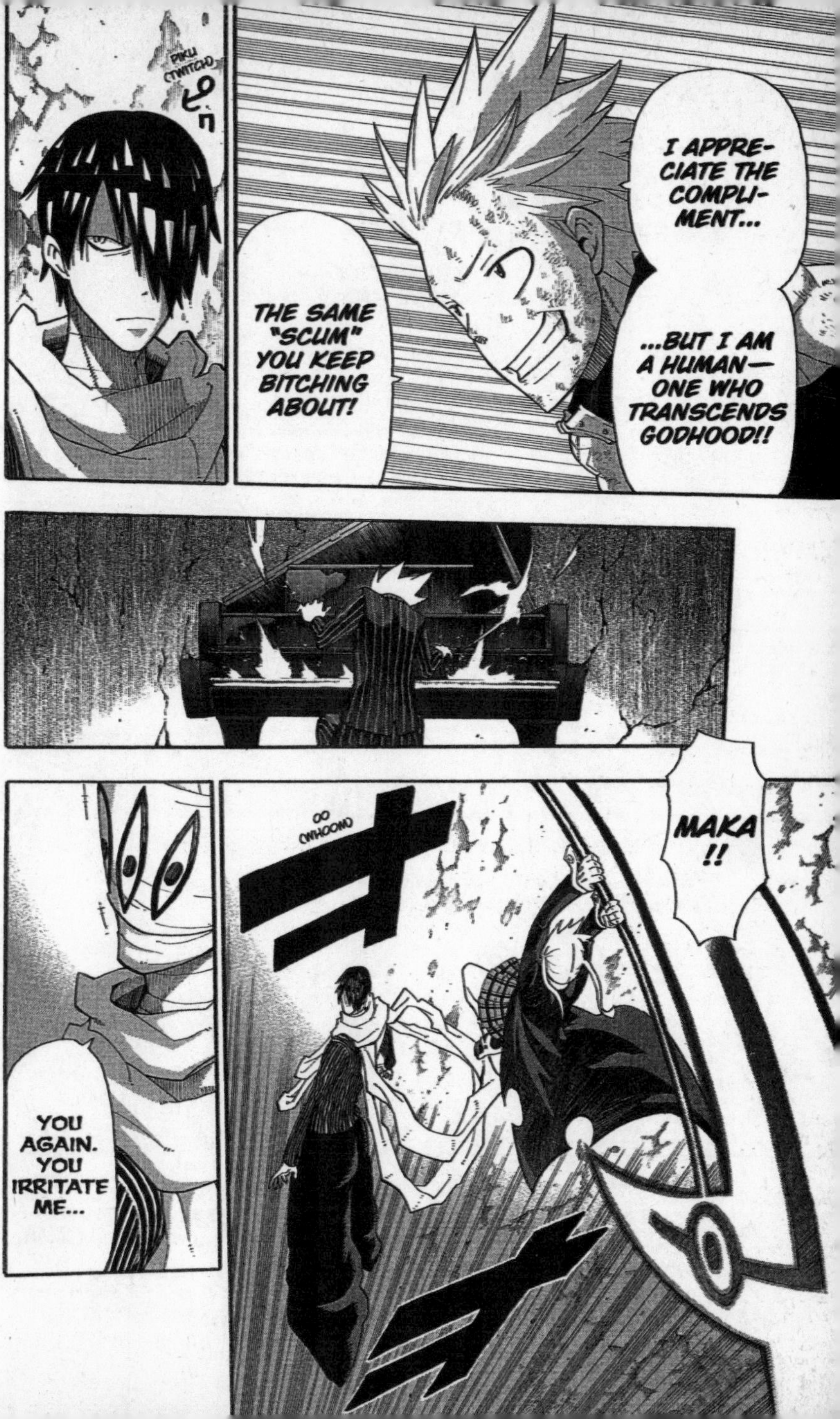
I APPRECIATE THE COMPLIMENT...
...BUT I AM A HUMAN—ONE WHO TRANSCENDS GODHOOD!!
THE SAME "SCUM" YOU KEEP BITCHING ABOUT!
PIKU (TWITCH)
MAKA!!
OO (WHOOM)
YOU AGAIN. YOU IRRITATE ME...

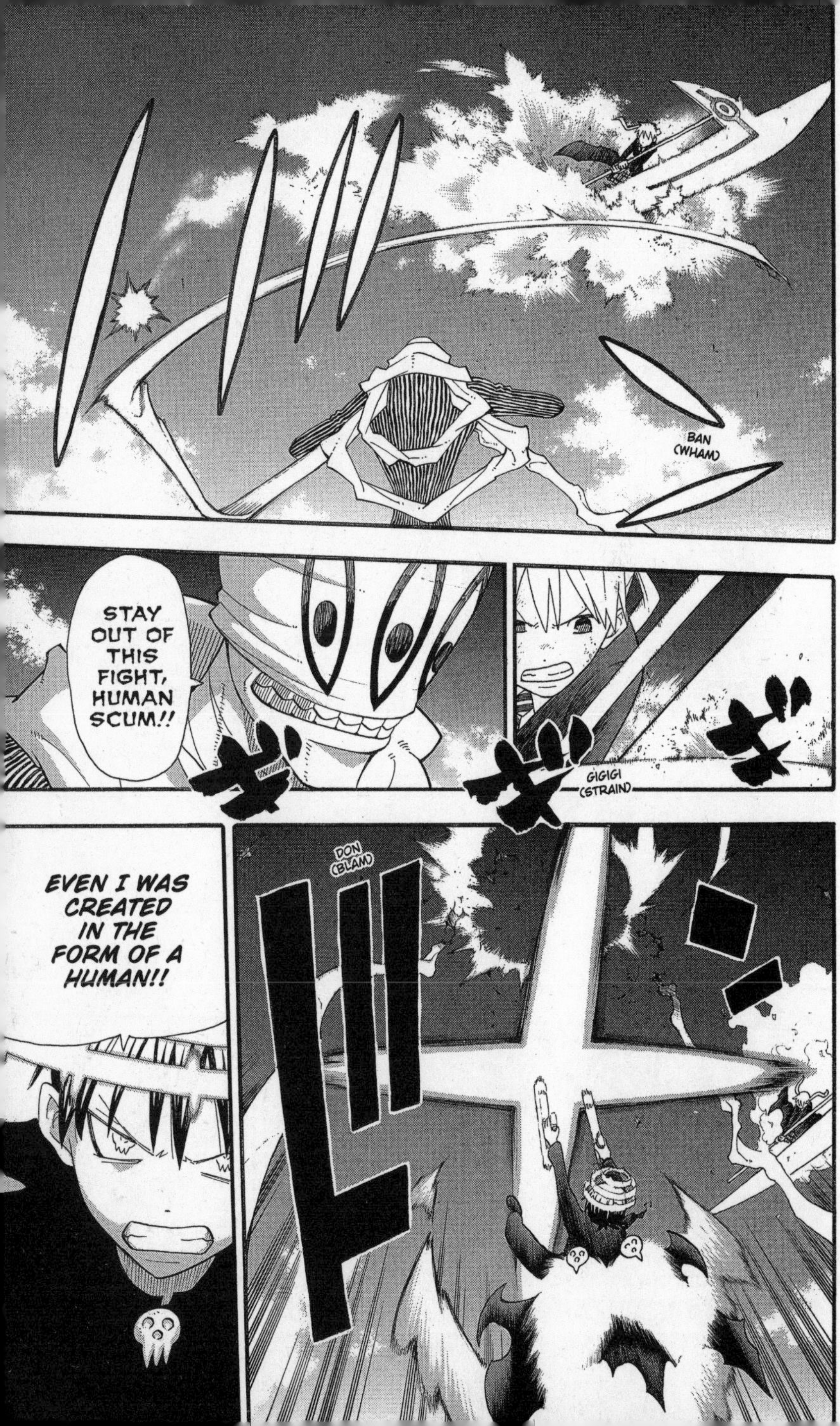
BAN (WHAM)
GIGIGI (STRAIN)
STAY OUT OF THIS FIGHT, HUMAN SCUM!!
DON (BLAM)
EVEN I WAS CREATED IN THE FORM OF A HUMAN!!

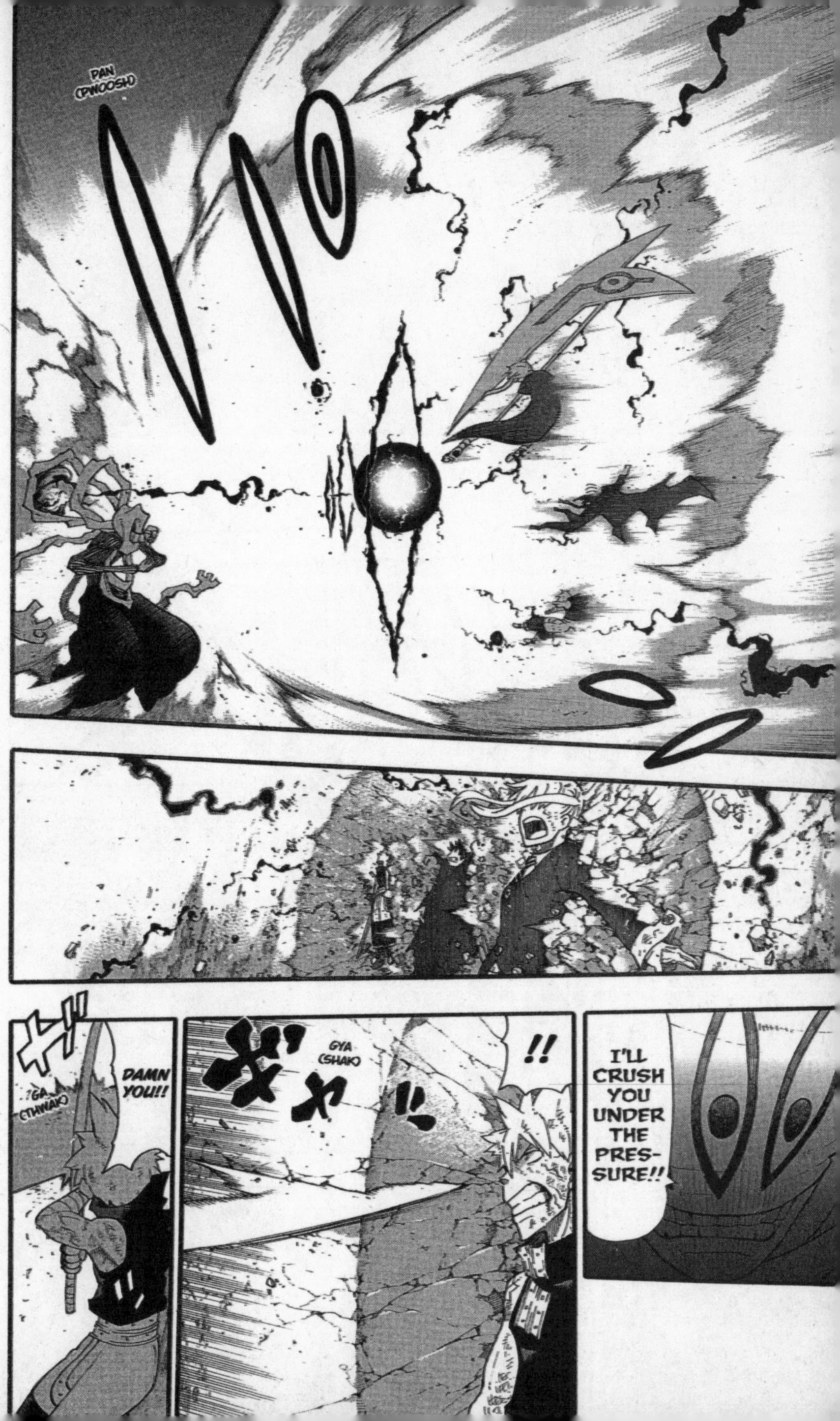
PAN (PWOOSH)
I'LL CRUSH YOU UNDER THE PRES-SURE!!
!!
GYA (SHAK)
DAMN YOU!!
GA (THWAK)

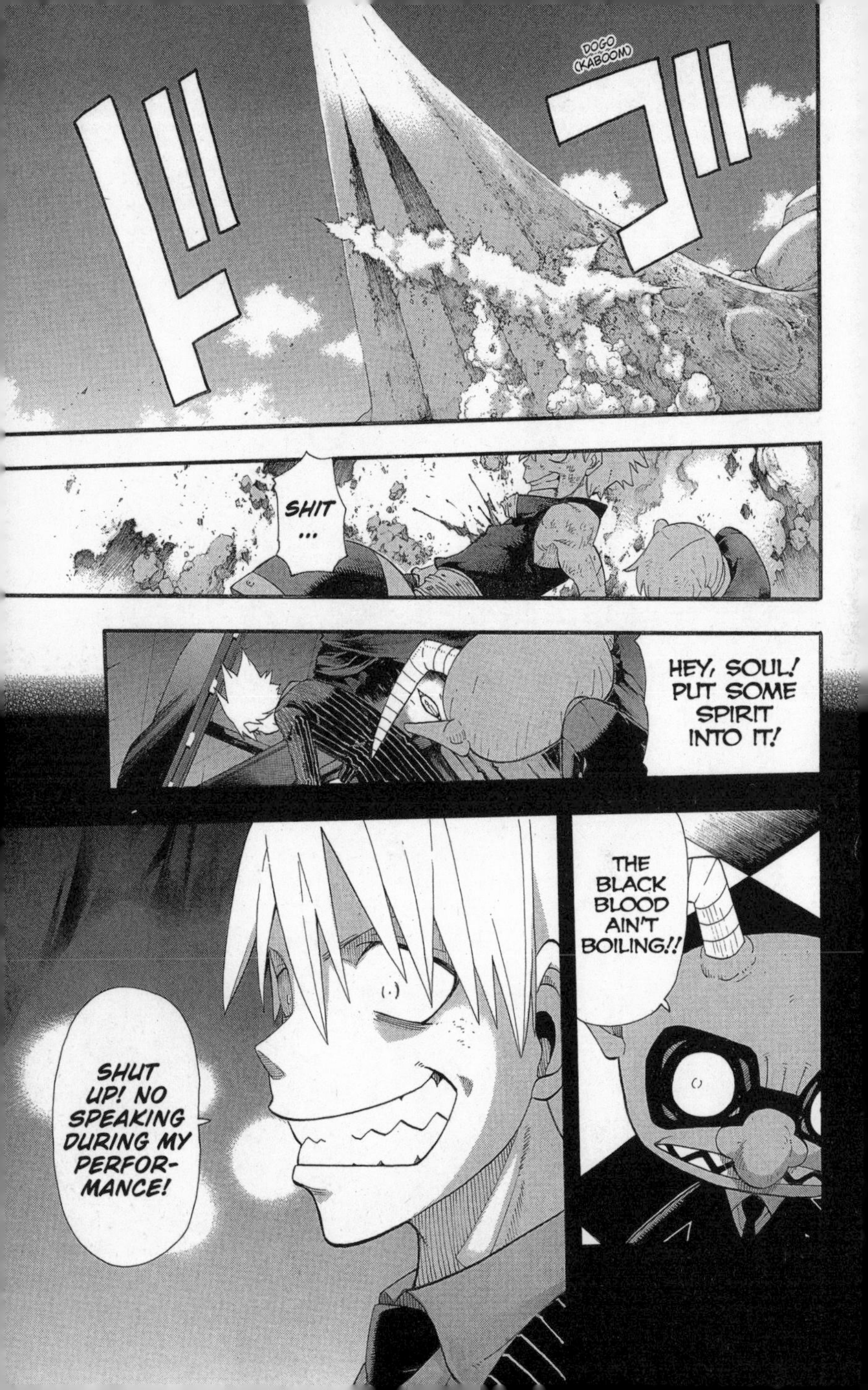
DOGO (KABOOM)
SHIT ...
HEY, SOUL! PUT SOME SPIRIT INTO IT!
THE BLACK BLOOD AIN'T BOILING!!
SHUT UP! NO SPEAKING DURING MY PERFOR-MANCE!

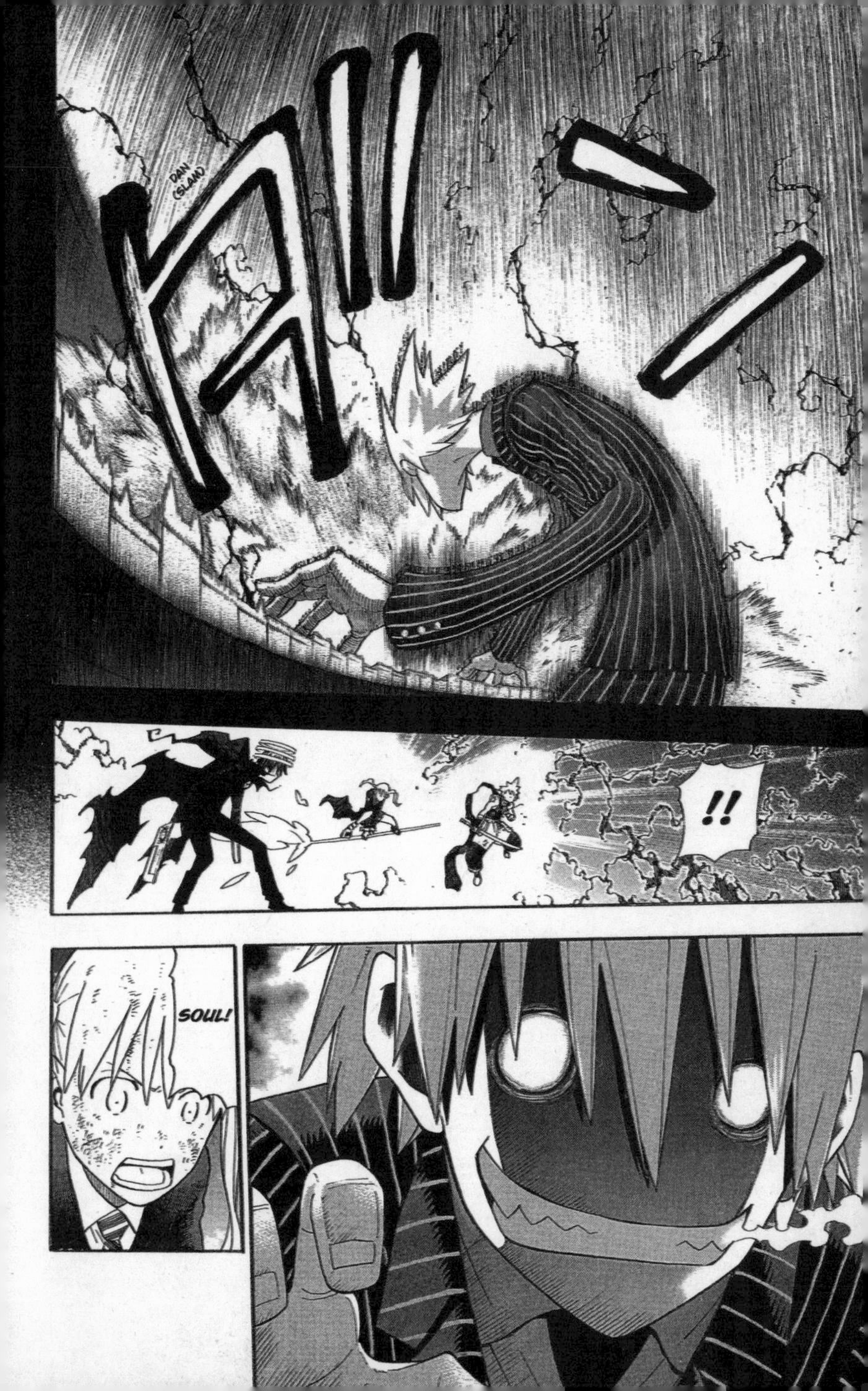
DAN (SLAM)
!!
SOUL!

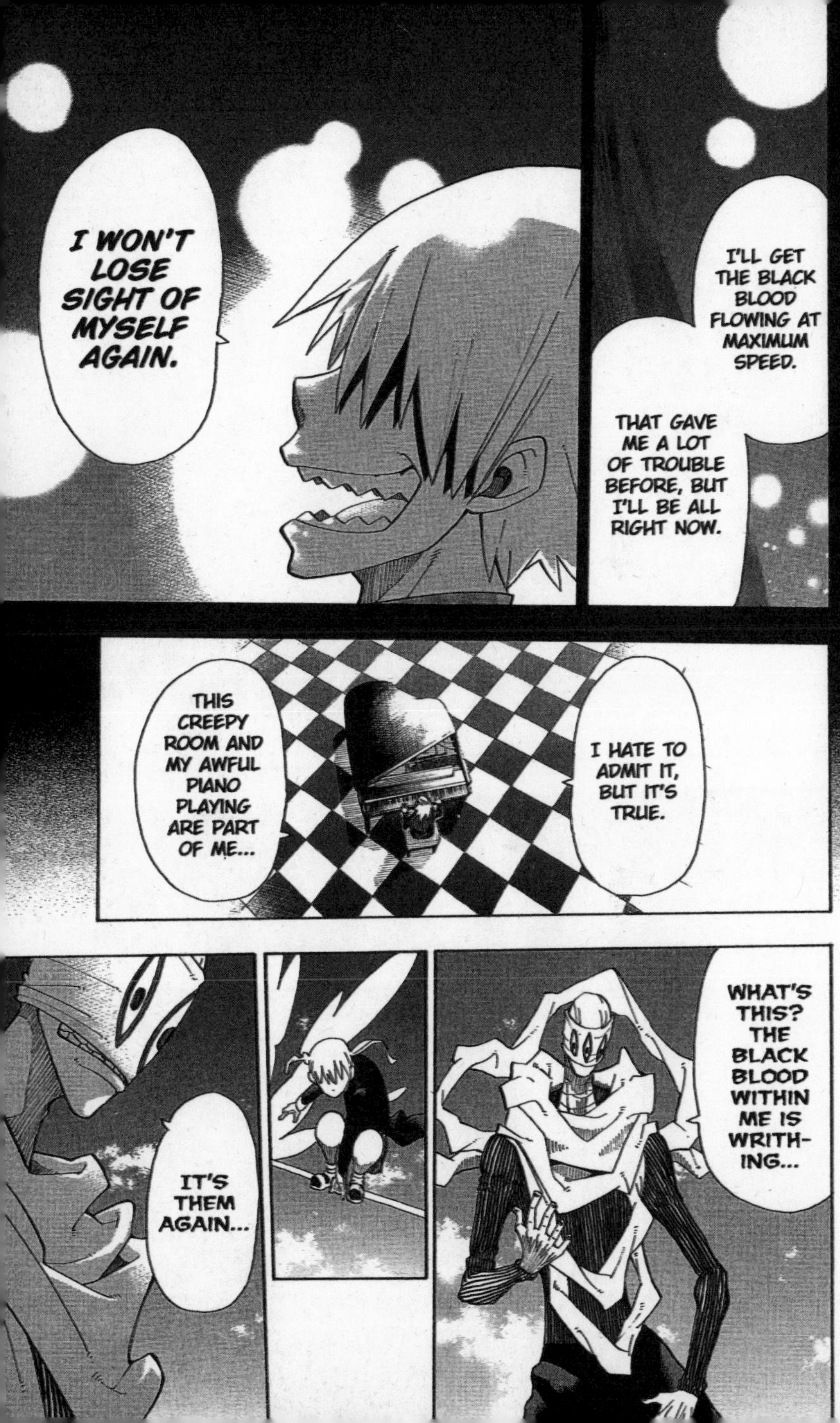
I'LL GET THE BLACK BLOOD FLOWING AT MAXIMUM SPEED.
THAT GAVE ME A LOT OF TROUBLE BEFORE, BUT I'LL BE ALL RIGHT NOW.
I WON'T LOSE SIGHT OF MYSELF AGAIN.
I HATE TO ADMIT IT, BUT IT'S TRUE.
THIS CREEPY ROOM AND MY AWFUL PIANO PLAYING ARE PART OF ME...
WHAT'S THIS? THE BLACK BLOOD WITHIN ME IS WRITH-ING...
IT'S THEM AGAIN...

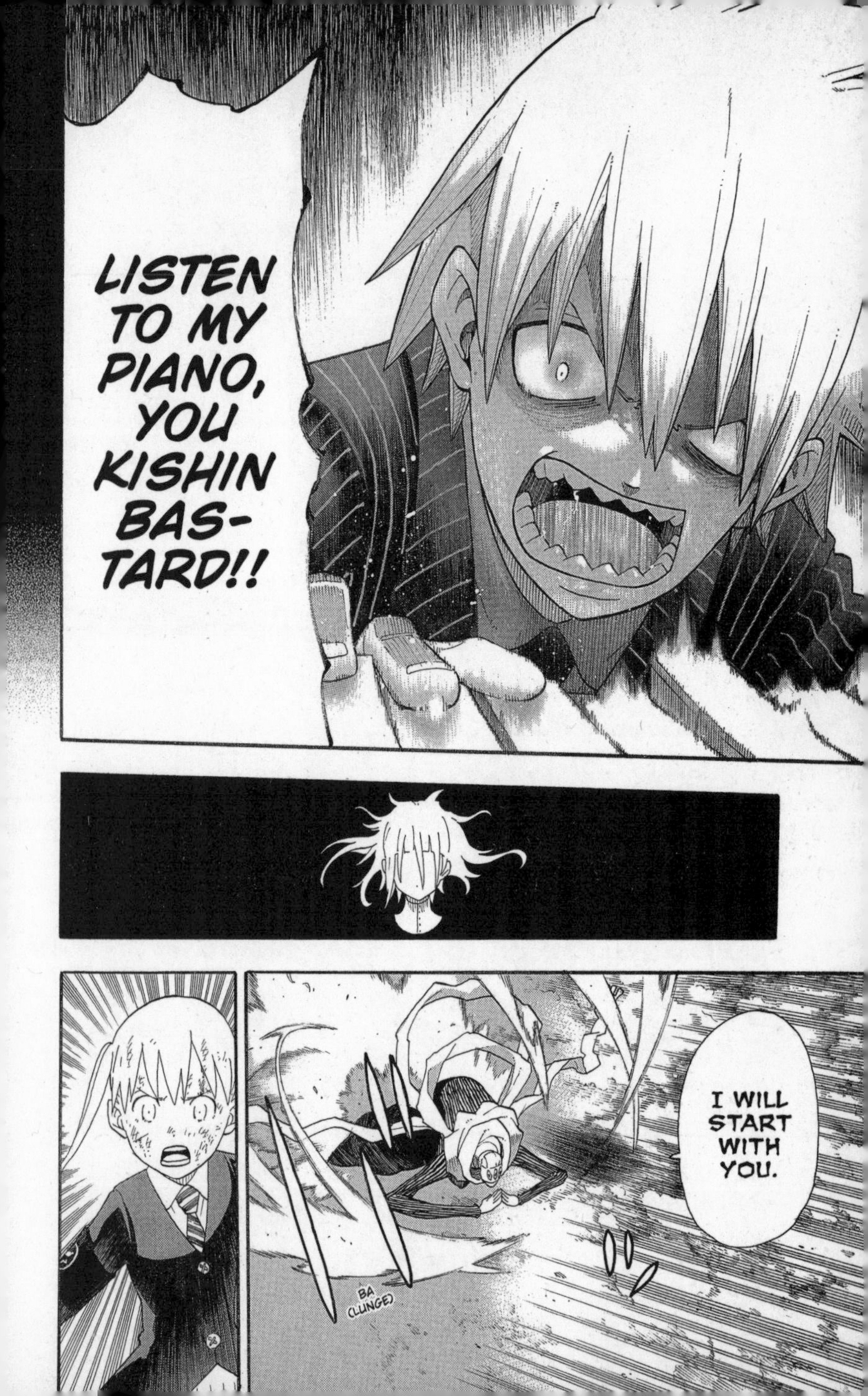
LISTEN TO MY PIANO, YOU KISHIN BAS-TARD!!
I WILL START WITH YOU.
BA (LUNGE)

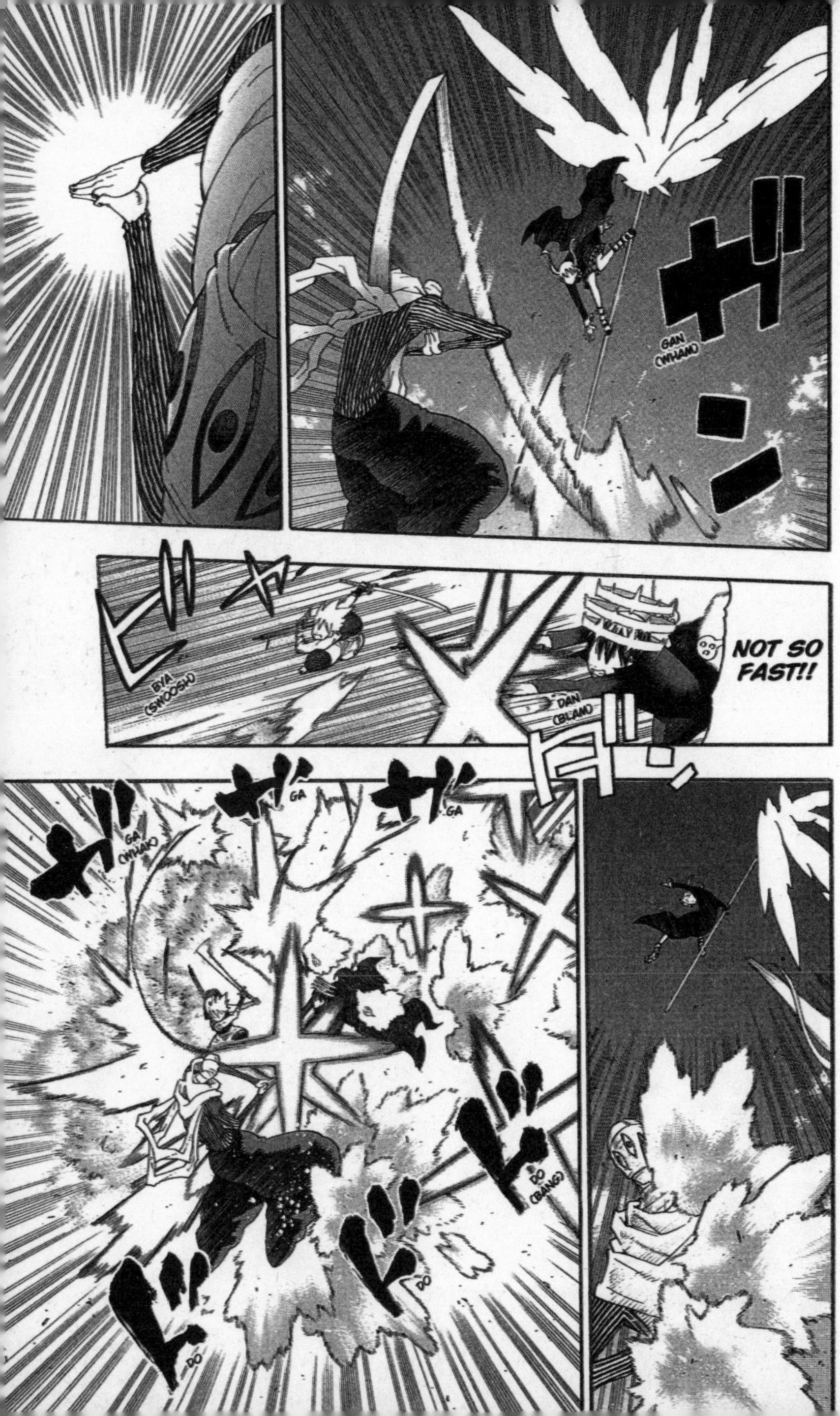
GAN (WHAM)
NOT SO FAST!!
DAN (BLAM)
BYA (SWOOSH)
GA
GA
GA (WHAM)
DO (BANG)
DO
DO

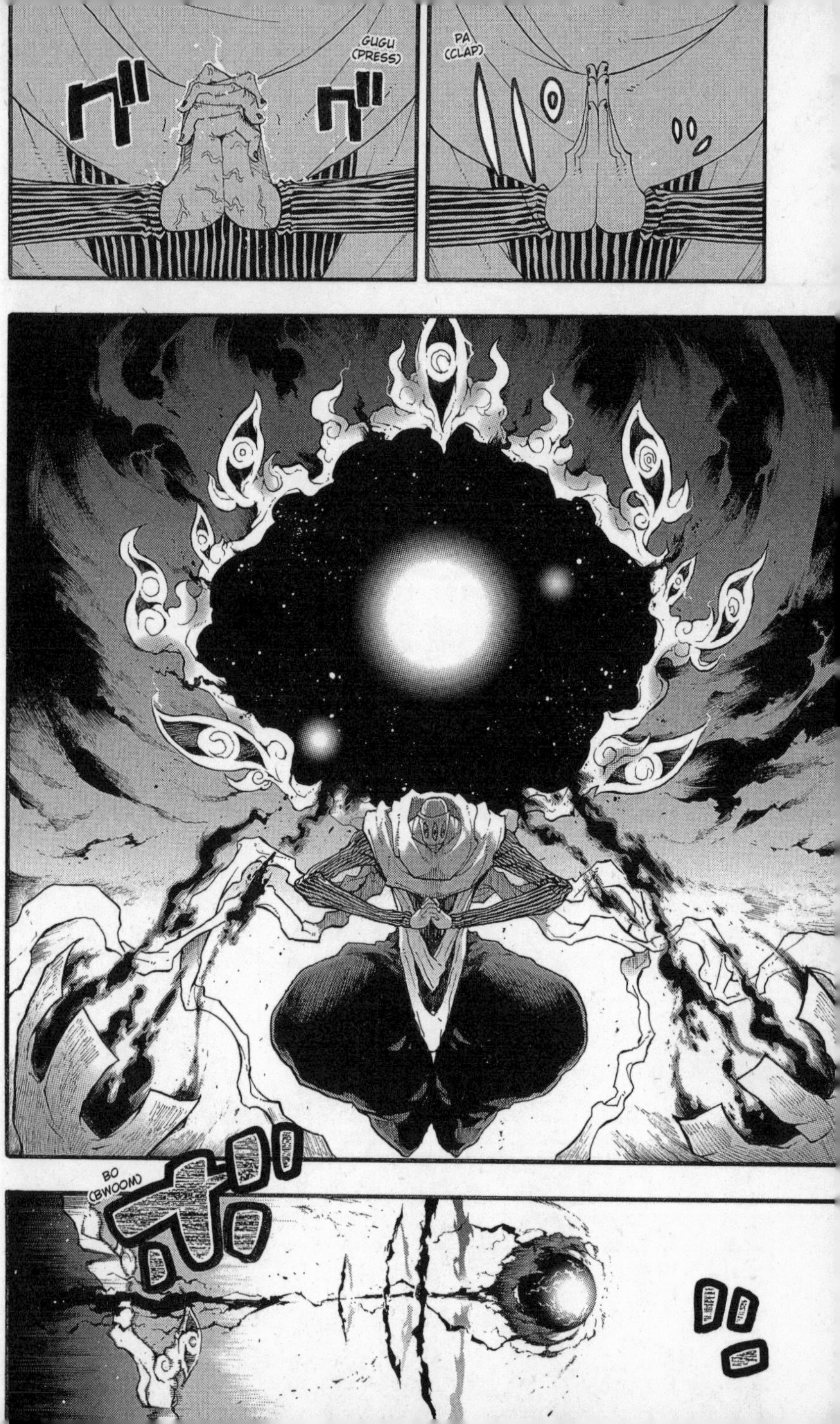
PA (CLAP)
GUGU (PRESS)
BO (BWOOM)

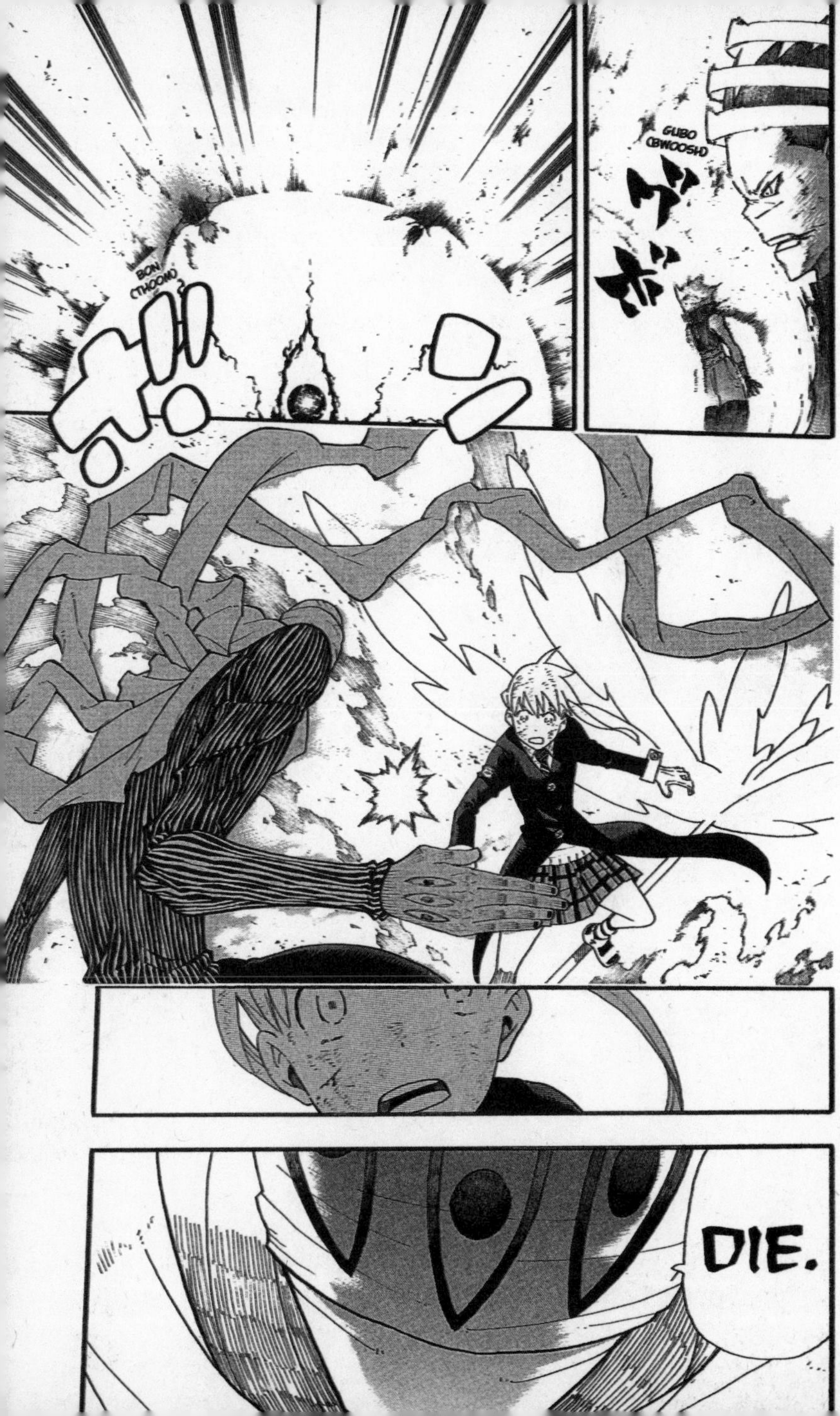
GUBO (BWOOSH)
BON (THOOM)
DIE.

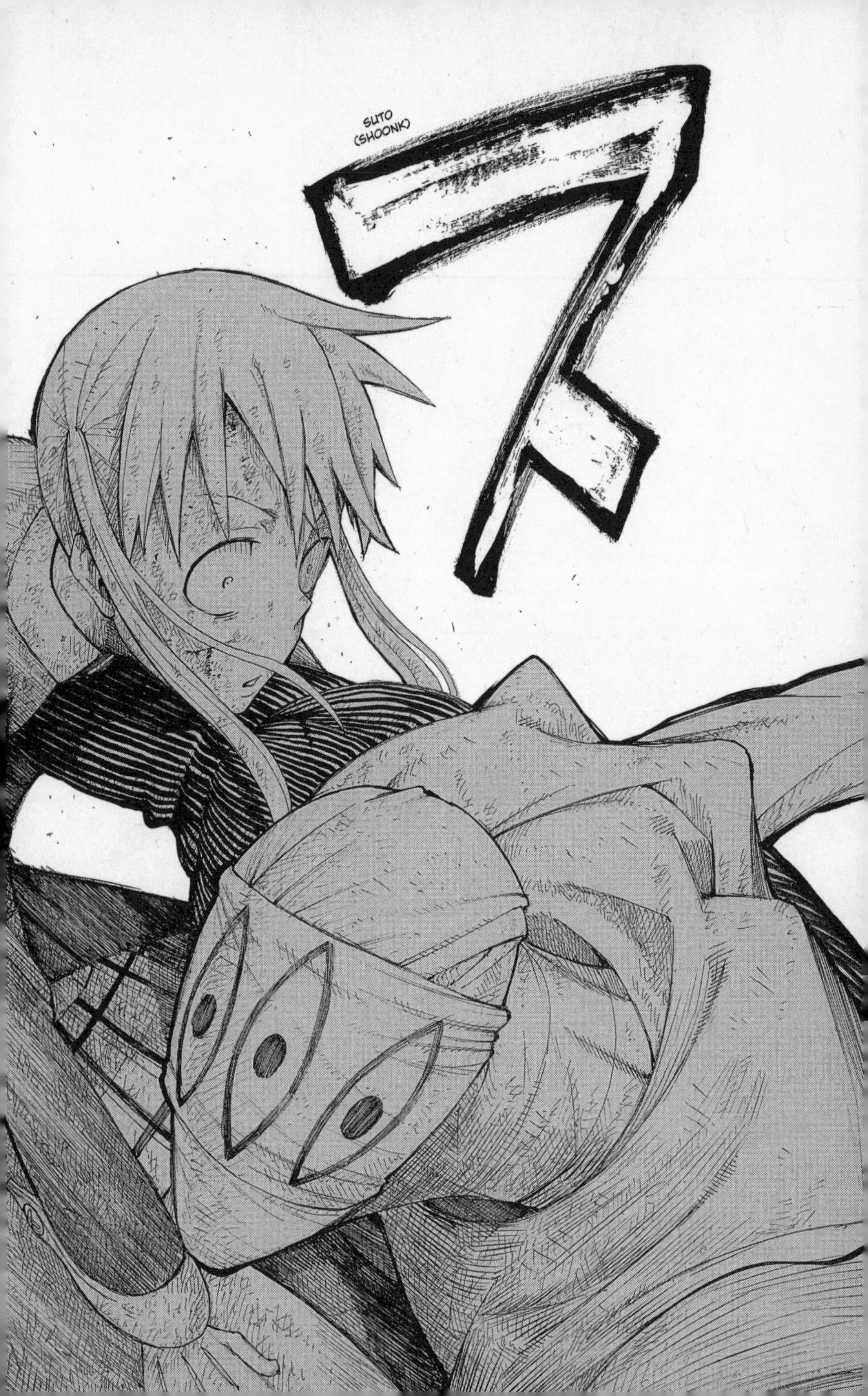
SUTO
(SHOONK)

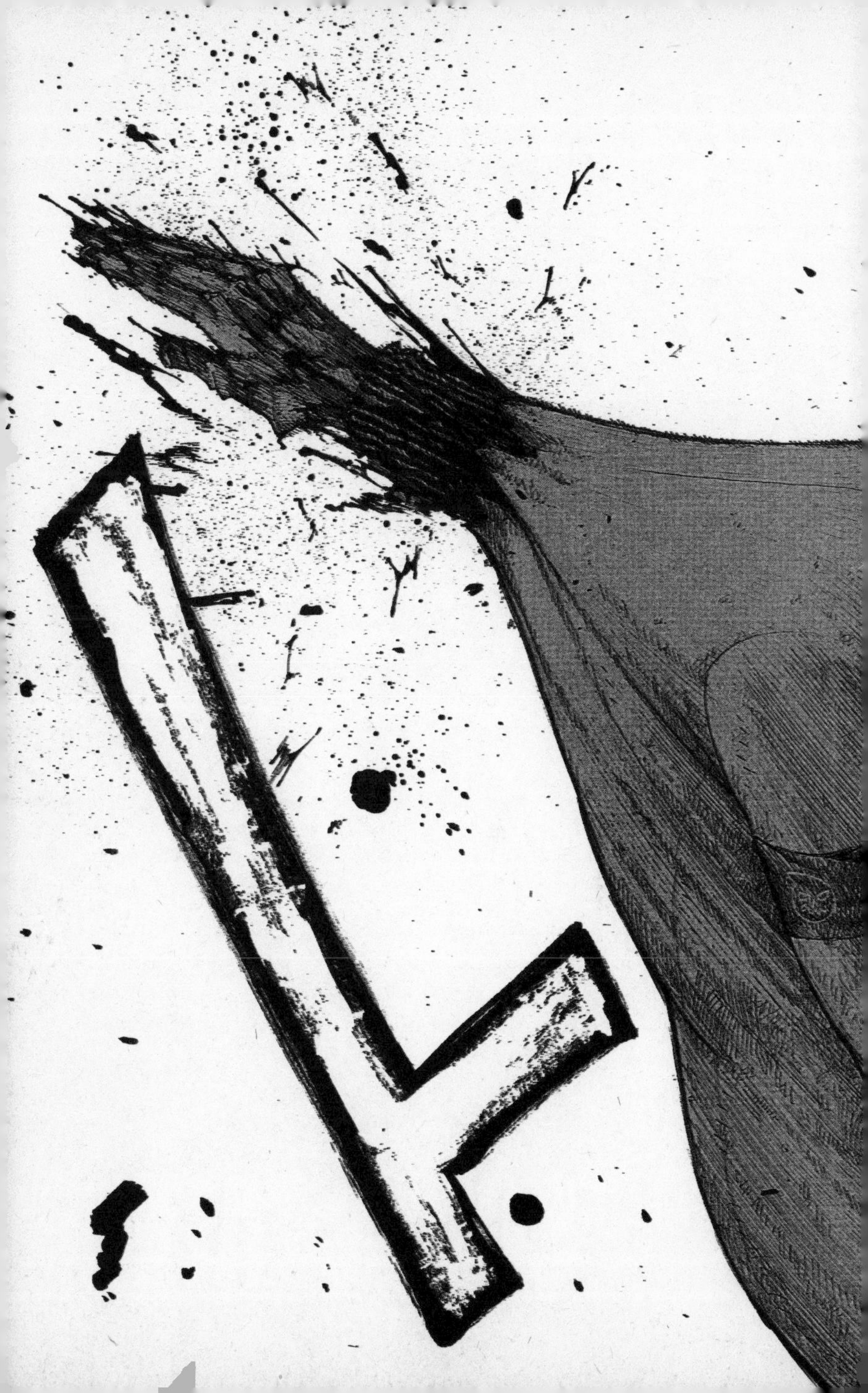

SOUL EATER

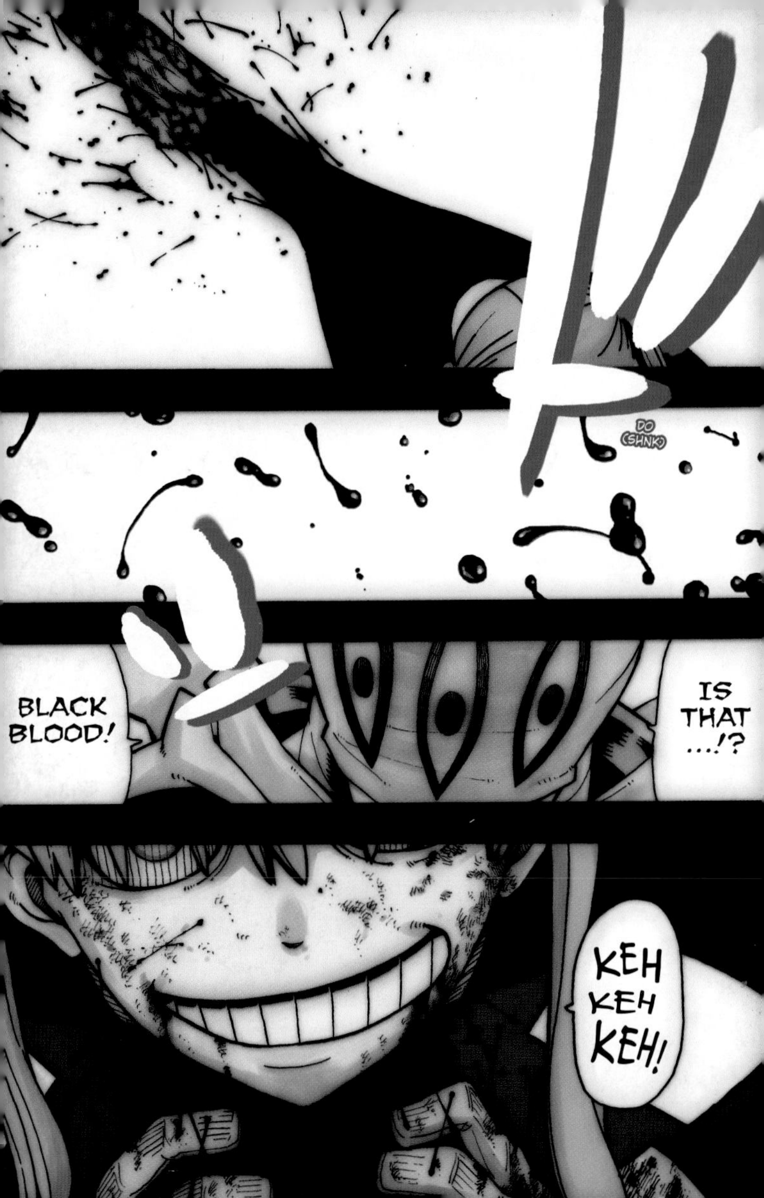
DO (SHNK)
IS THAT ...!?
BLACK BLOOD!
KEH KEH KEH!

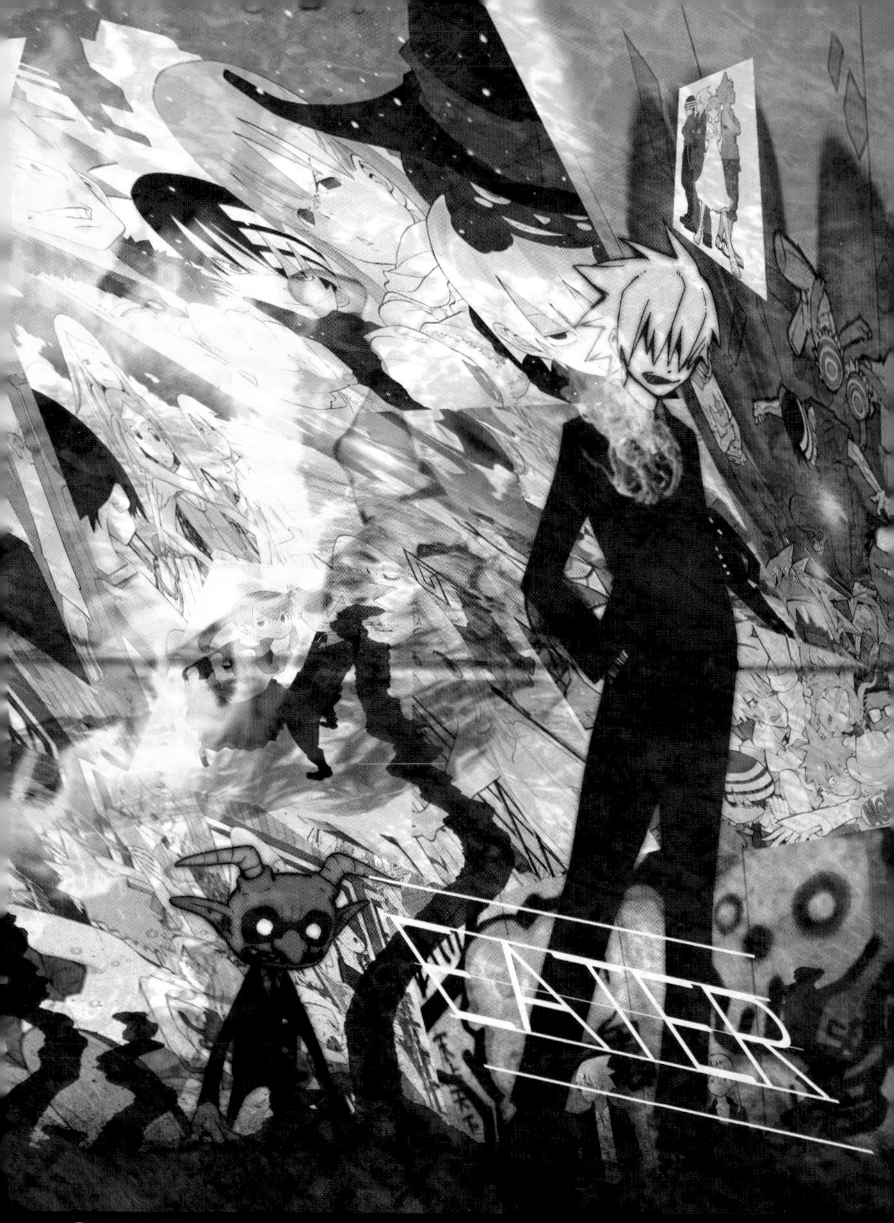

CHAPTER 111: THE DARK SIDE OF THE MOON VIII

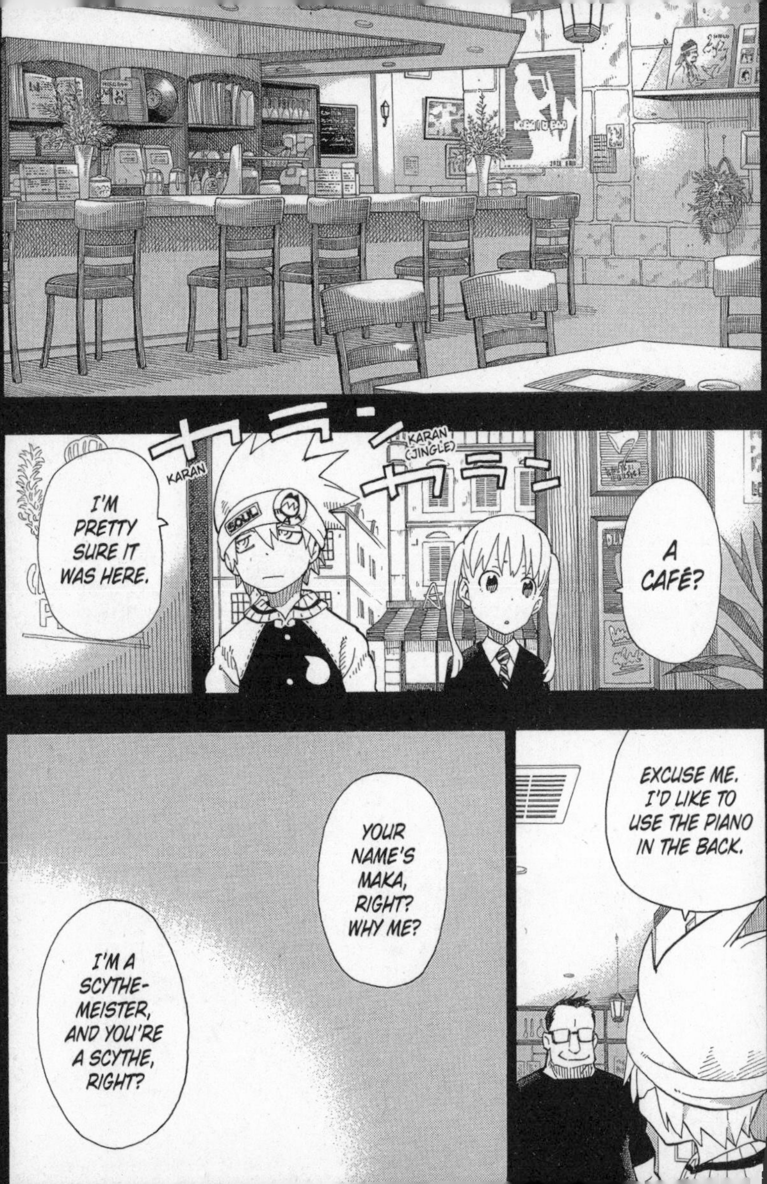
A CAFÉ?
KARAN (JINGLE)
KARAN
I'M PRETTY SURE IT WAS HERE.
EXCUSE ME. I'D LIKE TO USE THE PIANO IN THE BACK.
YOUR NAME'S MAKA, RIGHT? WHY ME?
I'M A SCYTHE-MEISTER, AND YOU'RE A SCYTHE, RIGHT?

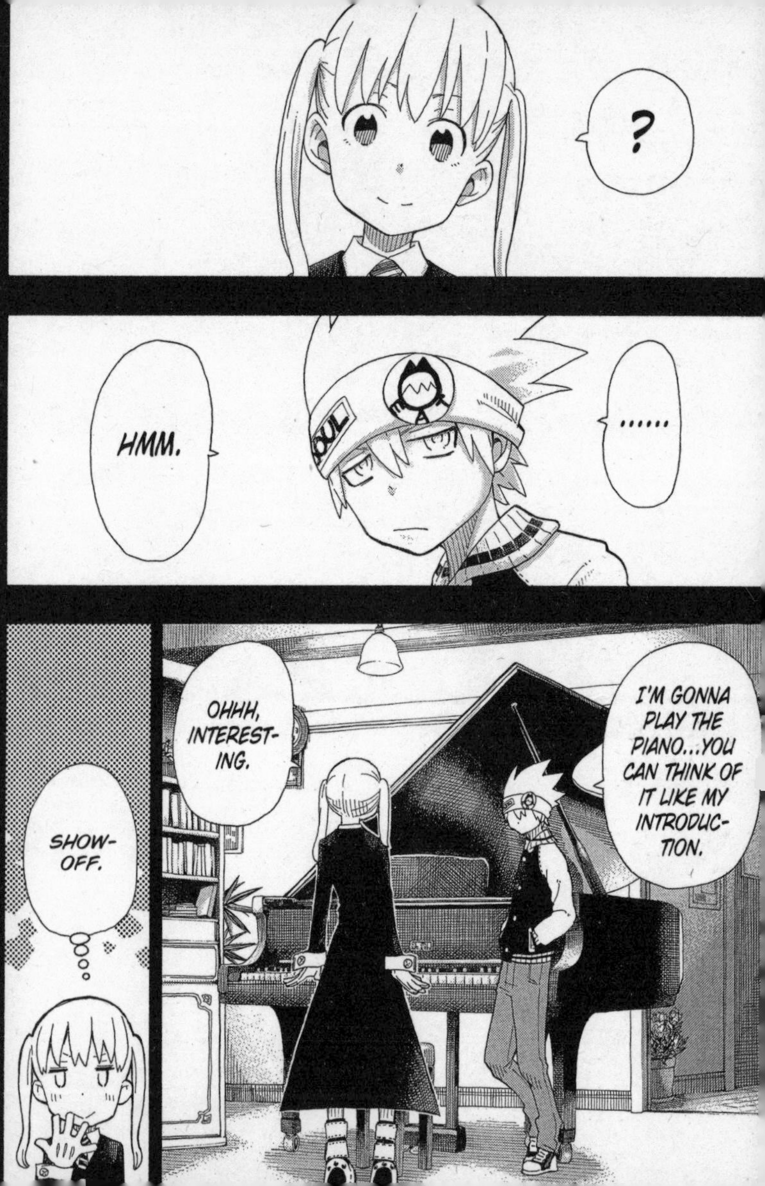
?
......
HMM.
I'M GONNA PLAY THE PIANO...YOU CAN THINK OF IT LIKE MY INTRODUCTION.
OHHH, INTERESTING.
SHOW-OFF.

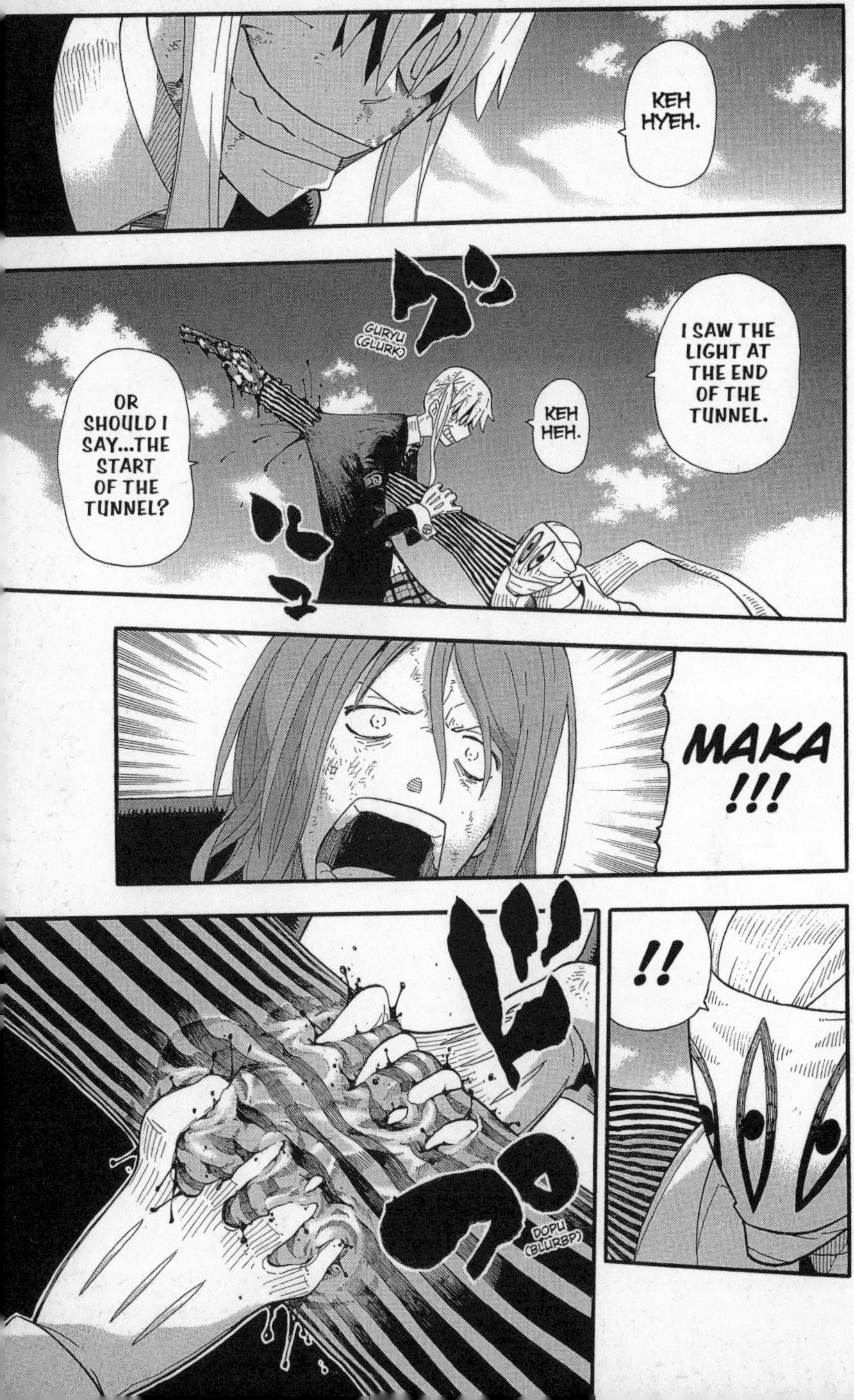
KEH HYEH.
I SAW THE LIGHT AT THE END OF THE TUNNEL.
KEH HEH.
GURYU (GLURK)
OR SHOULD I SAY...THE START OF THE TUNNEL?
MAKA!!!
!!
DOPU (BLURBP)

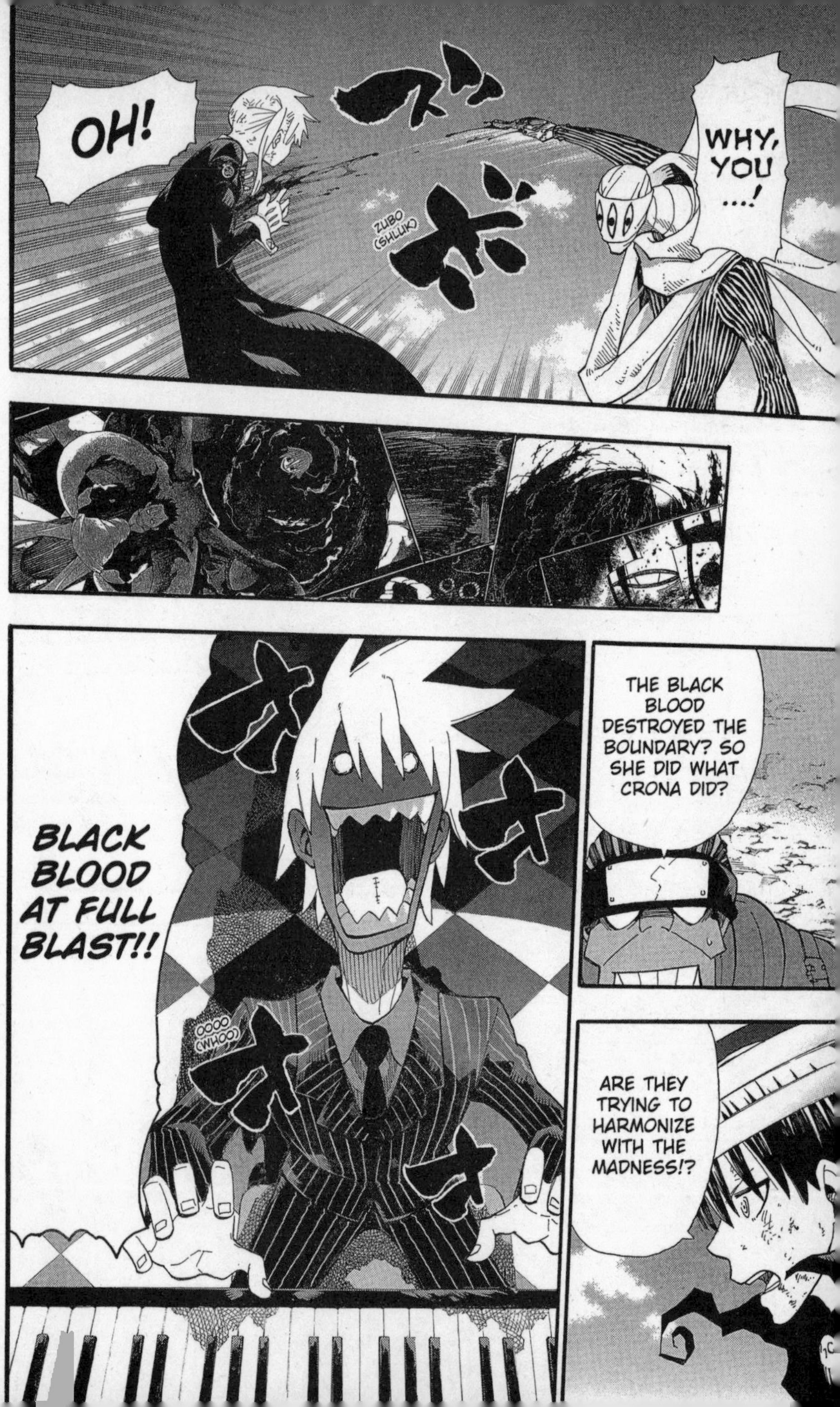
WHY, YOU ...!
OH!
ZUBO (SHLUK)
THE BLACK BLOOD DESTROYED THE BOUNDARY? SO SHE DID WHAT CRONA DID?
ARE THEY TRYING TO HARMONIZE WITH THE MADNESS!?
BLACK BLOOD AT FULL BLAST!!
OOOO (WHOO)

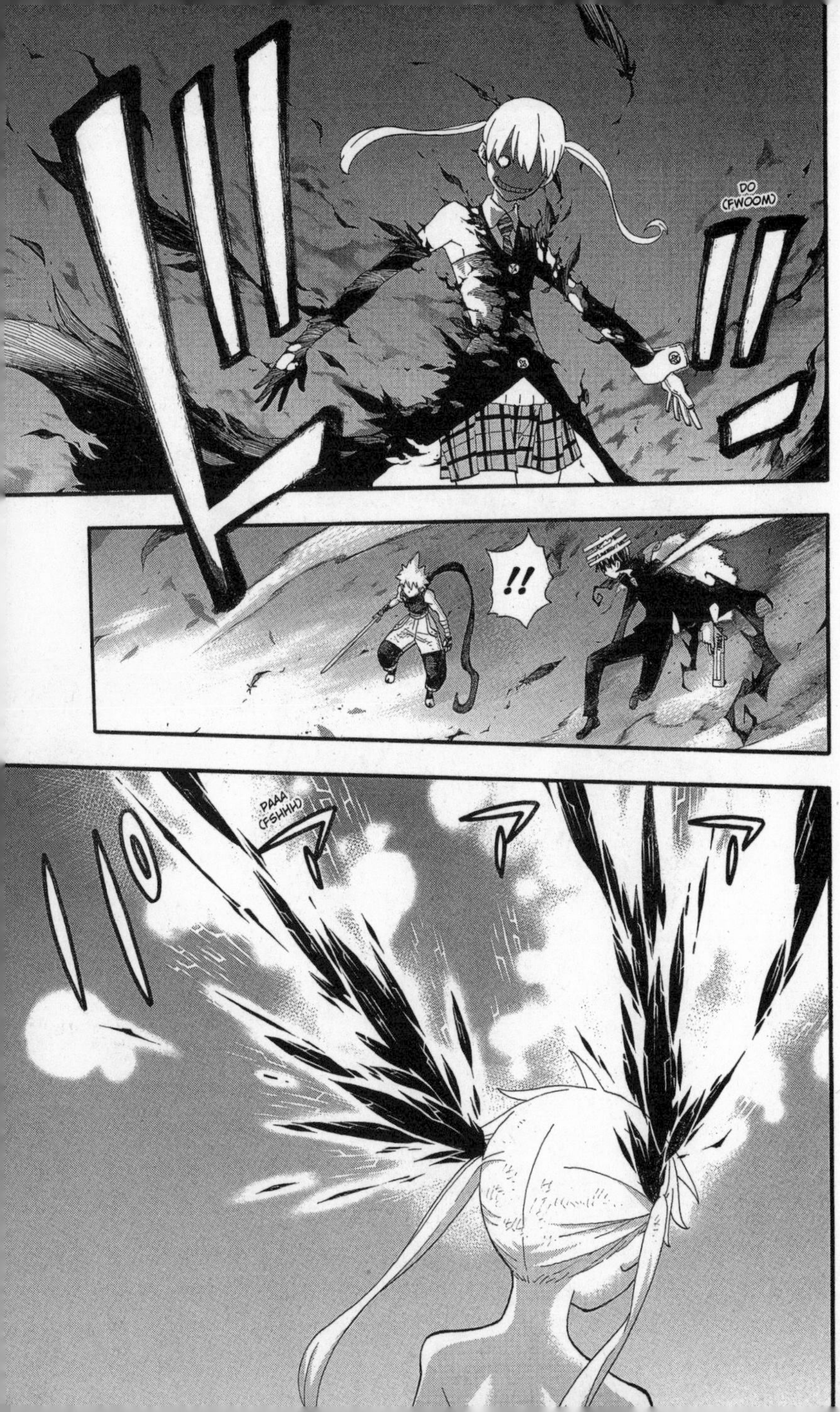
DO
(FWOOM)
!!
PAAA
(FSHHH)

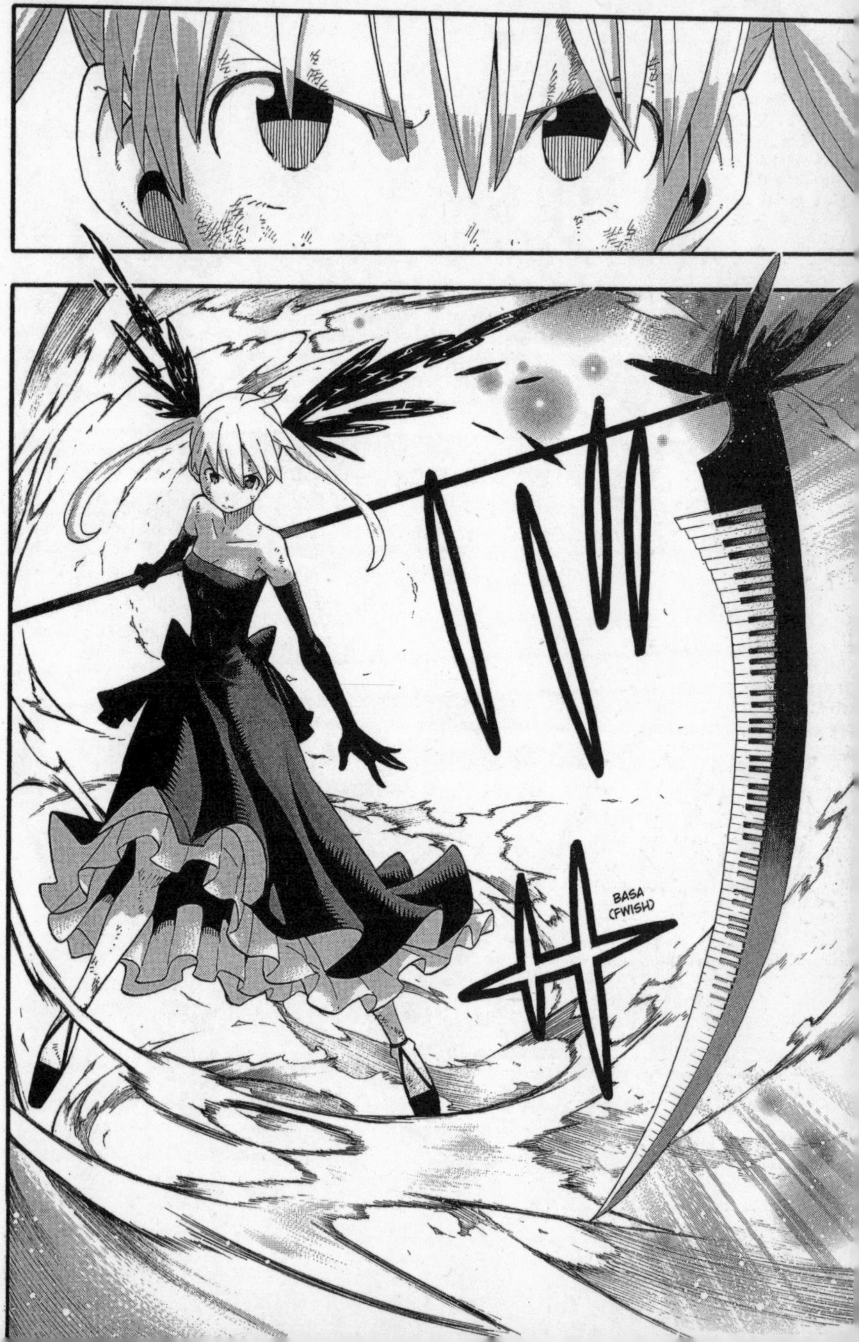
BASA
(FWISH)

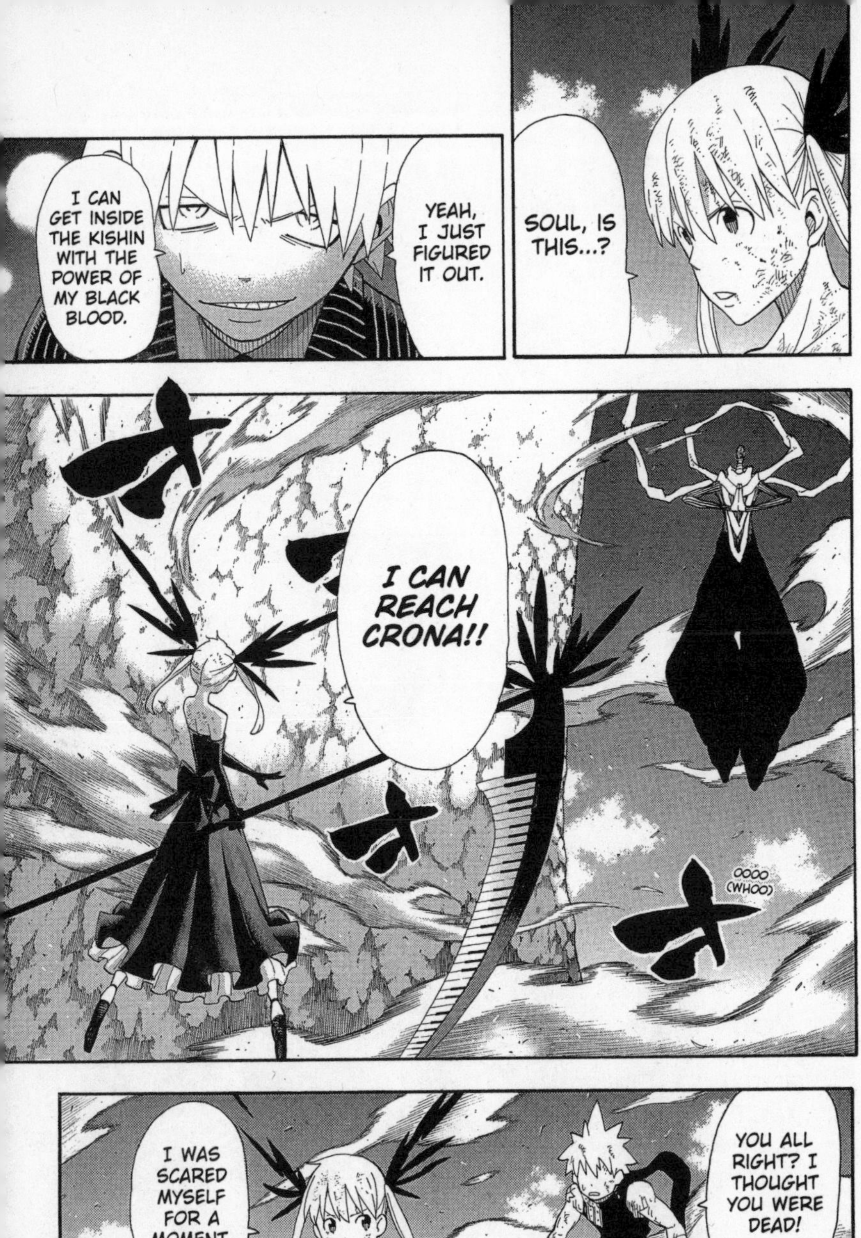
SOUL, IS THIS...?
YEAH, I JUST FIGURED IT OUT.
I CAN GET INSIDE THE KISHIN WITH THE POWER OF MY BLACK BLOOD.
I CAN REACH CRONA!!
OOOO (WHOO)
YOU ALL RIGHT? I THOUGHT YOU WERE DEAD!
I WAS SCARED MYSELF FOR A MOMENT.

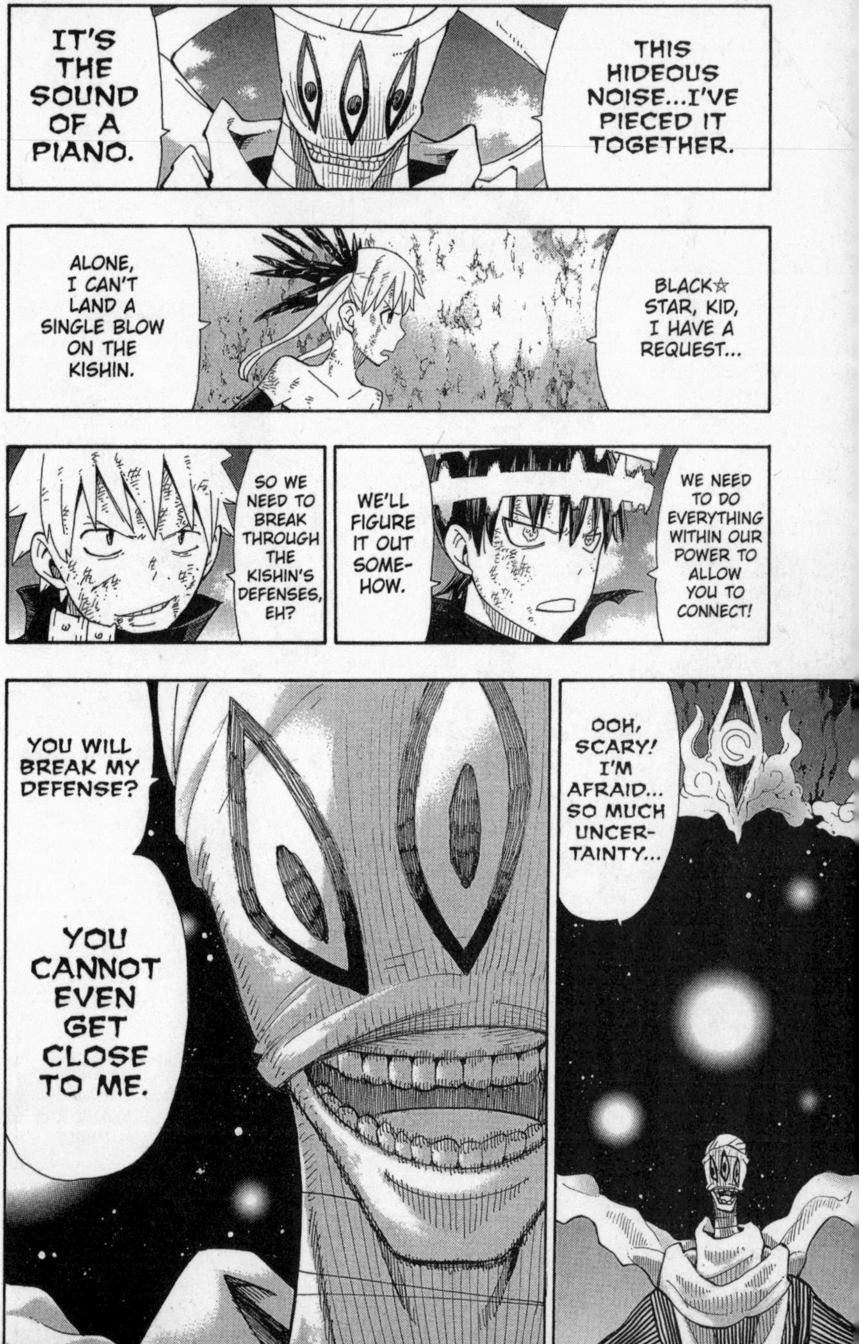
THIS HIDEOUS NOISE...I'VE PIECED IT TOGETHER.
IT'S THE SOUND OF A PIANO.
BLACK☆ STAR, KID, I HAVE A REQUEST...
ALONE, I CAN'T LAND A SINGLE BLOW ON THE KISHIN.
WE NEED TO DO EVERYTHING WITHIN OUR POWER TO ALLOW YOU TO CONNECT!
WE'LL FIGURE IT OUT SOMEHOW.
SO WE NEED TO BREAK THROUGH THE KISHIN'S DEFENSES, EH?
OOH, SCARY! I'M AFRAID... SO MUCH UNCERTAINTY...
YOU WILL BREAK MY DEFENSE?
YOU CANNOT EVEN GET CLOSE TO ME.

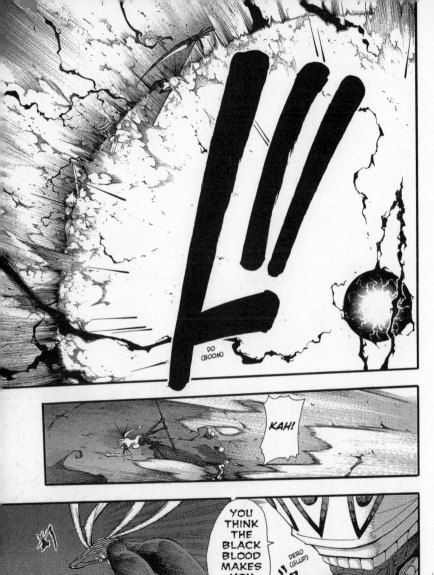
DO
(BOOM)

KAH!

YOU THINK THE BLACK BLOOD MAKES YOU IMMORTAL?

DERO
(GLUP)

BA
(WHOOSH)

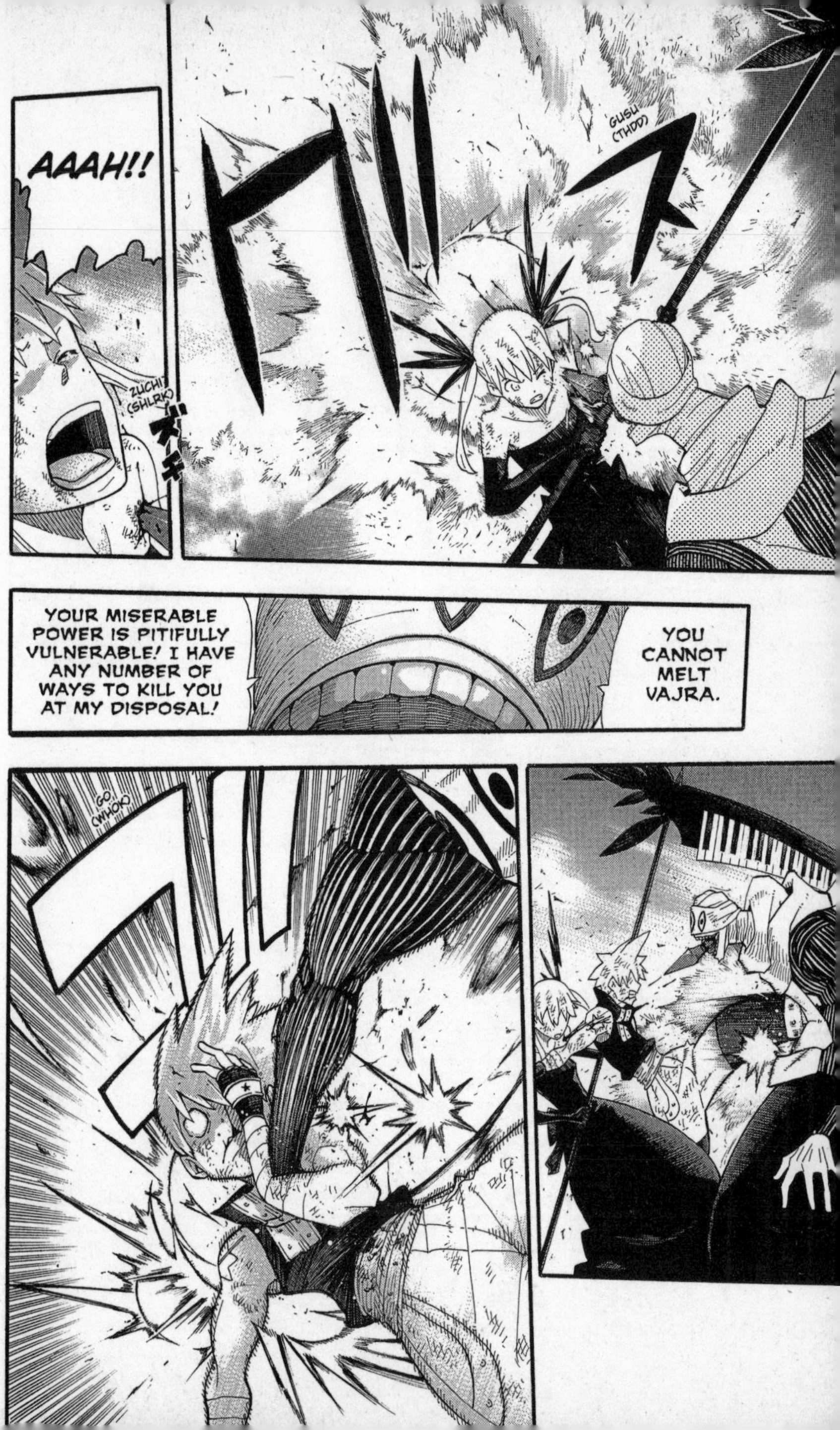
GUSU (THDD)
AAAH!!
ZUCHI (SHLRK)
YOU CANNOT MELT VAJRA.
YOUR MISERABLE POWER IS PITIFULLY VULNERABLE! I HAVE ANY NUMBER OF WAYS TO KILL YOU AT MY DISPOSAL!
GO (WHOK)

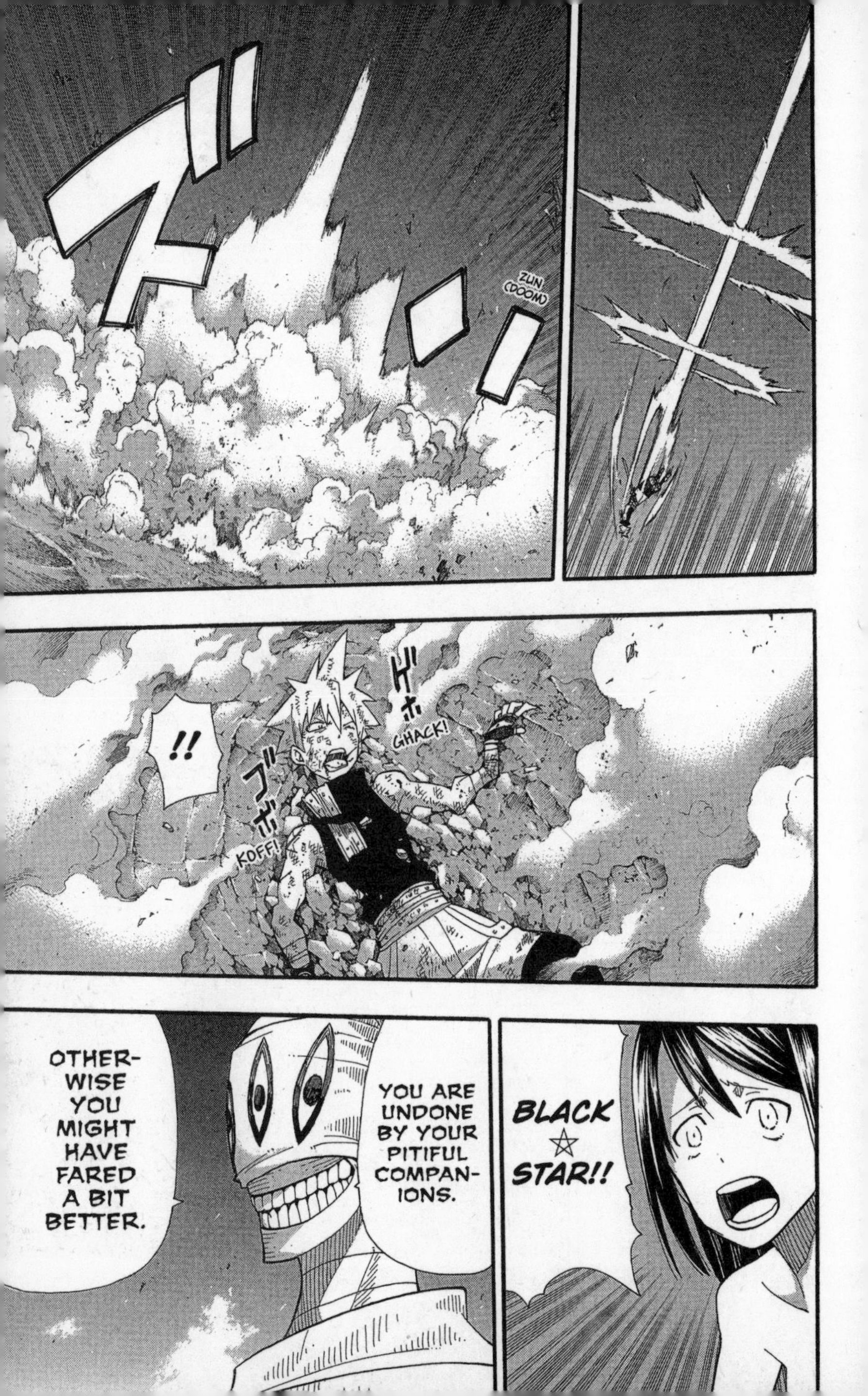
ZUN (DOOM)
!!
GHACK!
KOFF!
BLACK ☆ STAR!!
YOU ARE UNDONE BY YOUR PITIFUL COMPANIONS.
OTHERWISE YOU MIGHT HAVE FARED A BIT BETTER.

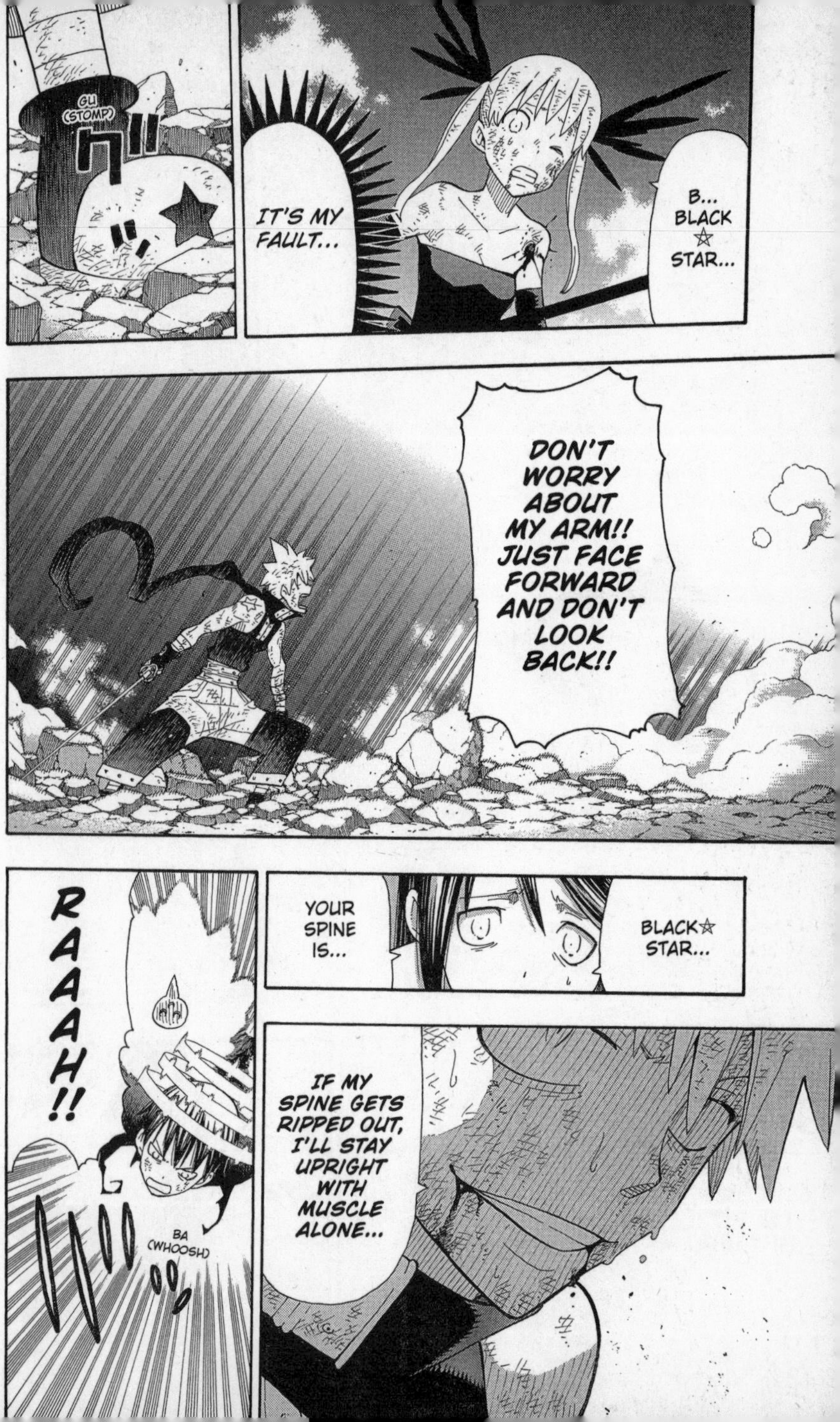
B... BLACK☆STAR...
IT'S MY FAULT...
GU (STOMP)
DON'T WORRY ABOUT MY ARM!! JUST FACE FORWARD AND DON'T LOOK BACK!!
BLACK☆STAR...
YOUR SPINE IS...
IF MY SPINE GETS RIPPED OUT, I'LL STAY UPRIGHT WITH MUSCLE ALONE...
RAAAAH!!
BA (WHOOSH)

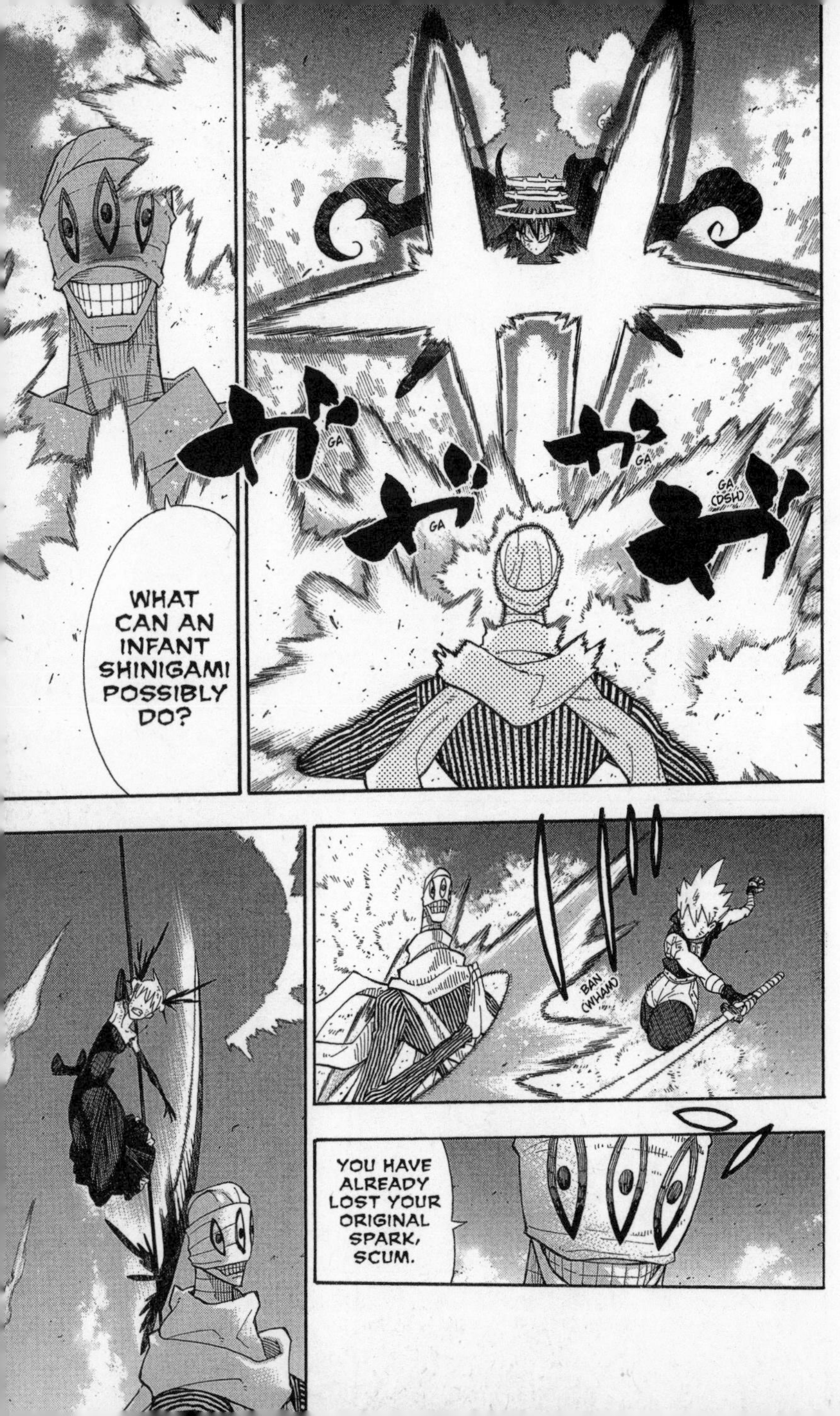
GA
GA
GA
GA (DSH)
WHAT CAN AN INFANT SHINIGAMI POSSIBLY DO?
BAN (WHAM)
YOU HAVE ALREADY LOST YOUR ORIGINAL SPARK, SCUM.

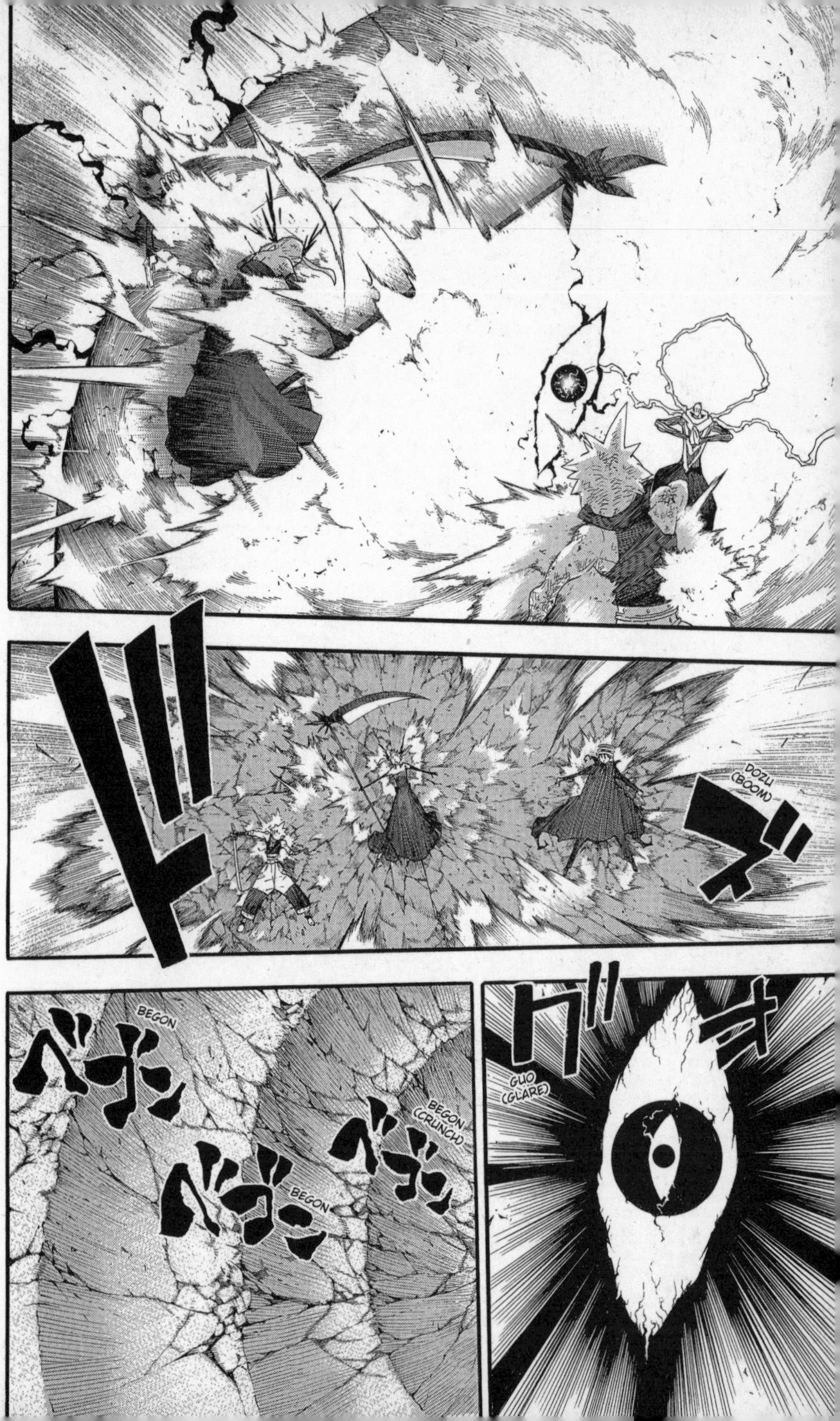
DOZU
(BOOM)
GUO
(GLARE)
BEGON
BEGON
(CRUNCH)
BEGON

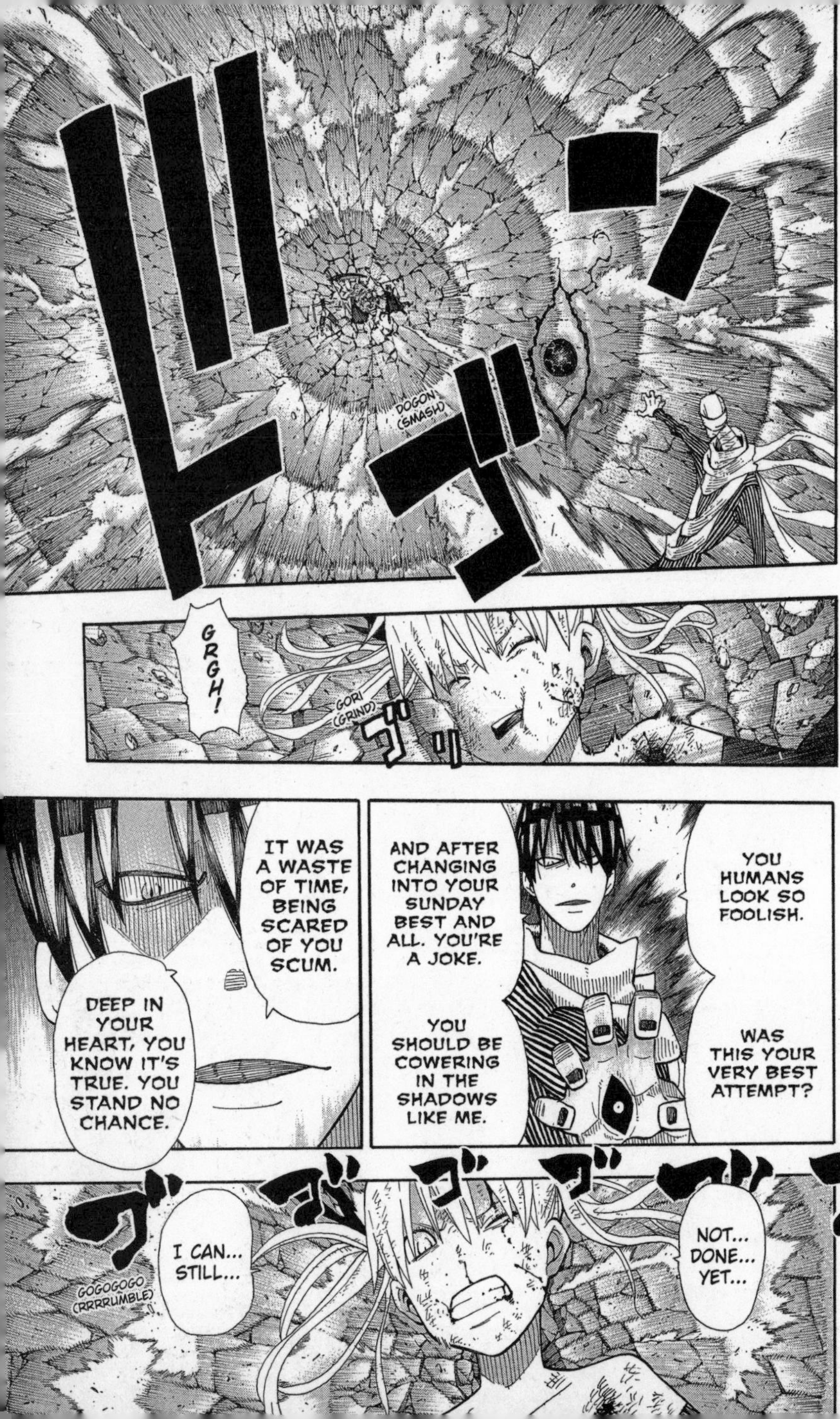
DOGON (SMASH)
GRGH!
GORI (GRIND)
YOU HUMANS LOOK SO FOOLISH.
AND AFTER CHANGING INTO YOUR SUNDAY BEST AND ALL. YOU'RE A JOKE.
WAS THIS YOUR VERY BEST ATTEMPT?
YOU SHOULD BE COWERING IN THE SHADOWS LIKE ME.
IT WAS A WASTE OF TIME, BEING SCARED OF YOU SCUM.
DEEP IN YOUR HEART, YOU KNOW IT'S TRUE. YOU STAND NO CHANCE.
NOT... DONE... YET...
I CAN... STILL...
GOGOGOGO (RRRRUMBLE)

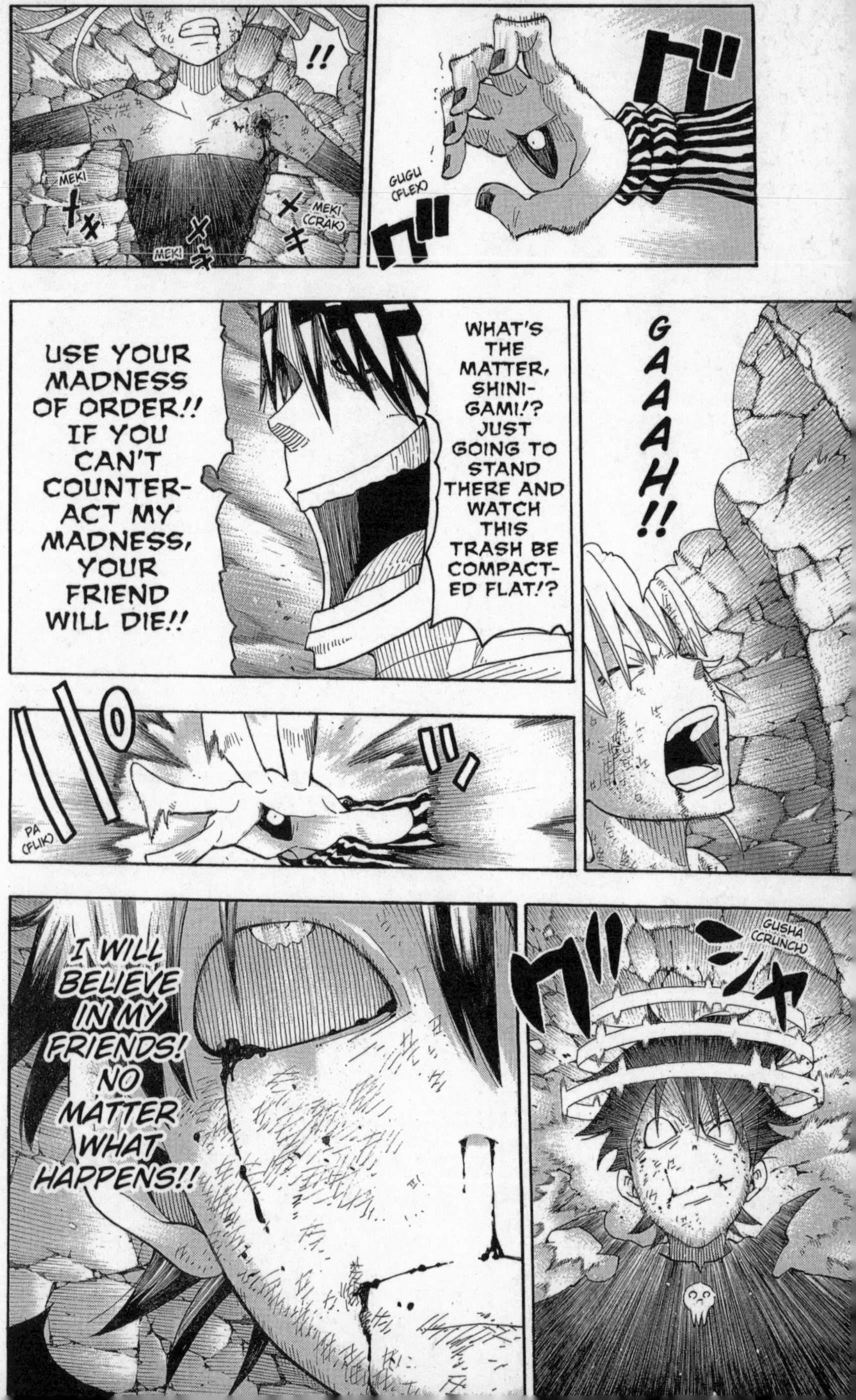
GUGU (FLEX)
!!
MEKI (CRAK)
MEKI
MEKI
GAAAH!!
WHAT'S THE MATTER, SHINIGAMI!? JUST GOING TO STAND THERE AND WATCH THIS TRASH BE COMPACTED FLAT!?
USE YOUR MADNESS OF ORDER!! IF YOU CAN'T COUNTERACT MY MADNESS, YOUR FRIEND WILL DIE!!
PA (FLIK)
GUSHA (CRUNCH)
I WILL BELIEVE IN MY FRIENDS! NO MATTER WHAT HAPPENS!!

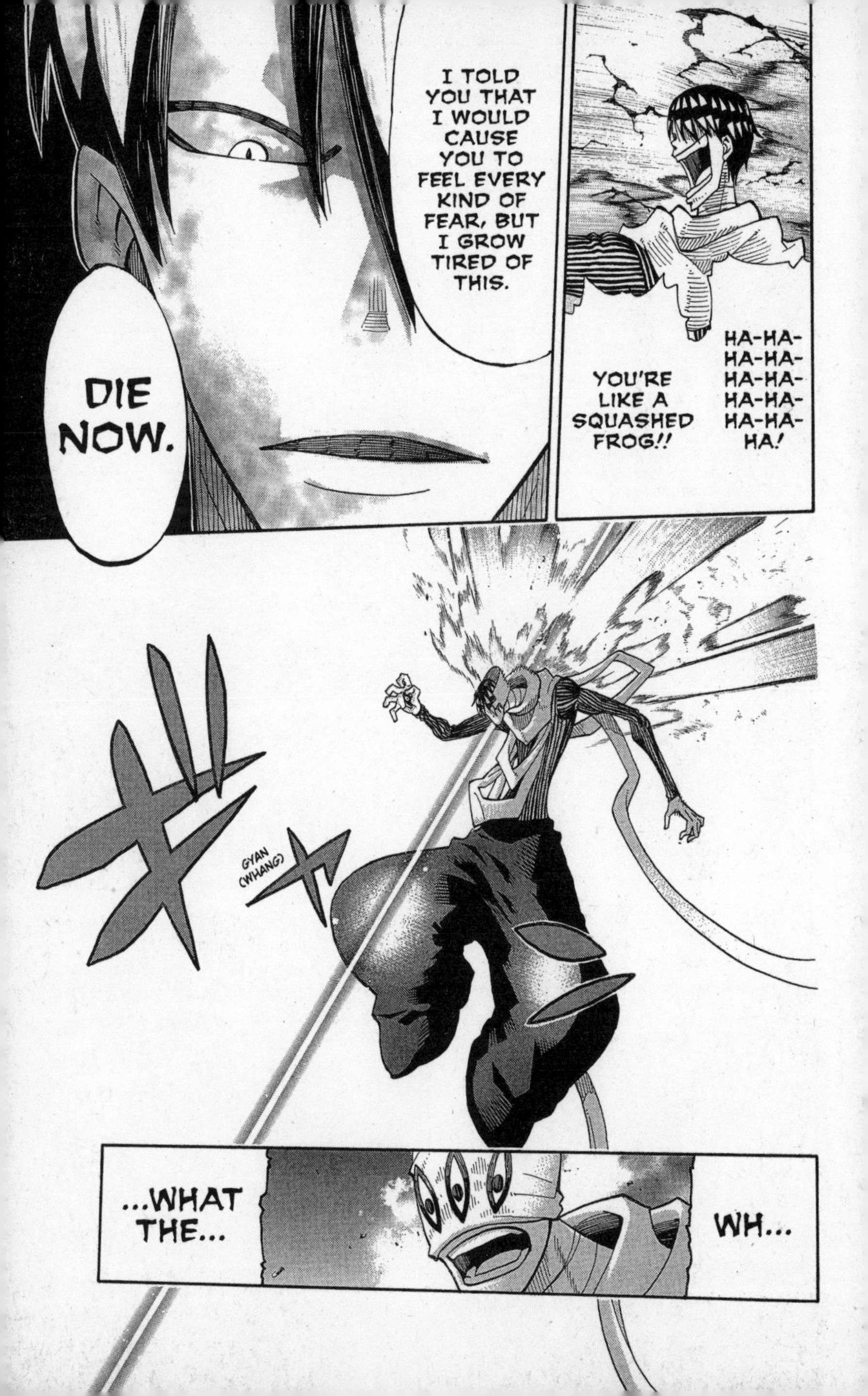
HA-HA-HA-HA-HA-HA-HA-HA-HA-HA-HA!
YOU'RE LIKE A SQUASHED FROG!!
I TOLD YOU THAT I WOULD CAUSE YOU TO FEEL EVERY KIND OF FEAR, BUT I GROW TIRED OF THIS.
DIE NOW.
GYAN (WHANG)
WH...
...WHAT THE...

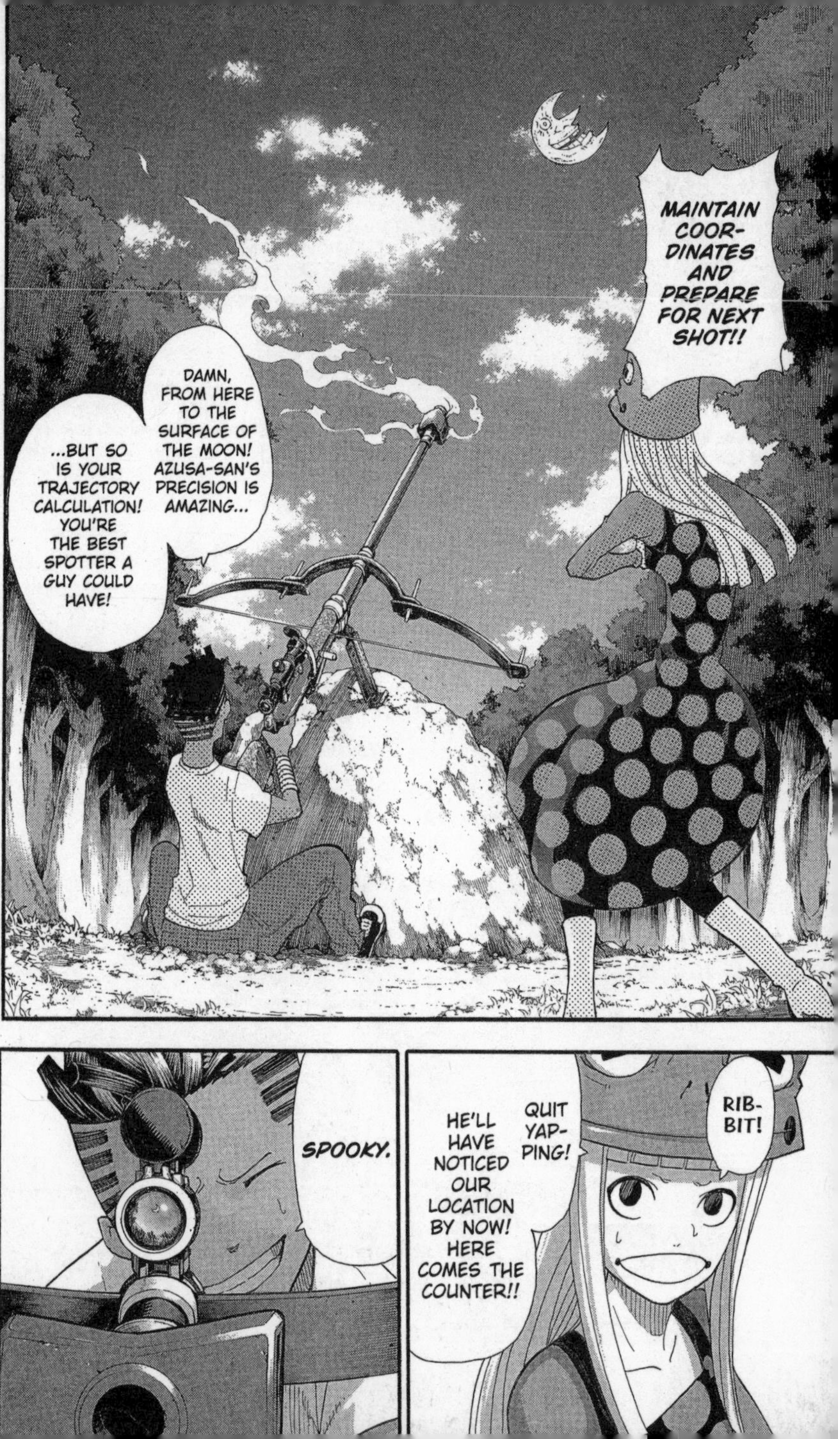
MAINTAIN COOR-DINATES AND PREPARE FOR NEXT SHOT!!
DAMN, FROM HERE TO THE SURFACE OF THE MOON! AZUSA-SAN'S PRECISION IS AMAZING...
...BUT SO IS YOUR TRAJECTORY CALCULATION! YOU'RE THE BEST SPOTTER A GUY COULD HAVE!
RIB-BIT!
QUIT YAP-PING!
HE'LL HAVE NOTICED OUR LOCATION BY NOW! HERE COMES THE COUNTER!!
SPOOKY.

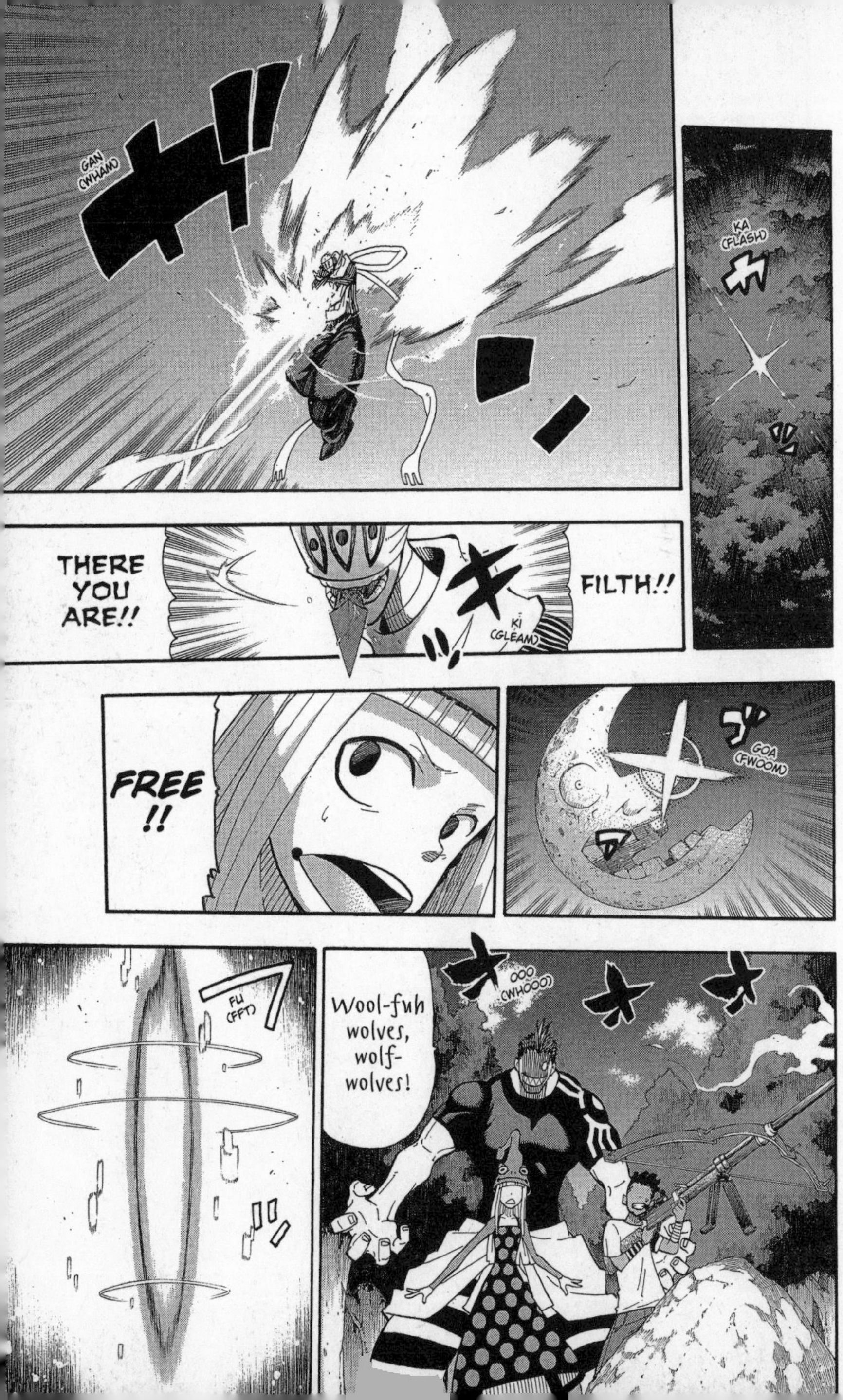

KA (FLASH)
GAN (WHAM)
FILTH!!
KI (GLEAM)
THERE YOU ARE!!
GOA (FWOOM)
FREE!!
OOO (WHOOO)
Wool-fuh wolves, wolf-wolves!
FU (FFT)

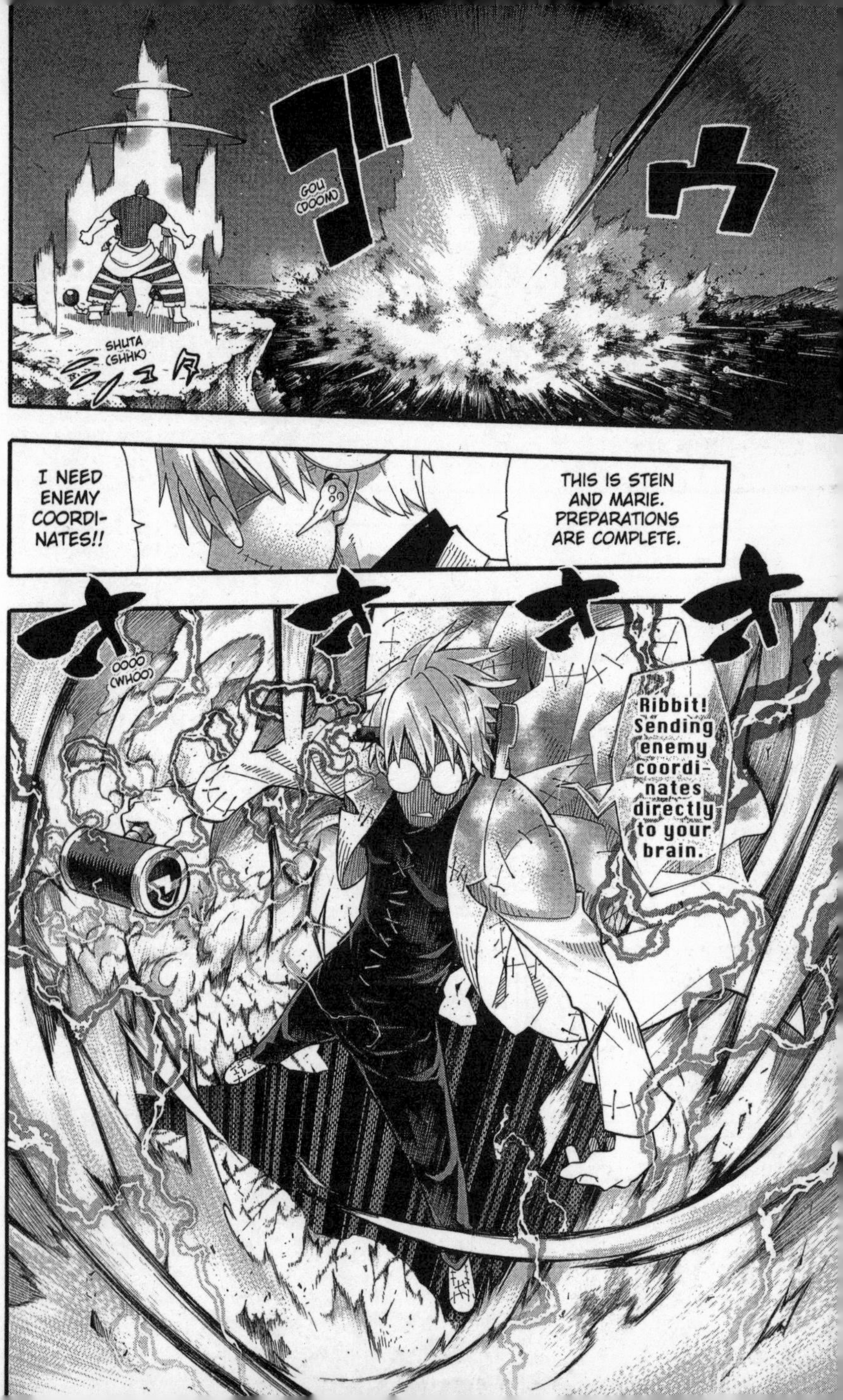
GOU (DOOM)
SHUTA (SHHK)
THIS IS STEIN AND MARIE. PREPARATIONS ARE COMPLETE.
I NEED ENEMY COORDINATES!!
OOOO (WHOO)
Ribbit! Sending enemy coordinates directly to your brain.

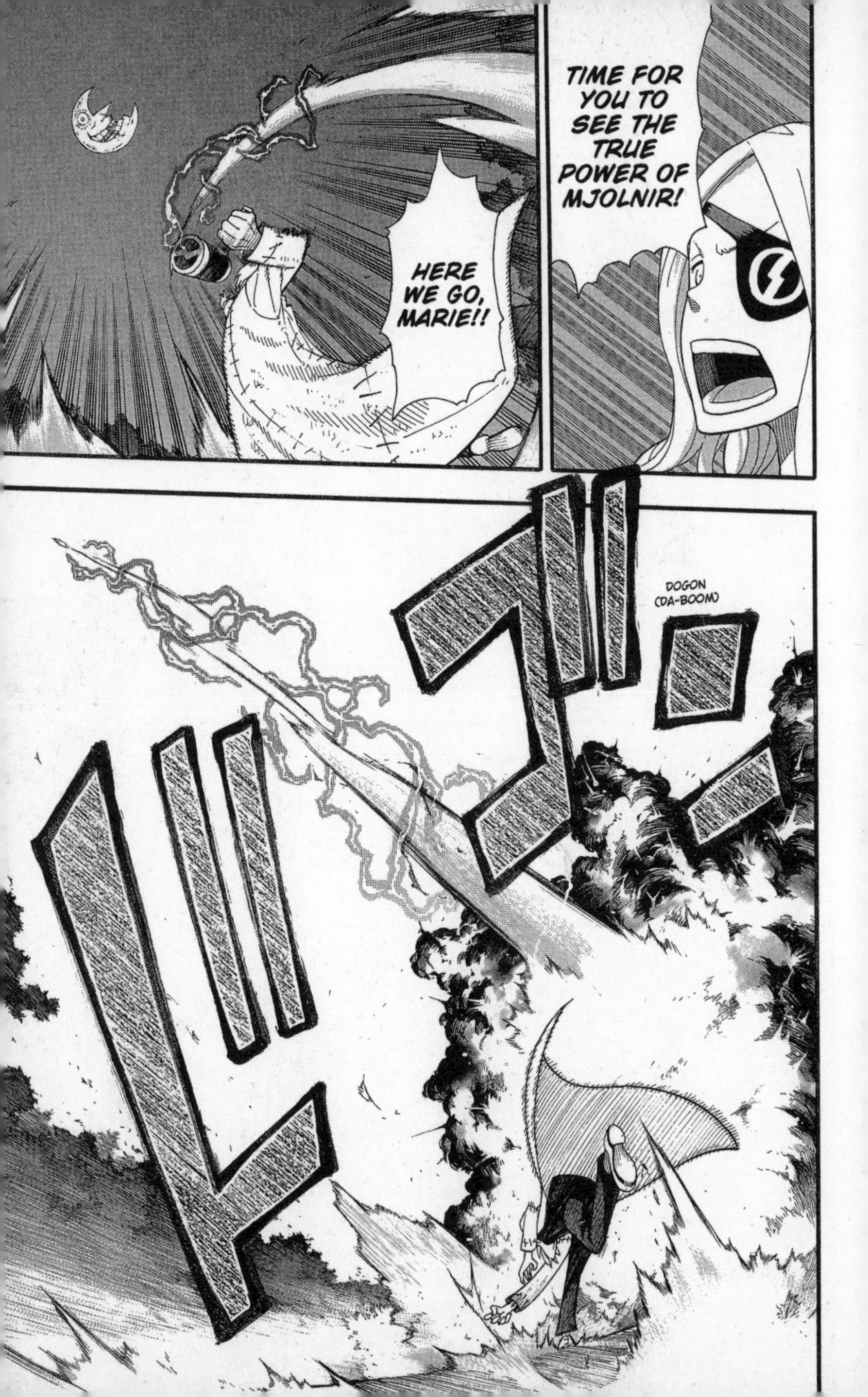
TIME FOR YOU TO SEE THE TRUE POWER OF MJOLNIR!
HERE WE GO, MARIE!!
DOGON (DA-BOOM)

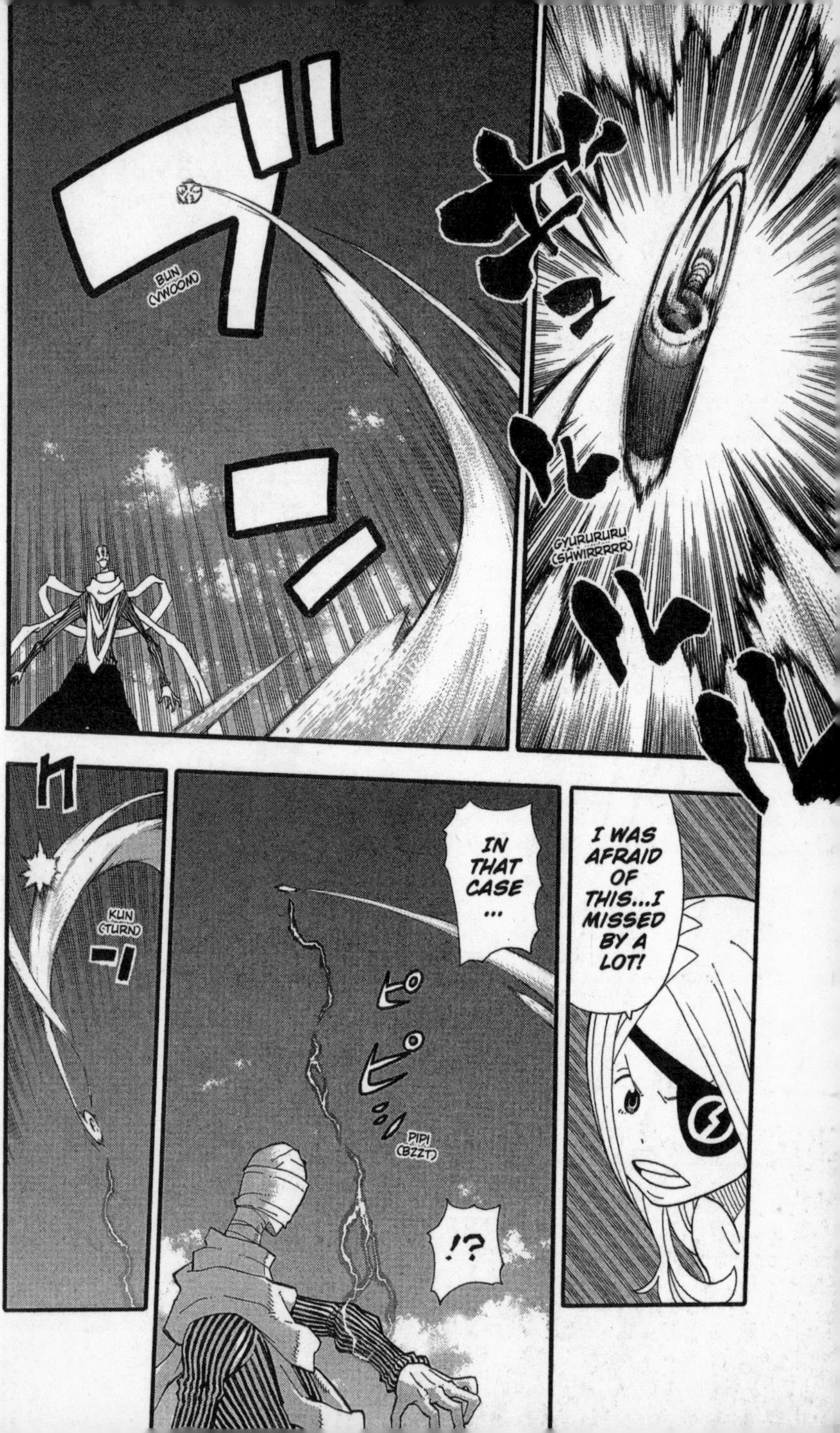
GYURURURU (SHWIRRRRR)
BUN (VWOOM)
I WAS AFRAID OF THIS...I MISSED BY A LOT!
IN THAT CASE...
PIPI (BZZT)
!?
KUN (TURN)

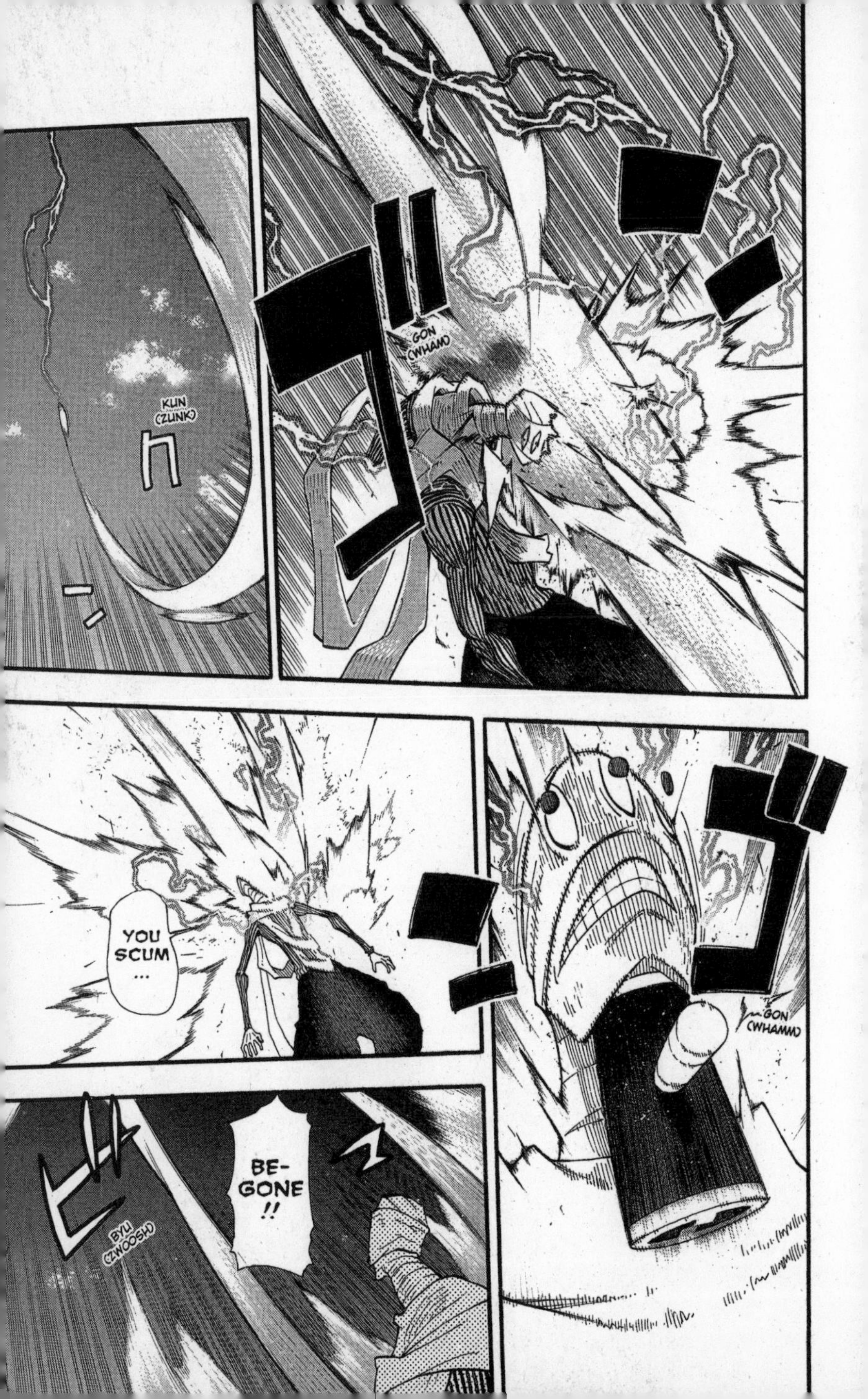
GON (WHAM)
KUN (ZUNK)
GON (WHAMM)
YOU SCUM ...
BE-GONE !!
BYU (ZWOOSH)

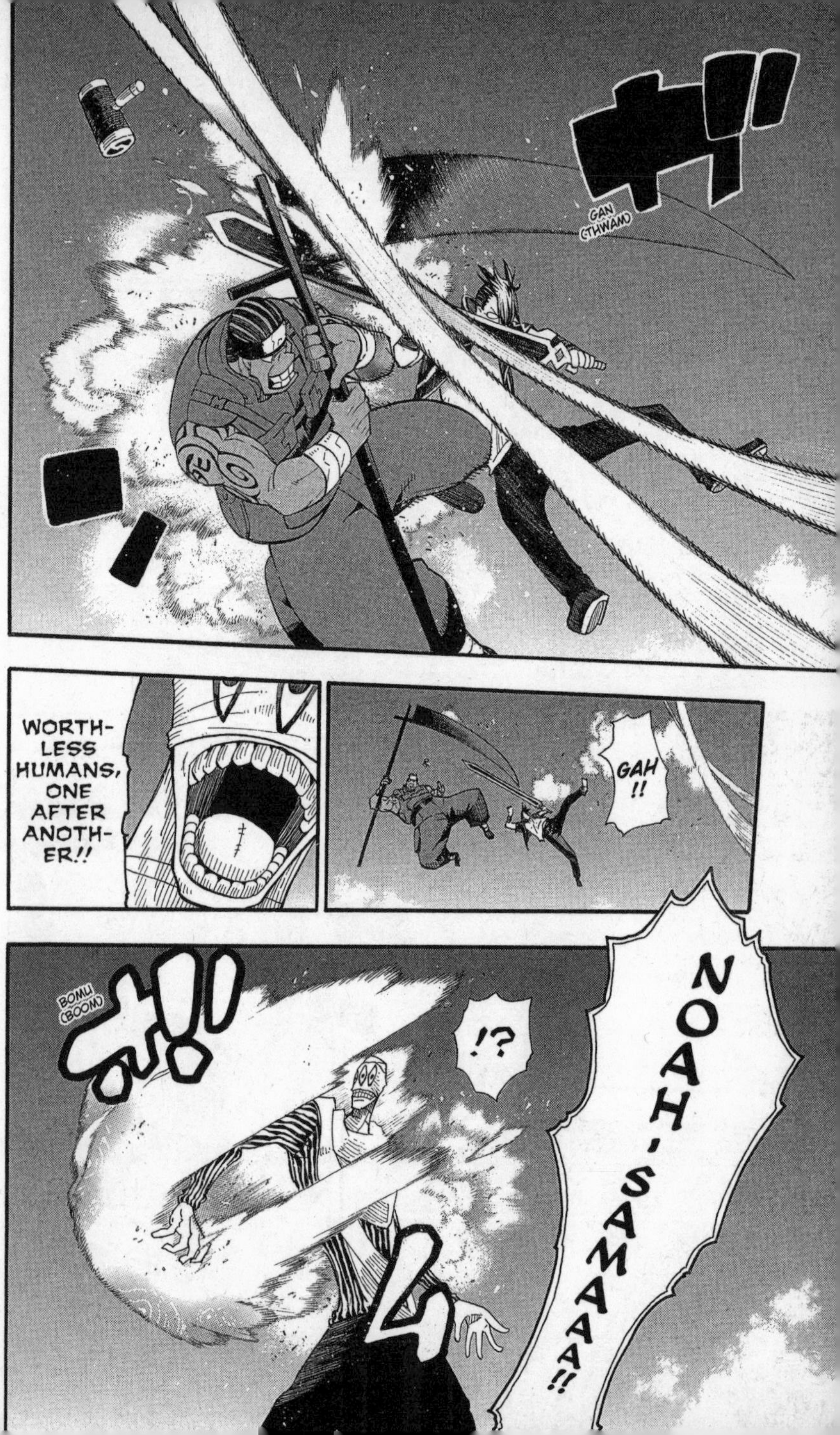
GAN
(THWAM)
GAH !!
WORTH-LESS HUMANS, ONE AFTER ANOTHER!!
NOAH-SAMAAAA!!
!?
BOMU
(BOOM)

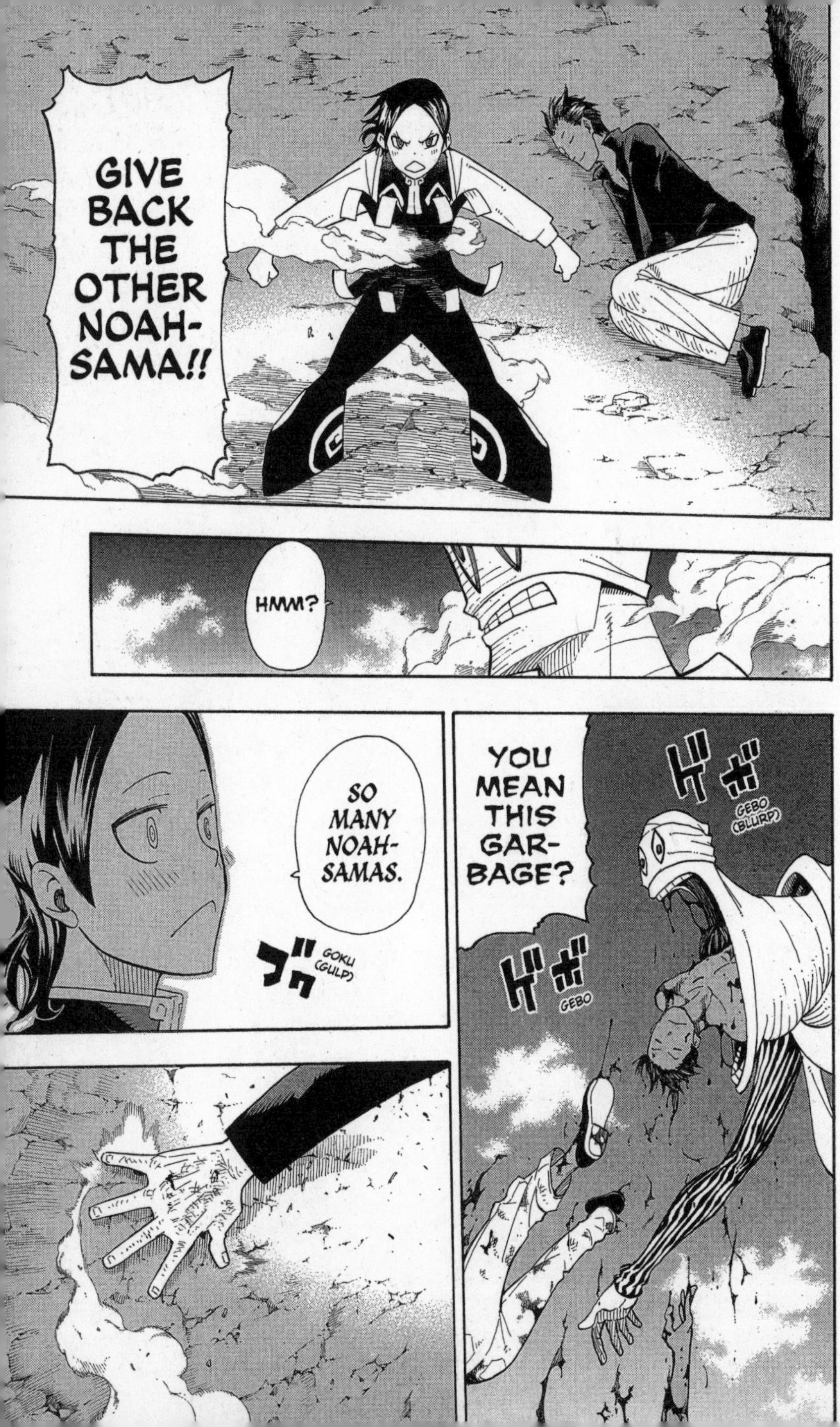
GIVE BACK THE OTHER NOAH-SAMA!!
HMM?
YOU MEAN THIS GAR-BAGE?
ゲボ
GEBO (BLURP)
ゲボ
GEBO
SO MANY NOAH-SAMAS.
ゴク
GOKU (GULP)

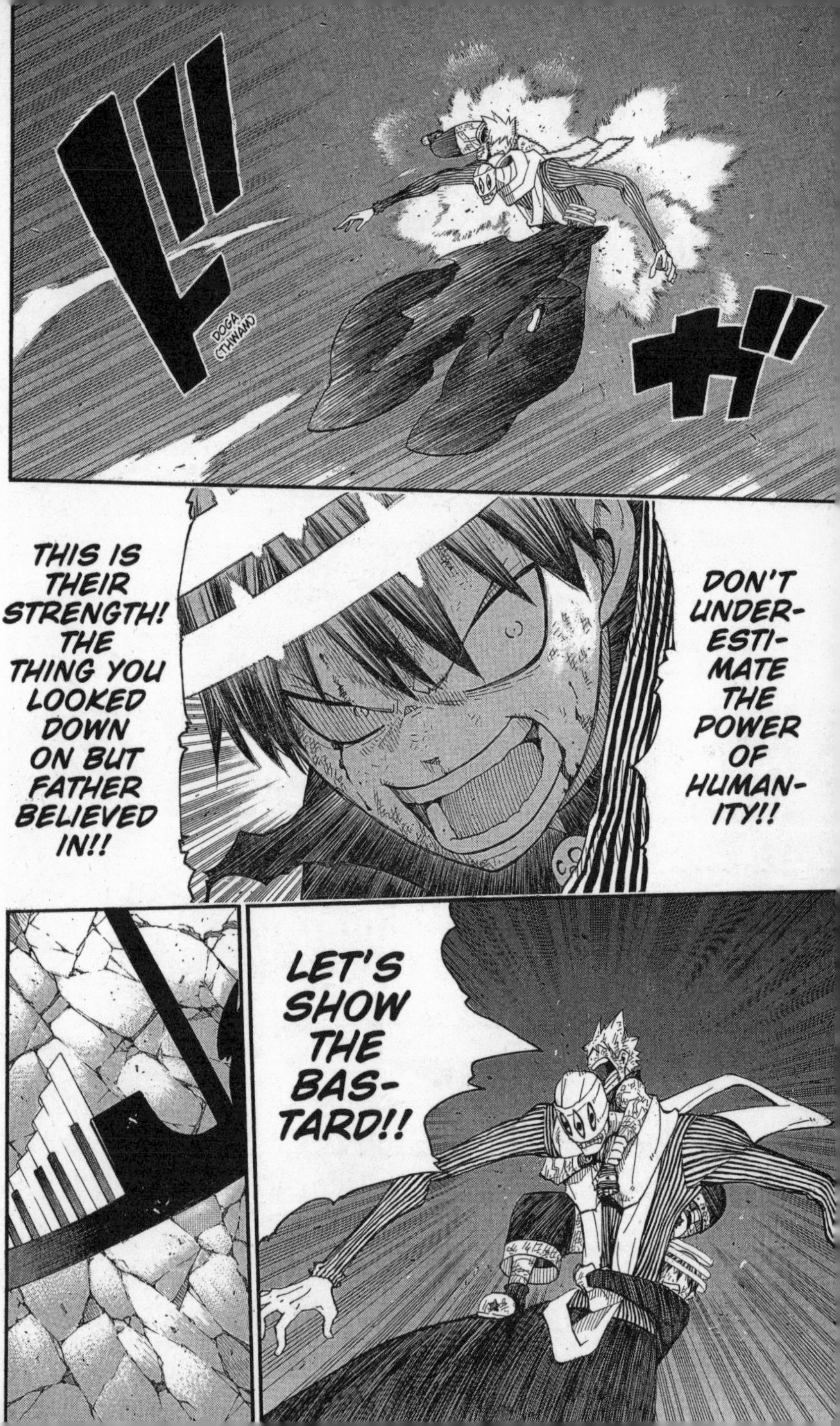
DOGA (THWAM)
DON'T UNDER-ESTI-MATE THE POWER OF HUMAN-ITY!!
THIS IS THEIR STRENGTH! THE THING YOU LOOKED DOWN ON BUT FATHER BELIEVED IN!!
LET'S SHOW THE BAS-TARD!!

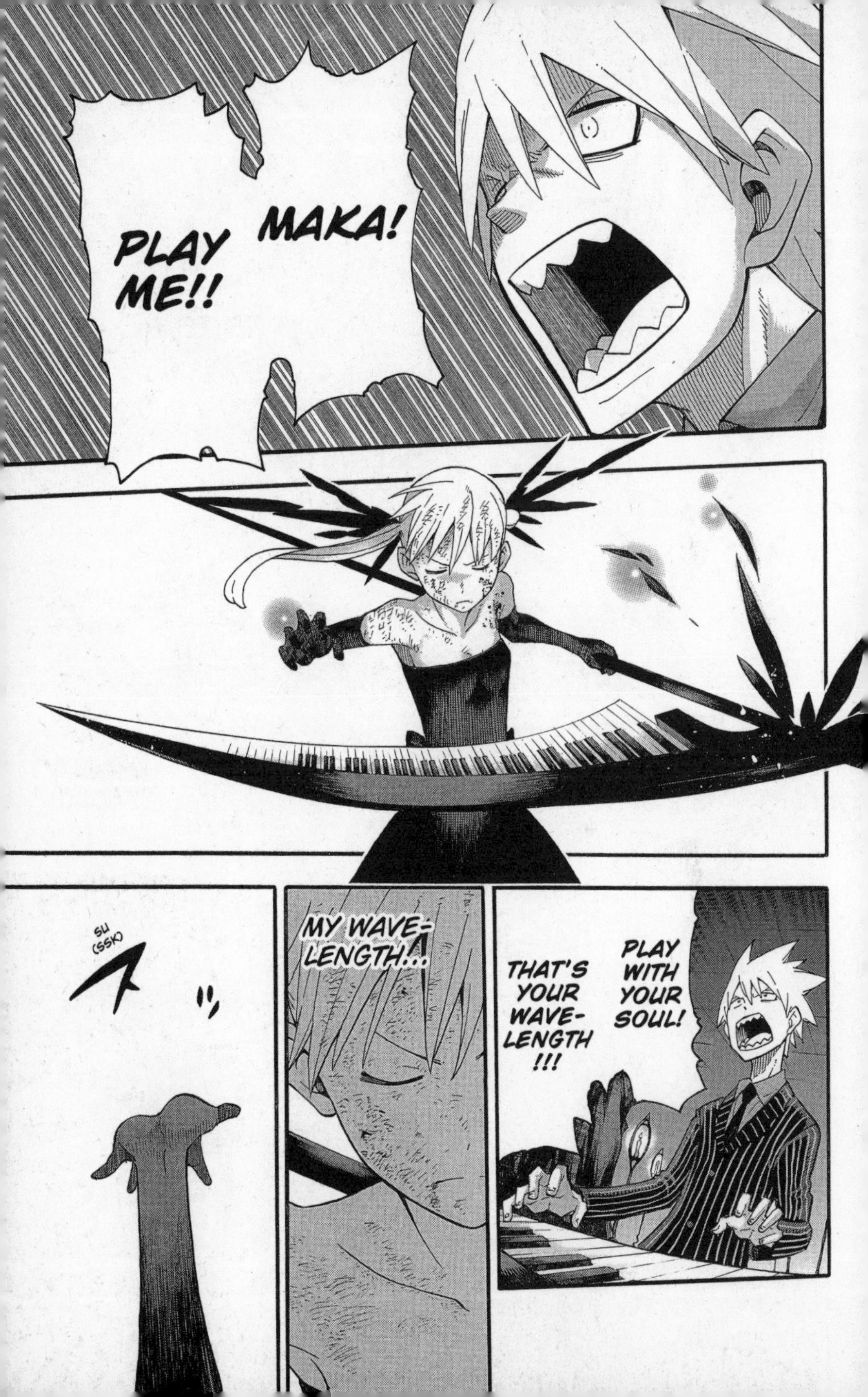
MAKA!
PLAY ME!!
PLAY WITH YOUR SOUL!
THAT'S YOUR WAVE-LENGTH!!!
MY WAVE-LENGTH...
SU (SSK)

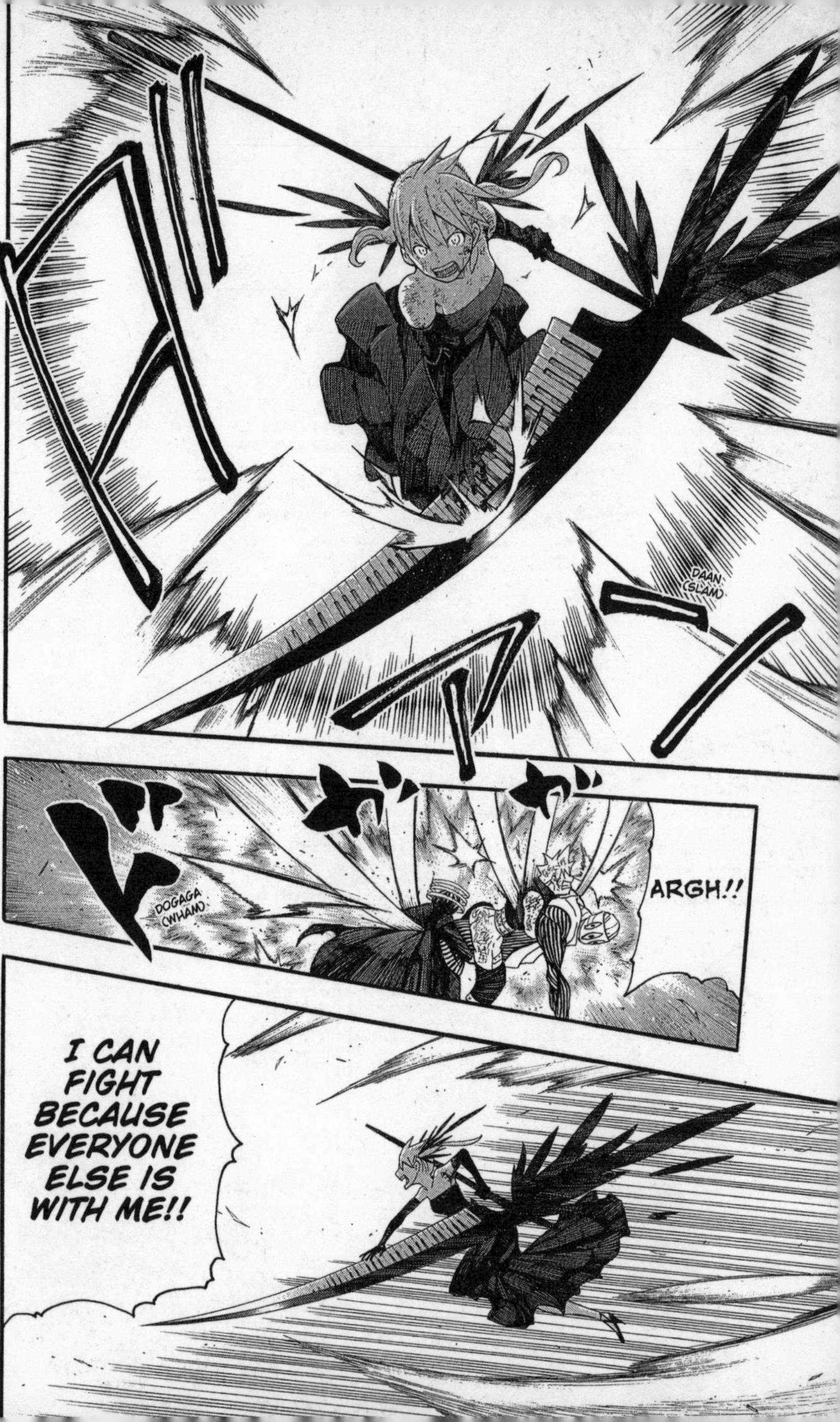
DAAN (SLAM)
ARGH!!
DOGAGA (WHAM)
I CAN FIGHT BECAUSE EVERYONE ELSE IS WITH ME!!

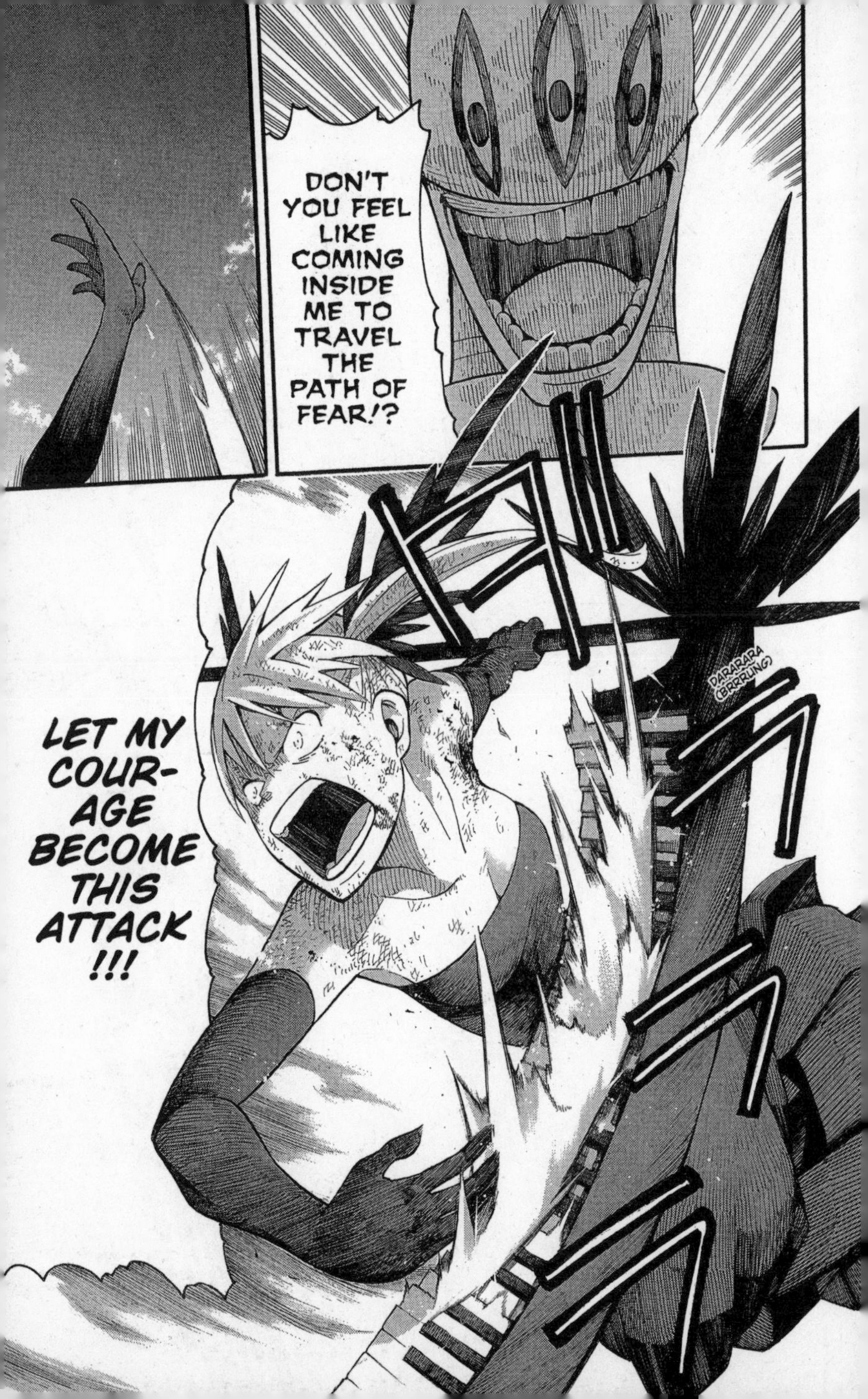
DON'T YOU FEEL LIKE COMING INSIDE ME TO TRAVEL THE PATH OF FEAR!?
DARARARA (BRRRUNG)
LET MY COURAGE BECOME THIS ATTACK!!!

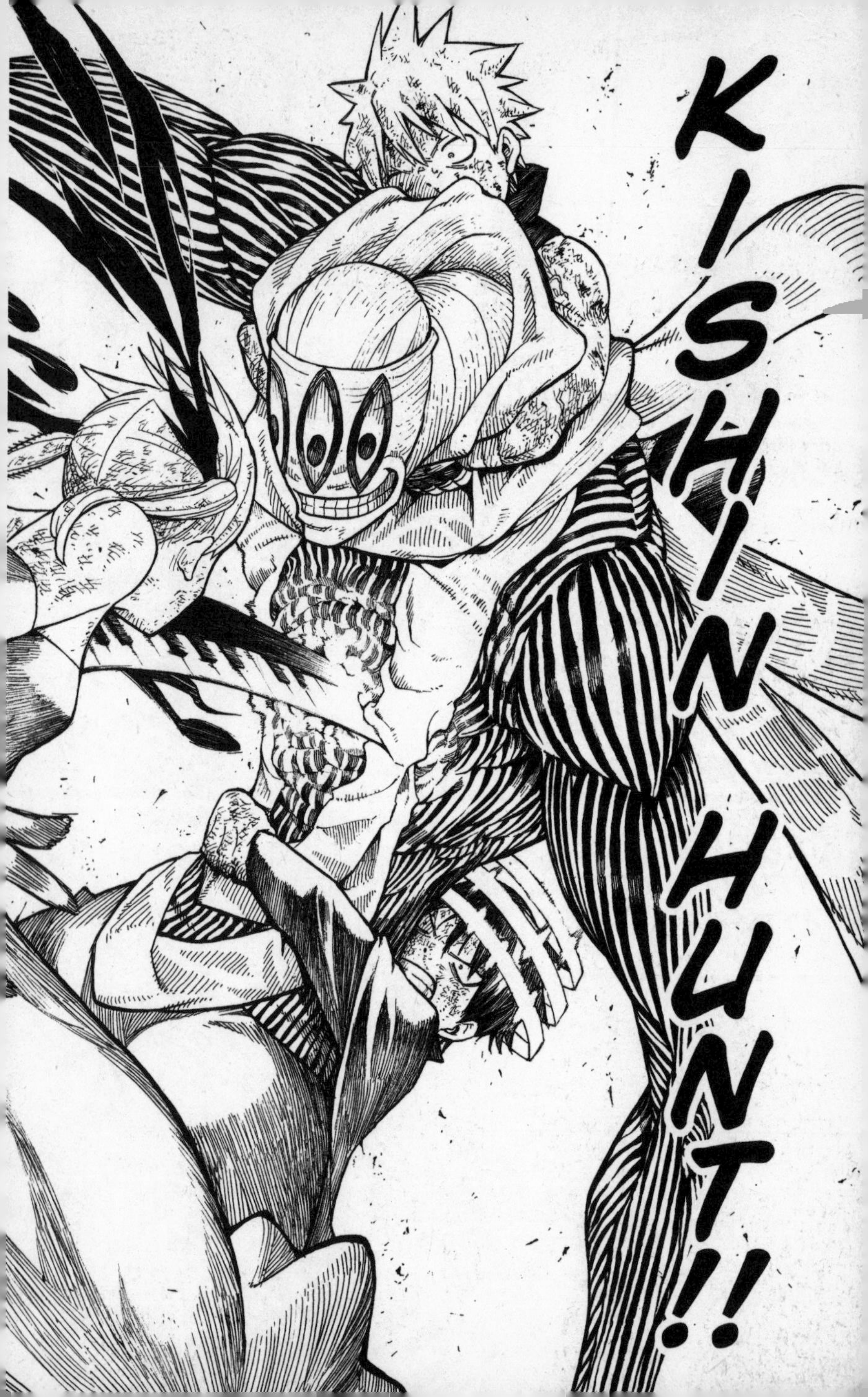
KI-SHHUNT!!

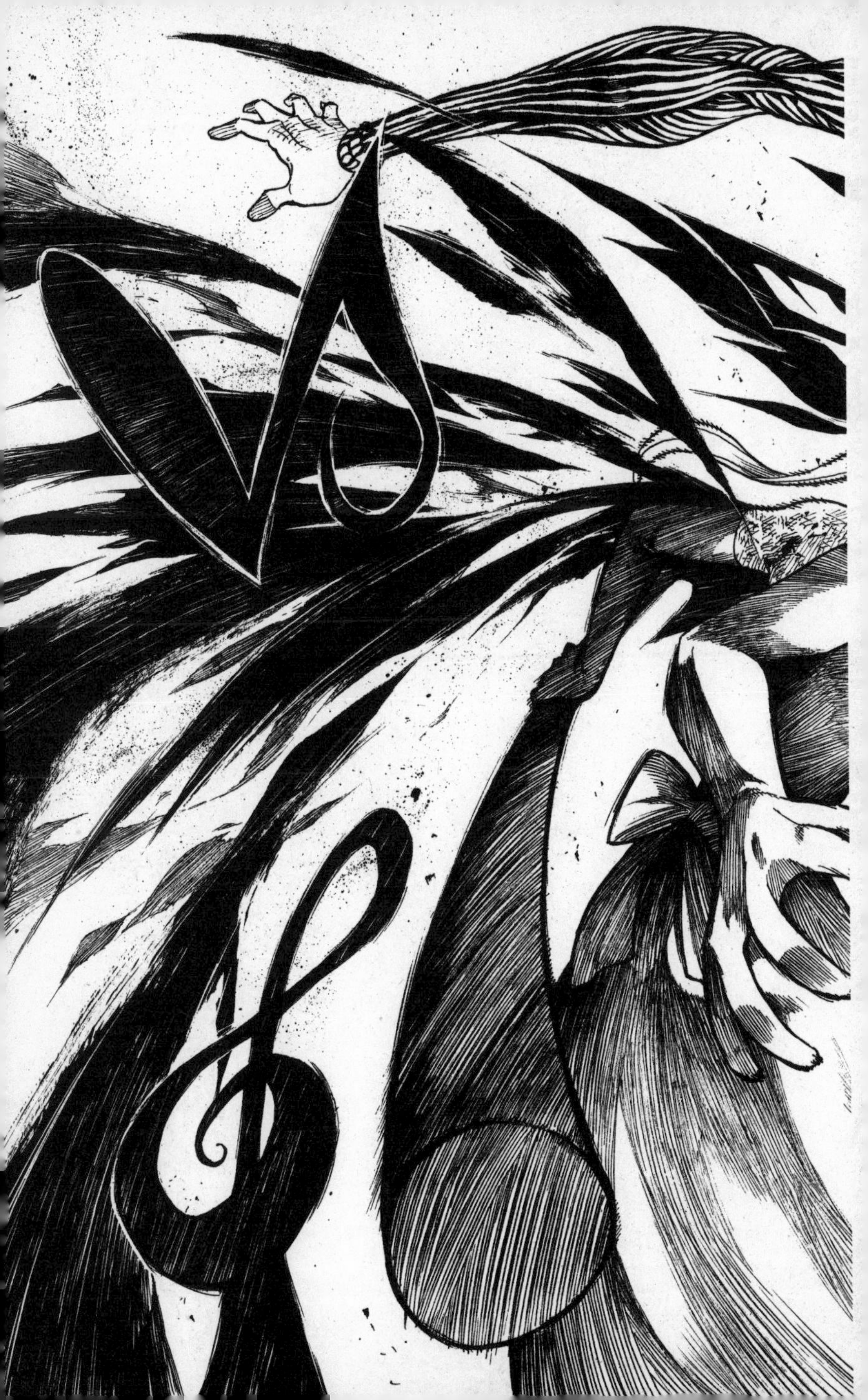

SOUL EATER

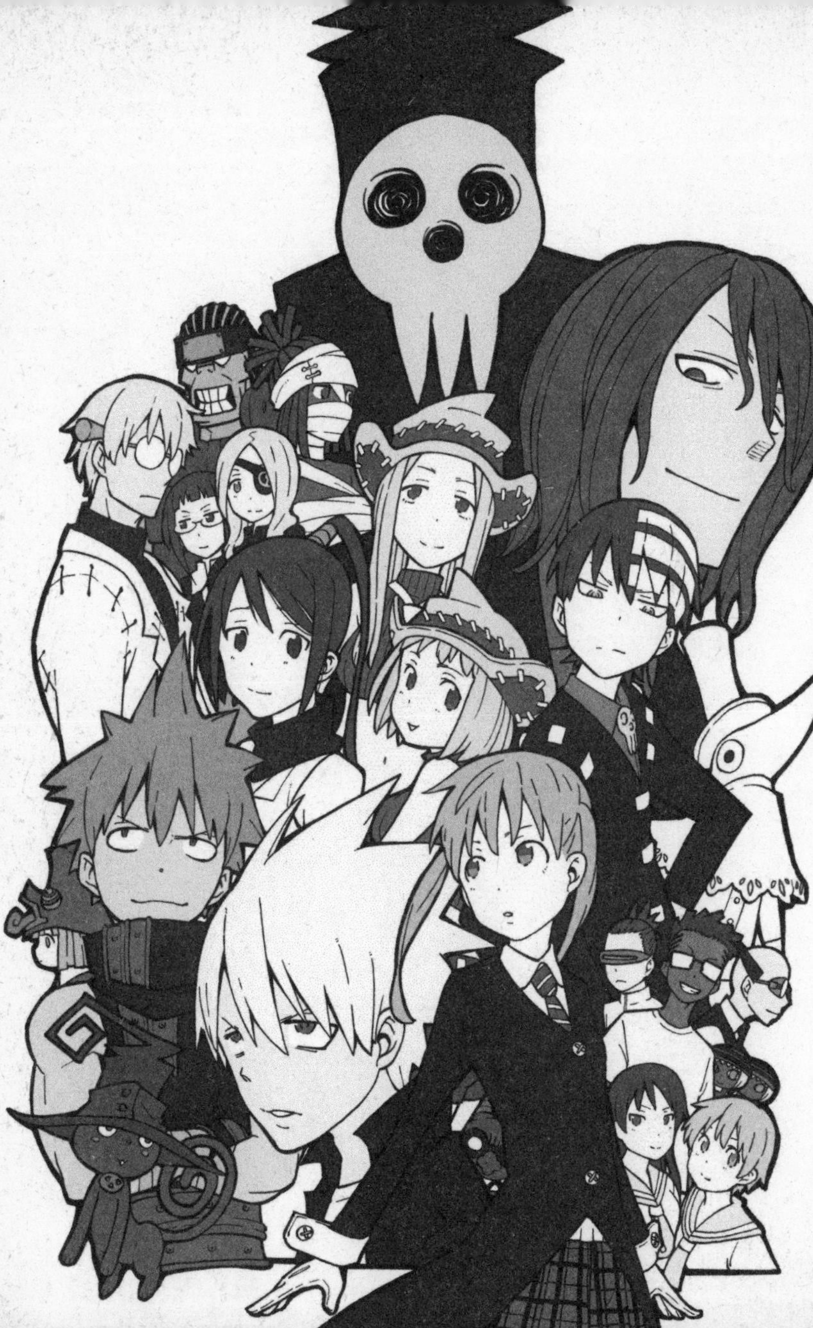

CHAPTER 112: THE DARK SIDE OF THE MOON IX

SOUL EATER

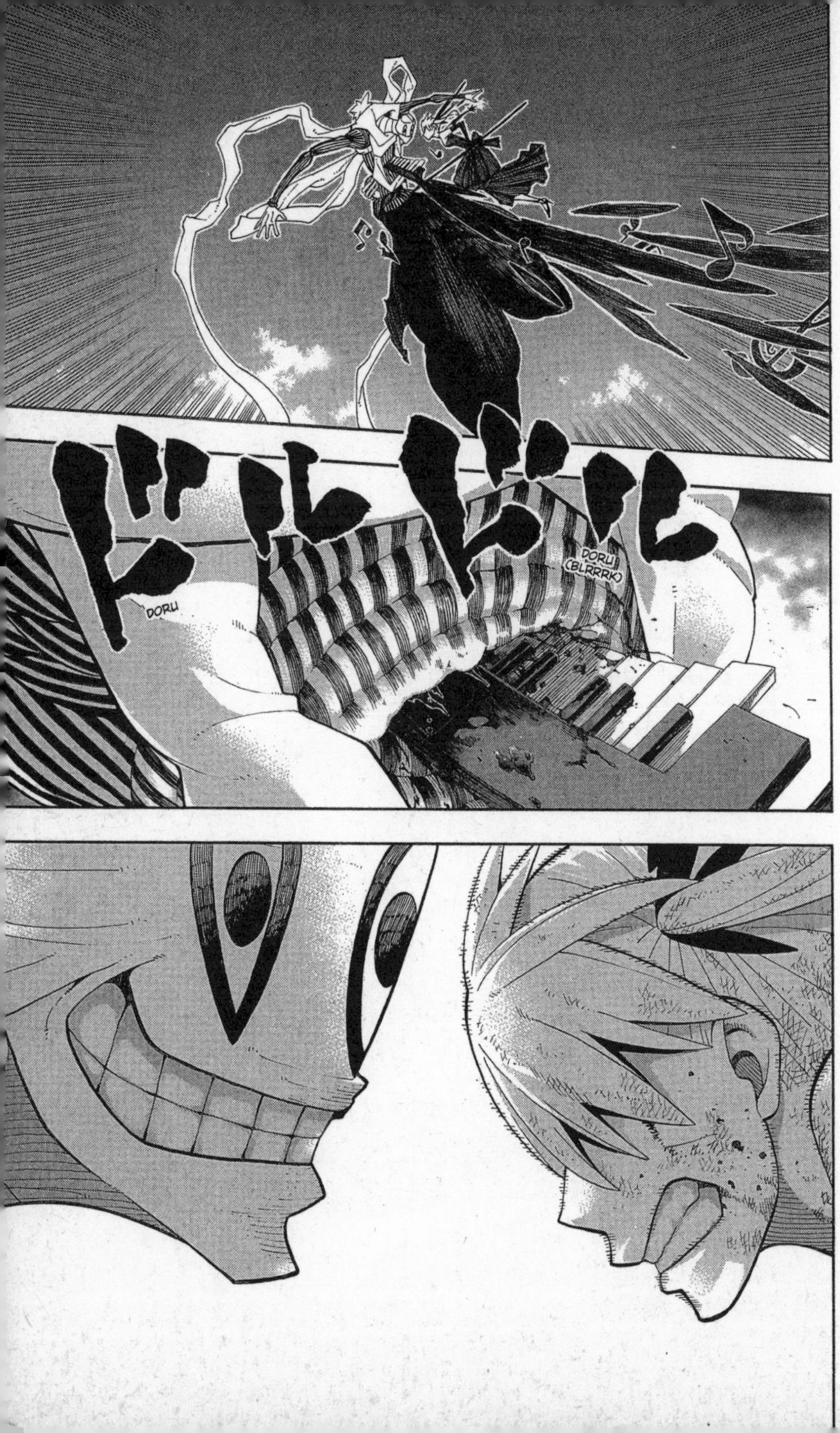
DORU
(BLRRRK)
DORU

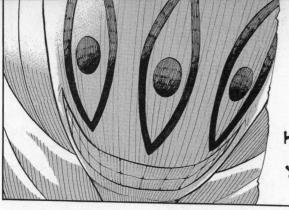

DO YOU FEEL LIKE VENTURING INSIDE!? LET'S SEE HOW YOU HANDLE THIS FEAR ON YOUR OWN!!

YOUR FEAR BROUGHT TOGETHER SOULS THAT HAD LONG BEEN SCATTERED— HUMANS, SHINIGAMI, WITCHES, AND WEIRD THINGS I CAN'T EVEN DESCRIBE!!

ZUBUBUBU (ZRRRPPP)

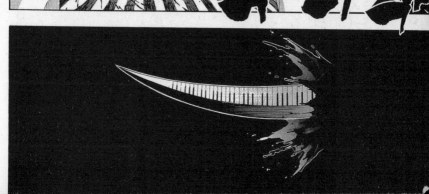

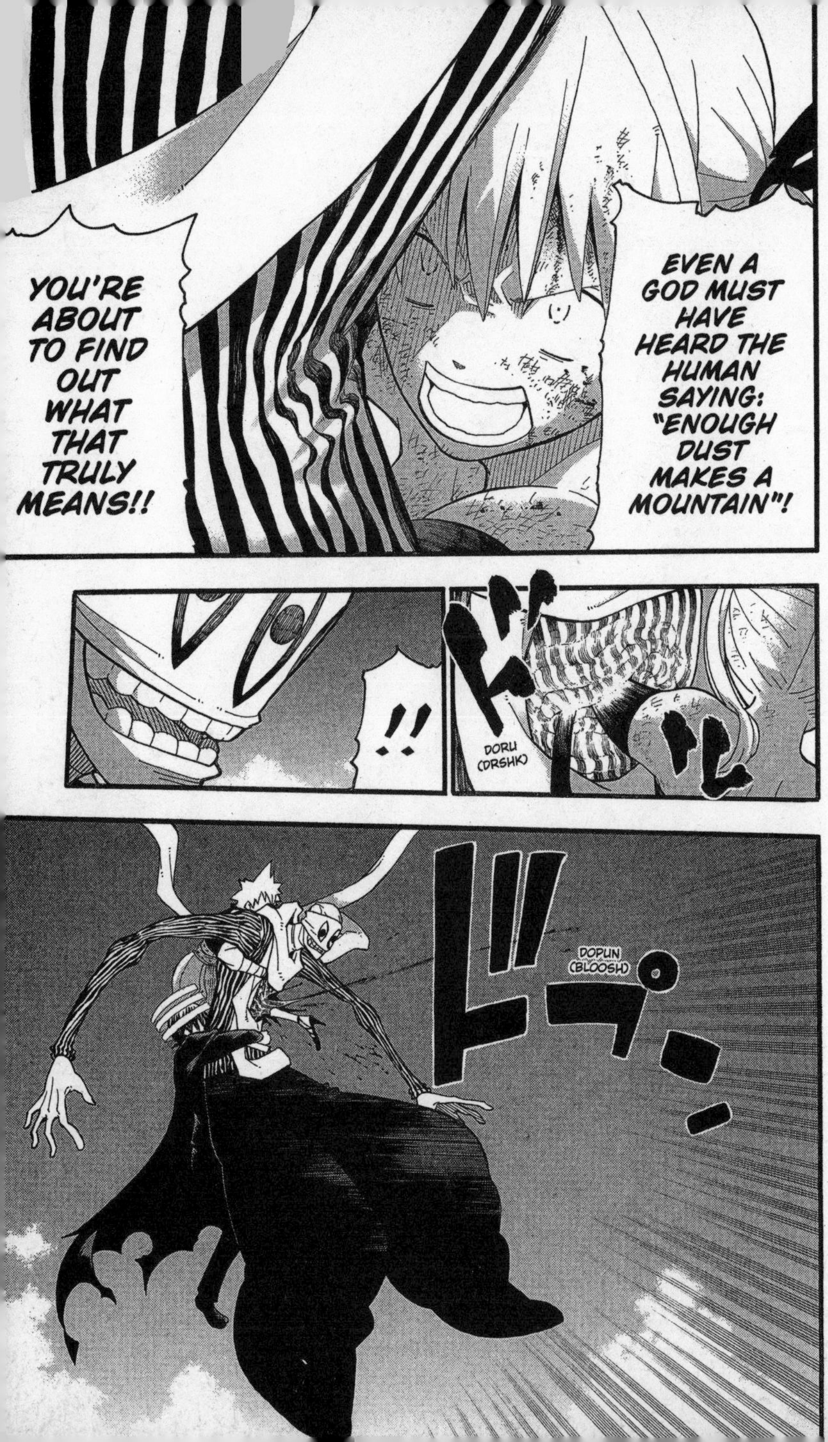
EVEN A GOD MUST HAVE HEARD THE HUMAN SAYING: "ENOUGH DUST MAKES A MOUNTAIN"!
YOU'RE ABOUT TO FIND OUT WHAT THAT TRULY MEANS!!
DORU (DRSHK)
!!
DOPUN (BLOOSH)

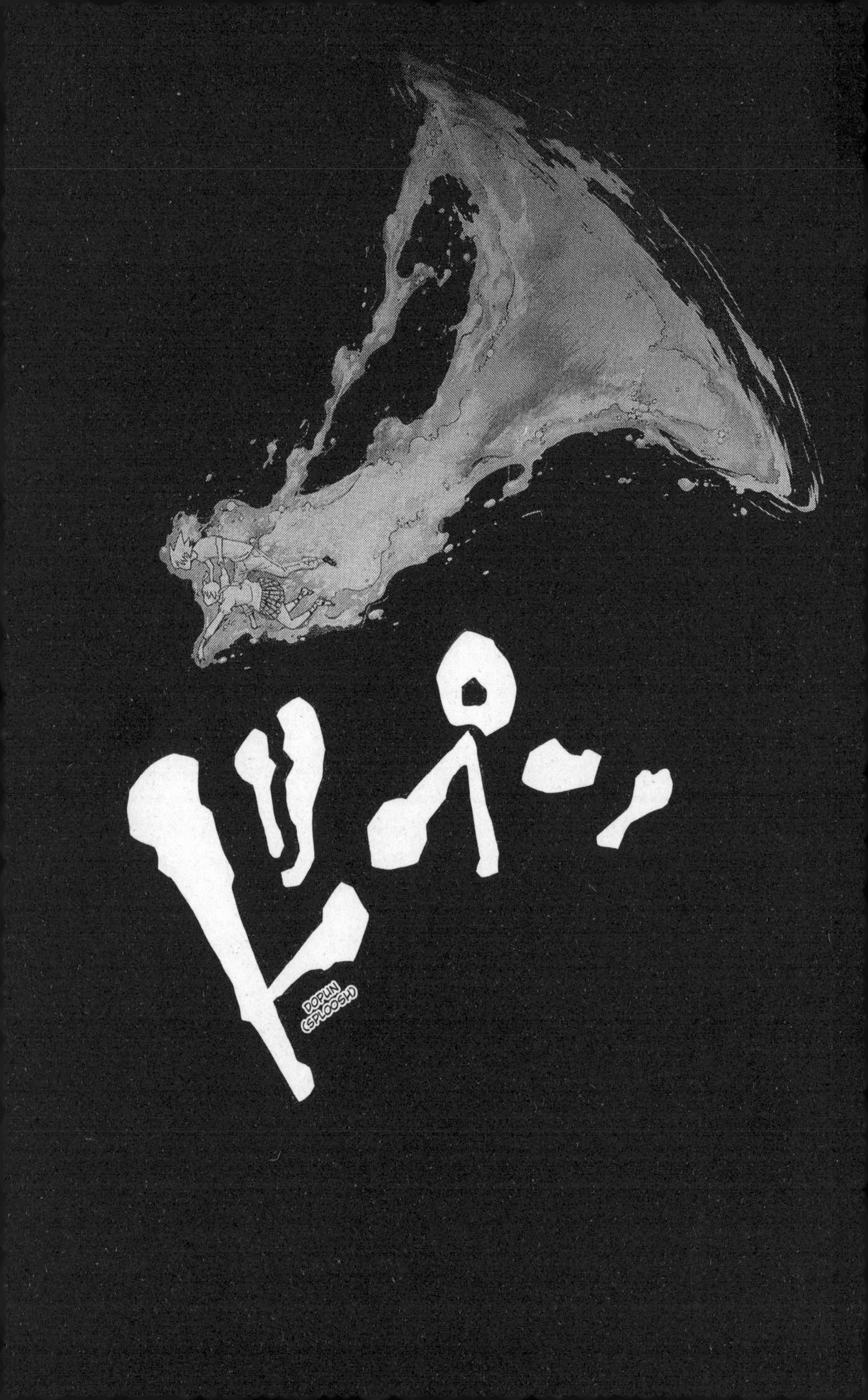
DOPUN
(SPLOOSH)

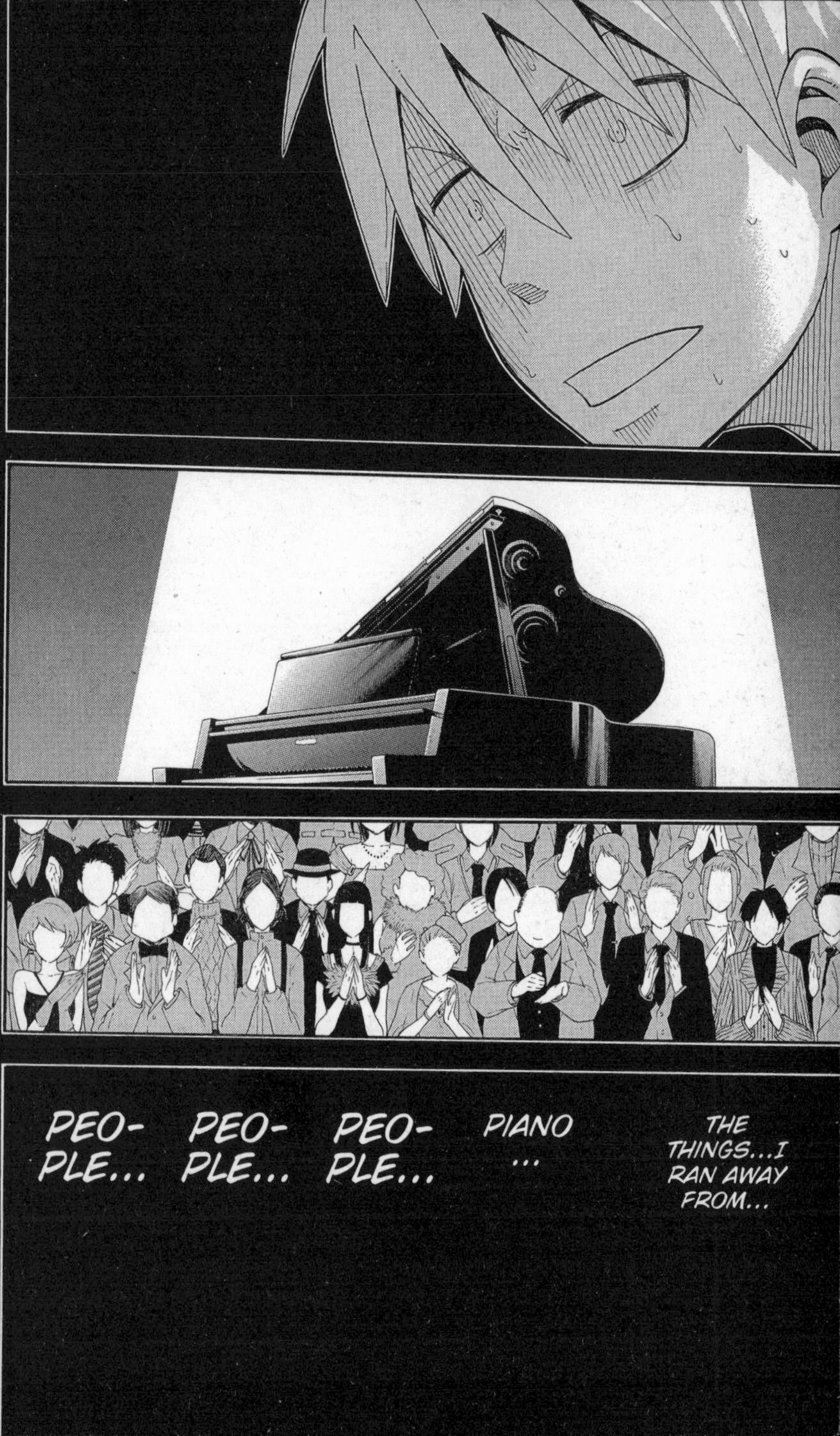
THE THINGS...I RAN AWAY FROM...
PIANO ...
PEO-PLE...
PEO-PLE...
PEO-PLE...

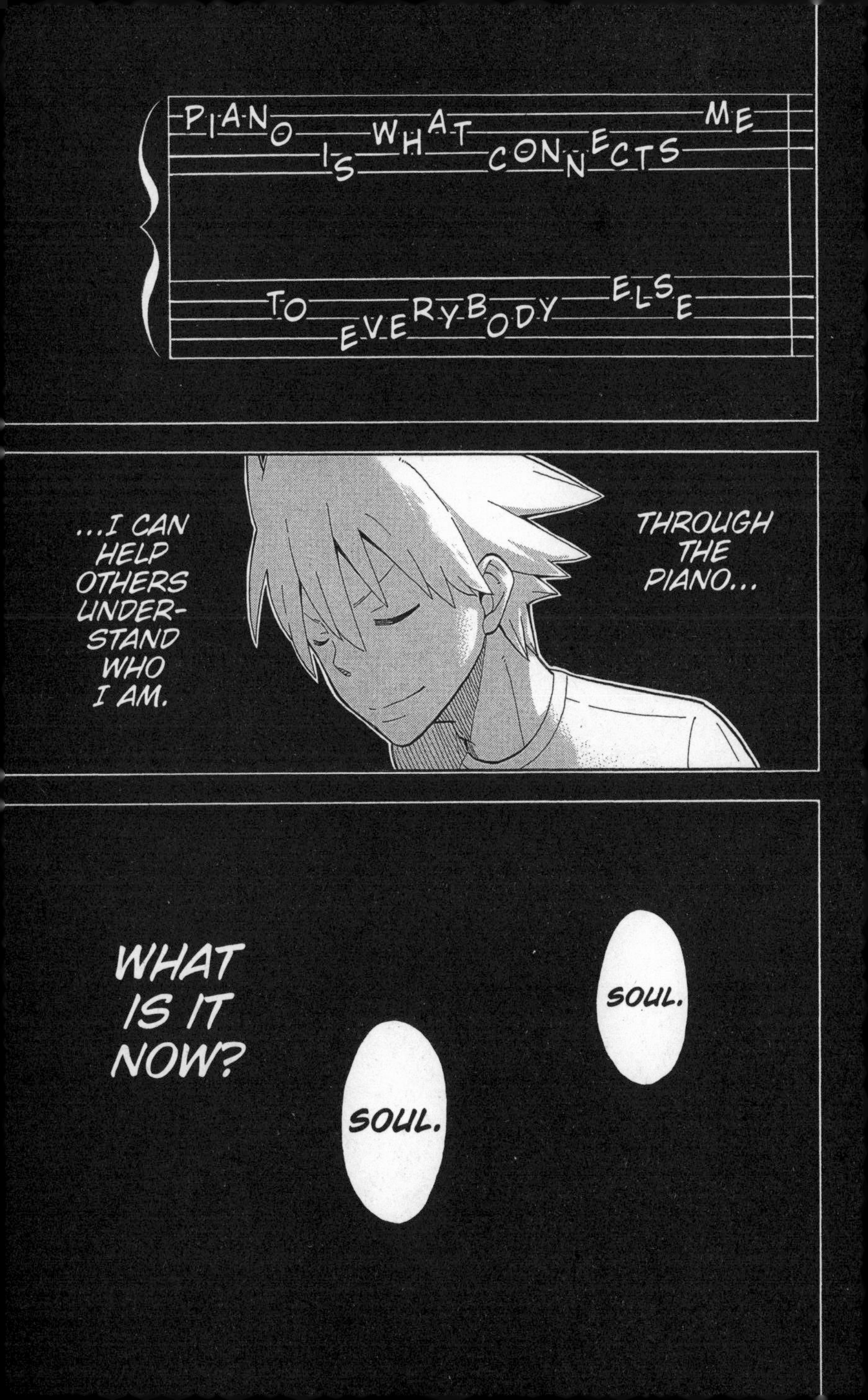
PIANO IS WHAT CONNECTS ME
TO EVERYBODY ELSE
THROUGH THE PIANO...
...I CAN HELP OTHERS UNDER-STAND WHO I AM.
SOUL.
SOUL.
WHAT IS IT NOW?

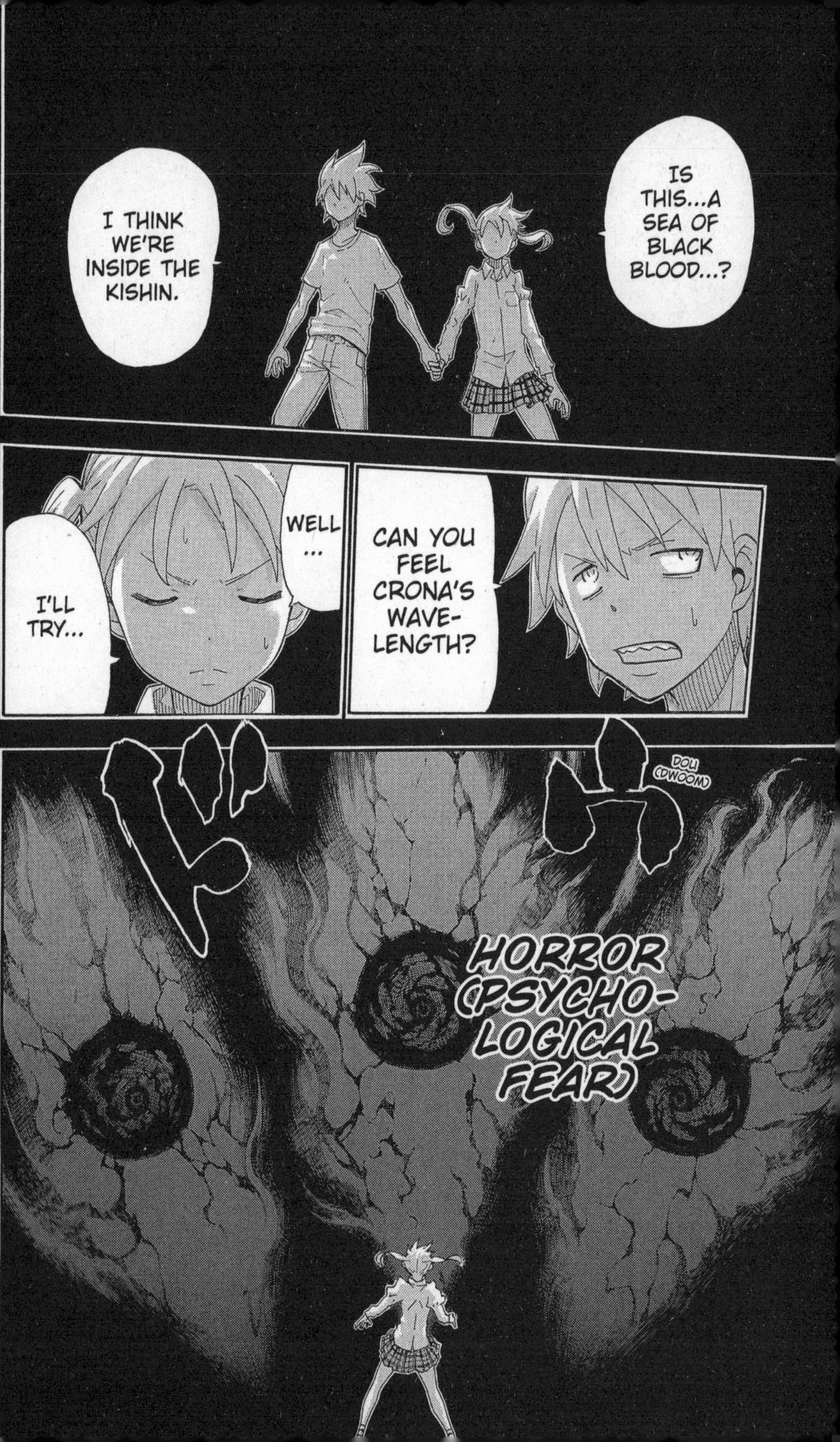
IS THIS...A SEA OF BLACK BLOOD...?
I THINK WE'RE INSIDE THE KISHIN.
CAN YOU FEEL CRONA'S WAVE-LENGTH?
WELL...
I'LL TRY...
DOU (DWOOM)
HORROR (PSYCHO-LOGICAL FEAR)

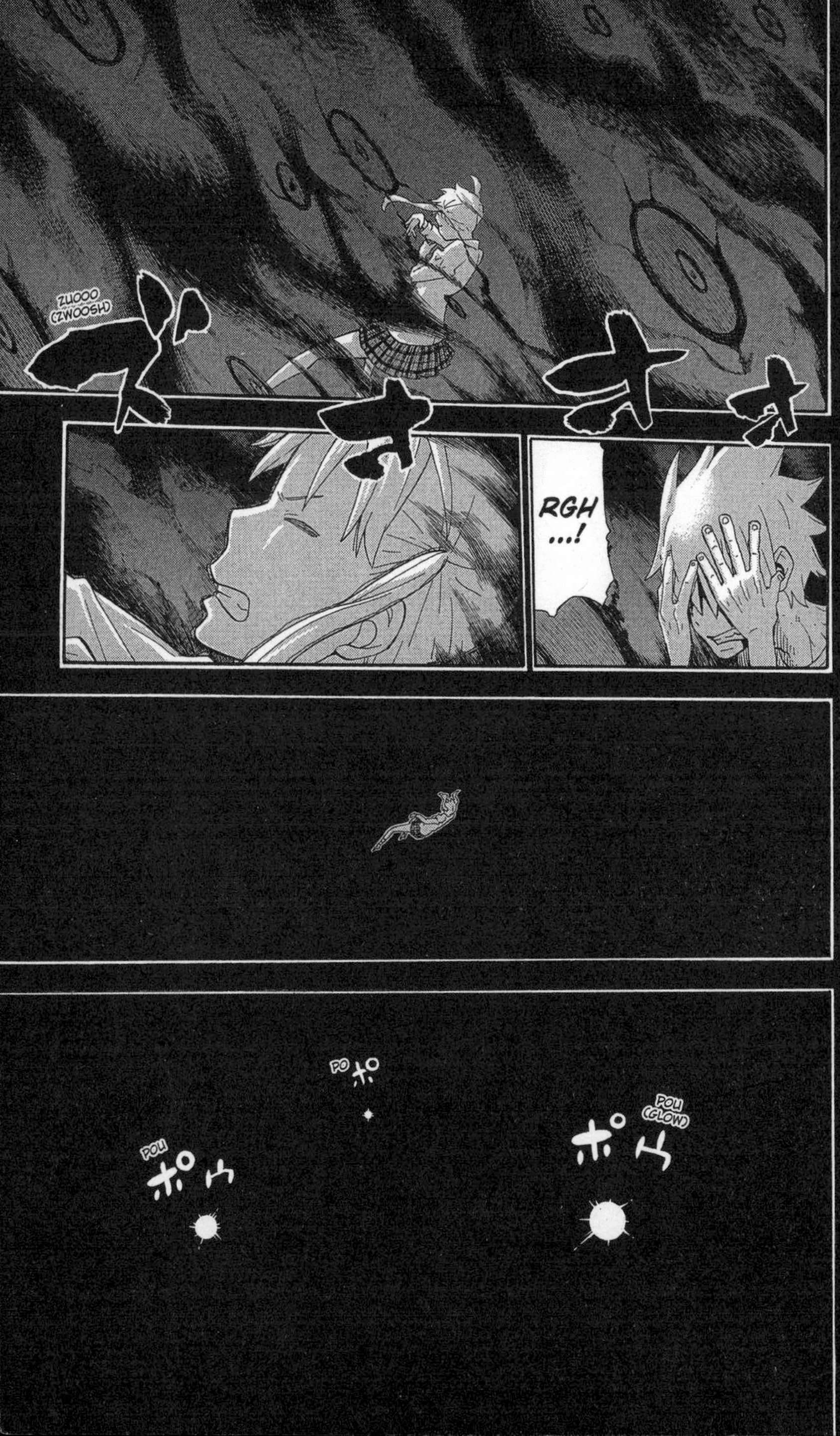
ZUOOO (ZWOOSH)
ズオオオ
RGH ...!
POU (GLOW)
ポウ
PO
ポ
POU
ポウ

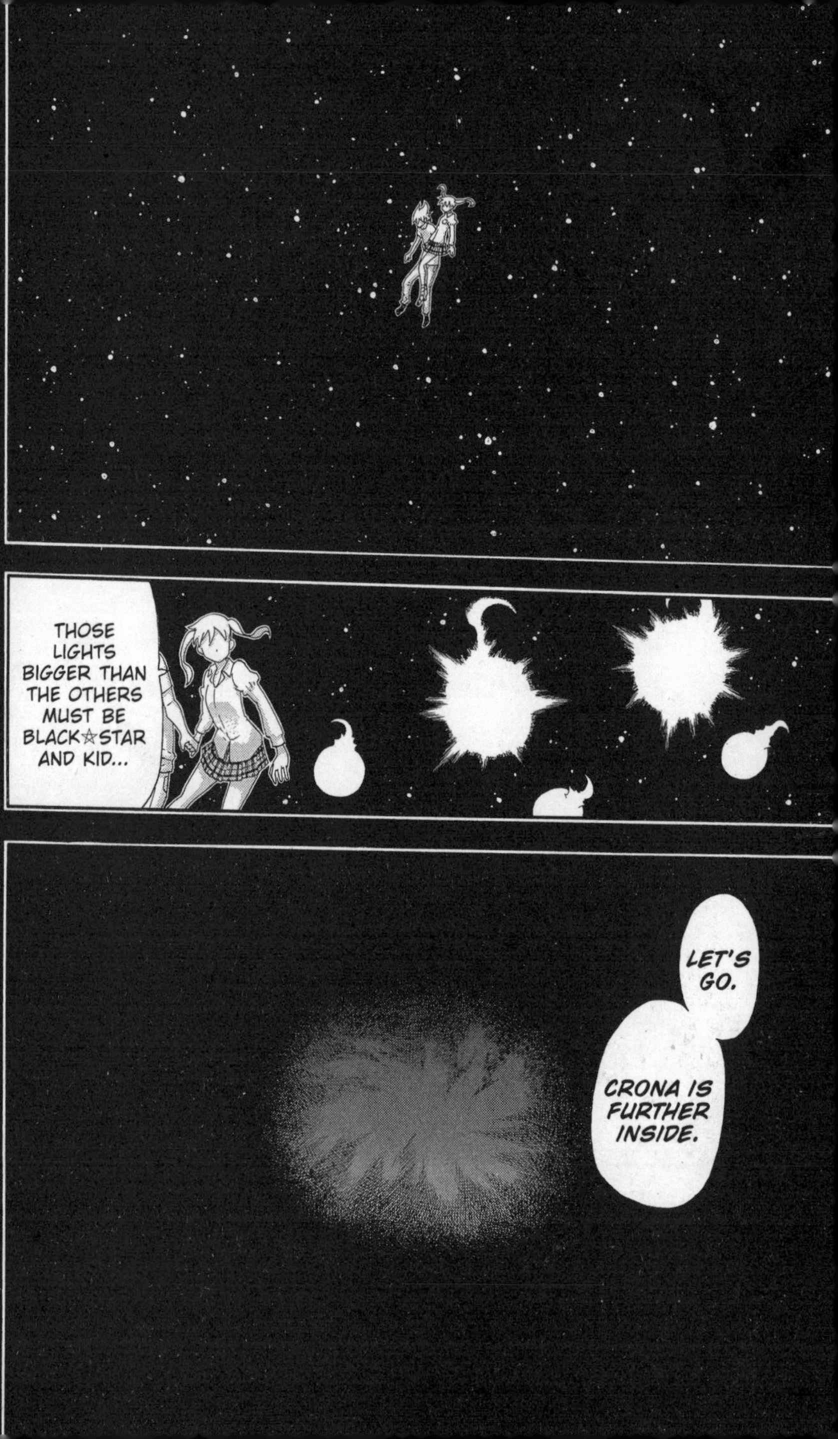
THOSE LIGHTS BIGGER THAN THE OTHERS MUST BE BLACK☆STAR AND KID...
LET'S GO.
CRONA IS FURTHER INSIDE.

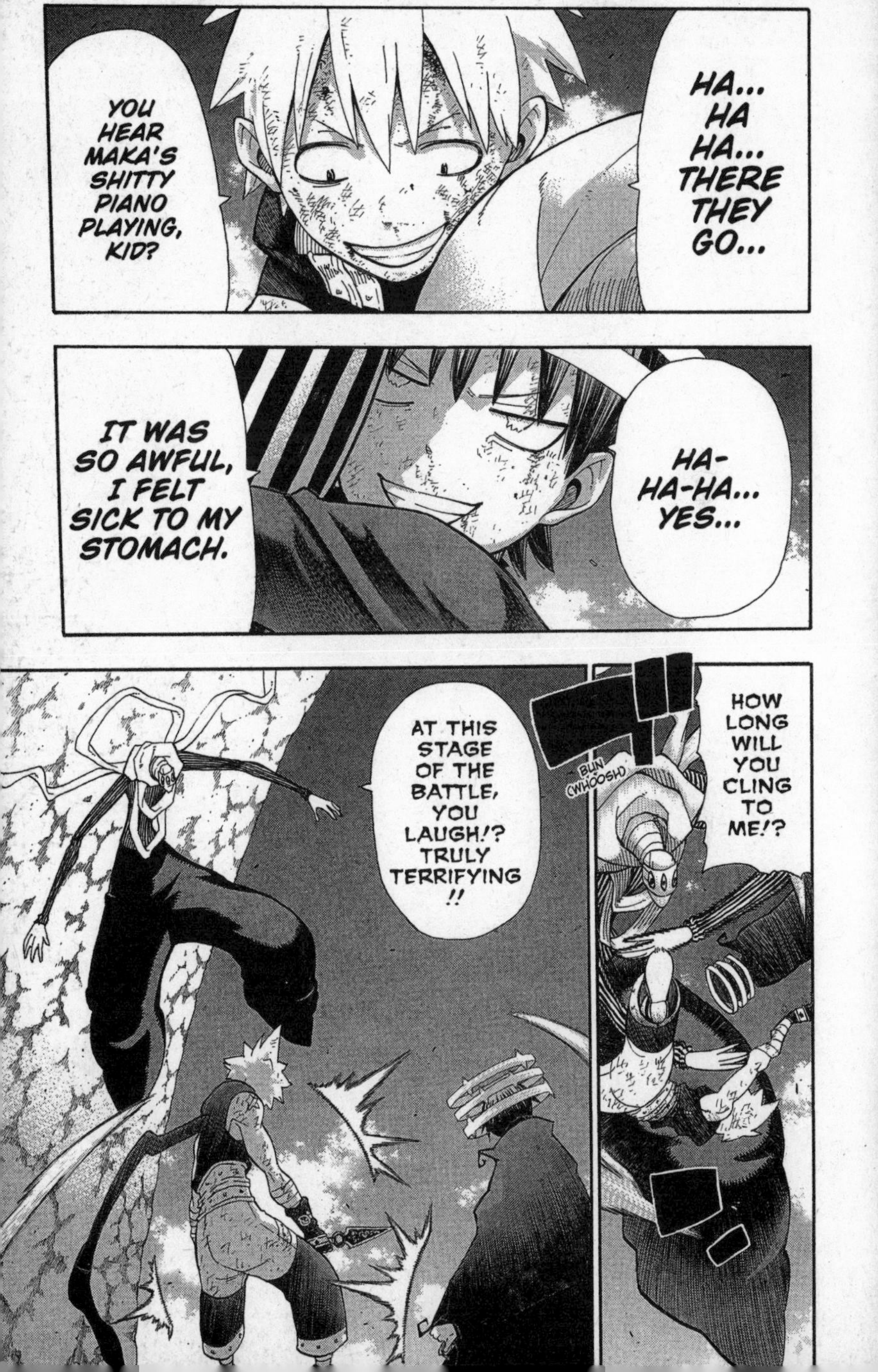
HA... HA HA... THERE THEY GO...
YOU HEAR MAKA'S SHITTY PIANO PLAYING, KID?
HA-HA-HA... YES...
IT WAS SO AWFUL, I FELT SICK TO MY STOMACH.
HOW LONG WILL YOU CLING TO ME!?
BUN (WHOOSH)
AT THIS STAGE OF THE BATTLE, YOU LAUGH!? TRULY TERRIFYING!!

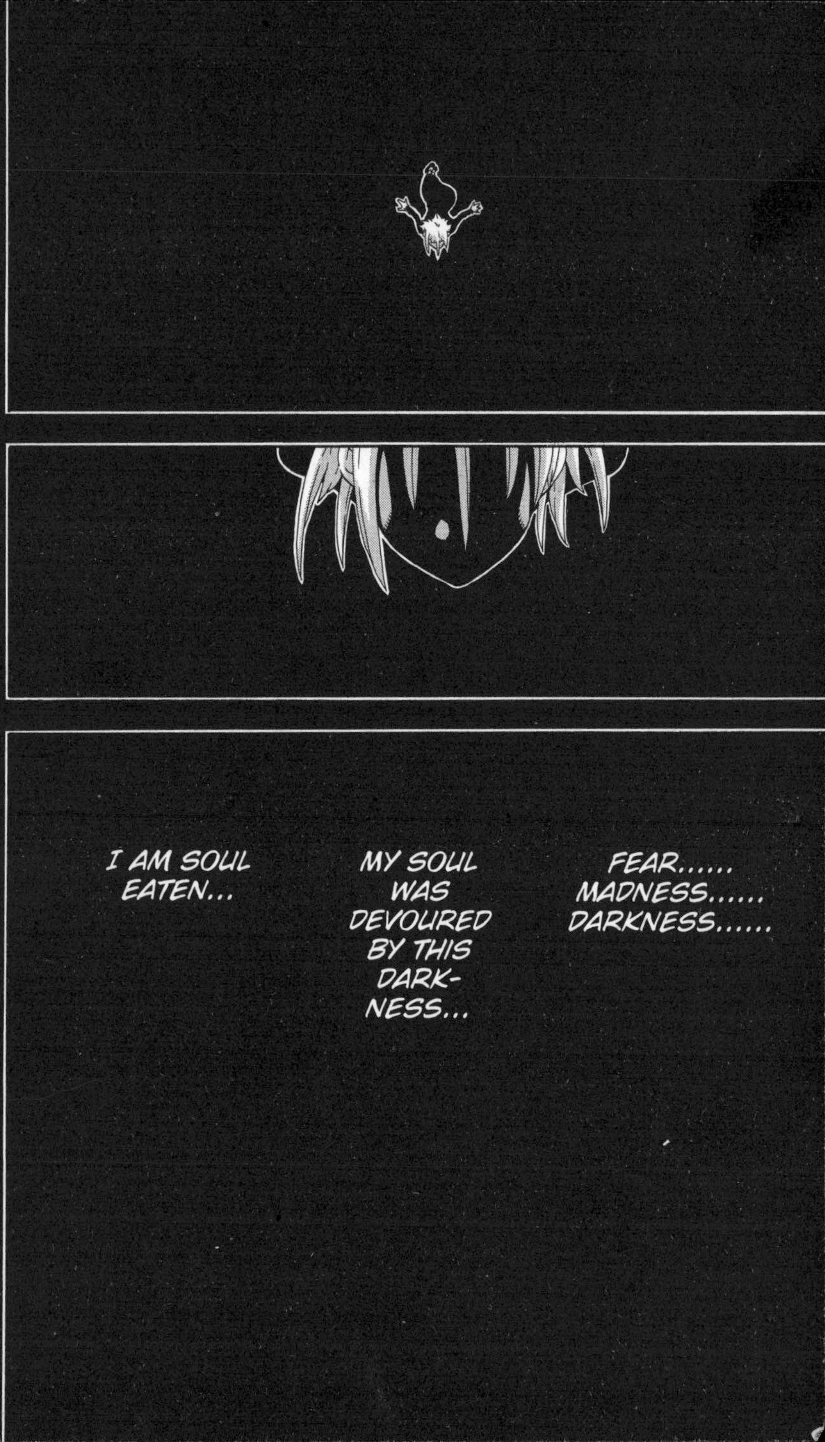
FEAR...... MADNESS...... DARKNESS......
MY SOUL WAS DEVOURED BY THIS DARK-NESS...
I AM SOUL EATEN...

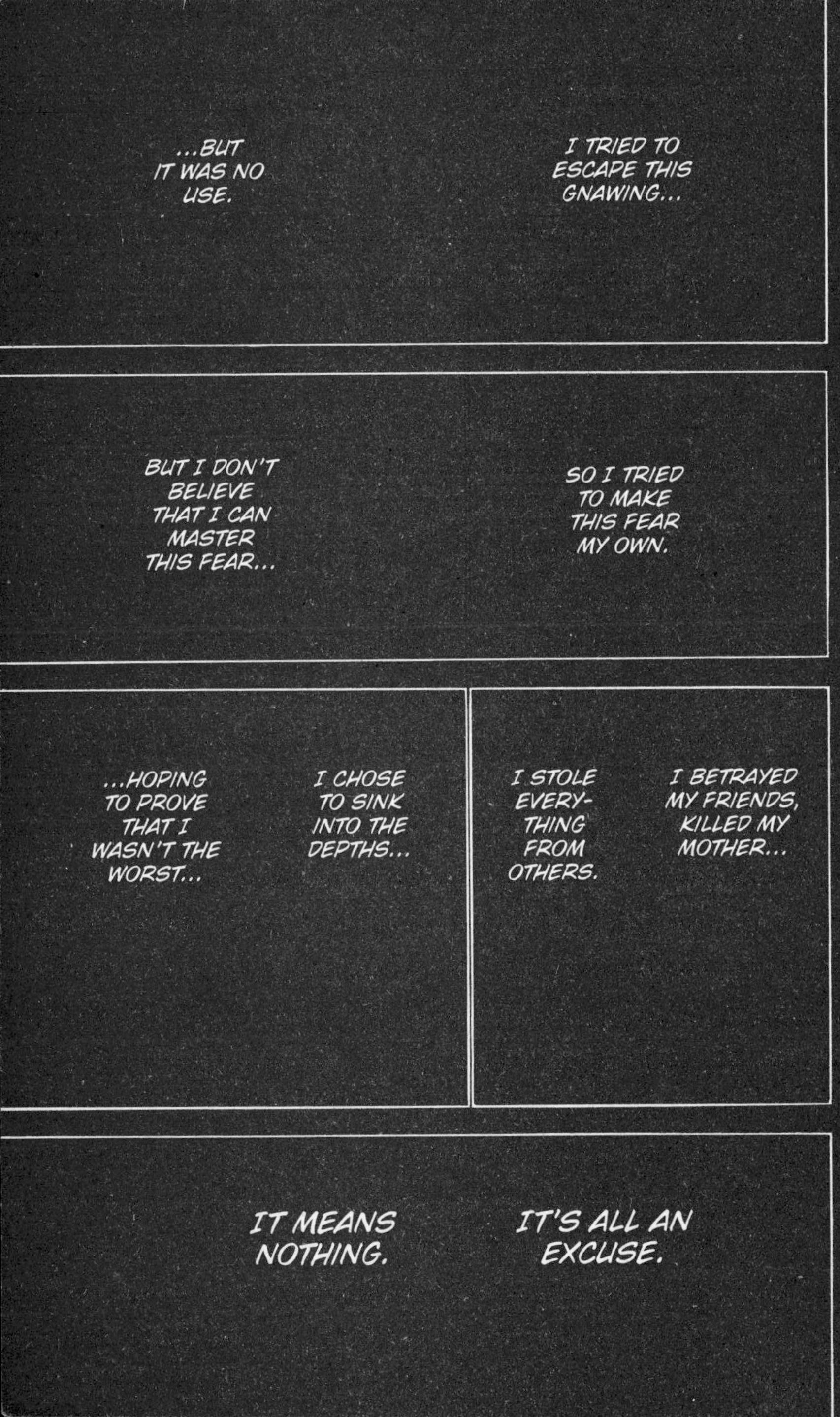
I TRIED TO ESCAPE THIS GNAWING...
...BUT IT WAS NO USE.
SO I TRIED TO MAKE THIS FEAR MY OWN.
BUT I DON'T BELIEVE THAT I CAN MASTER THIS FEAR...
I BETRAYED MY FRIENDS, KILLED MY MOTHER...
I STOLE EVERY-THING FROM OTHERS.
I CHOSE TO SINK INTO THE DEPTHS...
...HOPING TO PROVE THAT I WASN'T THE WORST...
IT'S ALL AN EXCUSE.
IT MEANS NOTHING.

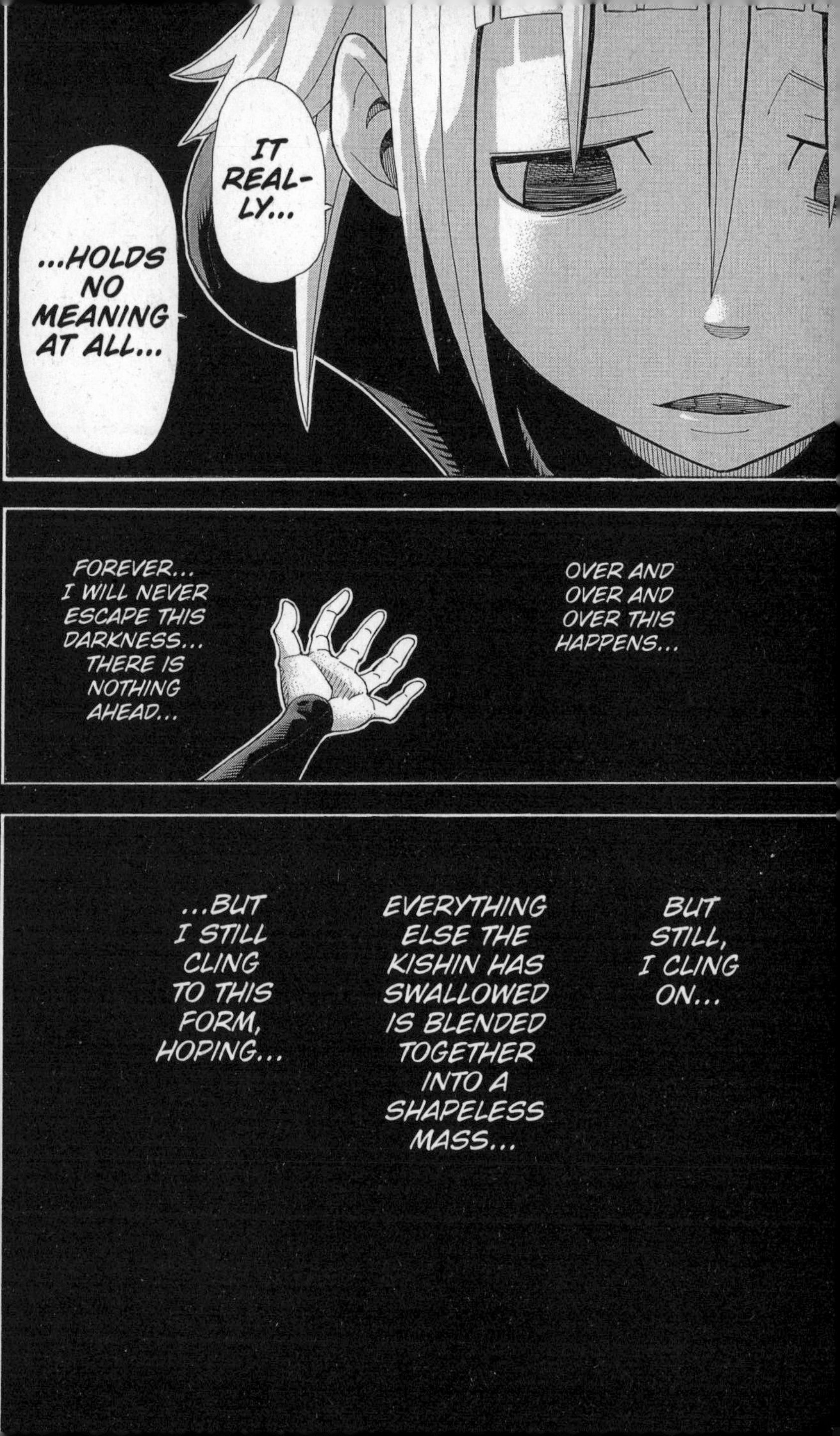
IT REALLY...
...HOLDS NO MEANING AT ALL...
OVER AND OVER AND OVER THIS HAPPENS...
FOREVER... I WILL NEVER ESCAPE THIS DARKNESS... THERE IS NOTHING AHEAD...
BUT STILL, I CLING ON...
EVERYTHING ELSE THE KISHIN HAS SWALLOWED IS BLENDED TOGETHER INTO A SHAPELESS MASS...
...BUT I STILL CLING TO THIS FORM, HOPING...

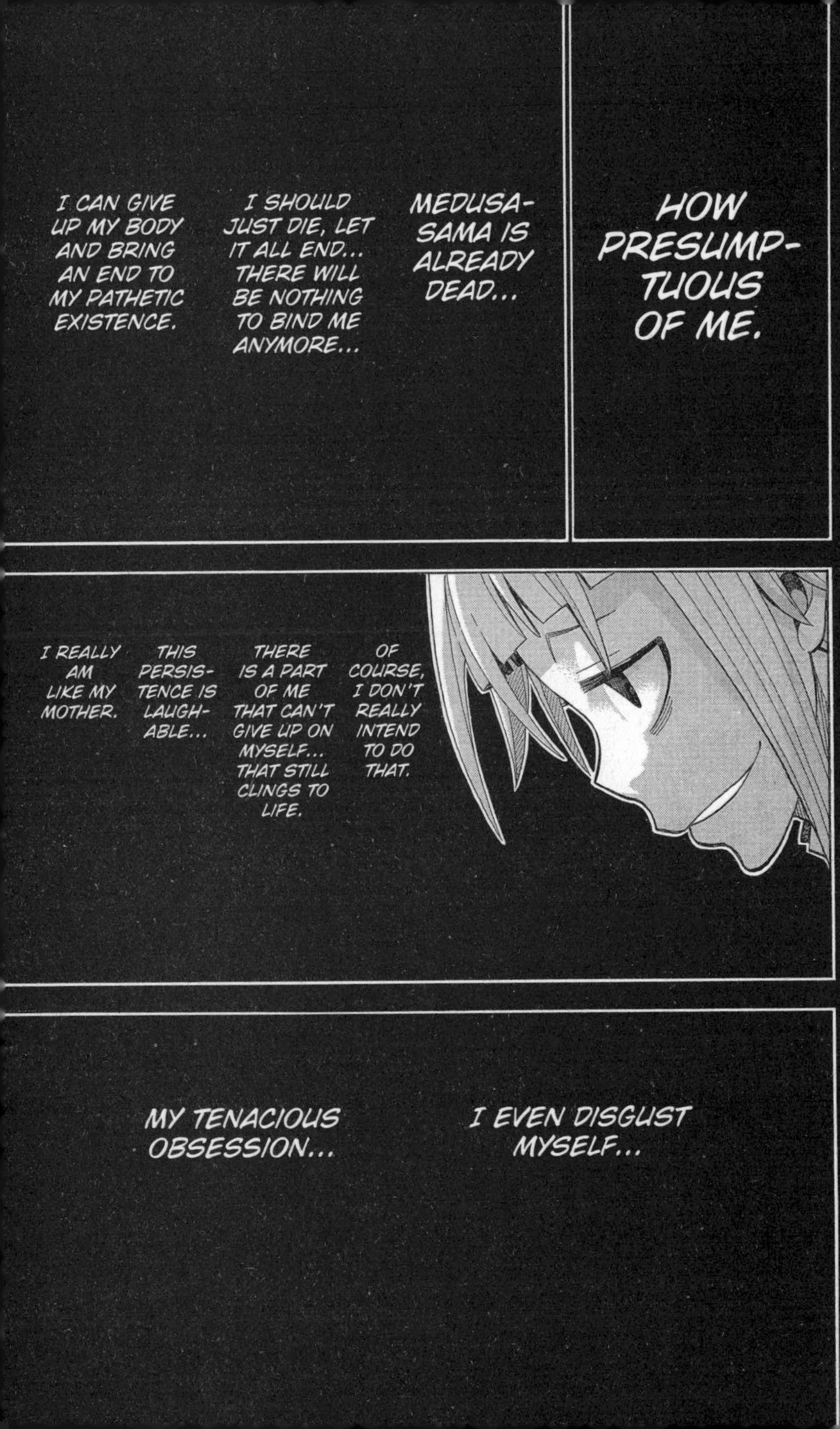
HOW PRESUMP-TUOUS OF ME.
MEDUSA-SAMA IS ALREADY DEAD...
I SHOULD JUST DIE, LET IT ALL END... THERE WILL BE NOTHING TO BIND ME ANYMORE...
I CAN GIVE UP MY BODY AND BRING AN END TO MY PATHETIC EXISTENCE.
OF COURSE, I DON'T REALLY INTEND TO DO THAT.
THERE IS A PART OF ME THAT CAN'T GIVE UP ON MYSELF... THAT STILL CLINGS TO LIFE.
THIS PERSIS-TENCE IS LAUGH-ABLE...
I REALLY AM LIKE MY MOTHER.
I EVEN DISGUST MYSELF...
MY TENACIOUS OBSESSION...

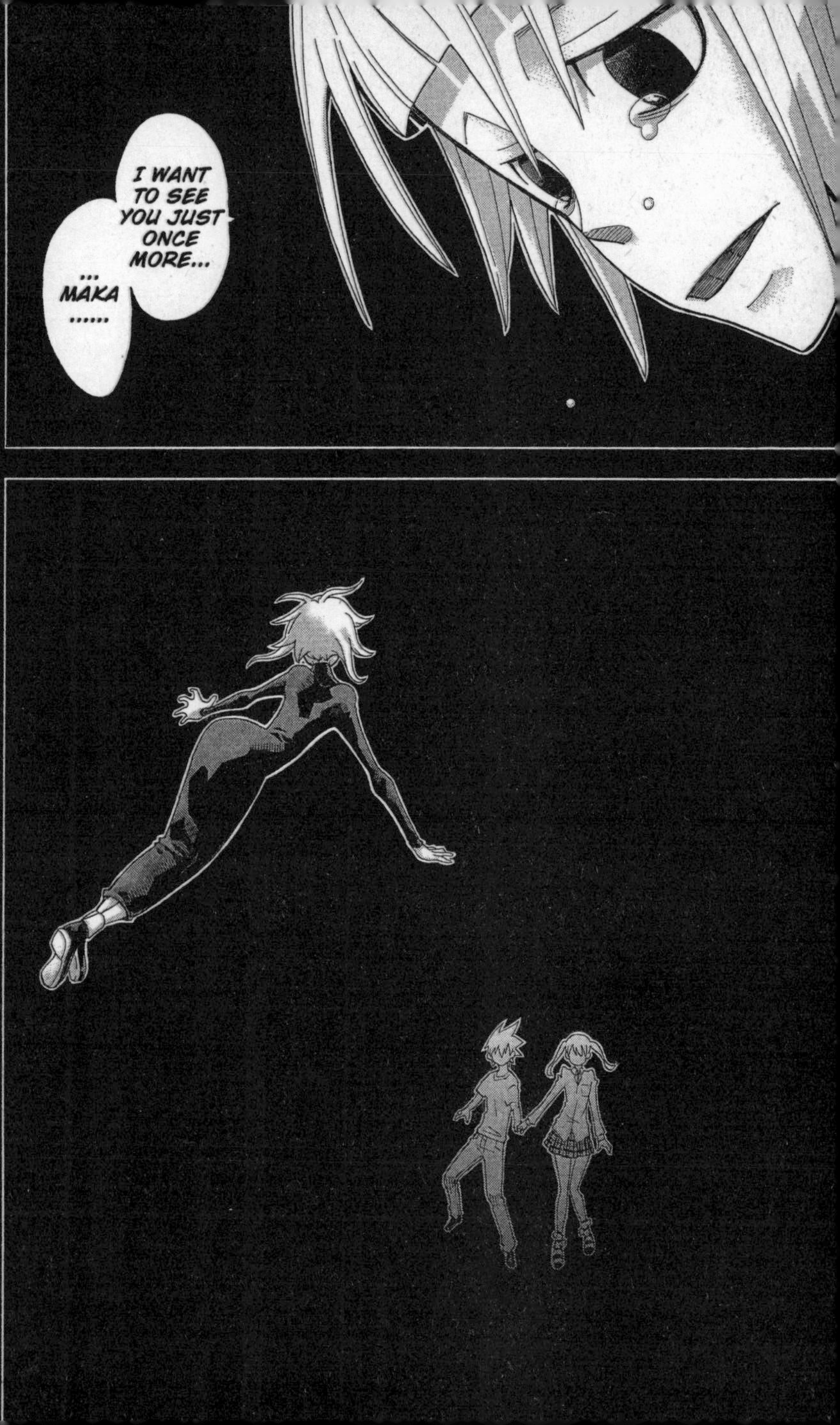
I WANT TO SEE YOU JUST ONCE MORE...
... MAKA ......

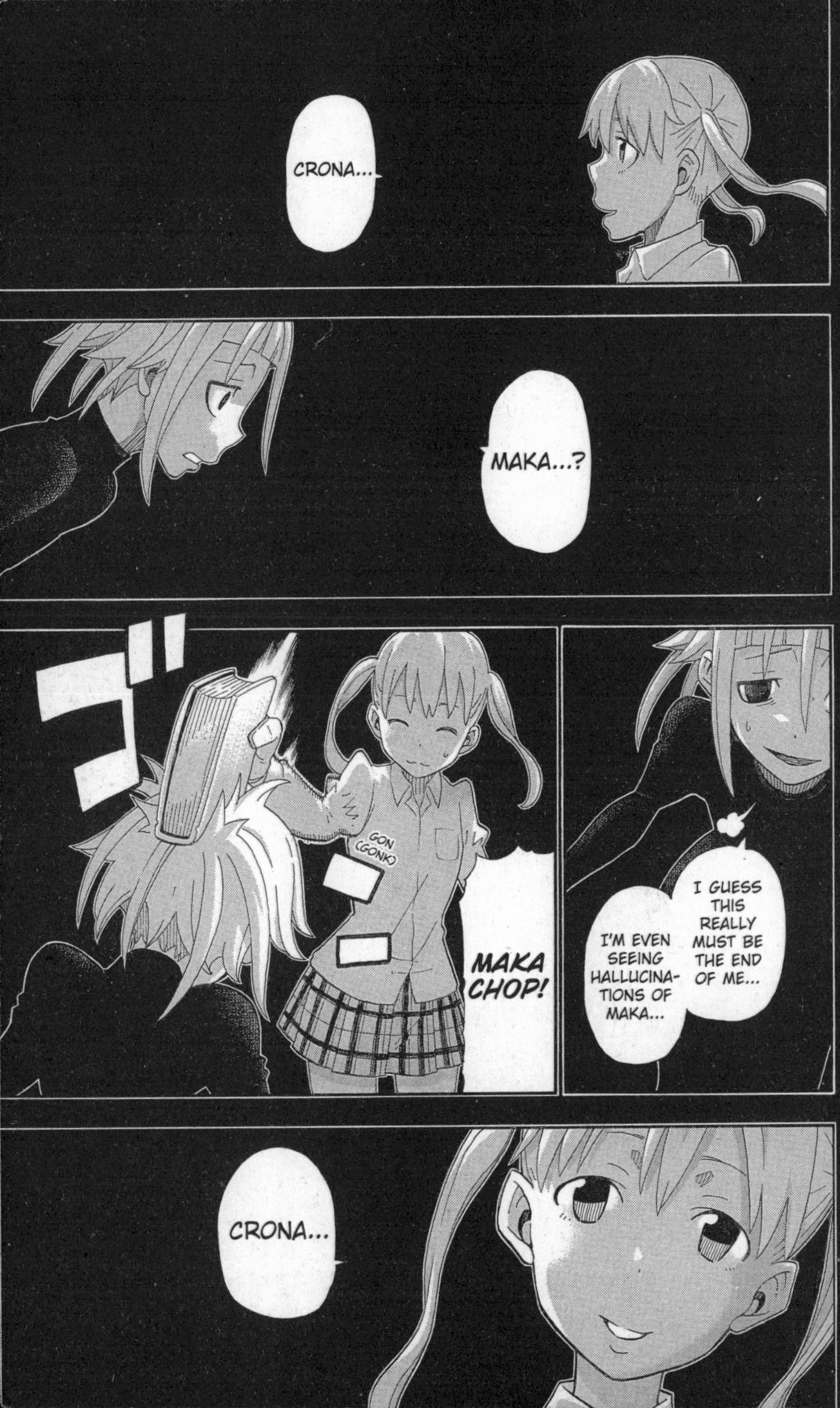
CRONA...
MAKA...?
I GUESS THIS REALLY MUST BE THE END OF ME...
I'M EVEN SEEING HALLUCINATIONS OF MAKA...
MAKA CHOP!
GON (GONK)
CRONA...

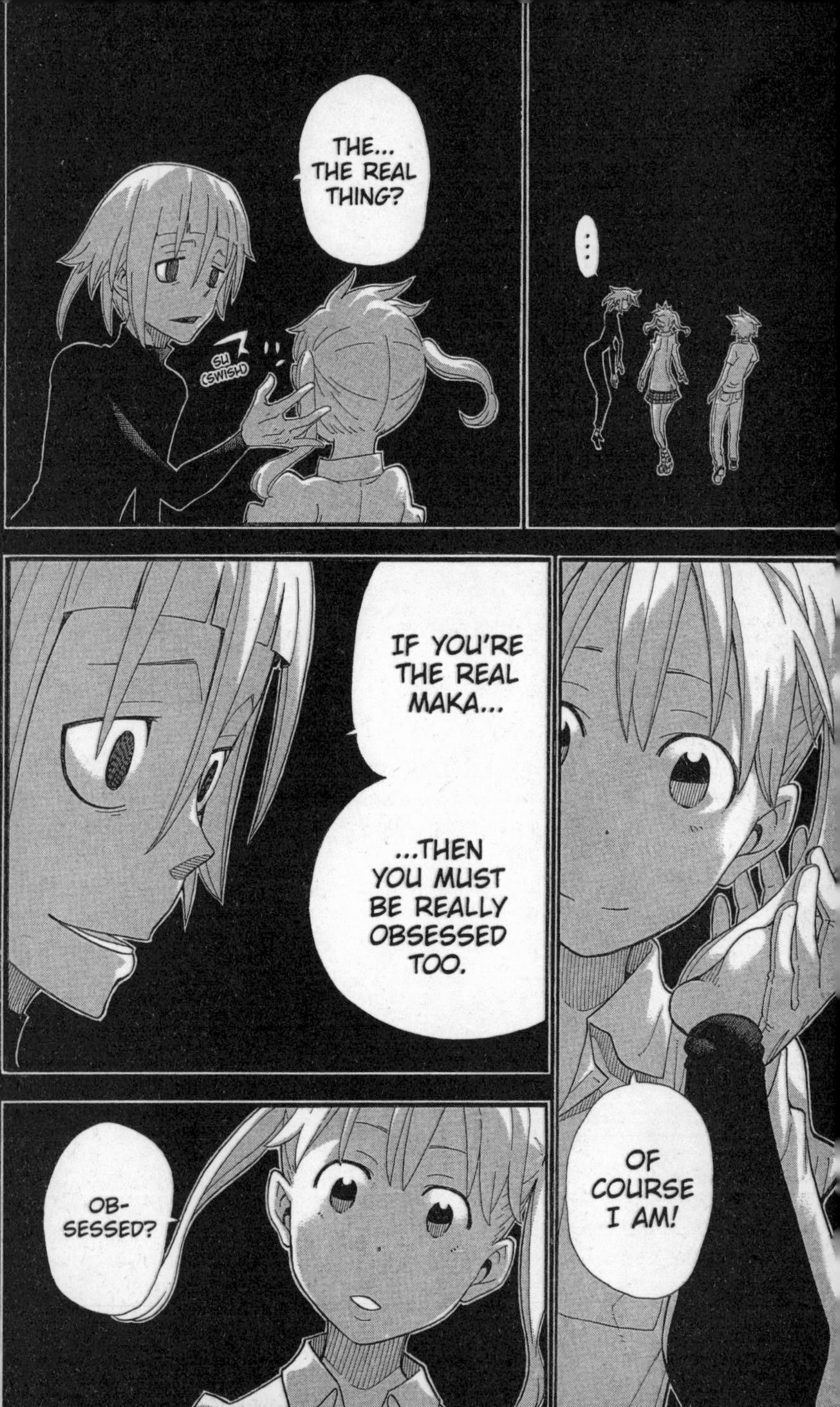

...
THE... THE REAL THING?
SU (SWISH)
OF COURSE I AM!
IF YOU'RE THE REAL MAKA...
...THEN YOU MUST BE REALLY OBSESSED TOO.
OB-SESSED?

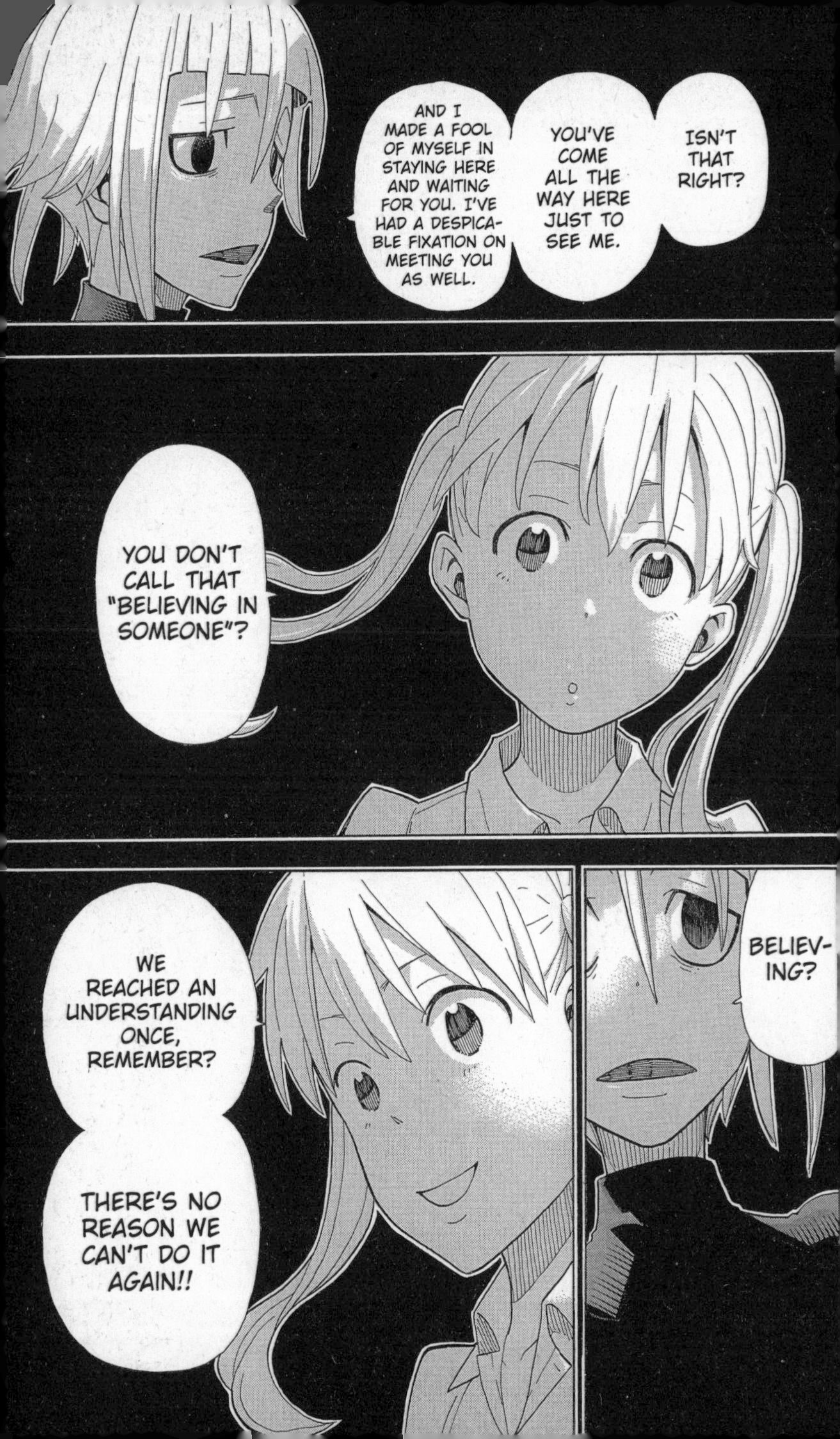
ISN'T THAT RIGHT?
YOU'VE COME ALL THE WAY HERE JUST TO SEE ME.
AND I MADE A FOOL OF MYSELF IN STAYING HERE AND WAITING FOR YOU. I'VE HAD A DESPICABLE FIXATION ON MEETING YOU AS WELL.
YOU DON'T CALL THAT "BELIEVING IN SOMEONE"?
BELIEVING?
WE REACHED AN UNDERSTANDING ONCE, REMEMBER?
THERE'S NO REASON WE CAN'T DO IT AGAIN!!

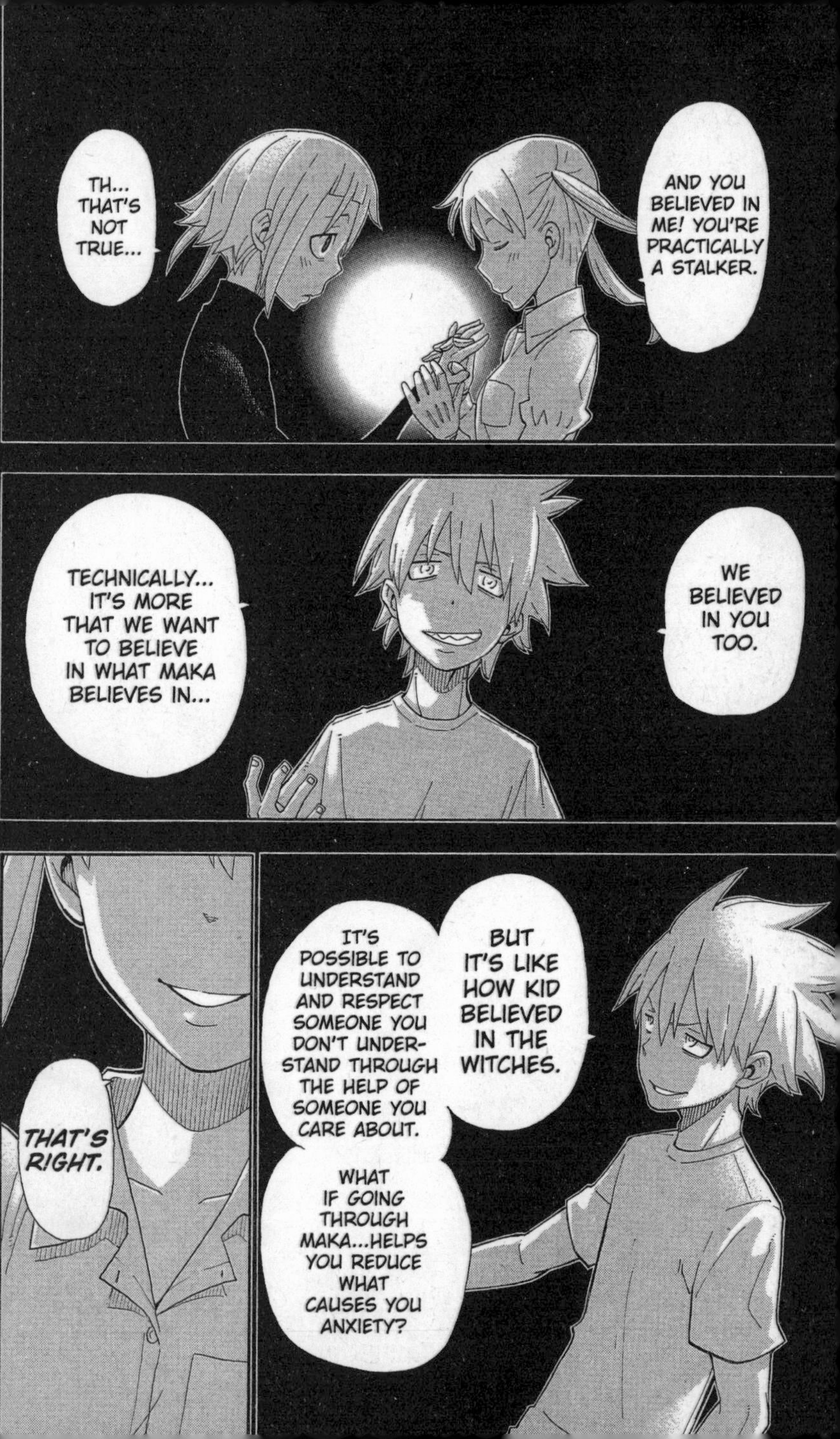
AND YOU BELIEVED IN ME! YOU'RE PRACTICALLY A STALKER.
TH... THAT'S NOT TRUE...
WE BELIEVED IN YOU TOO.
TECHNICALLY... IT'S MORE THAT WE WANT TO BELIEVE IN WHAT MAKA BELIEVES IN...
BUT IT'S LIKE HOW KID BELIEVED IN THE WITCHES.
IT'S POSSIBLE TO UNDERSTAND AND RESPECT SOMEONE YOU DON'T UNDER-STAND THROUGH THE HELP OF SOMEONE YOU CARE ABOUT.
WHAT IF GOING THROUGH MAKA...HELPS YOU REDUCE WHAT CAUSES YOU ANXIETY?
THAT'S RIGHT.

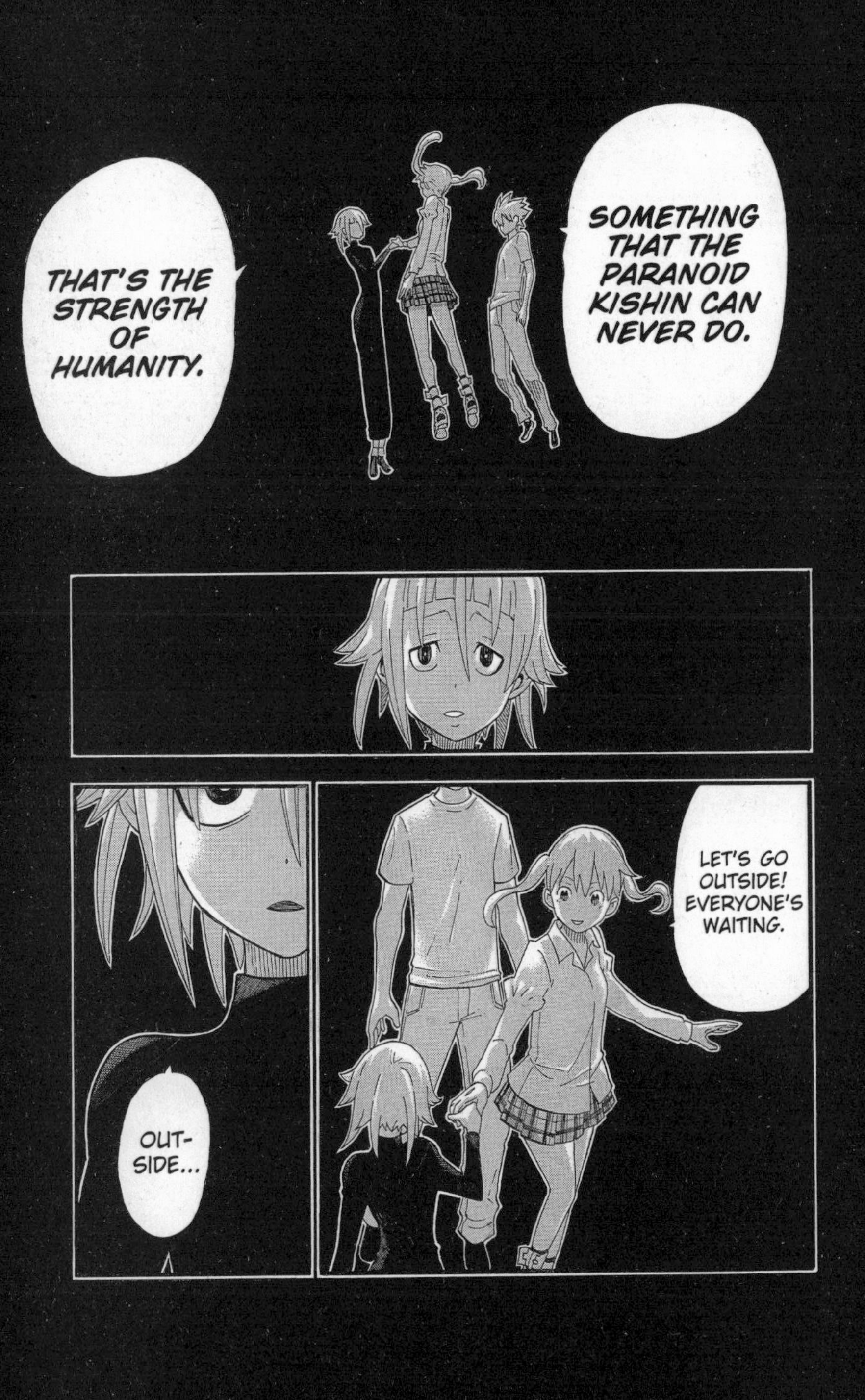
SOMETHING THAT THE PARANOID KISHIN CAN NEVER DO.
THAT'S THE STRENGTH OF HUMANITY.
LET'S GO OUTSIDE! EVERYONE'S WAITING.
OUT-SIDE...

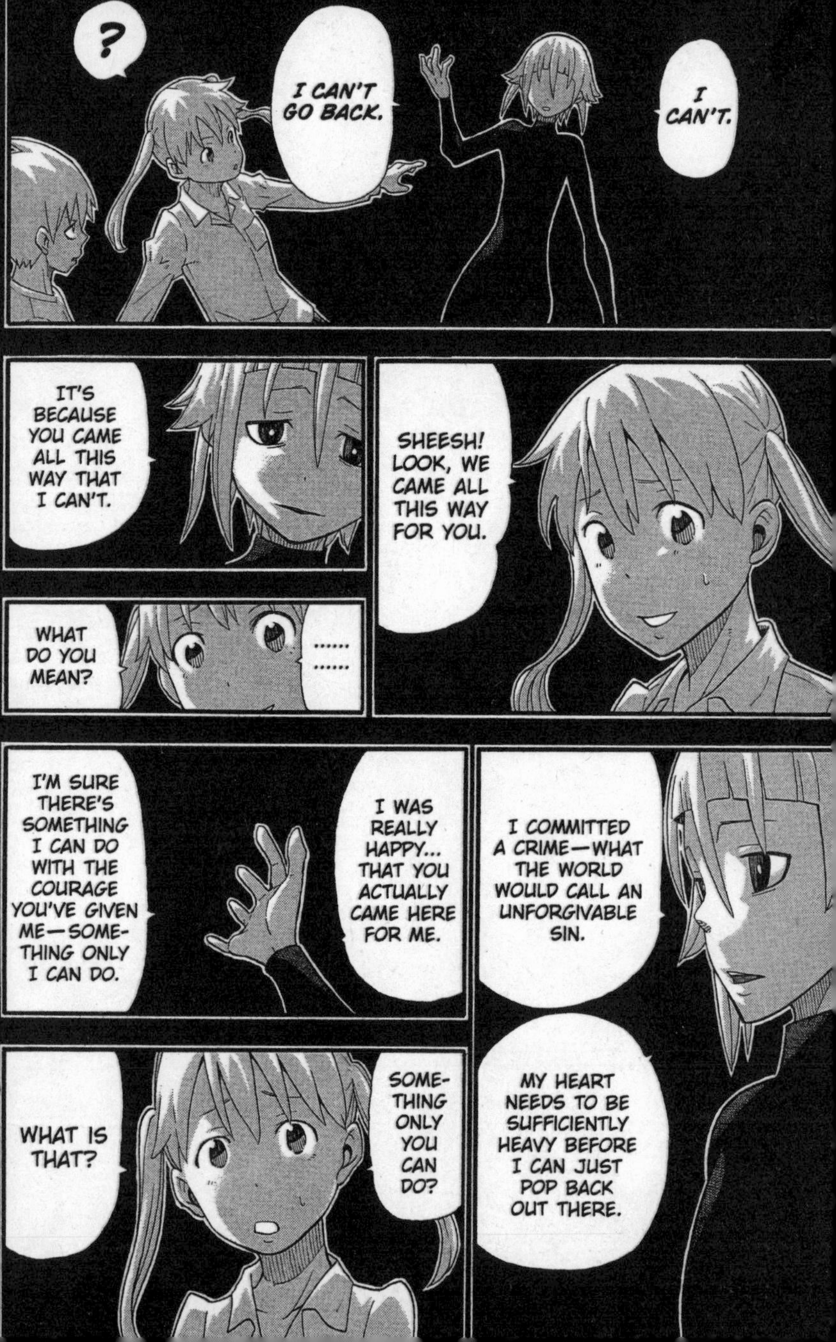
I CAN'T.
I CAN'T GO BACK.
?
SHEESH! LOOK, WE CAME ALL THIS WAY FOR YOU.
IT'S BECAUSE YOU CAME ALL THIS WAY THAT I CAN'T.
......
......
WHAT DO YOU MEAN?
I COMMITTED A CRIME—WHAT THE WORLD WOULD CALL AN UNFORGIVABLE SIN.
MY HEART NEEDS TO BE SUFFICIENTLY HEAVY BEFORE I CAN JUST POP BACK OUT THERE.
I WAS REALLY HAPPY... THAT YOU ACTUALLY CAME HERE FOR ME.
I'M SURE THERE'S SOMETHING I CAN DO WITH THE COURAGE YOU'VE GIVEN ME—SOMETHING ONLY I CAN DO.
SOMETHING ONLY YOU CAN DO?
WHAT IS THAT?

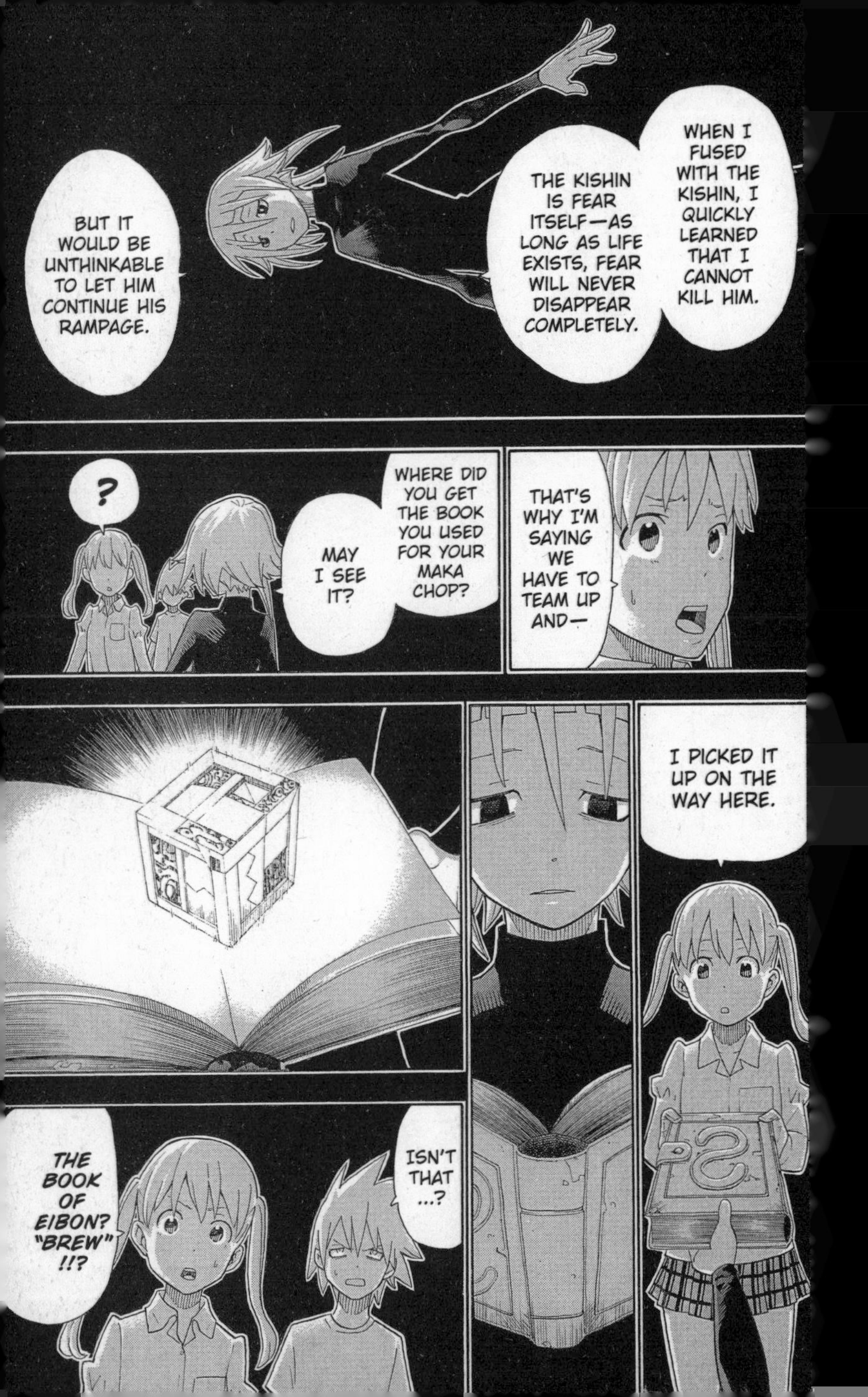
WHEN I FUSED WITH THE KISHIN, I QUICKLY LEARNED THAT I CANNOT KILL HIM.
THE KISHIN IS FEAR ITSELF—AS LONG AS LIFE EXISTS, FEAR WILL NEVER DISAPPEAR COMPLETELY.
BUT IT WOULD BE UNTHINKABLE TO LET HIM CONTINUE HIS RAMPAGE.
THAT'S WHY I'M SAYING WE HAVE TO TEAM UP AND—
WHERE DID YOU GET THE BOOK YOU USED FOR YOUR MAKA CHOP?
MAY I SEE IT?
?
I PICKED IT UP ON THE WAY HERE.
ISN'T THAT ...?
THE BOOK OF EIBON? "BREW" !!?

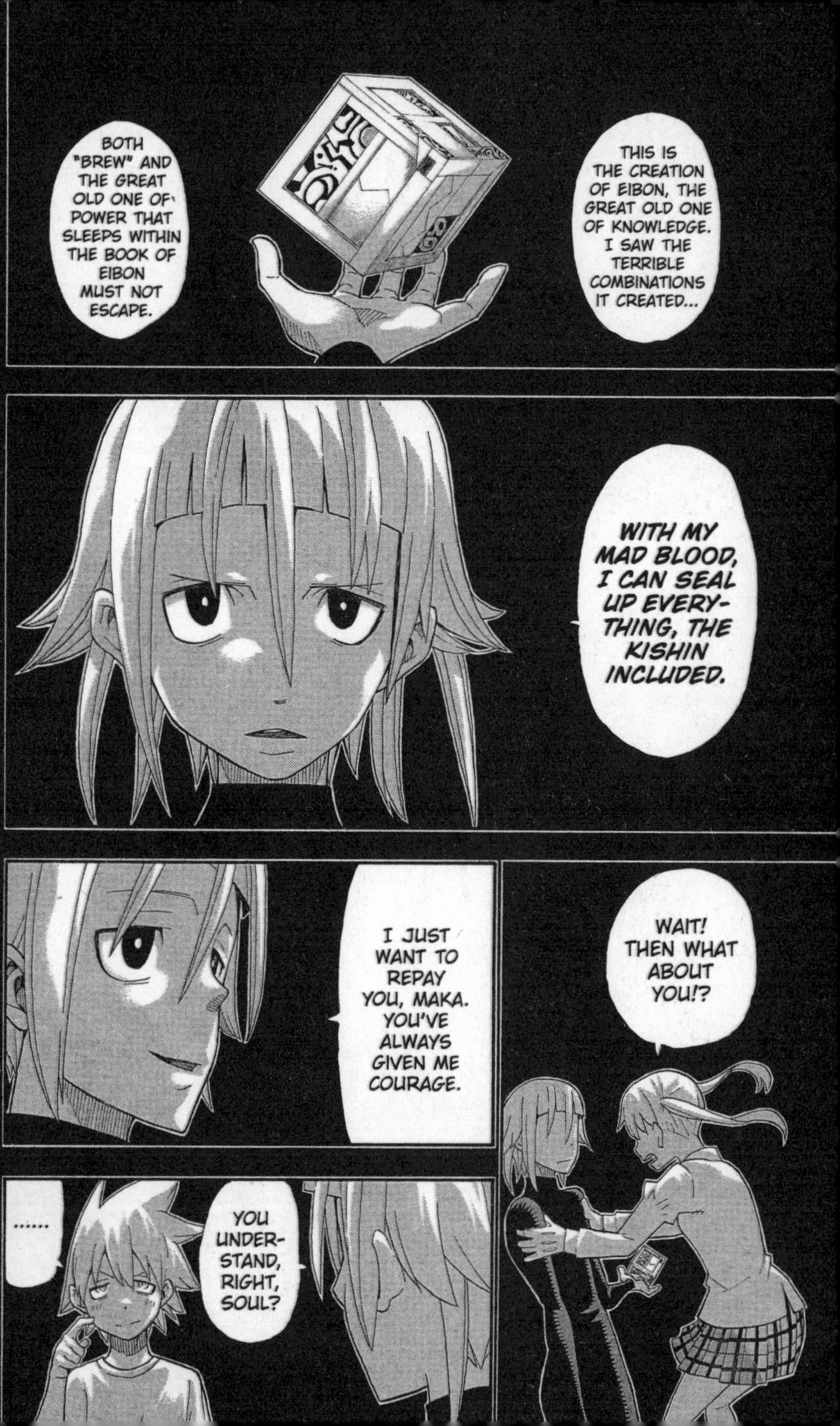
THIS IS THE CREATION OF EIBON, THE GREAT OLD ONE OF KNOWLEDGE. I SAW THE TERRIBLE COMBINATIONS IT CREATED...
BOTH "BREW" AND THE GREAT OLD ONE OF POWER THAT SLEEPS WITHIN THE BOOK OF EIBON MUST NOT ESCAPE.
WITH MY MAD BLOOD, I CAN SEAL UP EVERY-THING, THE KISHIN INCLUDED.
WAIT! THEN WHAT ABOUT YOU!?
I JUST WANT TO REPAY YOU, MAKA. YOU'VE ALWAYS GIVEN ME COURAGE.
YOU UNDER-STAND, RIGHT, SOUL?
......

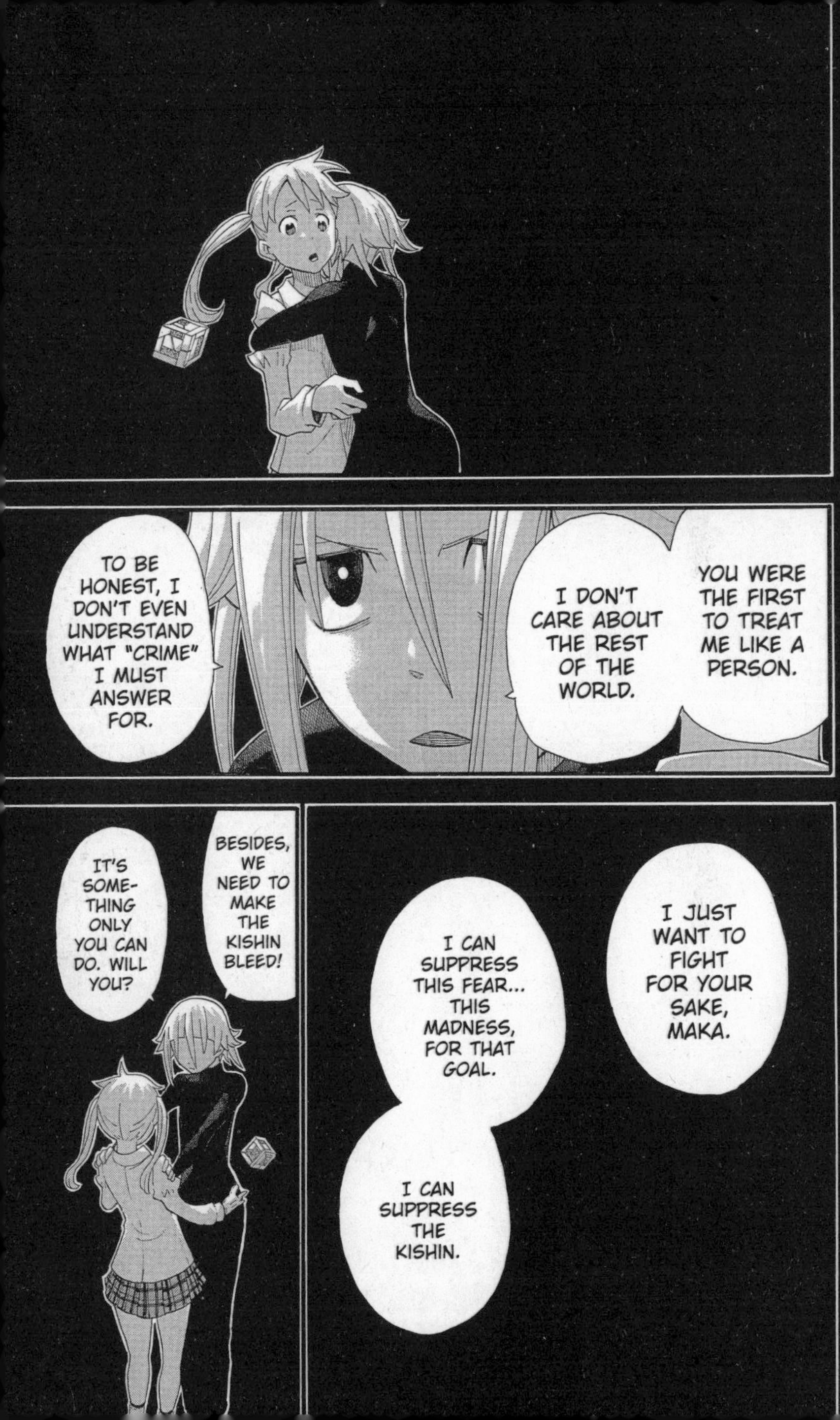
YOU WERE THE FIRST TO TREAT ME LIKE A PERSON.
I DON'T CARE ABOUT THE REST OF THE WORLD.
TO BE HONEST, I DON'T EVEN UNDERSTAND WHAT "CRIME" I MUST ANSWER FOR.
I JUST WANT TO FIGHT FOR YOUR SAKE, MAKA.
I CAN SUPPRESS THIS FEAR... THIS MADNESS, FOR THAT GOAL.
I CAN SUPPRESS THE KISHIN.
BESIDES, WE NEED TO MAKE THE KISHIN BLEED!
IT'S SOME-THING ONLY YOU CAN DO. WILL YOU?

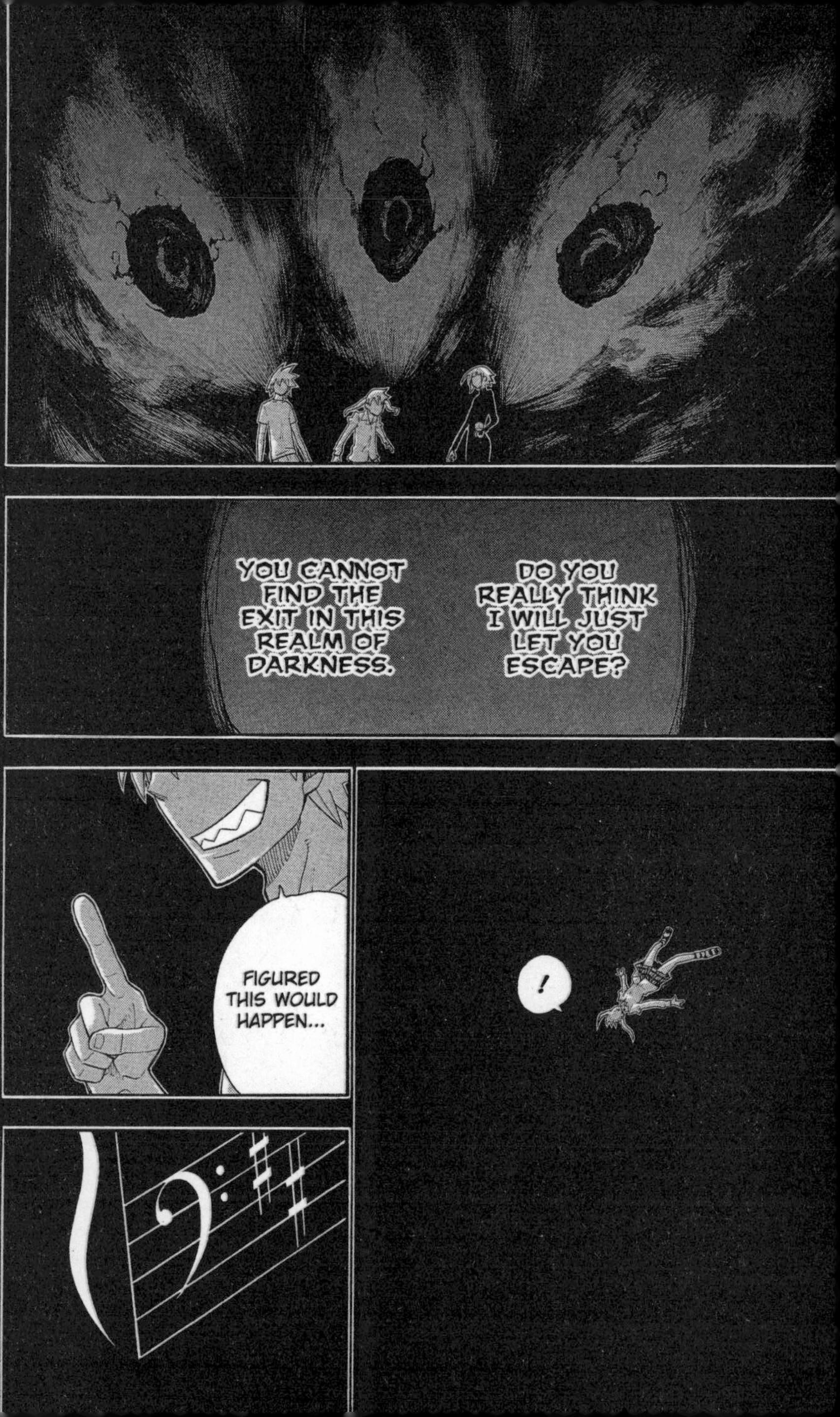
DO YOU REALLY THINK I WILL JUST LET YOU ESCAPE?
YOU CANNOT FIND THE EXIT IN THIS REALM OF DARKNESS.
!
FIGURED THIS WOULD HAPPEN...

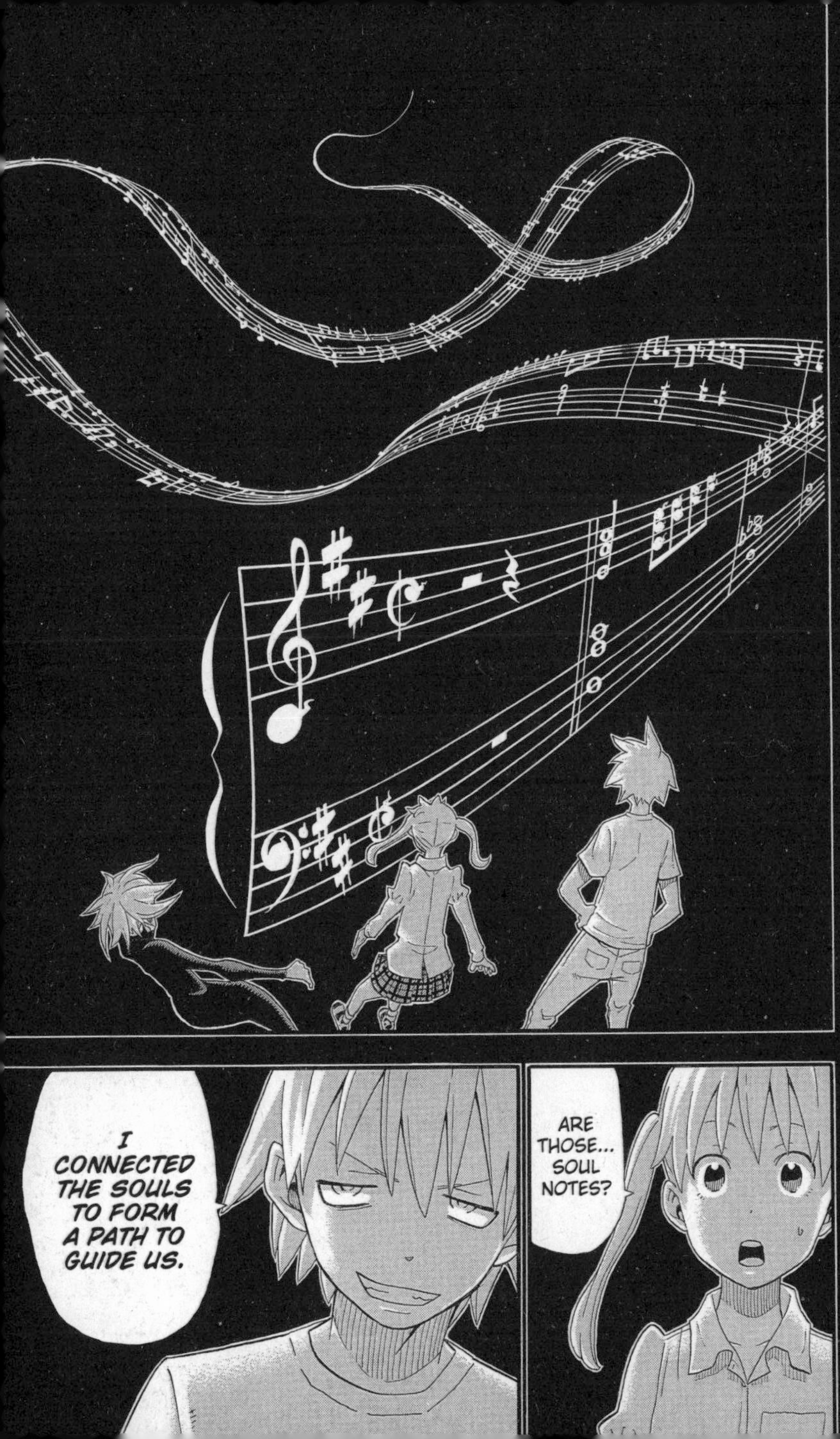
ARE THOSE... SOUL NOTES?
I CONNECTED THE SOULS TO FORM A PATH TO GUIDE US.

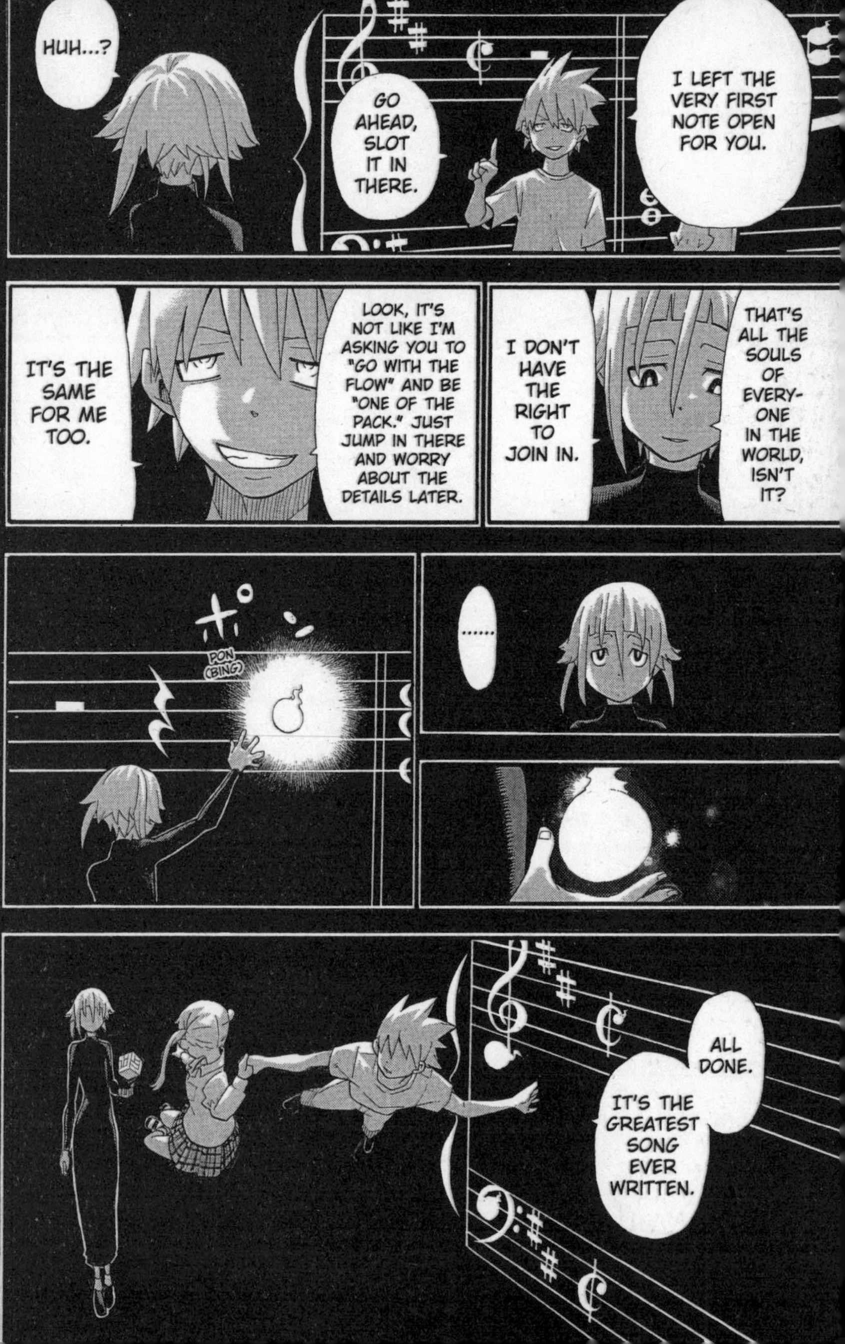
I LEFT THE VERY FIRST NOTE OPEN FOR YOU.
GO AHEAD, SLOT IT IN THERE.
HUH...?
THAT'S ALL THE SOULS OF EVERYONE IN THE WORLD, ISN'T IT?
I DON'T HAVE THE RIGHT TO JOIN IN.
LOOK, IT'S NOT LIKE I'M ASKING YOU TO "GO WITH THE FLOW" AND BE "ONE OF THE PACK." JUST JUMP IN THERE AND WORRY ABOUT THE DETAILS LATER.
IT'S THE SAME FOR ME TOO.
......
PON (BING)
ALL DONE.
IT'S THE GREATEST SONG EVER WRITTEN.

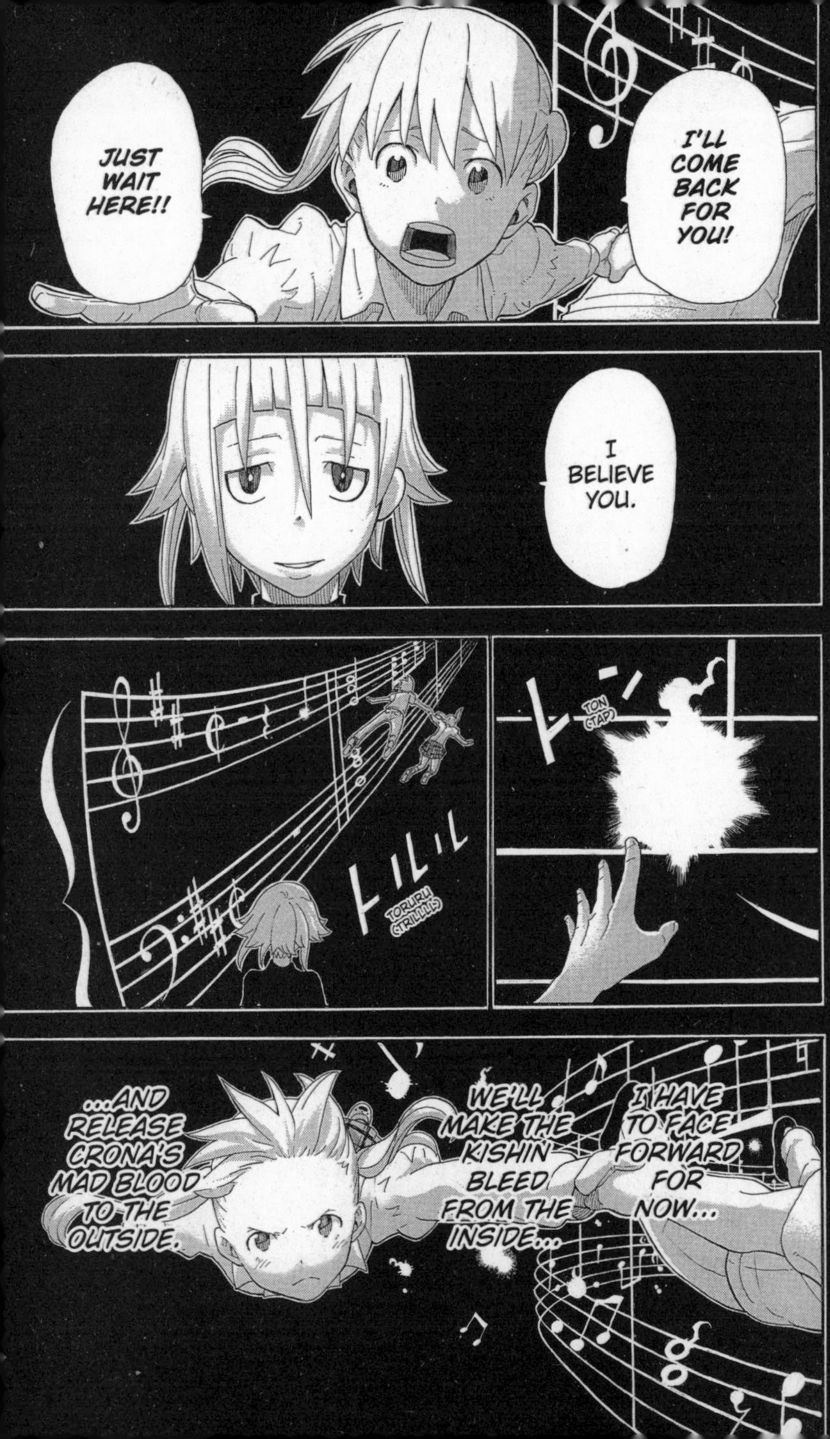
I'LL COME BACK FOR YOU!
JUST WAIT HERE!!
I BELIEVE YOU.
TON (TAP)
TORURU (TRILLLL)
I HAVE TO FACE FORWARD FOR NOW...
WE'LL MAKE THE KISHIN BLEED FROM THE INSIDE...
...AND RELEASE CRONA'S MAD BLOOD TO THE OUTSIDE.

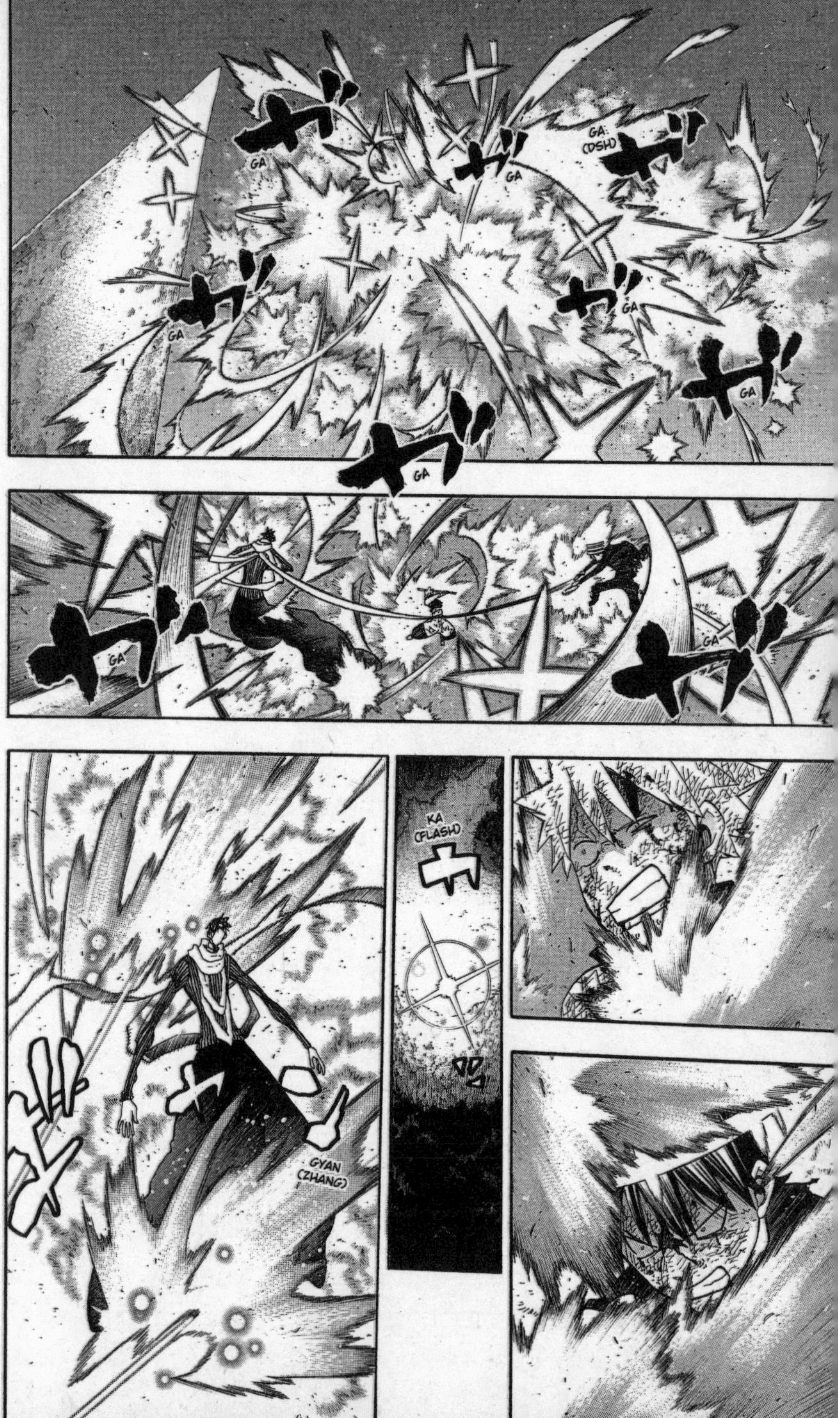
GA (DSH)
GA
GA
GA
GA
GA
GA
GA
GA
KA (FLASH)
GYAN (ZHANG)

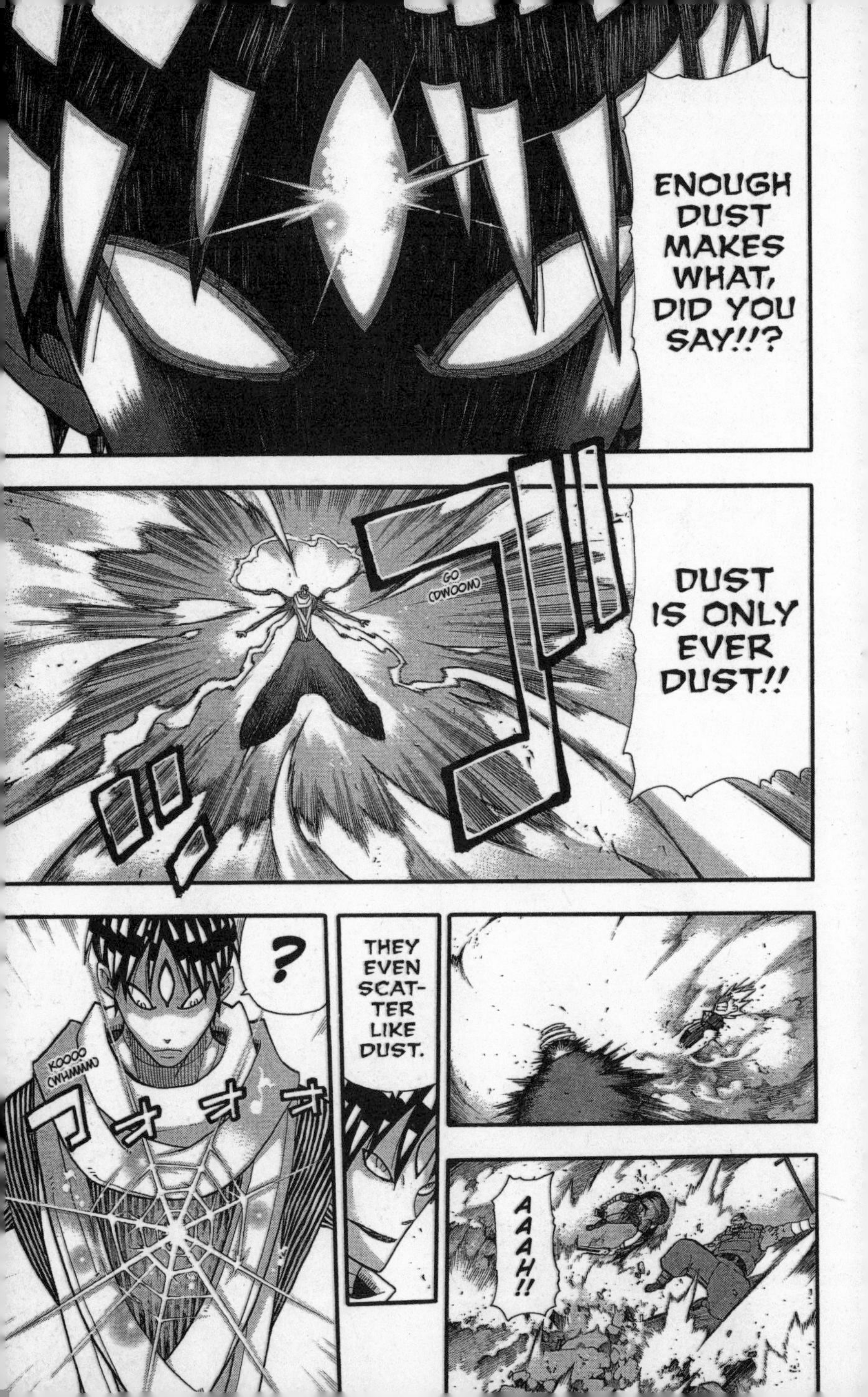
ENOUGH DUST MAKES WHAT, DID YOU SAY!!?
DUST IS ONLY EVER DUST!!
GO (DWOOM)
AAAH!!
THEY EVEN SCAT-TER LIKE DUST.
?
KOOOO (WHMMM)

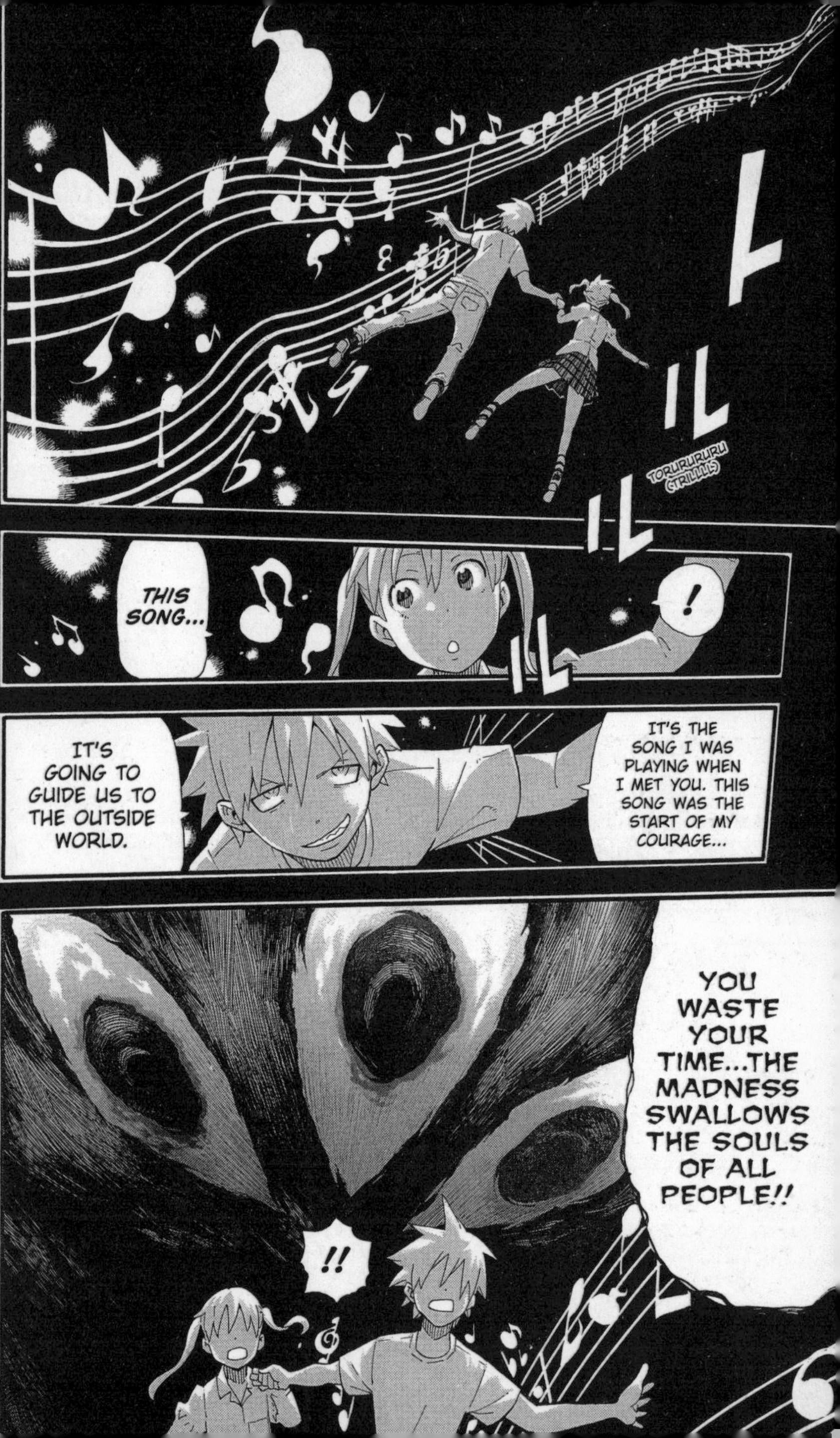
TORURURURU (TRILLLLS)
!
THIS SONG...
IT'S THE SONG I WAS PLAYING WHEN I MET YOU. THIS SONG WAS THE START OF MY COURAGE...
IT'S GOING TO GUIDE US TO THE OUTSIDE WORLD.
YOU WASTE YOUR TIME...THE MADNESS SWALLOWS THE SOULS OF ALL PEOPLE!!
!!

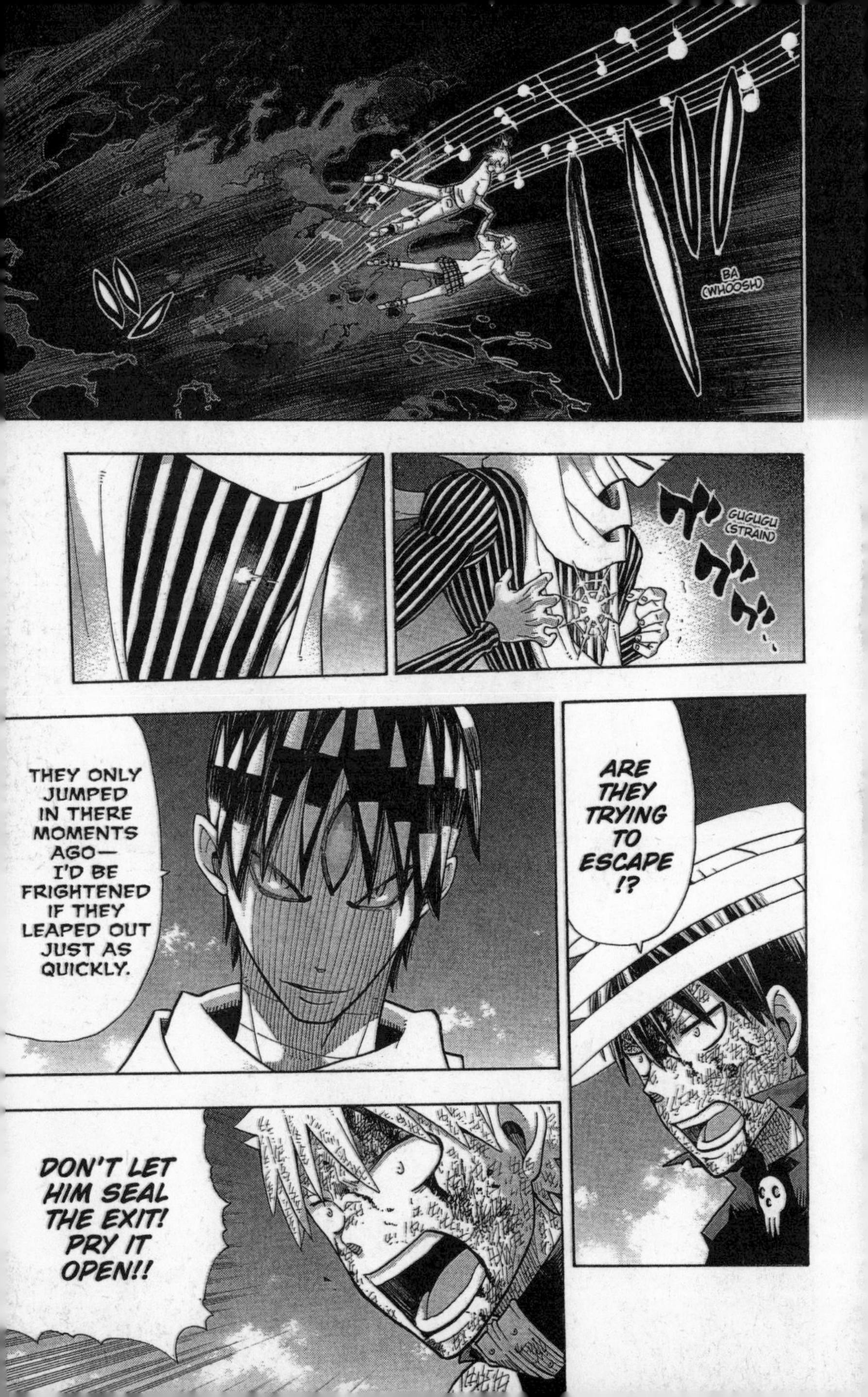
BA (WHOOSH)
GUGUGU (STRAIN)
ARE THEY TRYING TO ESCAPE!?
THEY ONLY JUMPED IN THERE MOMENTS AGO— I'D BE FRIGHTENED IF THEY LEAPED OUT JUST AS QUICKLY.
DON'T LET HIM SEAL THE EXIT! PRY IT OPEN!!

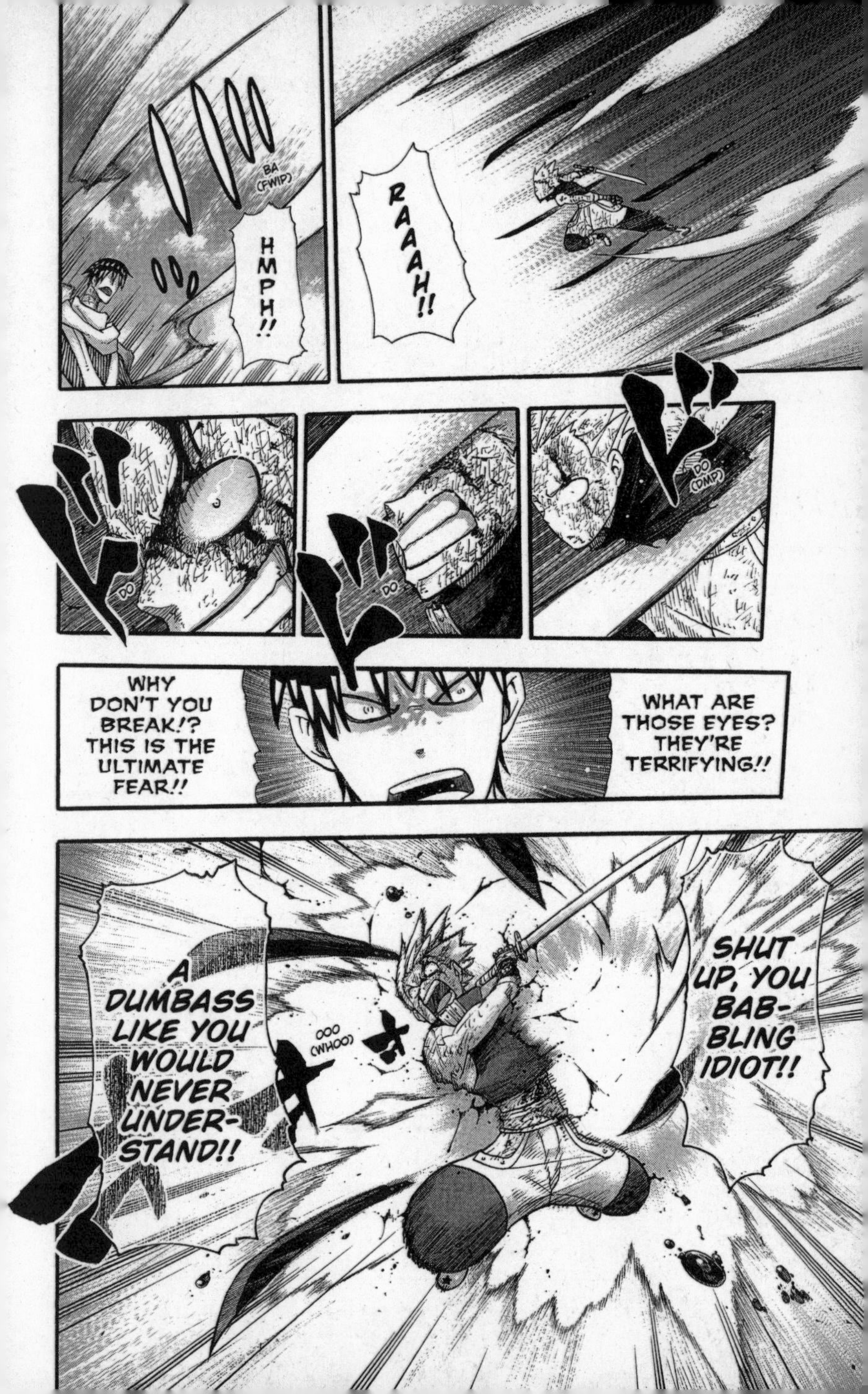
RAAAH!!
BA
(FWIP)
HMPH!!
DO
(DMP)
DO
DO
WHAT ARE THOSE EYES? THEY'RE TERRIFYING!!
WHY DON'T YOU BREAK!? THIS IS THE ULTIMATE FEAR!!
SHUT UP, YOU BAB-BLING IDIOT!!
OOO
(WHOO)
A DUMBASS LIKE YOU WOULD NEVER UNDER-STAND!!

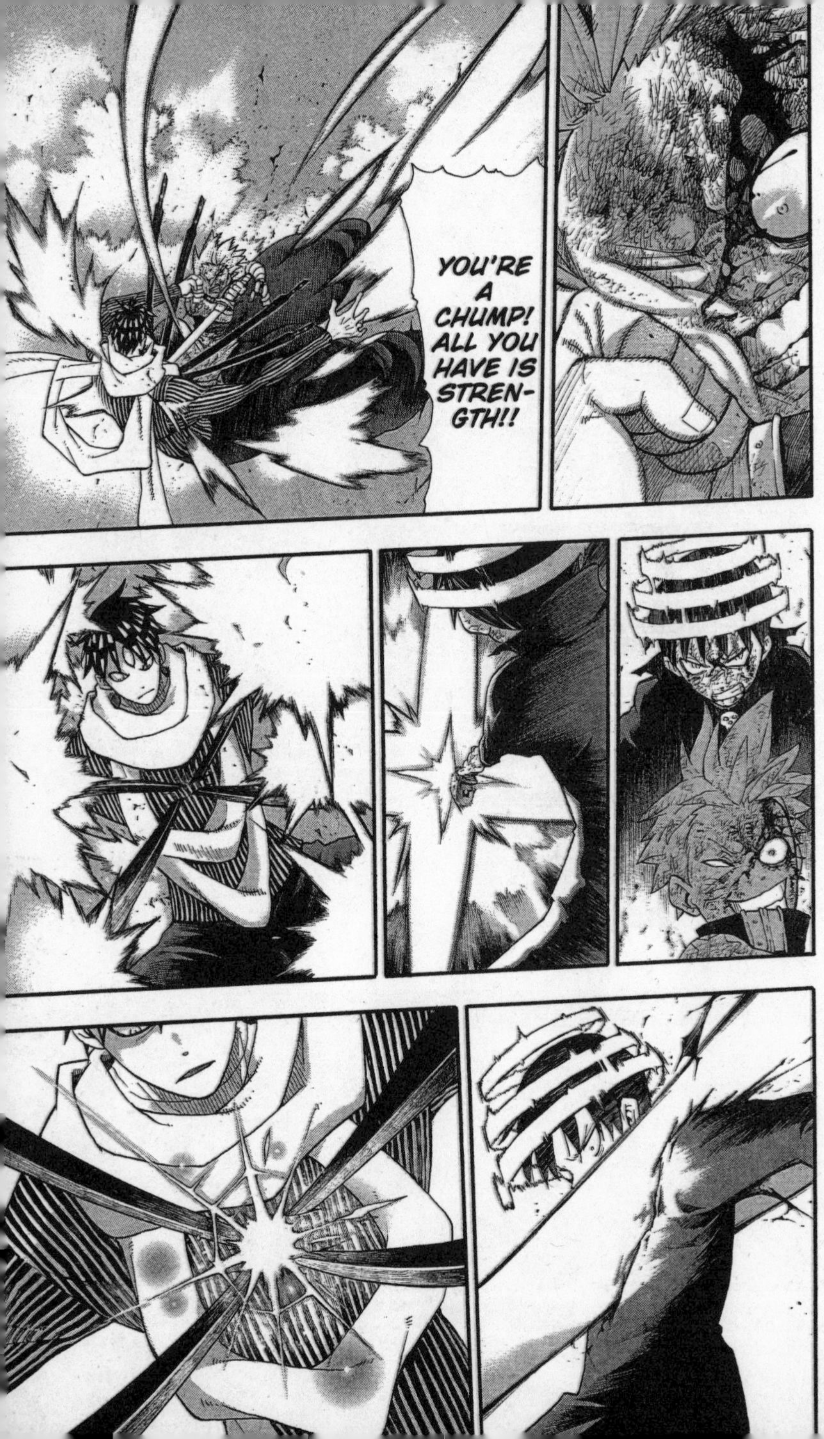
YOU'RE A CHUMP! ALL YOU HAVE IS STREN-GTH!!

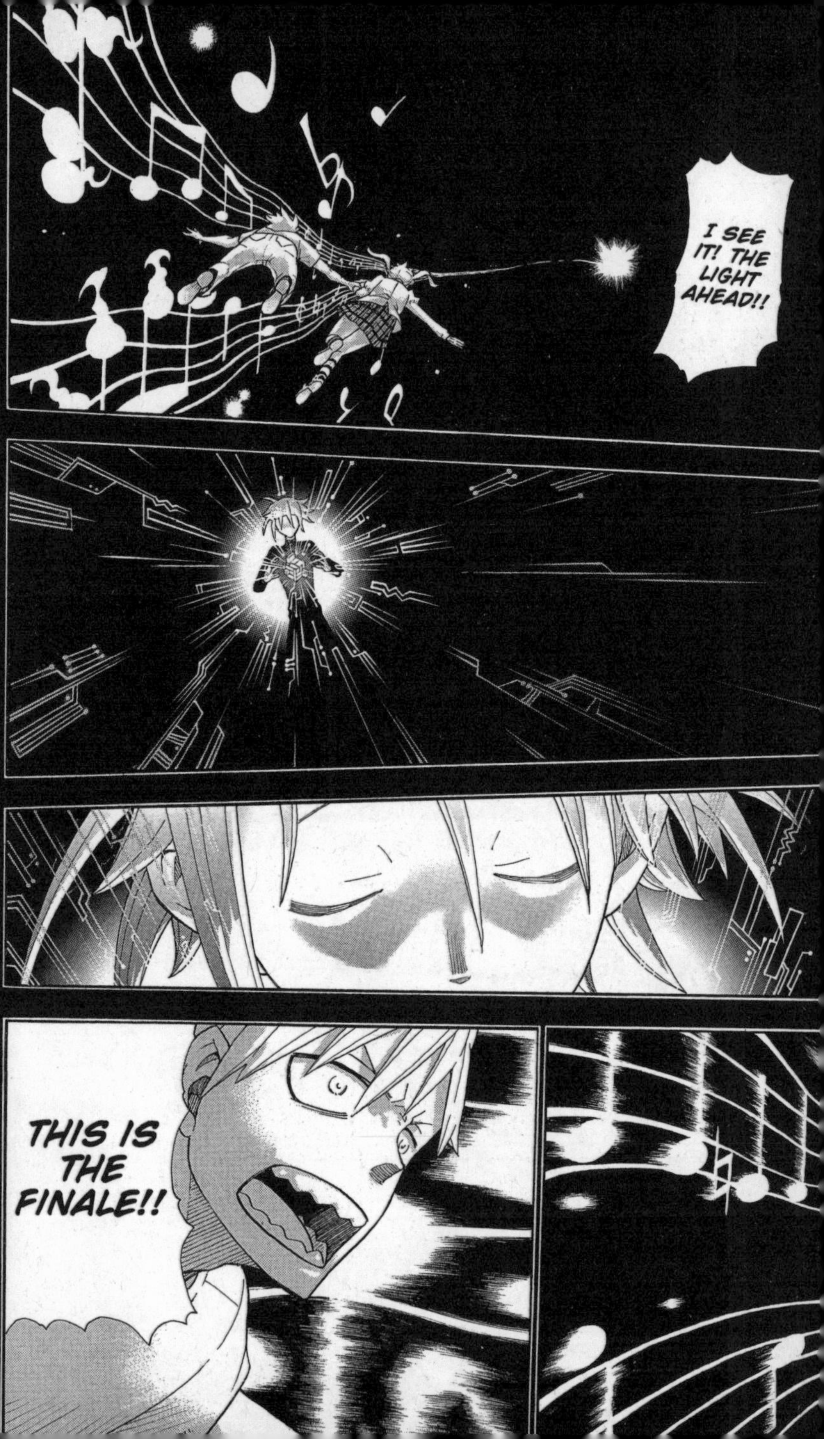
I SEE IT! THE LIGHT AHEAD!!
THIS IS THE FINALE!!

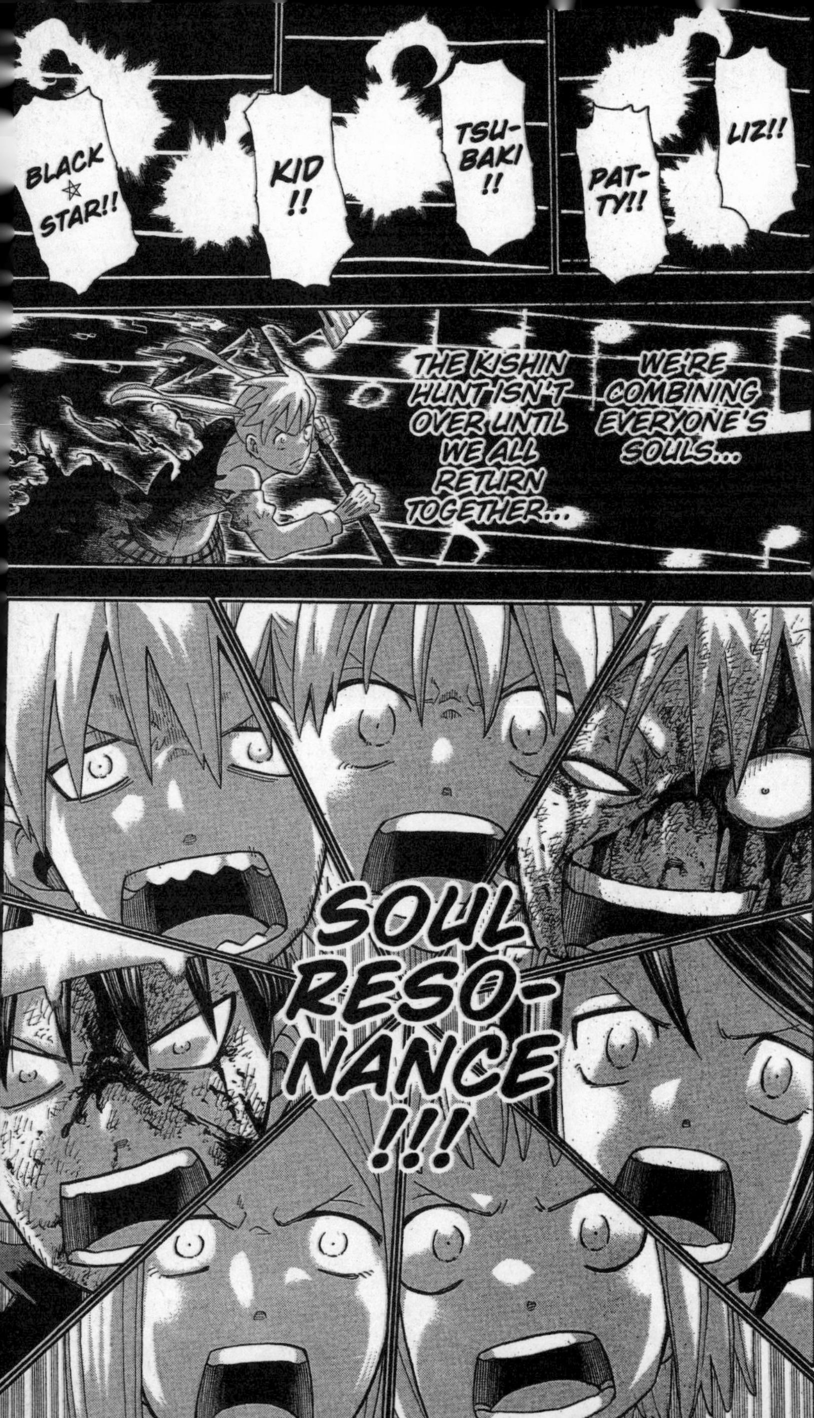
LIZ!!
PAT-TY!!
TSU-BAKI!!
KID!!
BLACK☆STAR!!
WE'RE COMBINING EVERYONE'S SOULS...
THE KISHIN HUNT ISN'T OVER UNTIL WE ALL RETURN TOGETHER...
SOUL RESO-NANCE!!!

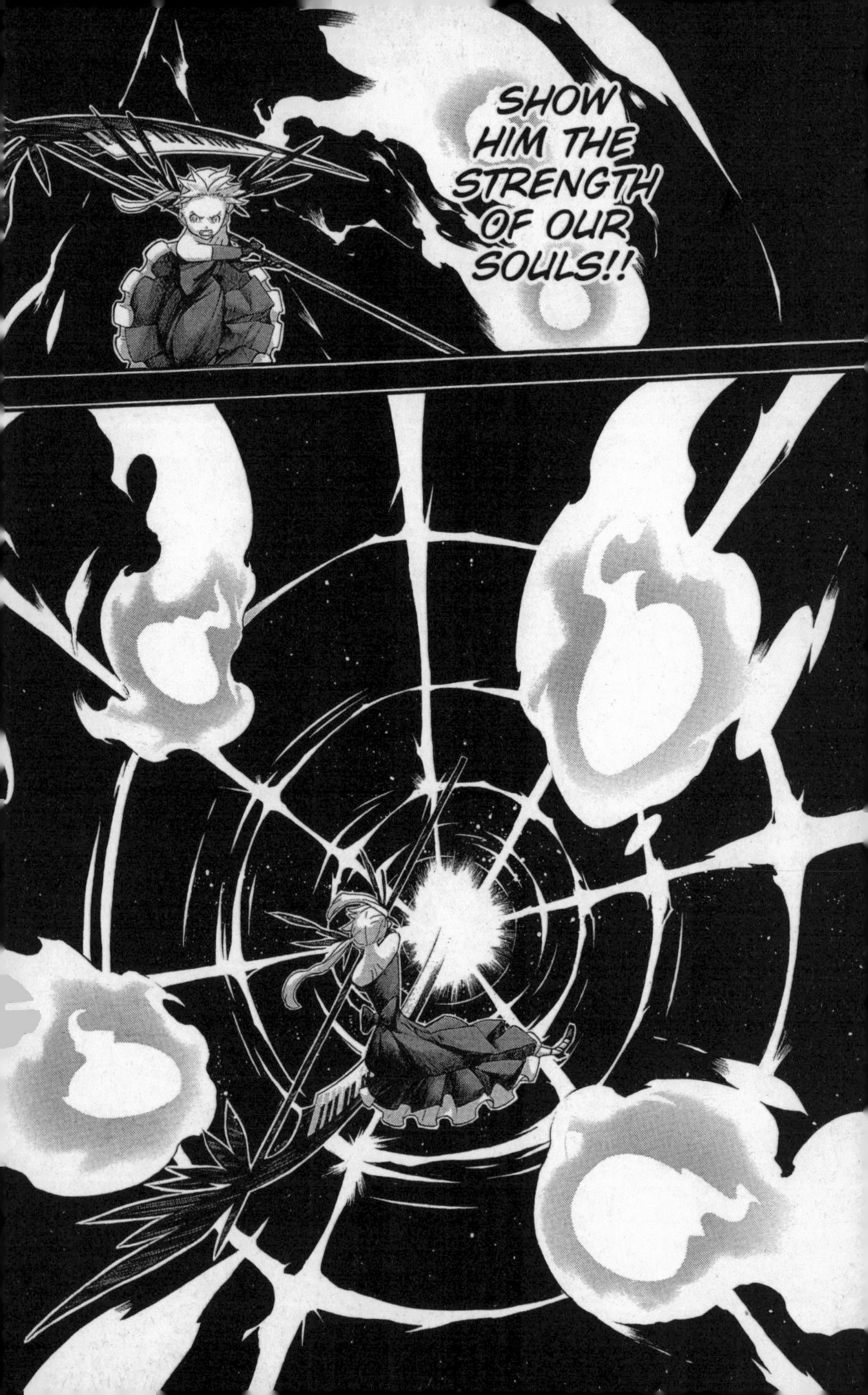
SHOW HIM THE STRENGTH OF OUR SOULS!!

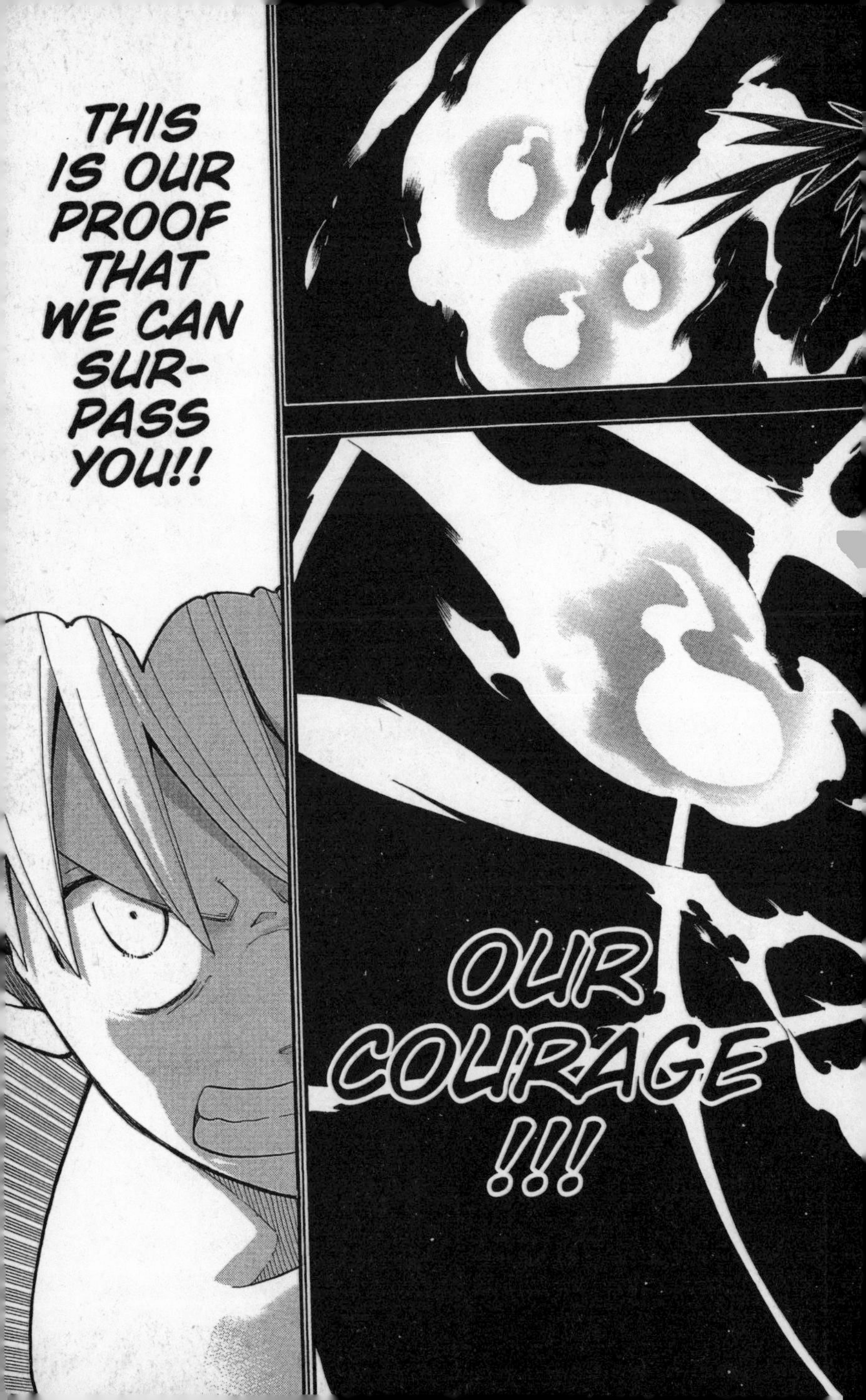
THIS IS OUR PROOF THAT WE CAN SUR-PASS YOU!!
OUR COURAGE !!!

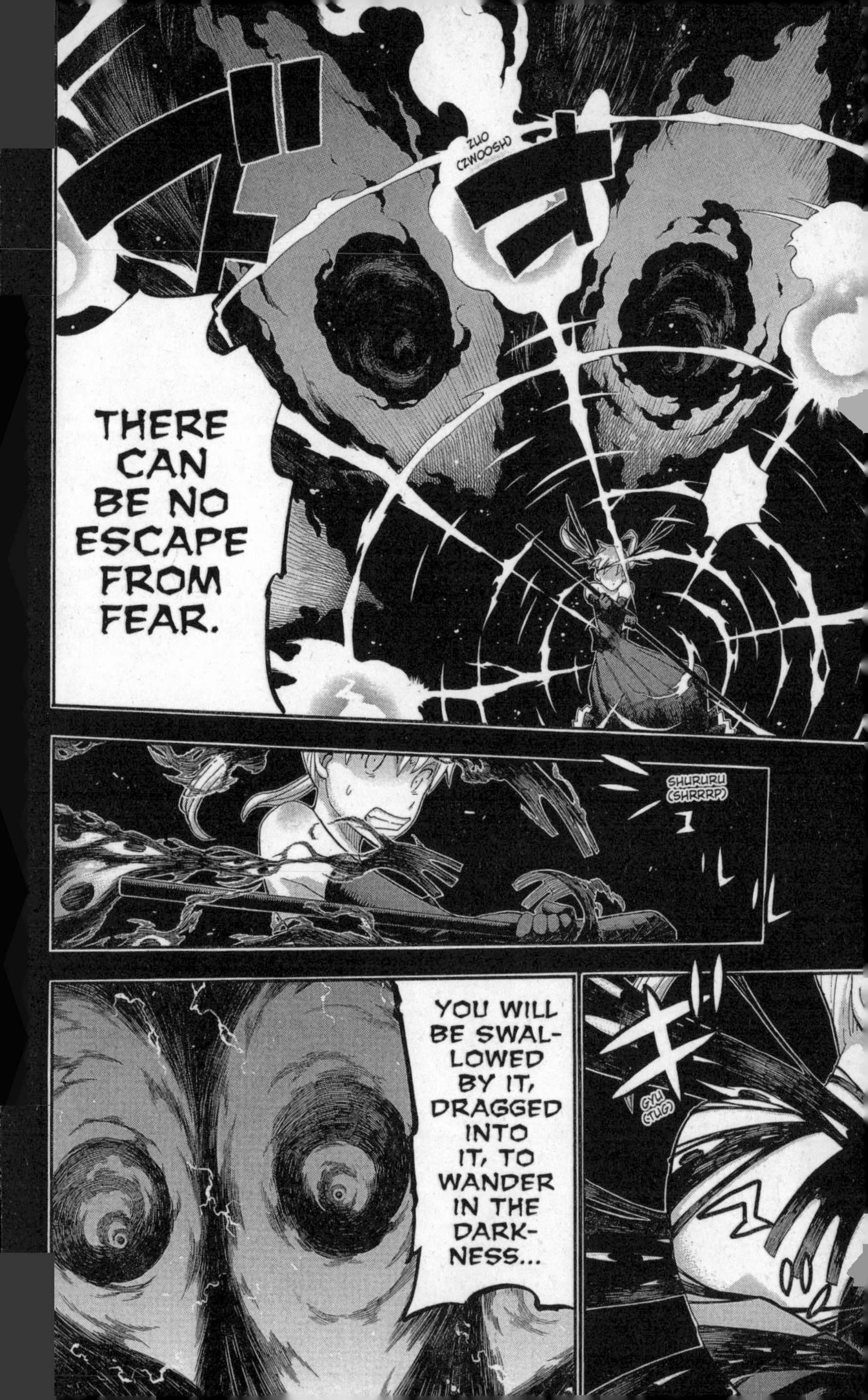
ZUO (ZWOOSH)
THERE CAN BE NO ESCAPE FROM FEAR.
SHURURU (SHRRRP)
GYU (TUG)
YOU WILL BE SWAL-LOWED BY IT, DRAGGED INTO IT, TO WANDER IN THE DARK-NESS...

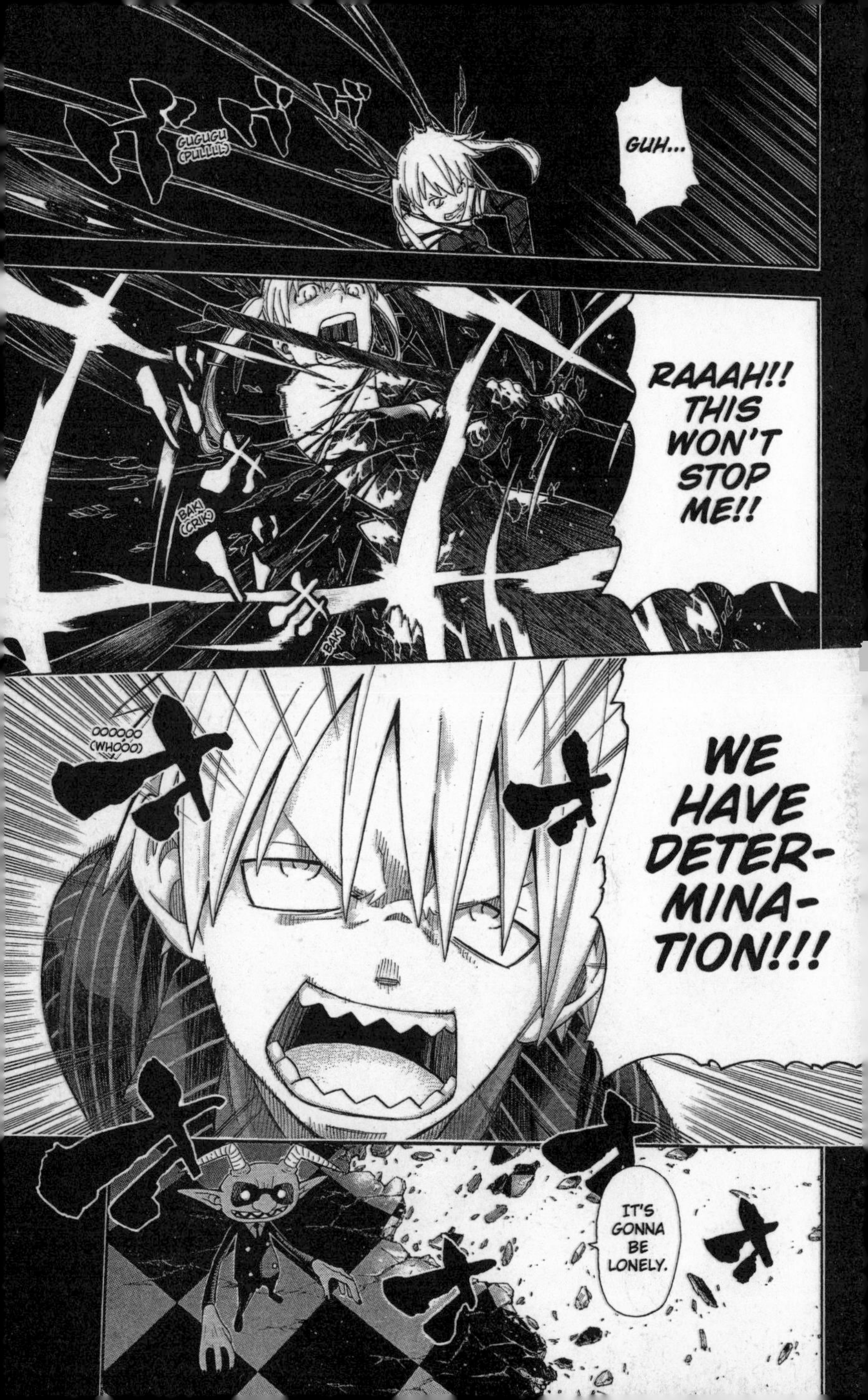
GUH...
GUGUGU (PULLLL)
RAAAH!! THIS WON'T STOP ME!!
BAKI (CRIK)
BAKI
WE HAVE DETER-MINA-TION!!!
OOOOOO (WHOOO)
IT'S GONNA BE LONELY.

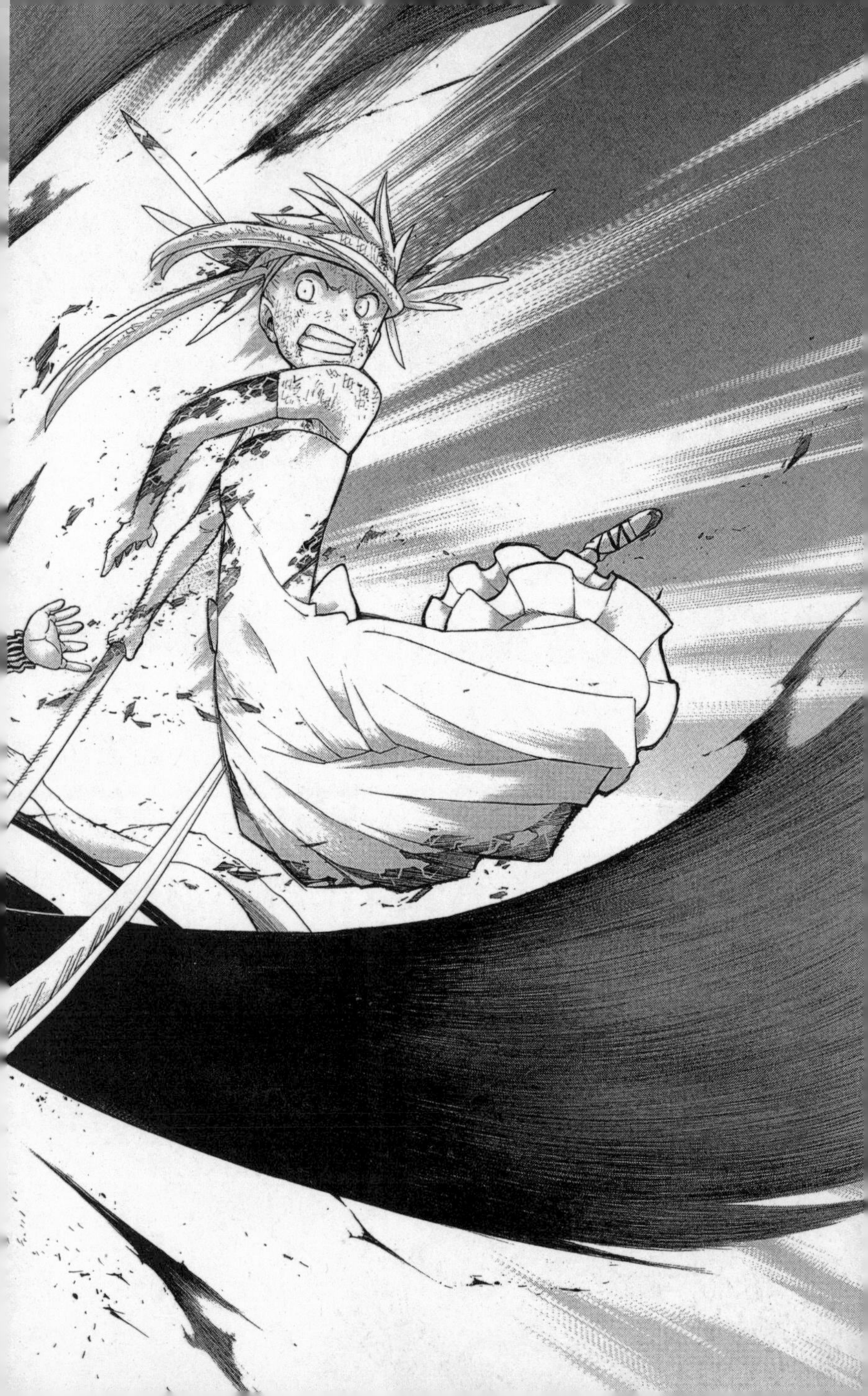

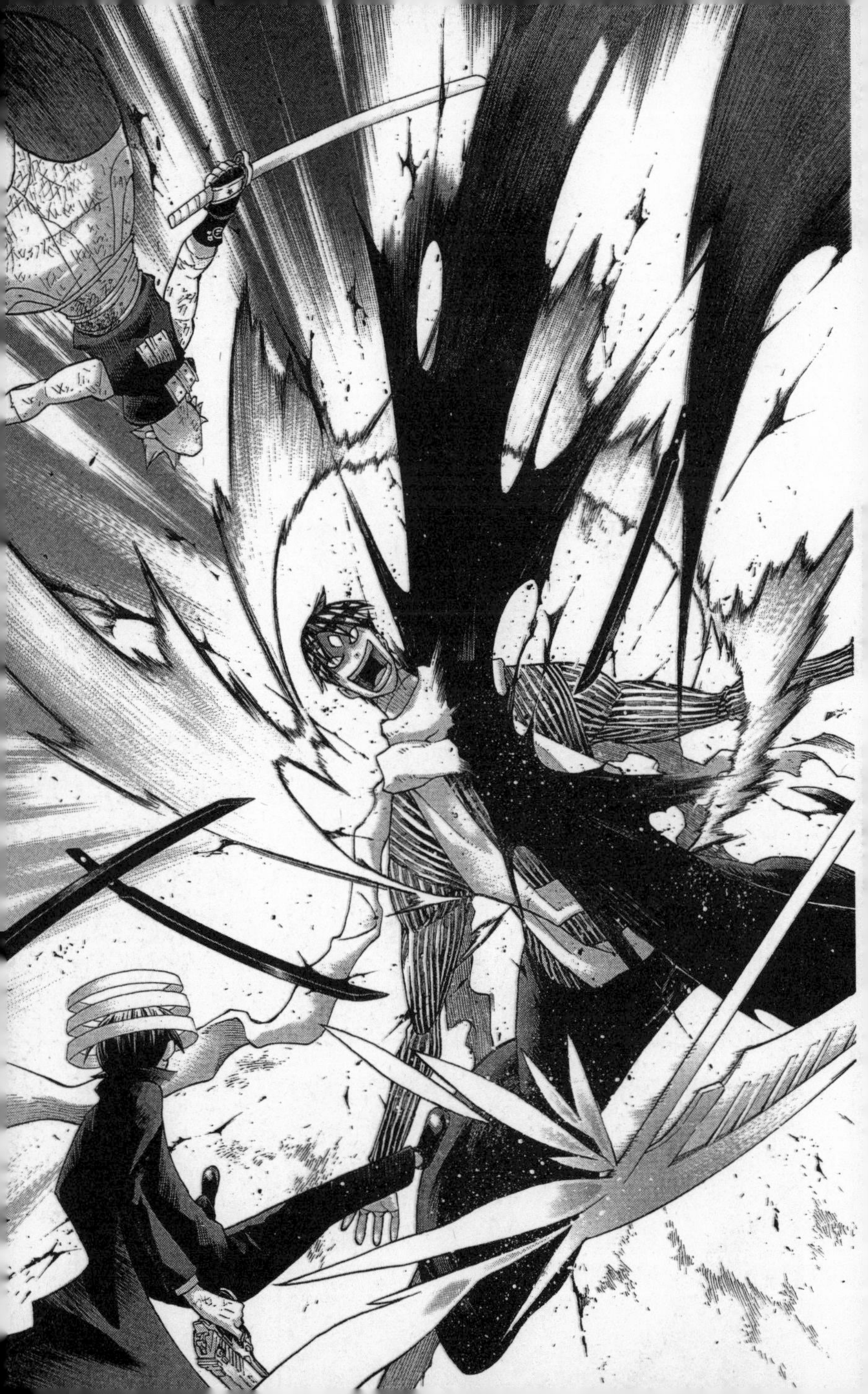

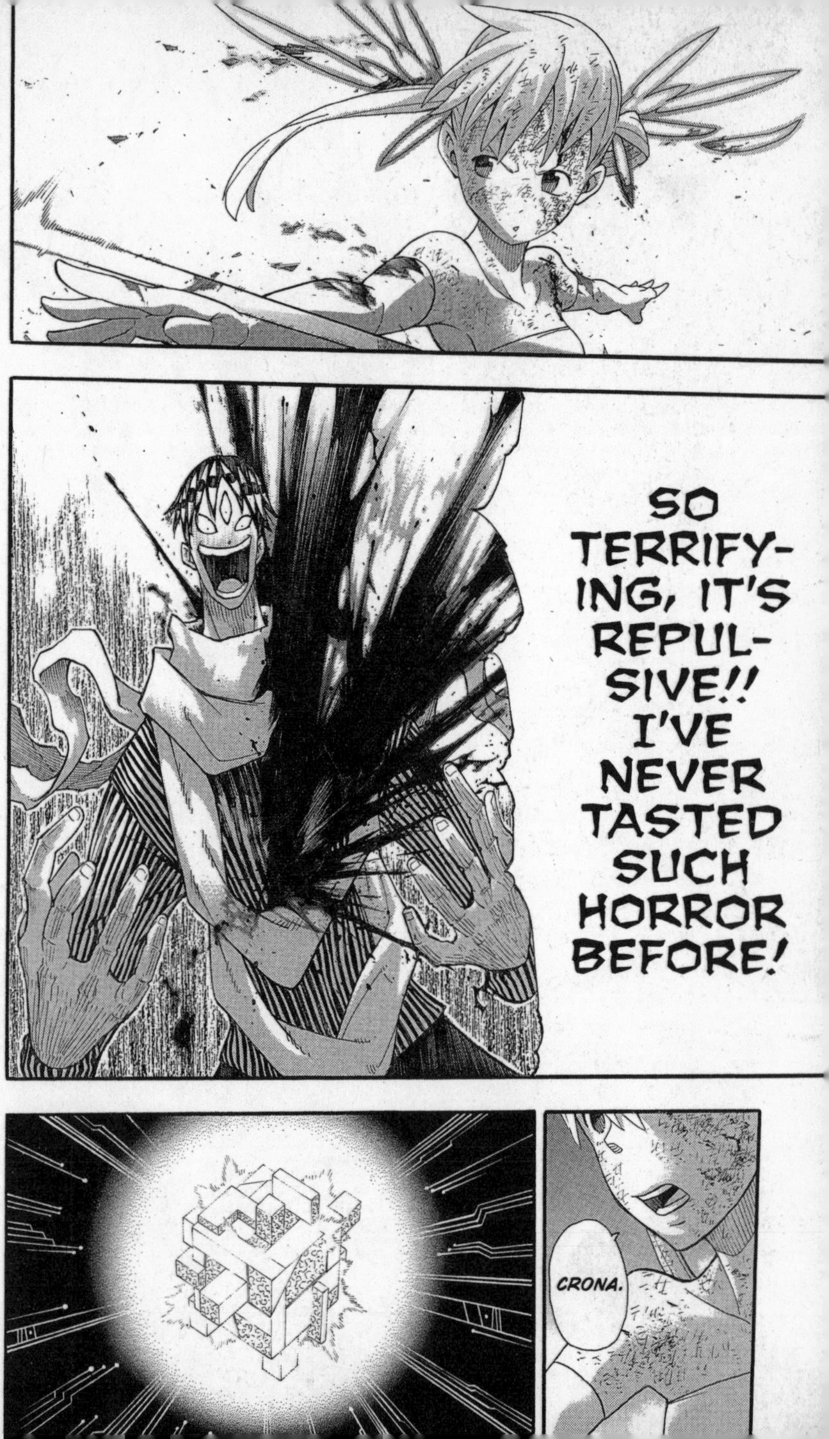
SO TERRIFYING, IT'S REPULSIVE!! I'VE NEVER TASTED SUCH HORROR BEFORE!
CRONA.

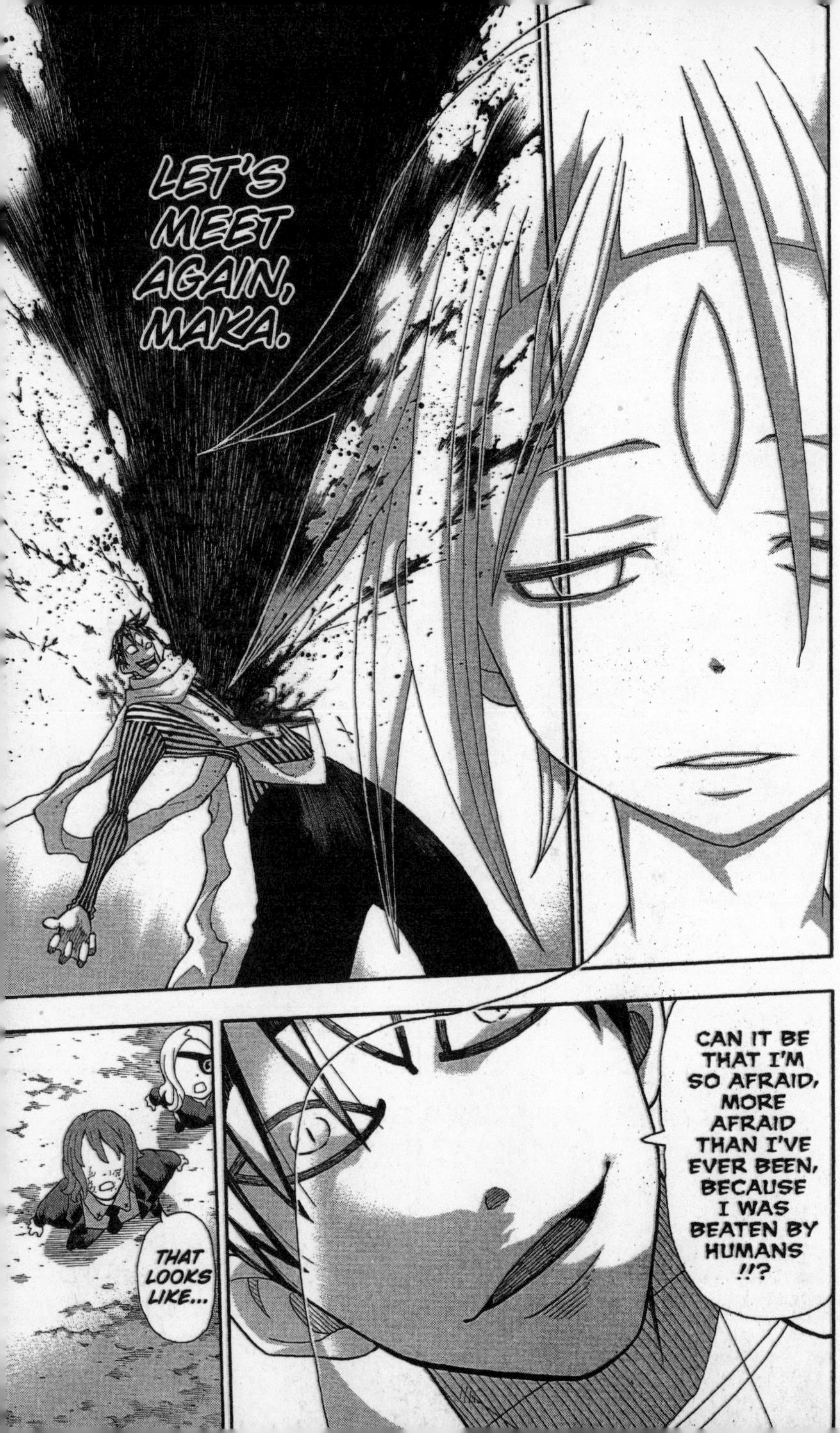
LET'S MEET AGAIN, MAKA.
CAN IT BE THAT I'M SO AFRAID, MORE AFRAID THAN I'VE EVER BEEN, BECAUSE I WAS BEATEN BY HUMANS !!?
THAT LOOKS LIKE...

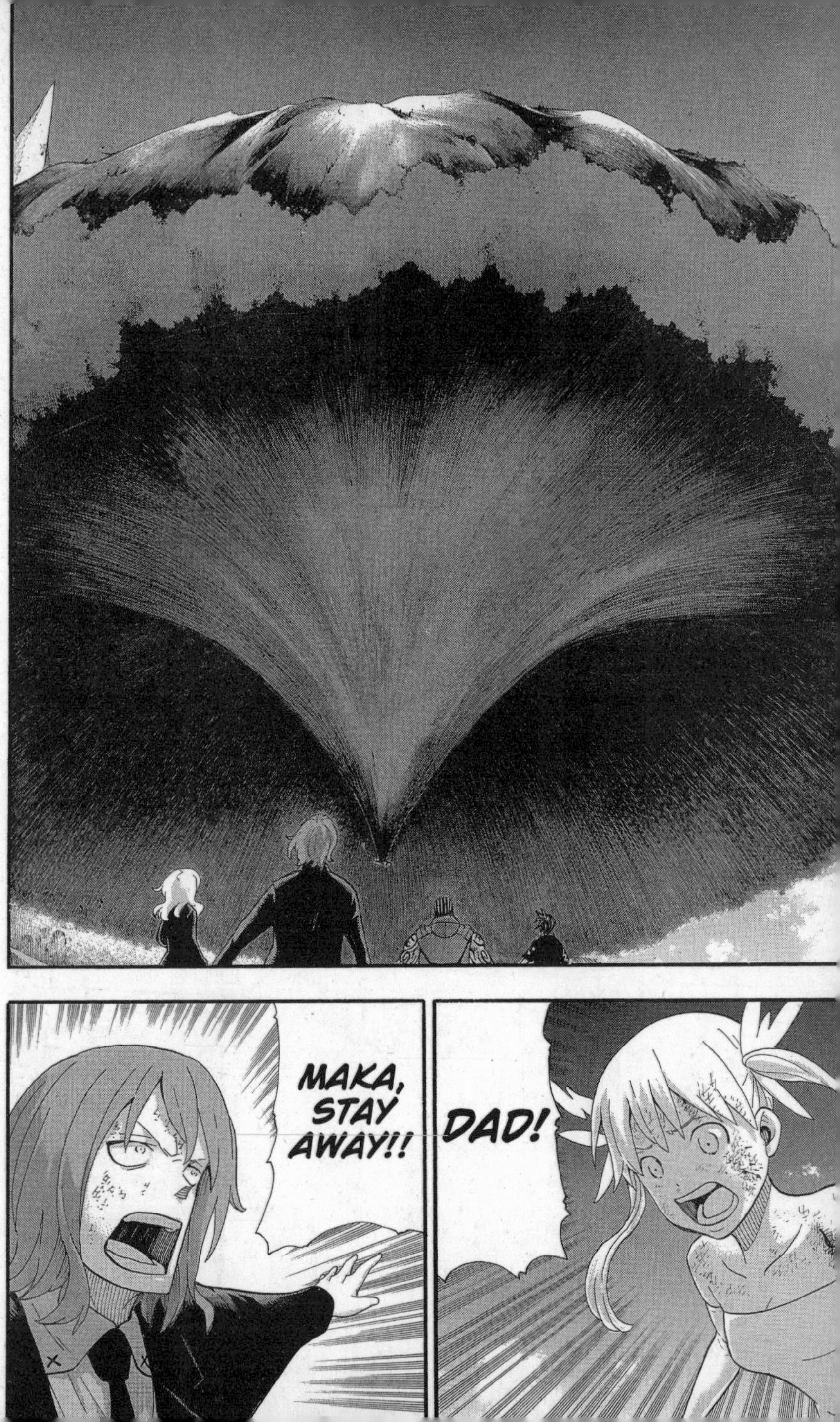
DAD!
MAKA, STAY AWAY!!

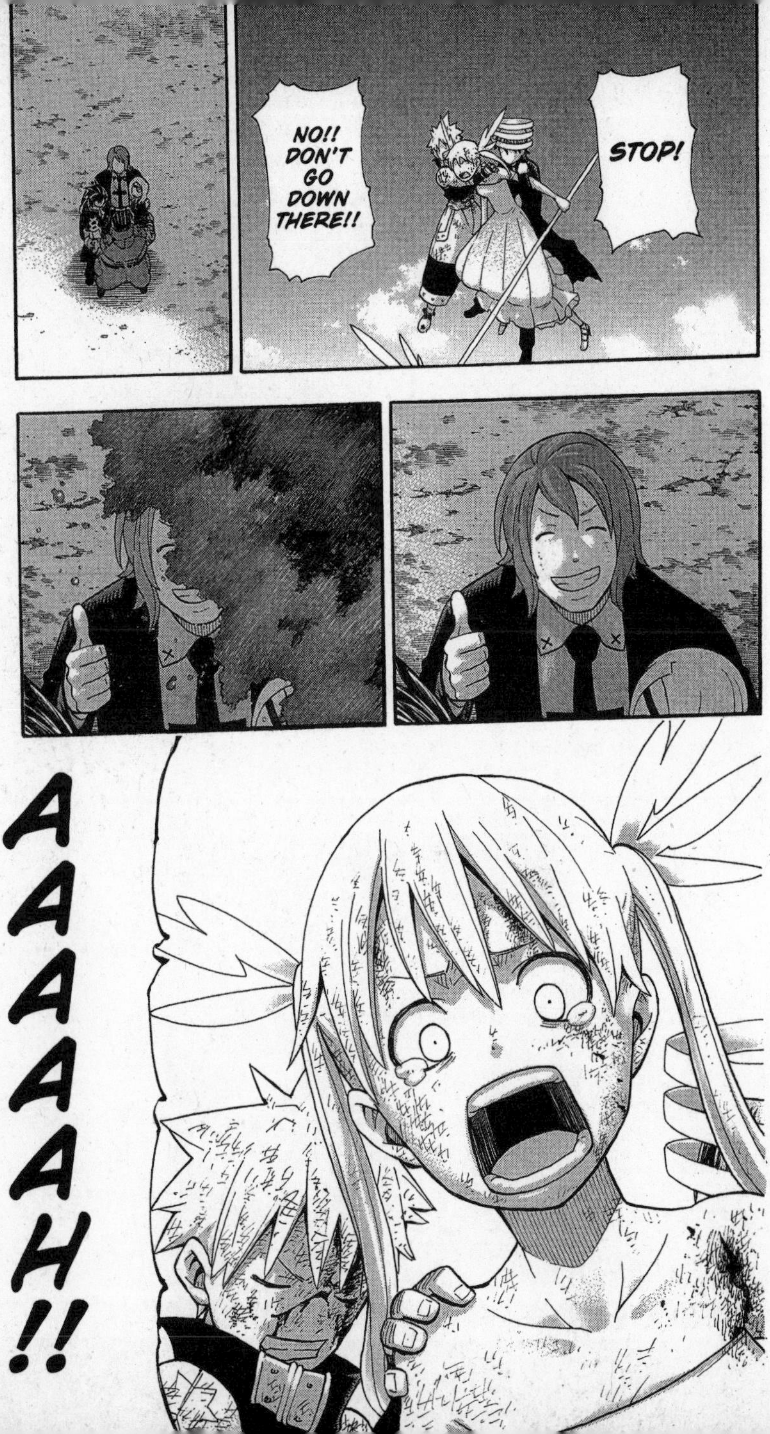
STOP!
NO!! DON'T GO DOWN THERE!!
AAAAAAH!!

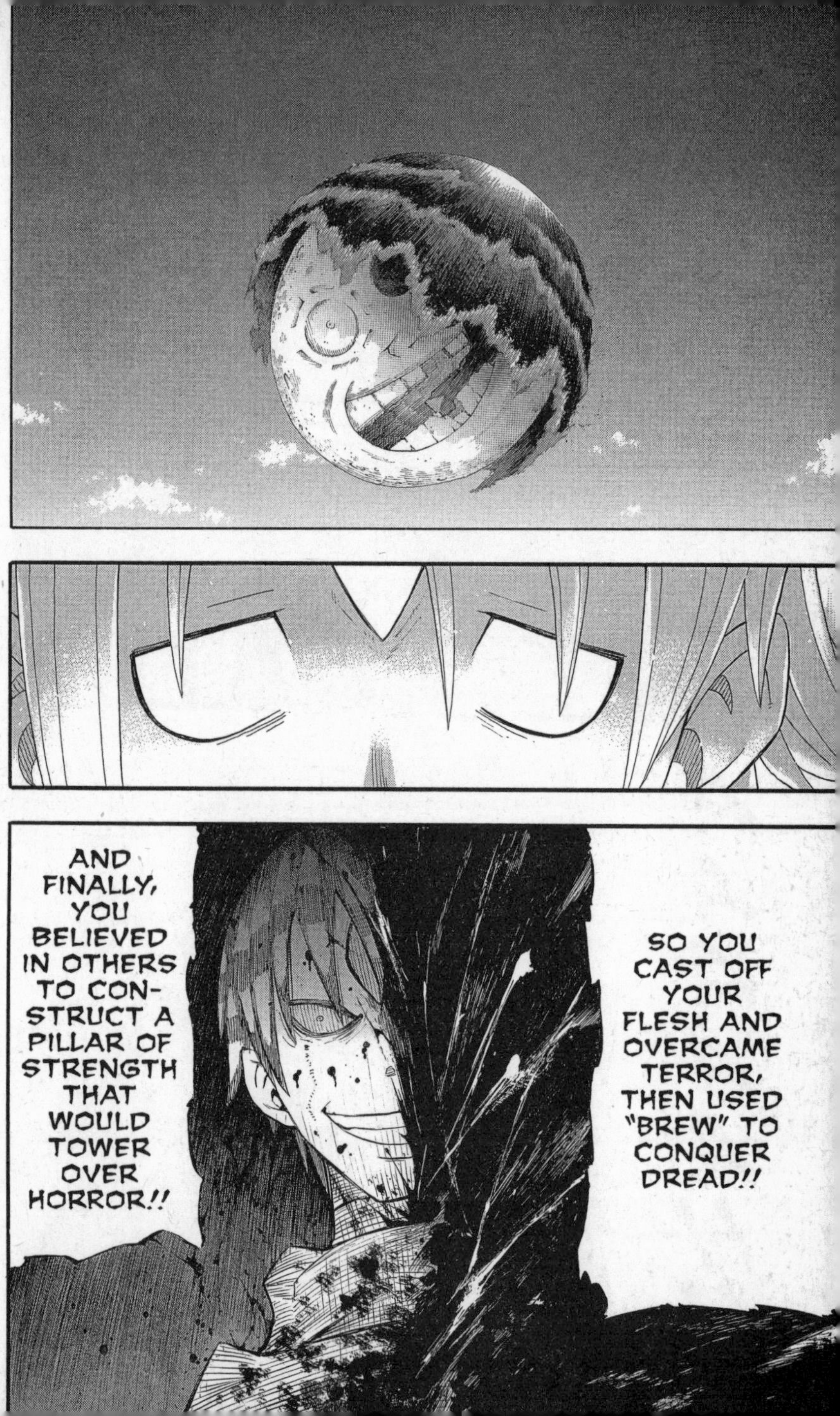
SO YOU CAST OFF YOUR FLESH AND OVERCAME TERROR, THEN USED "BREW" TO CONQUER DREAD!!
AND FINALLY, YOU BELIEVED IN OTHERS TO CONSTRUCT A PILLAR OF STRENGTH THAT WOULD TOWER OVER HORROR!!

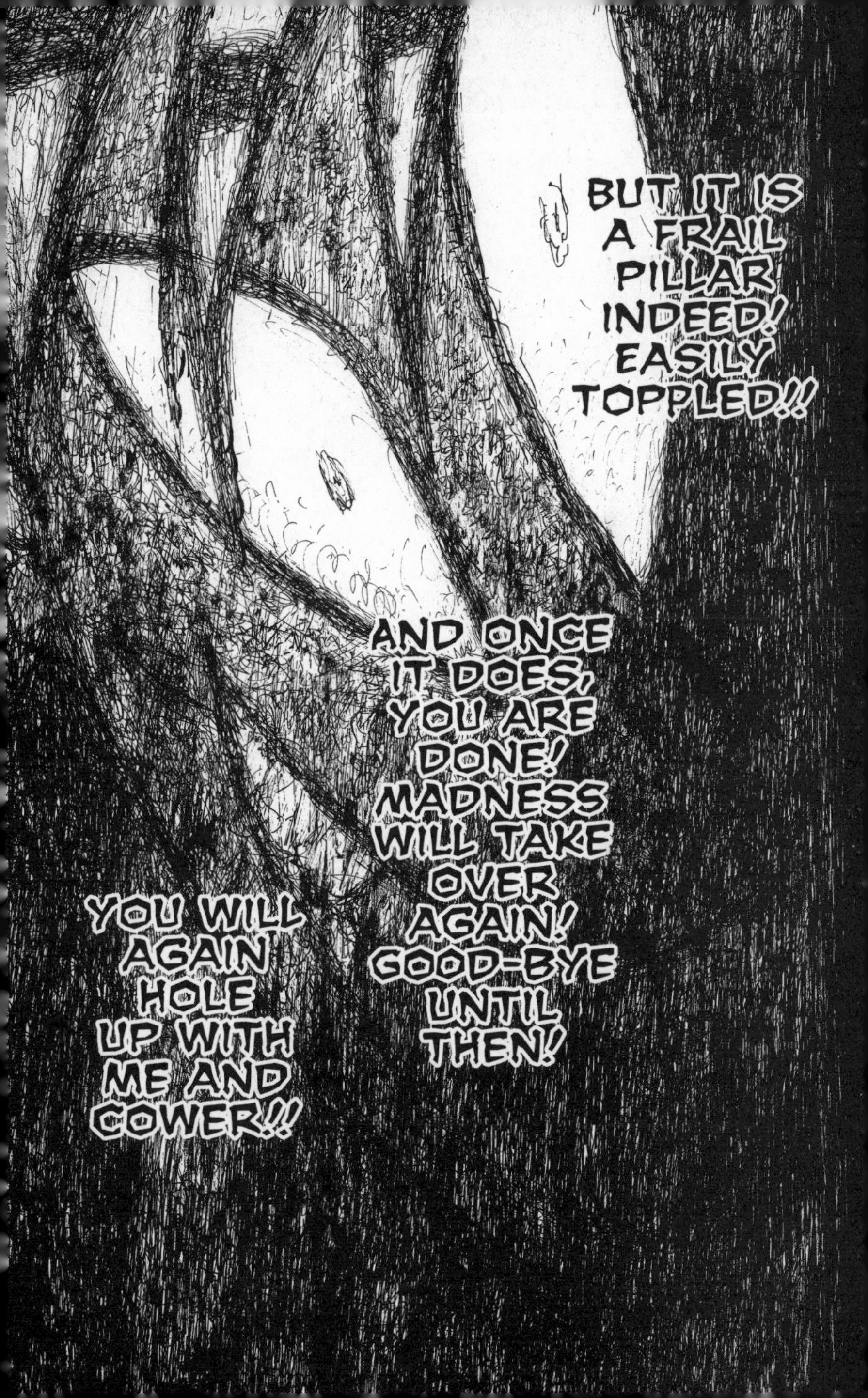
BUT IT IS A FRAIL PILLAR INDEED! EASILY TOPPLED!!
AND ONCE IT DOES, YOU ARE DONE! MADNESS WILL TAKE OVER AGAIN! GOOD-BYE UNTIL THEN!
YOU WILL AGAIN HOLE UP WITH ME AND COWER!!

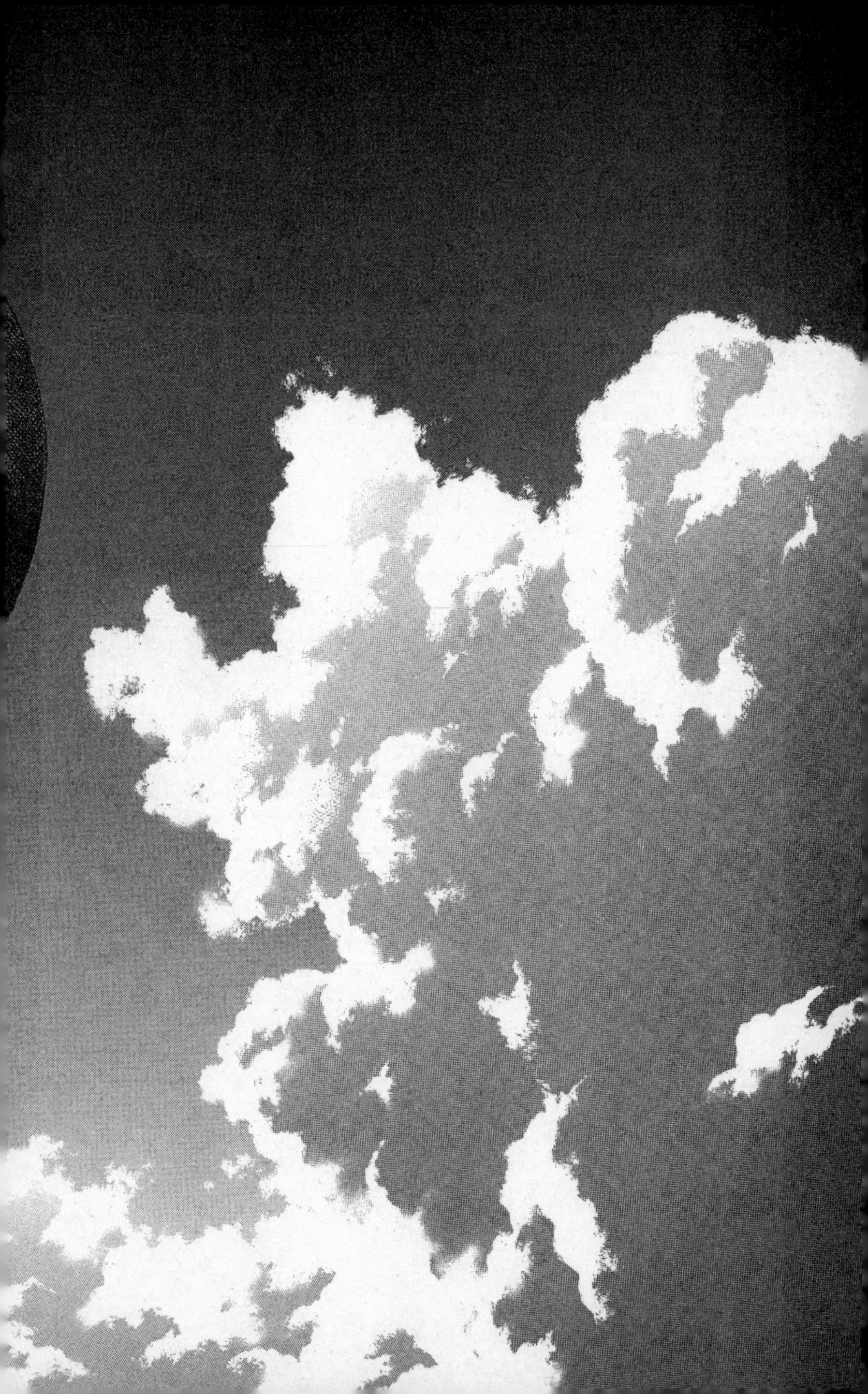

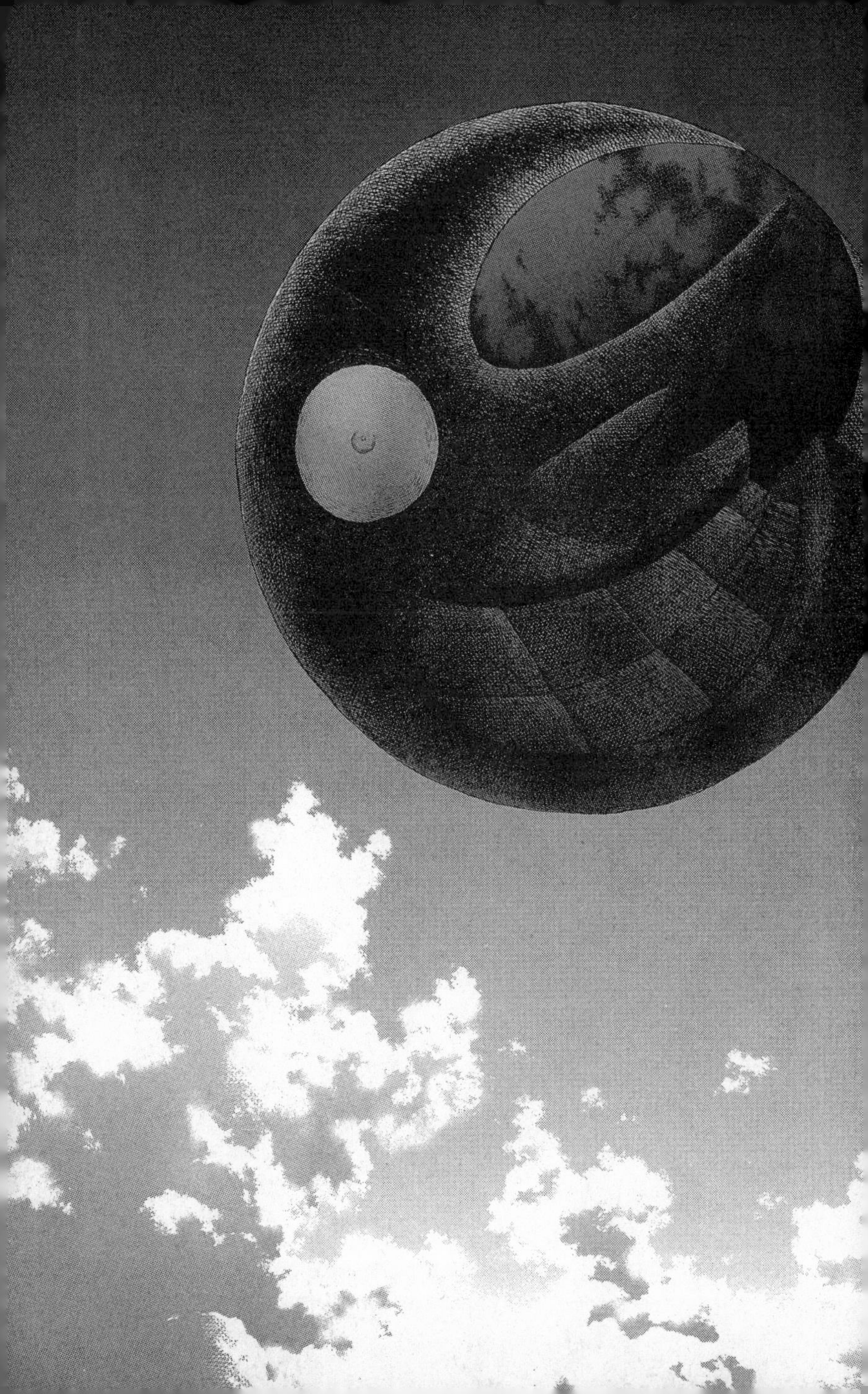

SOUL EATER

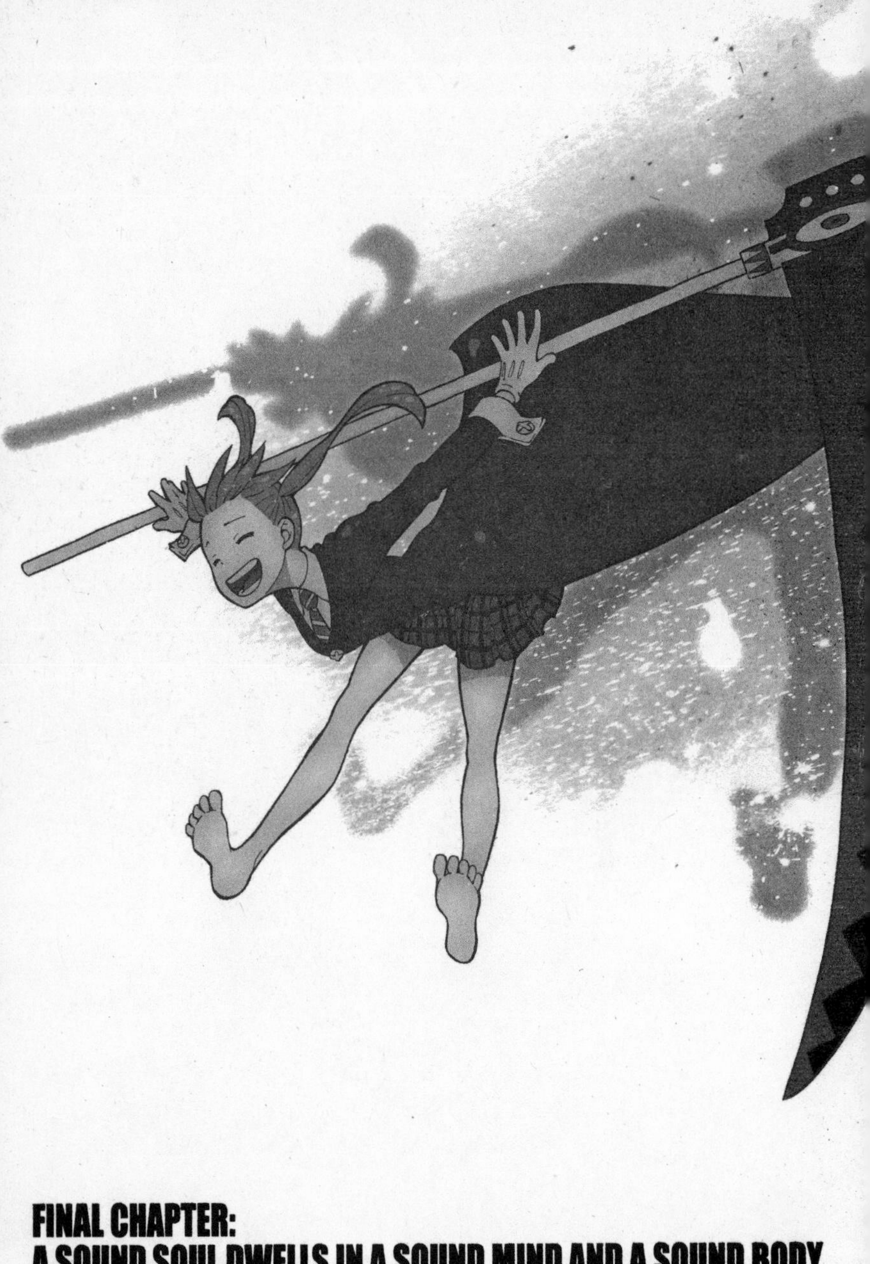

FINAL CHAPTER:
A SOUND SOUL DWELLS IN A SOUND MIND AND A SOUND BODY

SOUL EATER

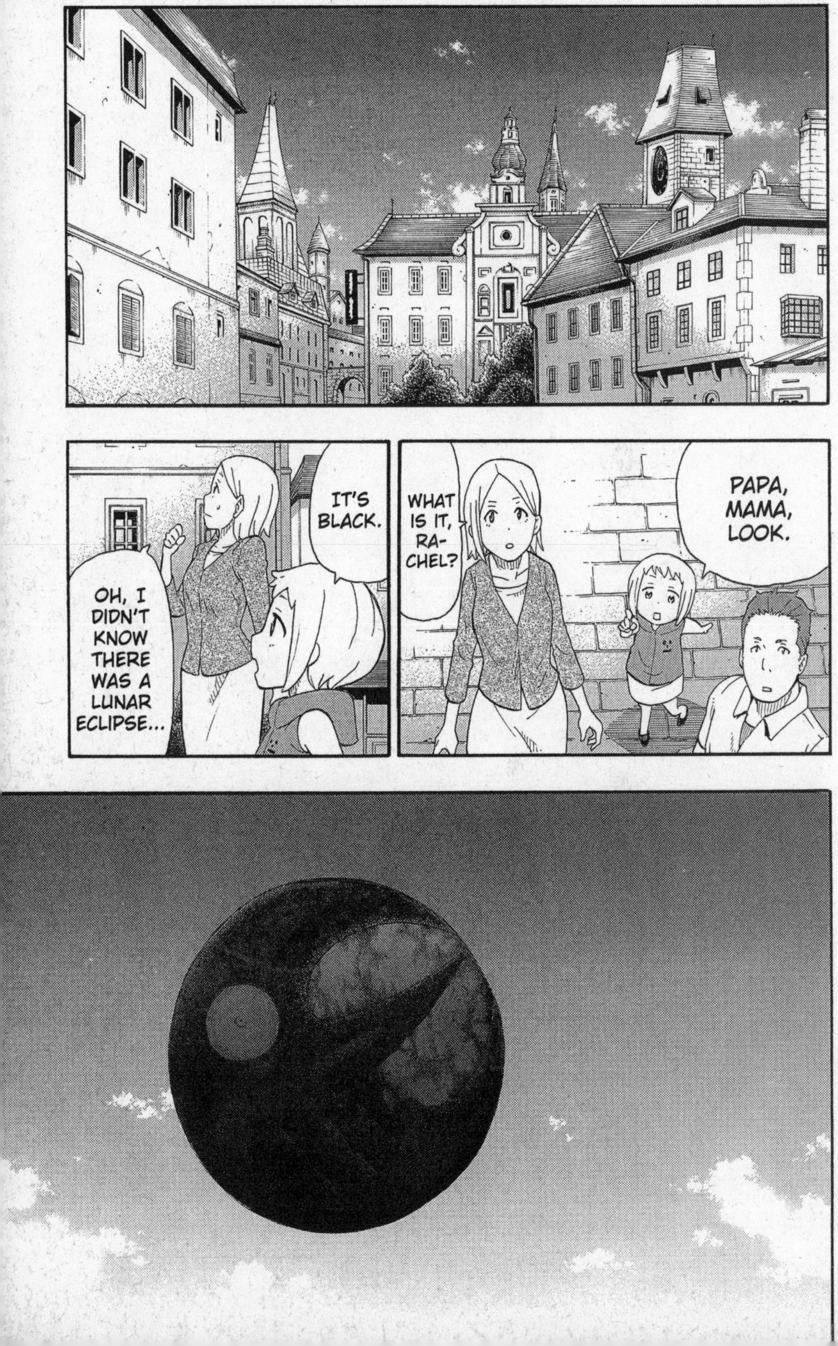
PAPA, MAMA, LOOK.
WHAT IS IT, RA-CHEL?
IT'S BLACK.
OH, I DIDN'T KNOW THERE WAS A LUNAR ECLIPSE...

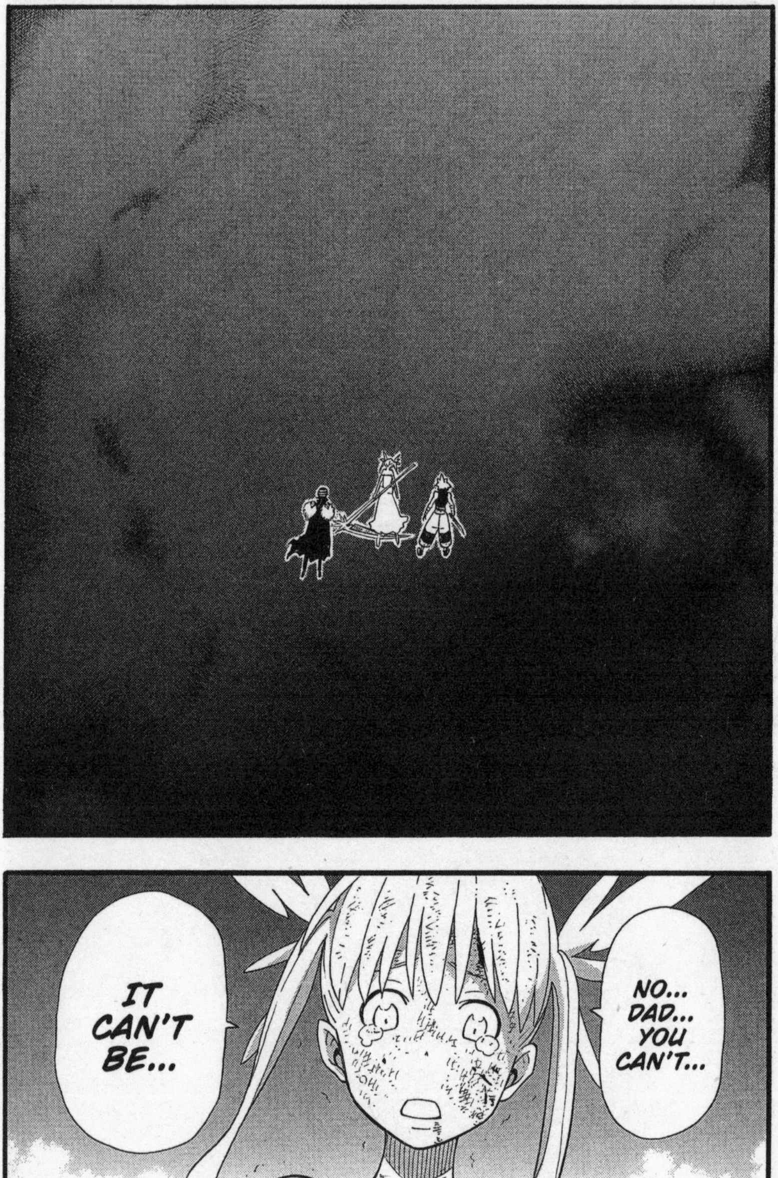
NO... DAD... YOU CAN'T...
IT CAN'T BE...

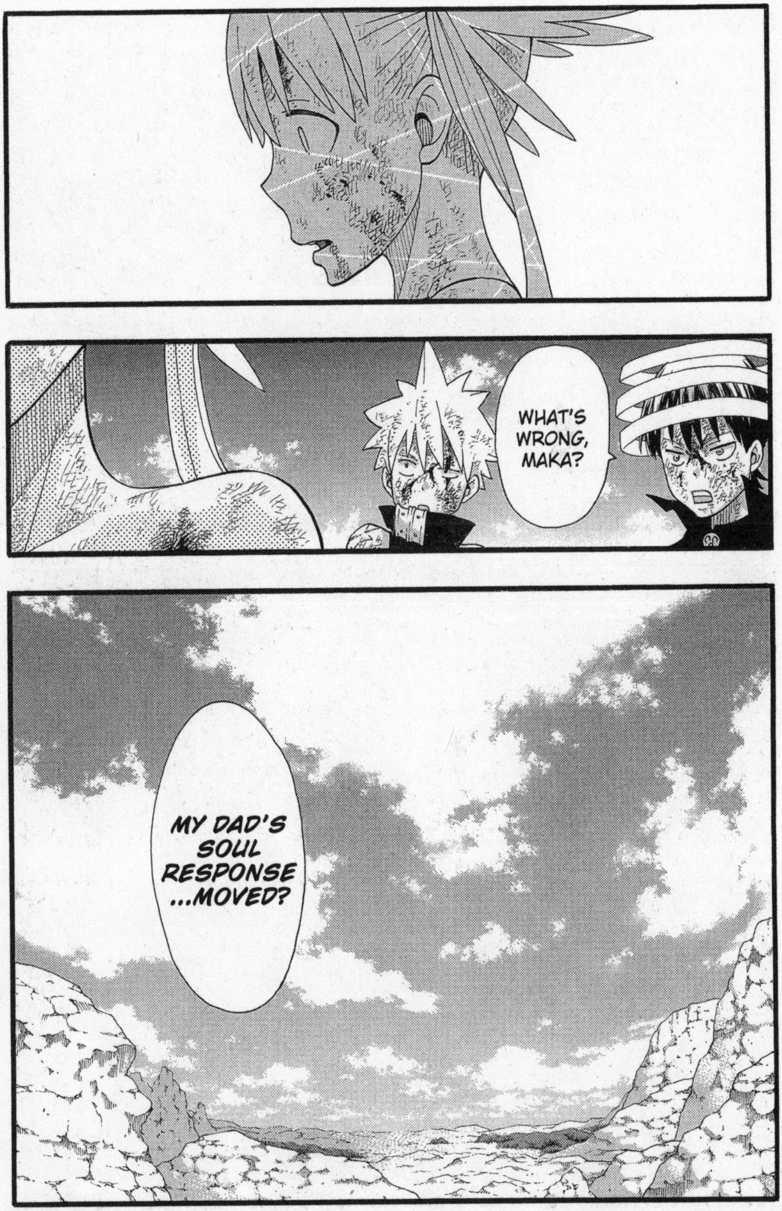
WHAT'S WRONG, MAKA?
MY DAD'S SOUL RESPONSE ...MOVED?

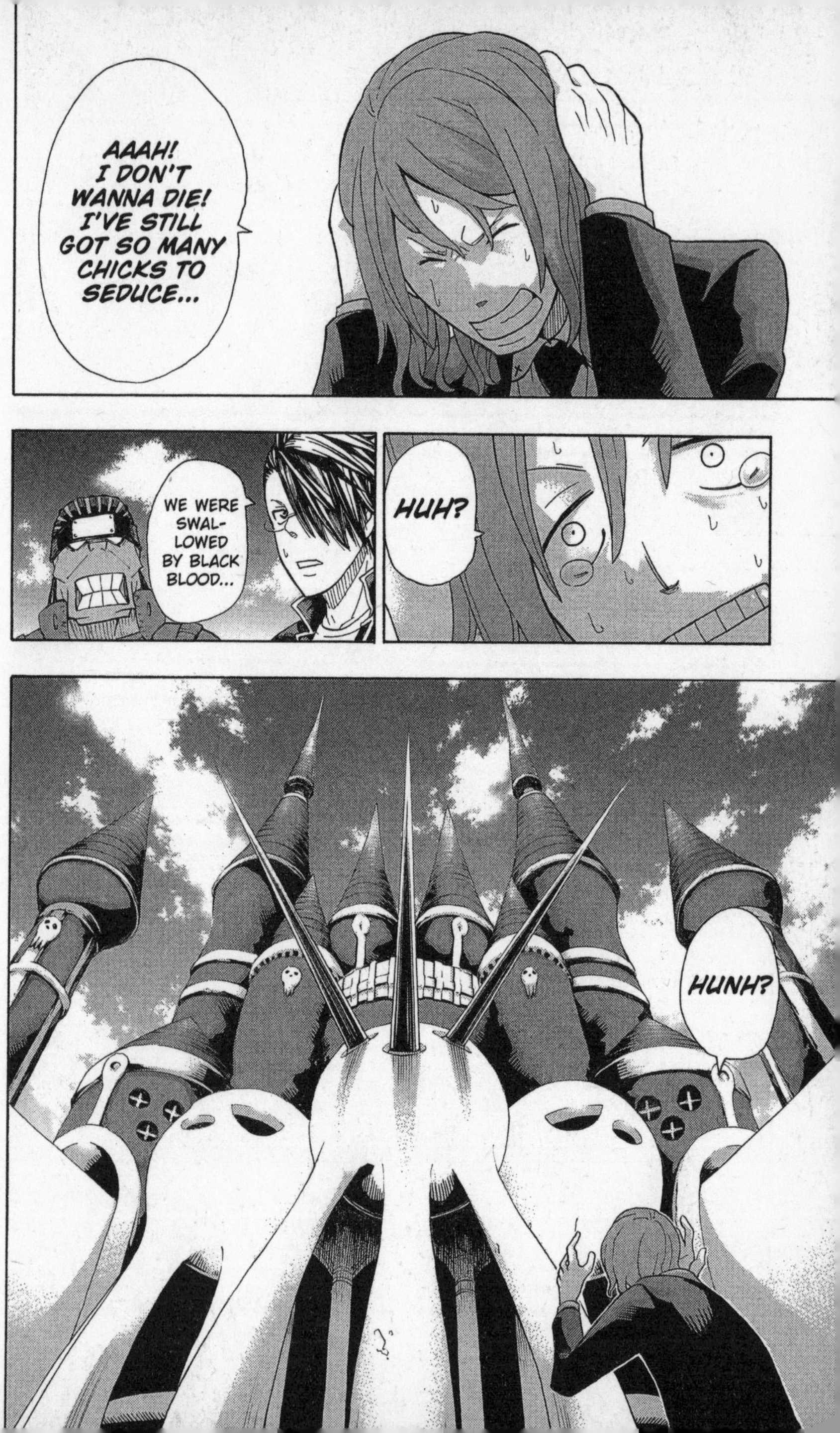
AAAH! I DON'T WANNA DIE! I'VE STILL GOT SO MANY CHICKS TO SEDUCE...
HUH?
WE WERE SWAL-LOWED BY BLACK BLOOD...
HUNH?

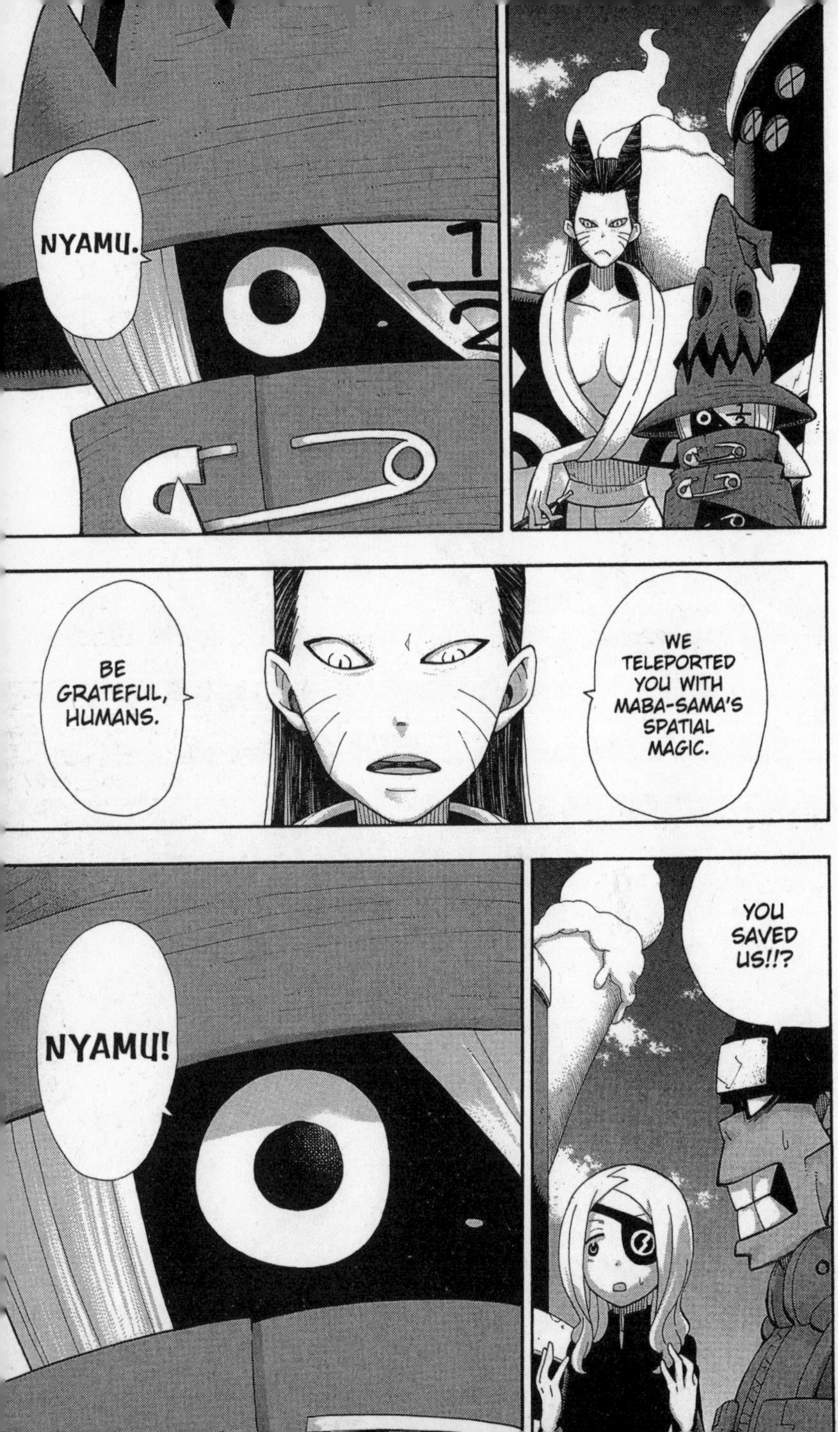
NYAMU.
WE TELEPORTED YOU WITH MABA-SAMA'S SPATIAL MAGIC.
BE GRATEFUL, HUMANS.
YOU SAVED US!!?
NYAMU!

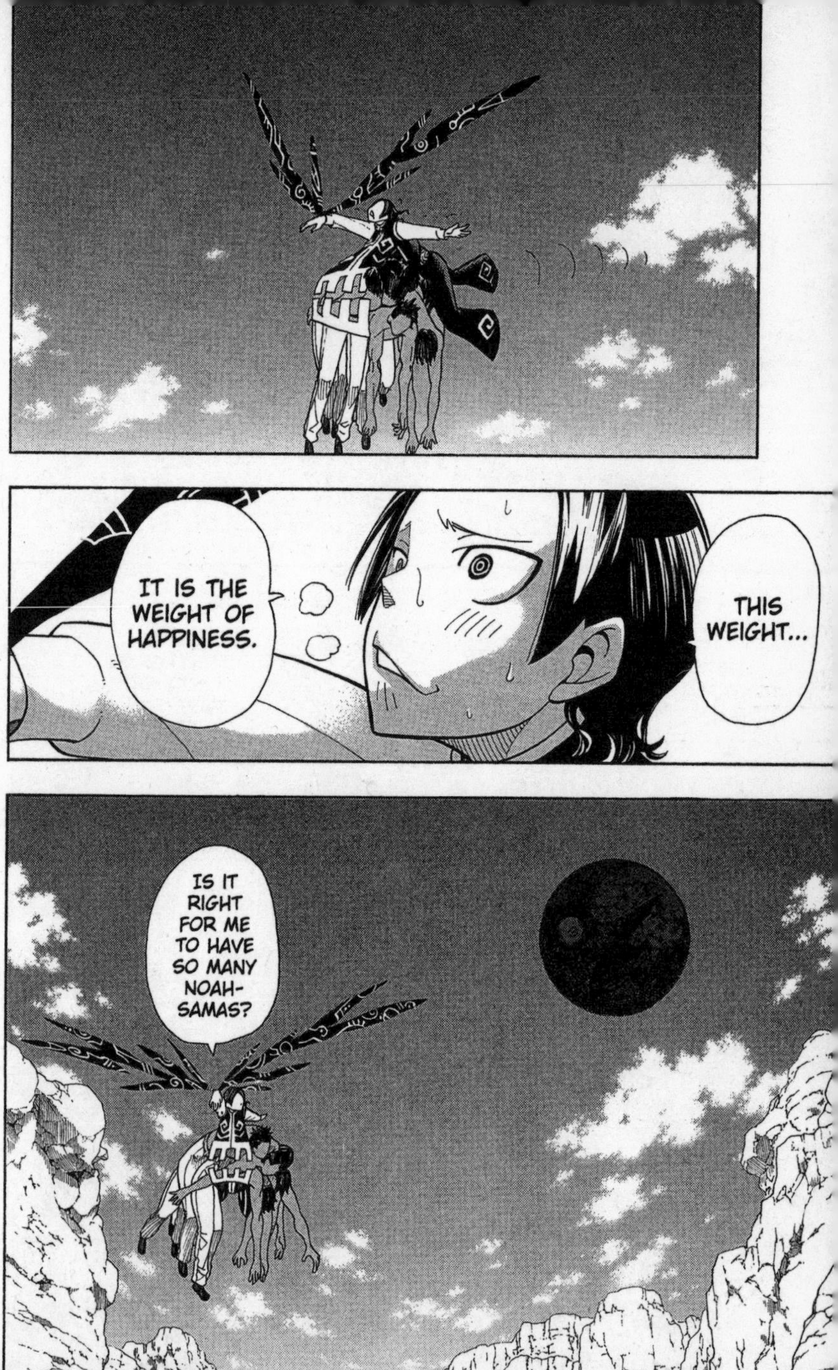
THIS WEIGHT...
IT IS THE WEIGHT OF HAPPINESS.
IS IT RIGHT FOR ME TO HAVE SO MANY NOAH-SAMAS?

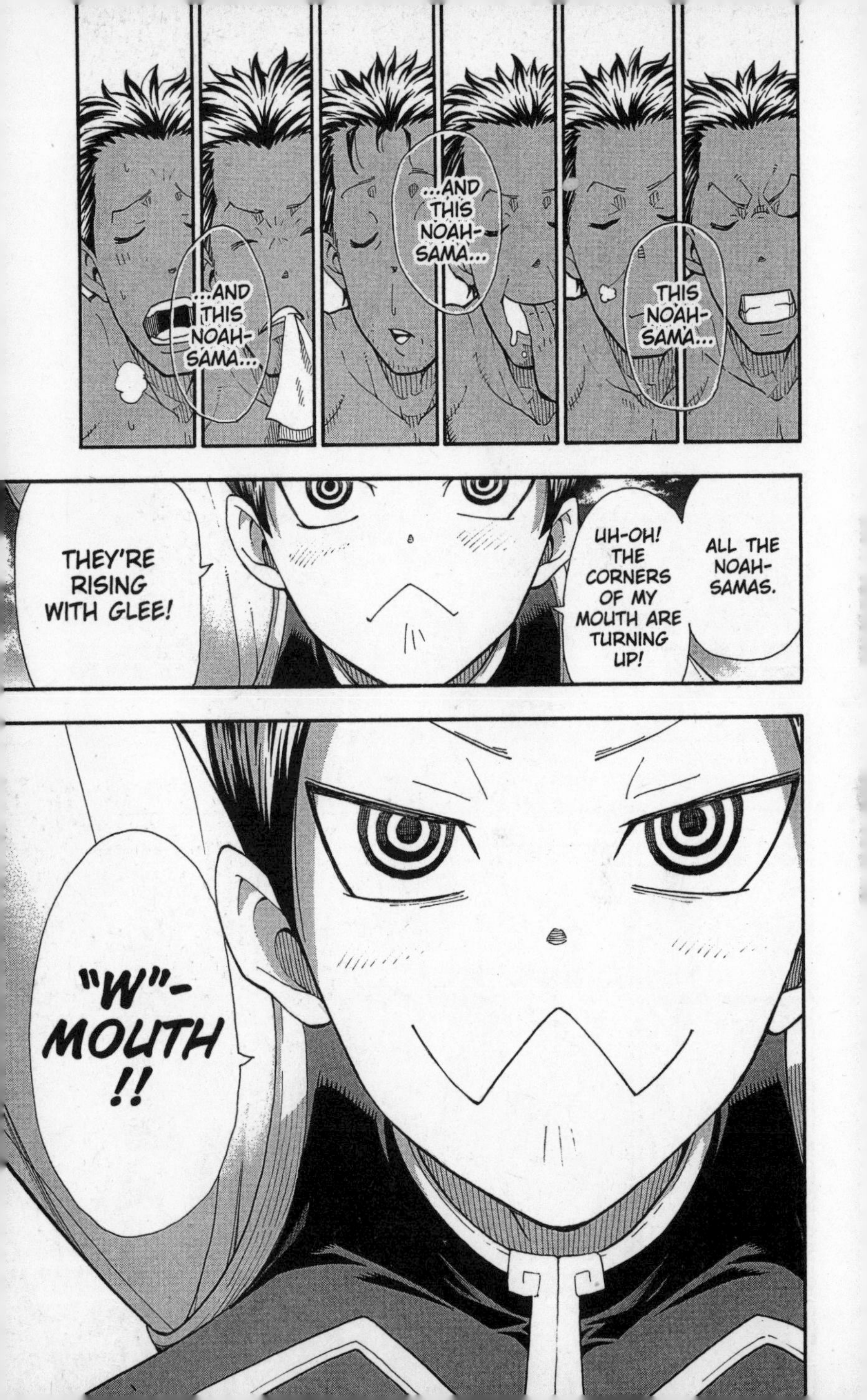

THIS NOAH-SAMA...
...AND THIS NOAH-SAMA...
...AND THIS NOAH-SAMA...
ALL THE NOAH-SAMAS.
UH-OH! THE CORNERS OF MY MOUTH ARE TURNING UP!
THEY'RE RISING WITH GLEE!
"W"-MOUTH!!

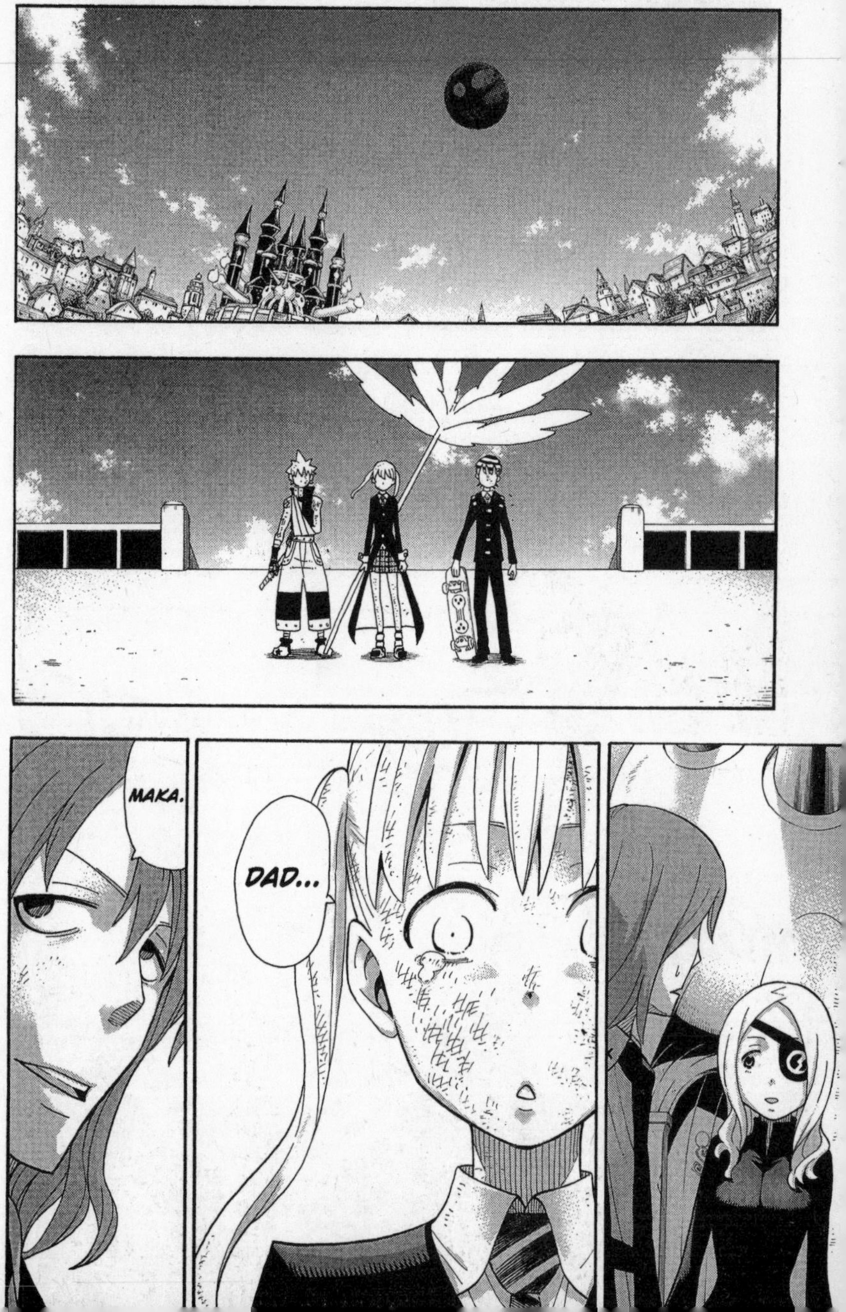
DAD...
MAKA.

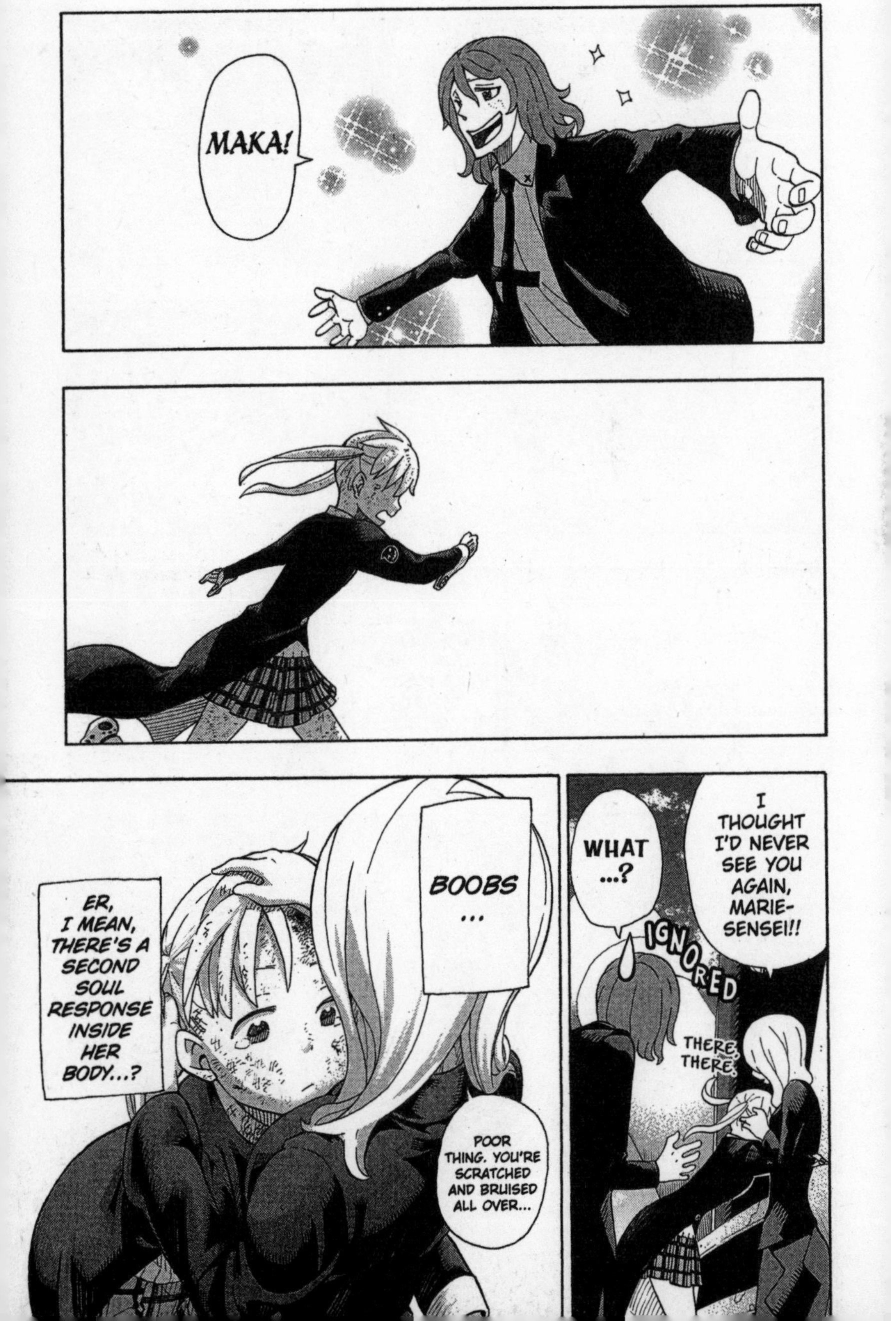
MAKA!
I THOUGHT I'D NEVER SEE YOU AGAIN, MARIE-SENSEI!!
WHAT ...?
IGNORED
THERE, THERE.
BOOBS ...
ER, I MEAN, THERE'S A SECOND SOUL RESPONSE INSIDE HER BODY...?
POOR THING. YOU'RE SCRATCHED AND BRUISED ALL OVER...

FA-THER?

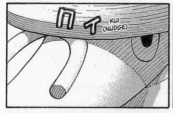
KUI (NUDGE)

WHAT DOES THIS MEAN? I DON'T FEEL HIS WAVE-LENGTH ANYMORE...

HE'S DEAD, YOU FOOL!

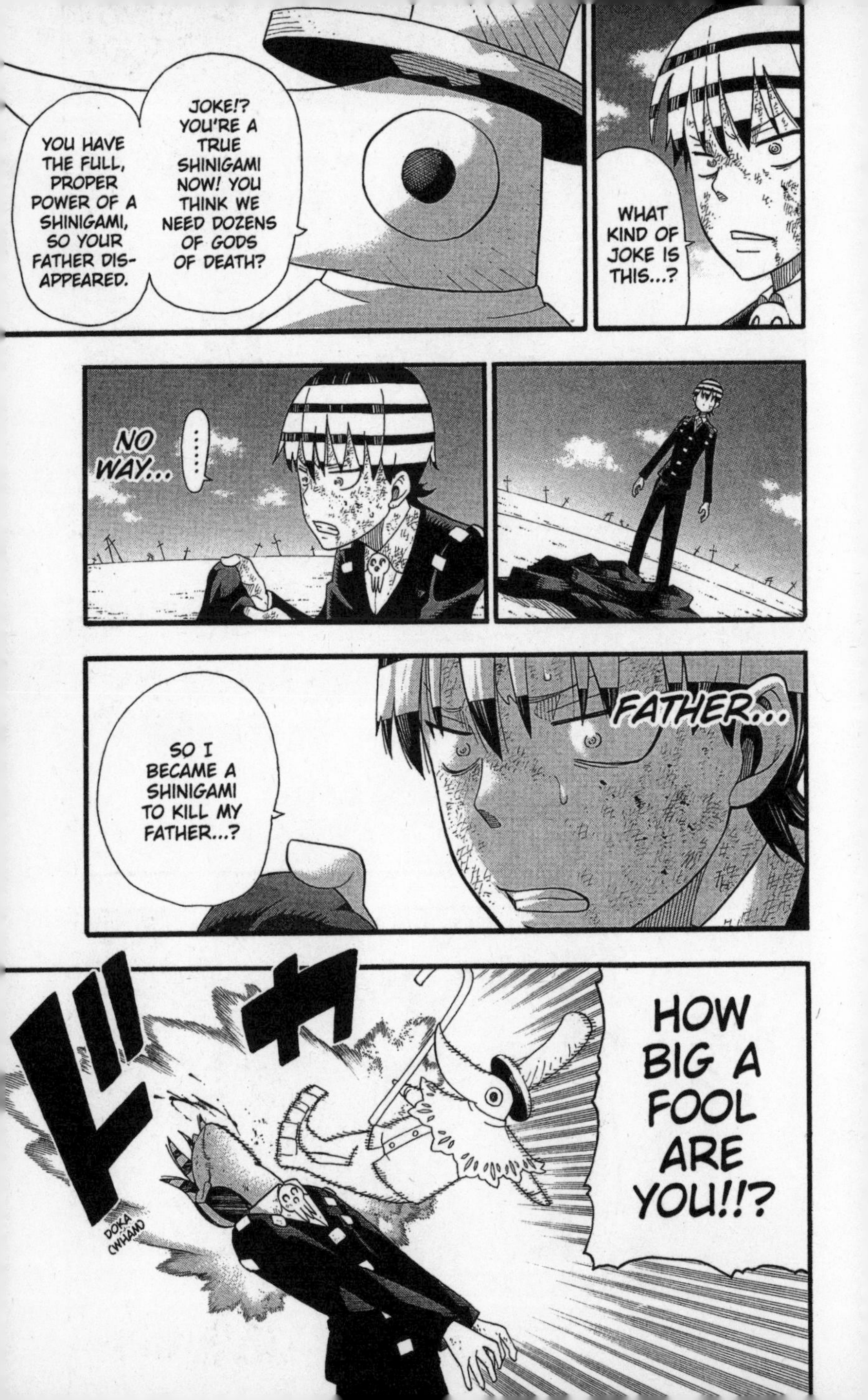
WHAT KIND OF JOKE IS THIS...?
JOKE!? YOU'RE A TRUE SHINIGAMI NOW! YOU THINK WE NEED DOZENS OF GODS OF DEATH?
YOU HAVE THE FULL, PROPER POWER OF A SHINIGAMI, SO YOUR FATHER DIS-APPEARED.
......
NO WAY...
FATHER...
SO I BECAME A SHINIGAMI TO KILL MY FATHER...?
HOW BIG A FOOL ARE YOU!!?
DOKA
WHAM

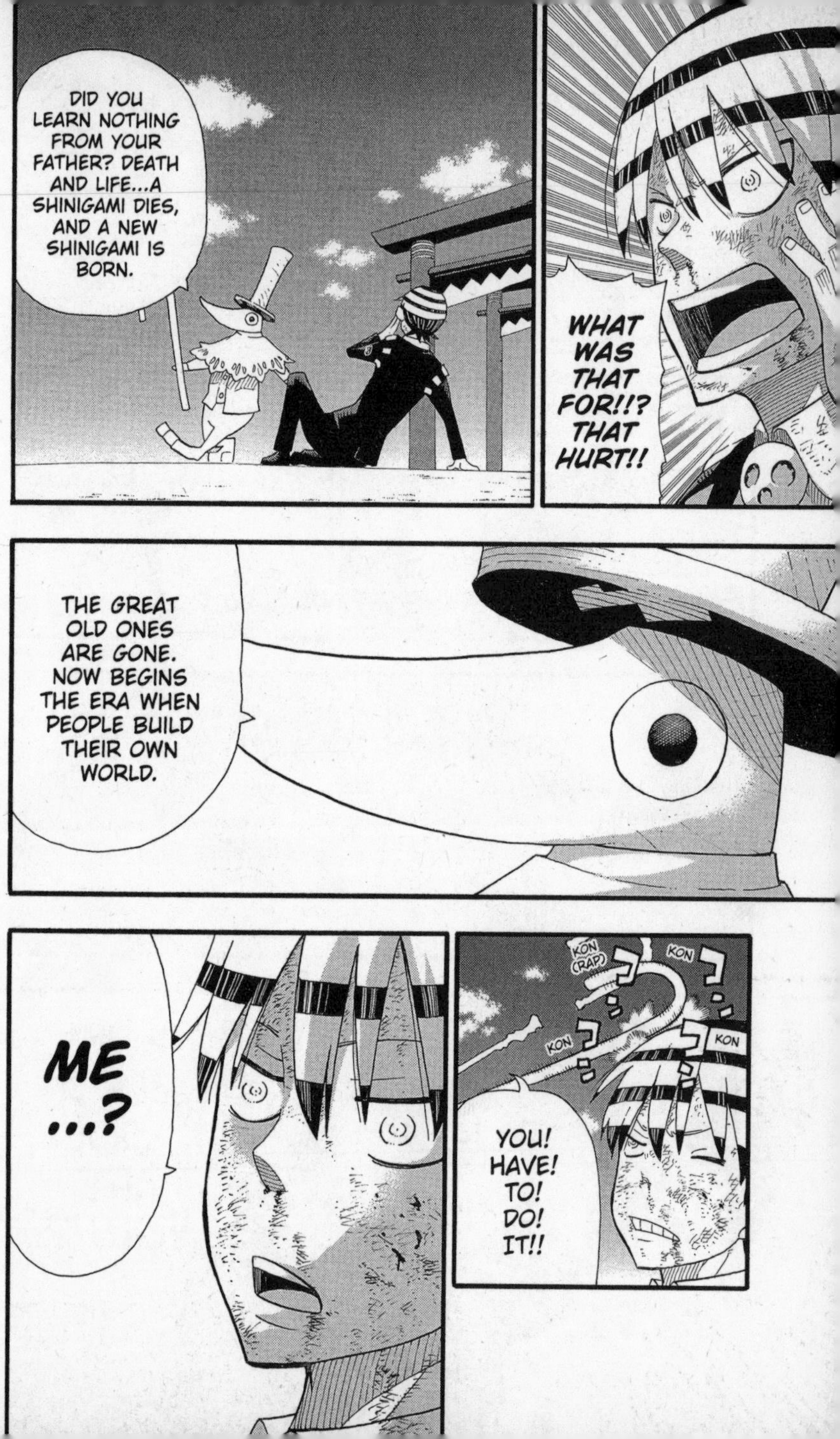
WHAT WAS THAT FOR!!? THAT HURT!!
DID YOU LEARN NOTHING FROM YOUR FATHER? DEATH AND LIFE...A SHINIGAMI DIES, AND A NEW SHINIGAMI IS BORN.
THE GREAT OLD ONES ARE GONE. NOW BEGINS THE ERA WHEN PEOPLE BUILD THEIR OWN WORLD.
KON
KON (RAP)
KON
KON
YOU! HAVE! TO! DO! IT!!
ME ...?

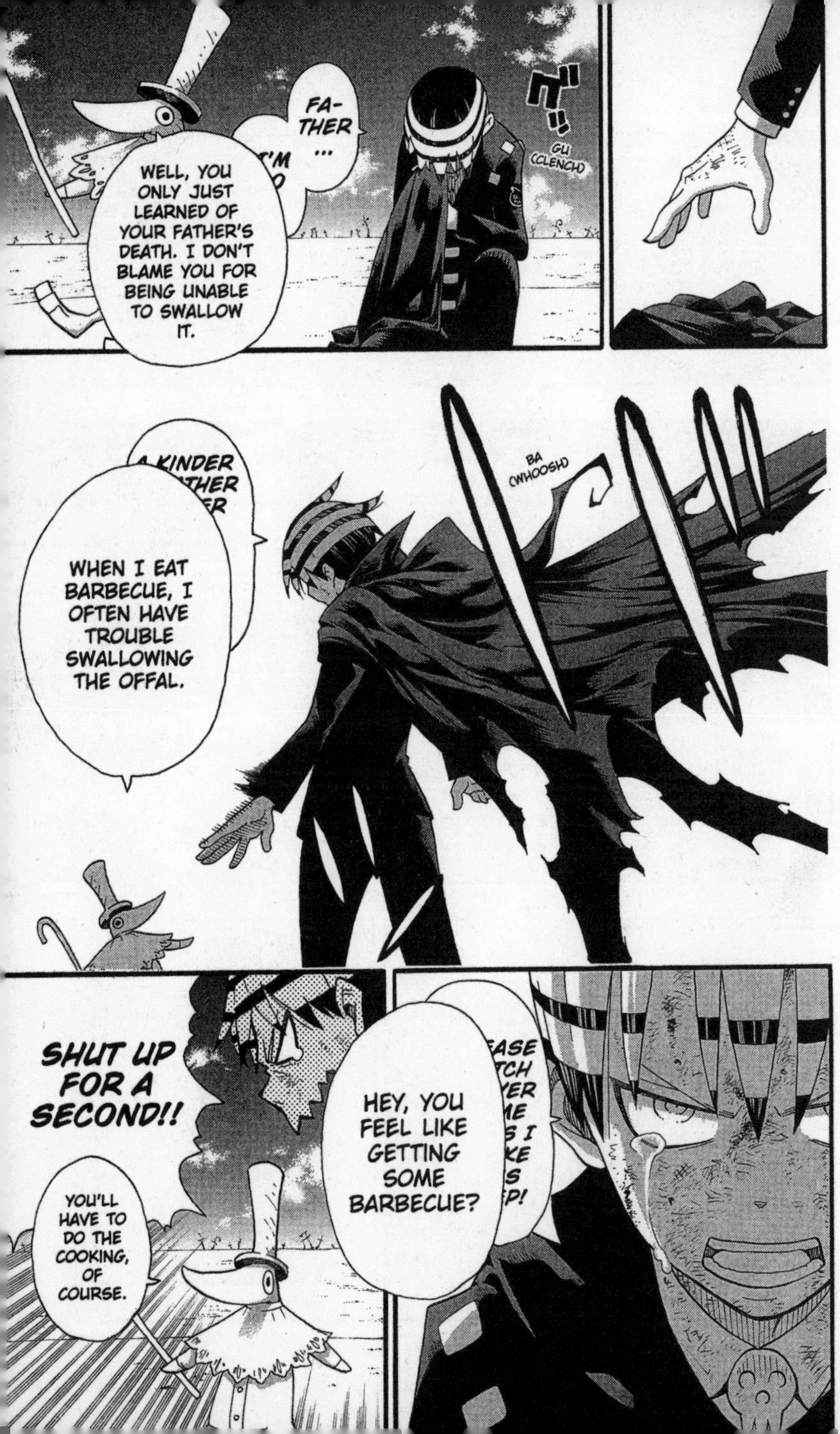
GU (CLENCH)
FA-THER ...
WELL, YOU ONLY JUST LEARNED OF YOUR FATHER'S DEATH. I DON'T BLAME YOU FOR BEING UNABLE TO SWALLOW IT.
BA (WHOOSH)
WHEN I EAT BARBECUE, I OFTEN HAVE TROUBLE SWALLOWING THE OFFAL.
HEY, YOU FEEL LIKE GETTING SOME BARBECUE?
SHUT UP FOR A SECOND!!
YOU'LL HAVE TO DO THE COOKING, OF COURSE.

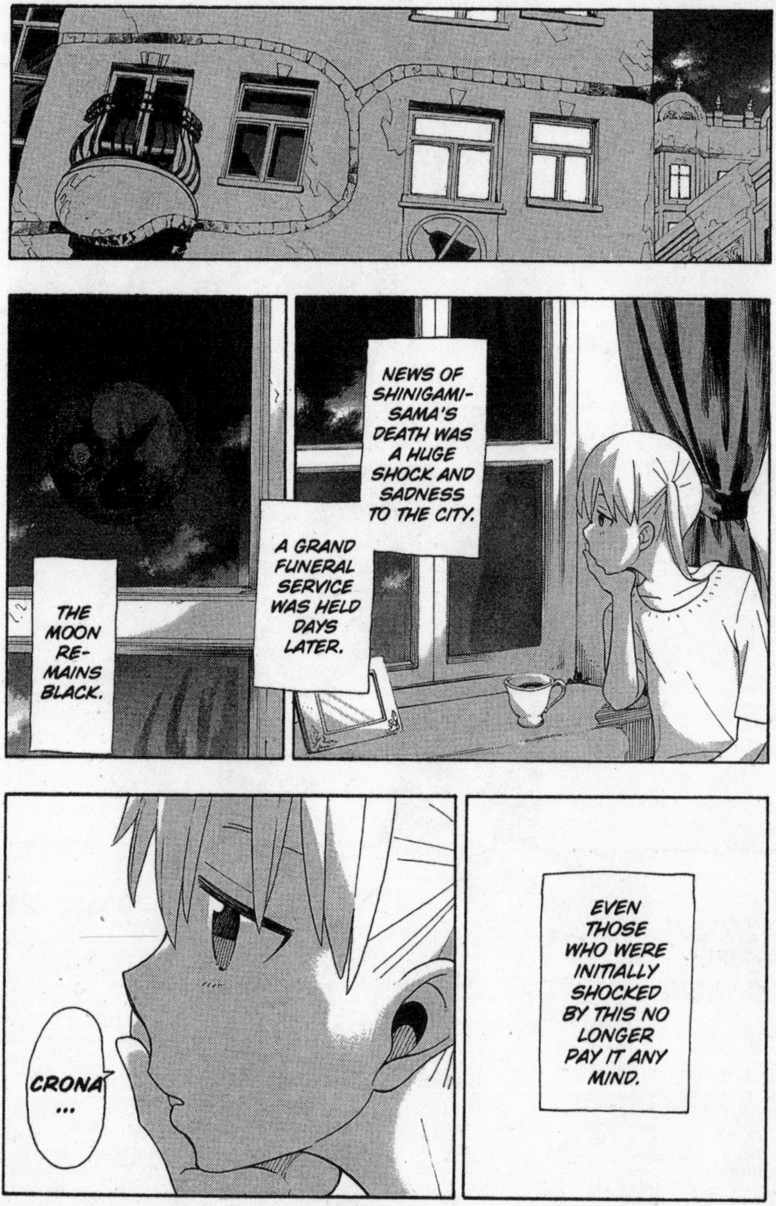
NEWS OF SHINIGAMI-SAMA'S DEATH WAS A HUGE SHOCK AND SADNESS TO THE CITY.
A GRAND FUNERAL SERVICE WAS HELD DAYS LATER.
THE MOON REMAINS BLACK.
EVEN THOSE WHO WERE INITIALLY SHOCKED BY THIS NO LONGER PAY IT ANY MIND.
CRONA...

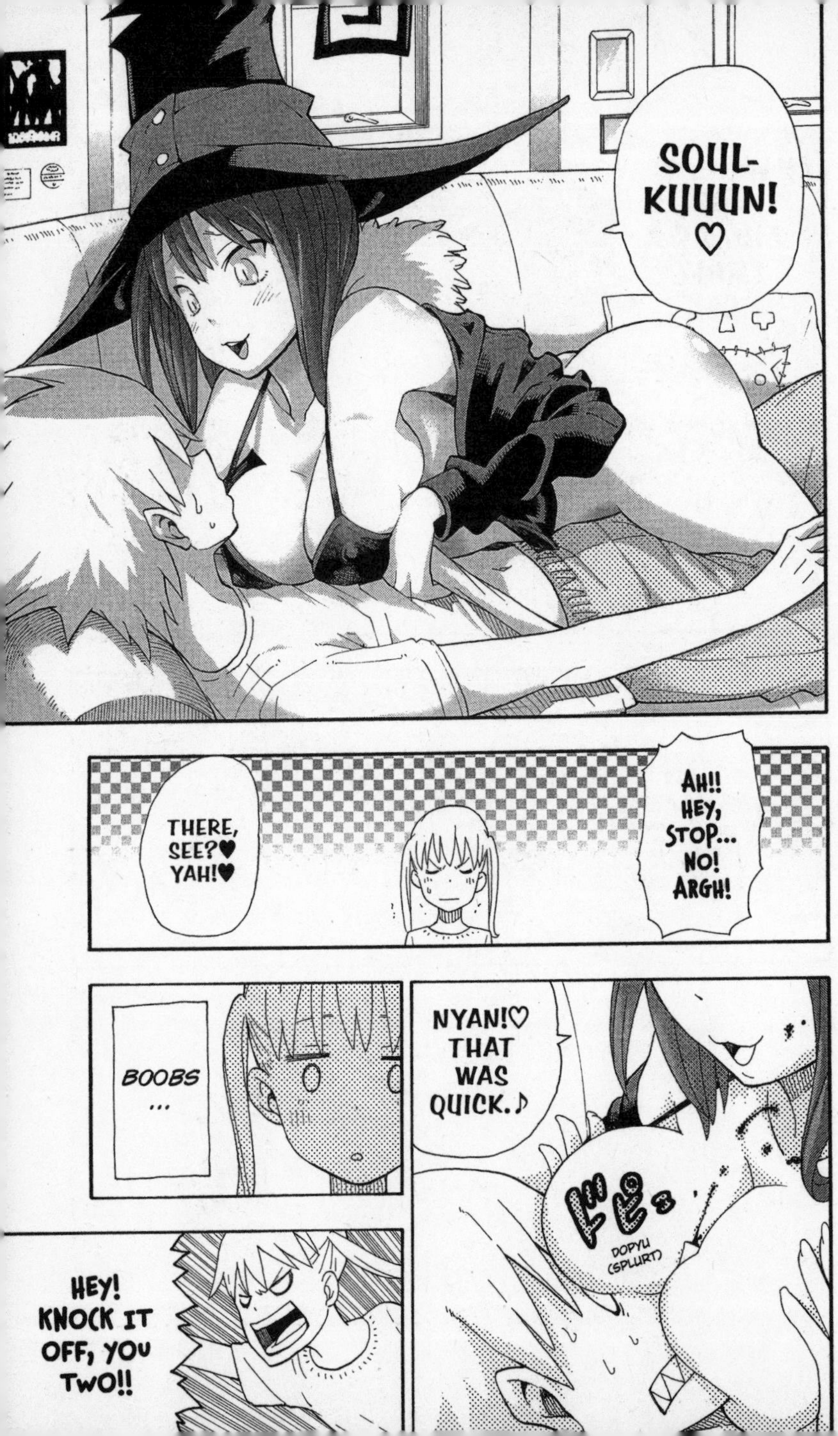
SOUL-KUUUN! ♡
AH!! HEY, STOP... NO! ARGH!
THERE, SEE?♥ YAH!♥
NYAN!♡ THAT WAS QUICK.♪
DOPYU (SPLURT)
BOOBS...
HEY! KNOCK IT OFF, YOU TWO!!

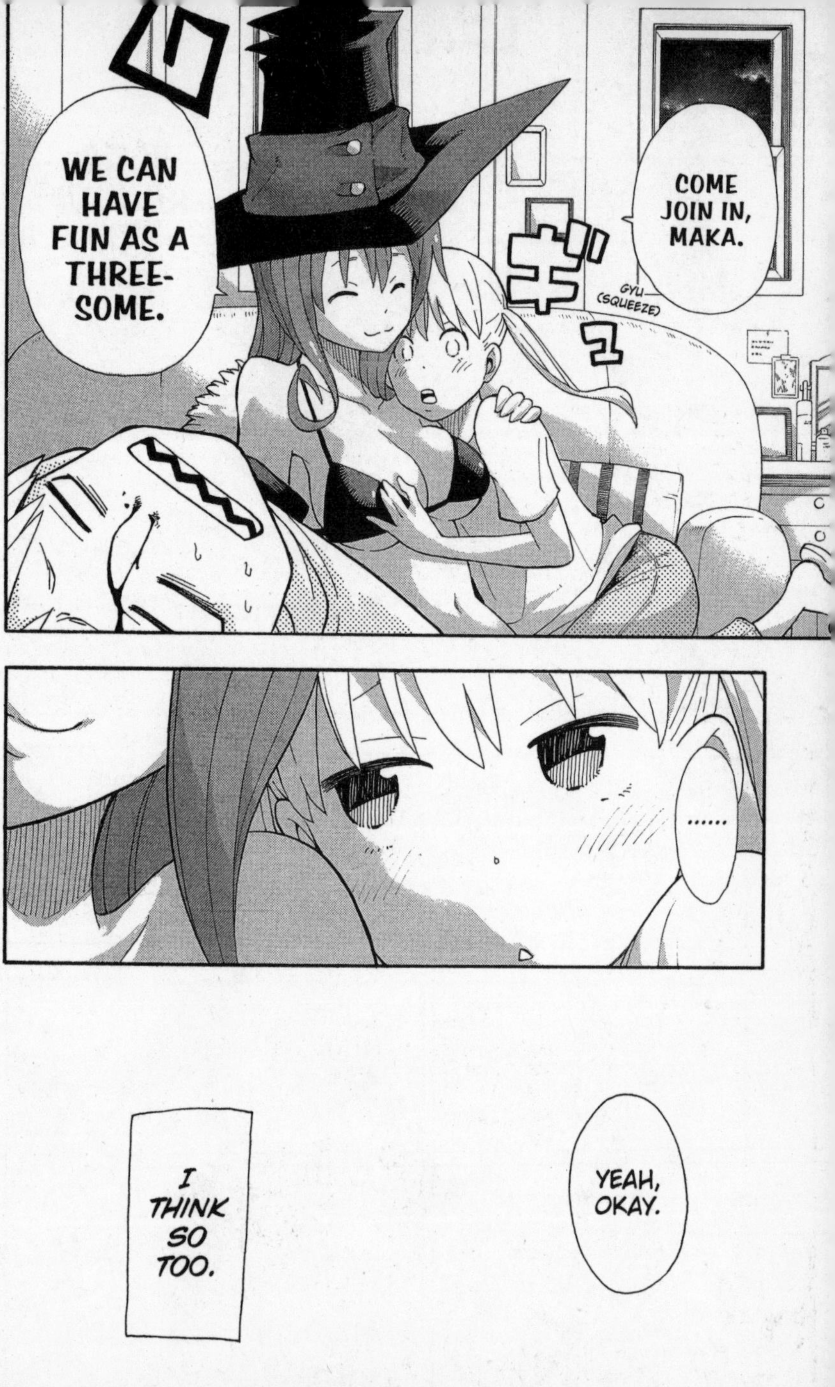
COME JOIN IN, MAKA.
GYU (SQUEEZE)
WE CAN HAVE FUN AS A THREE-SOME.
......
YEAH, OKAY.
I THINK SO TOO.

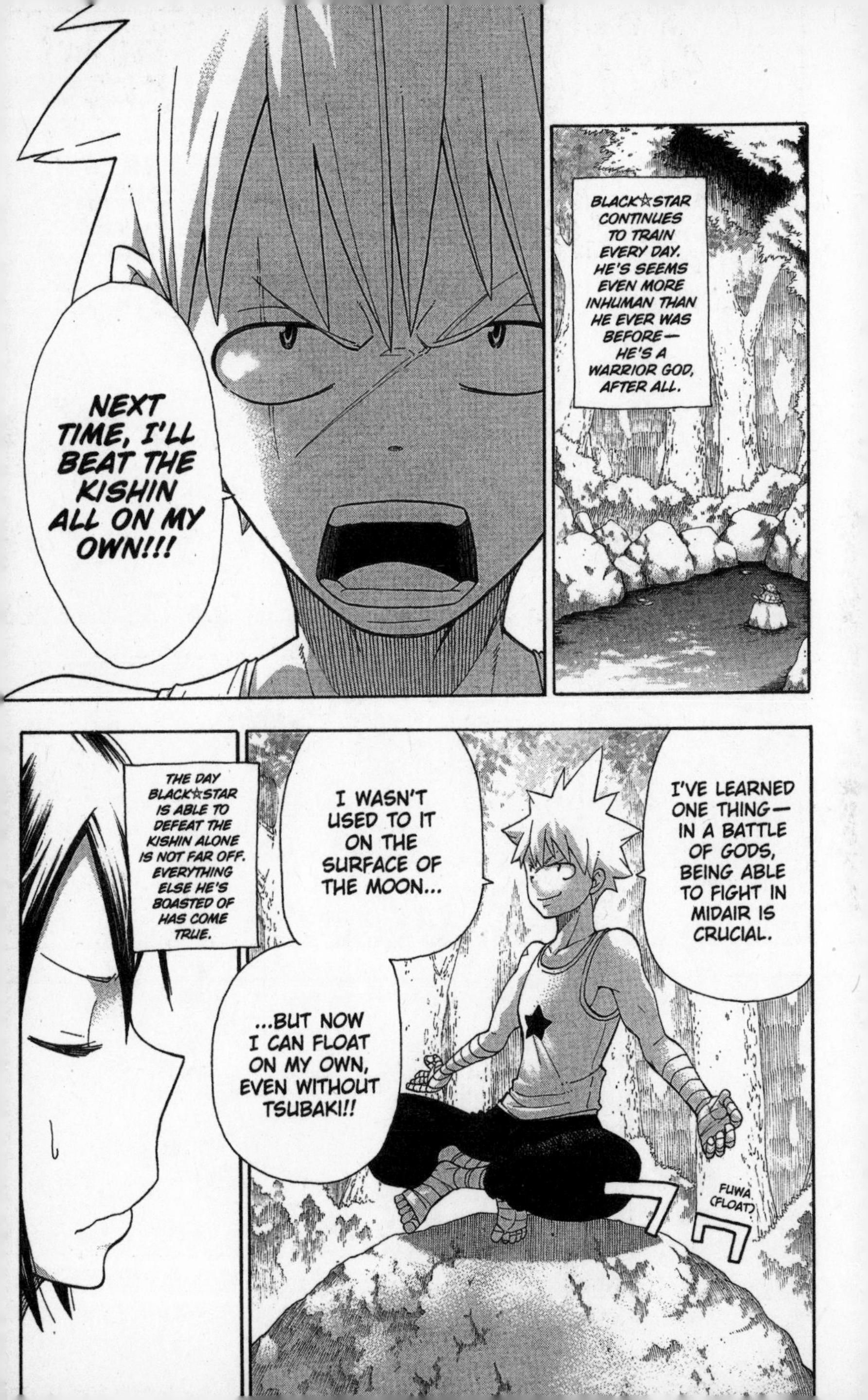
BLACK☆STAR CONTINUES TO TRAIN EVERY DAY. HE'S SEEMS EVEN MORE INHUMAN THAN HE EVER WAS BEFORE—HE'S A WARRIOR GOD, AFTER ALL.
NEXT TIME, I'LL BEAT THE KISHIN ALL ON MY OWN!!!
I'VE LEARNED ONE THING—IN A BATTLE OF GODS, BEING ABLE TO FIGHT IN MIDAIR IS CRUCIAL.
I WASN'T USED TO IT ON THE SURFACE OF THE MOON...
...BUT NOW I CAN FLOAT ON MY OWN, EVEN WITHOUT TSUBAKI!!
FUWA. (FLOAT)
THE DAY BLACK☆STAR IS ABLE TO DEFEAT THE KISHIN ALONE IS NOT FAR OFF. EVERYTHING ELSE HE'S BOASTED OF HAS COME TRUE.

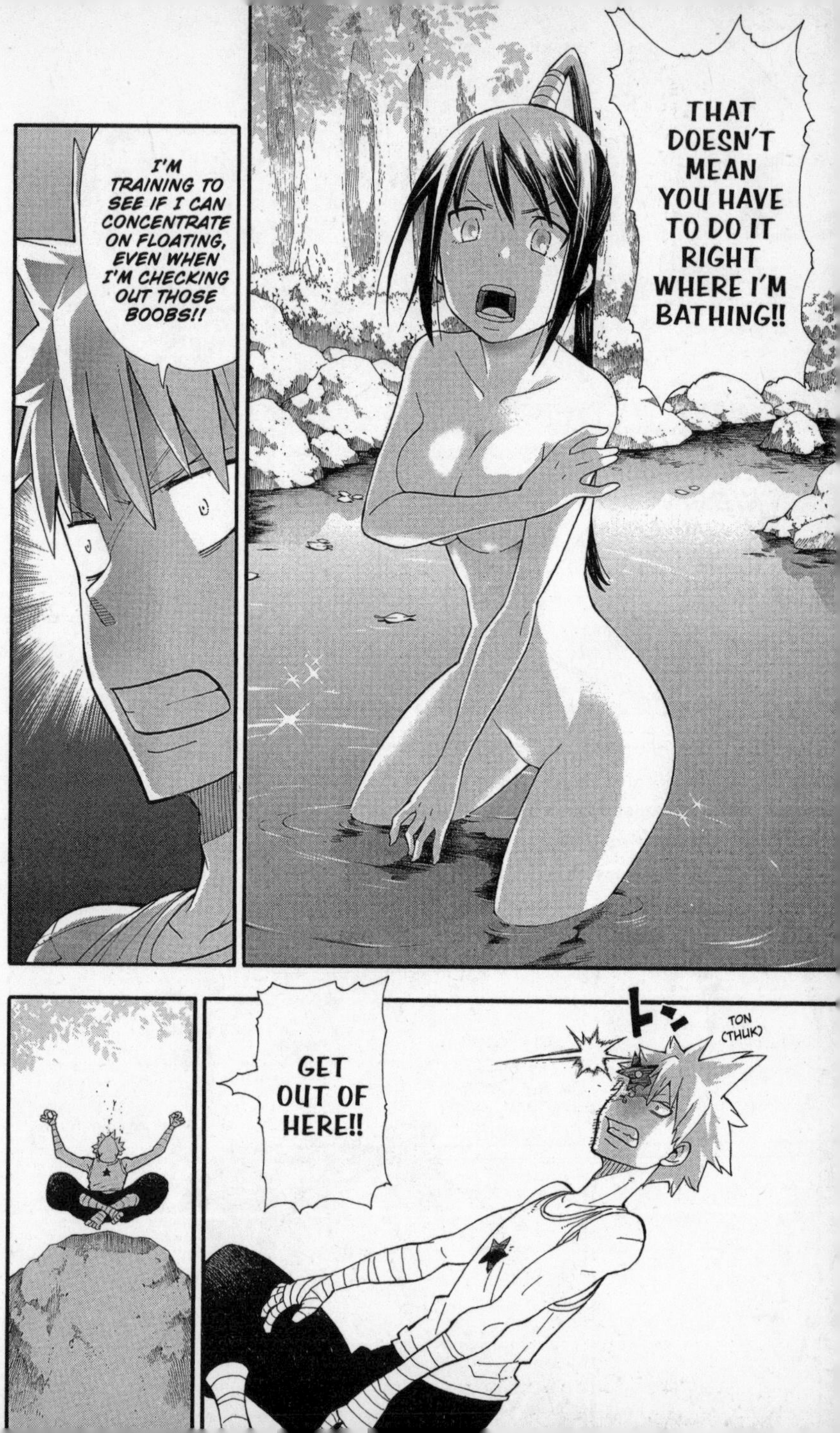
THAT DOESN'T MEAN YOU HAVE TO DO IT RIGHT WHERE I'M BATHING!!
I'M TRAINING TO SEE IF I CAN CONCENTRATE ON FLOATING, EVEN WHEN I'M CHECKING OUT THOSE BOOBS!!
TON (THUK)
トン
GET OUT OF HERE!!

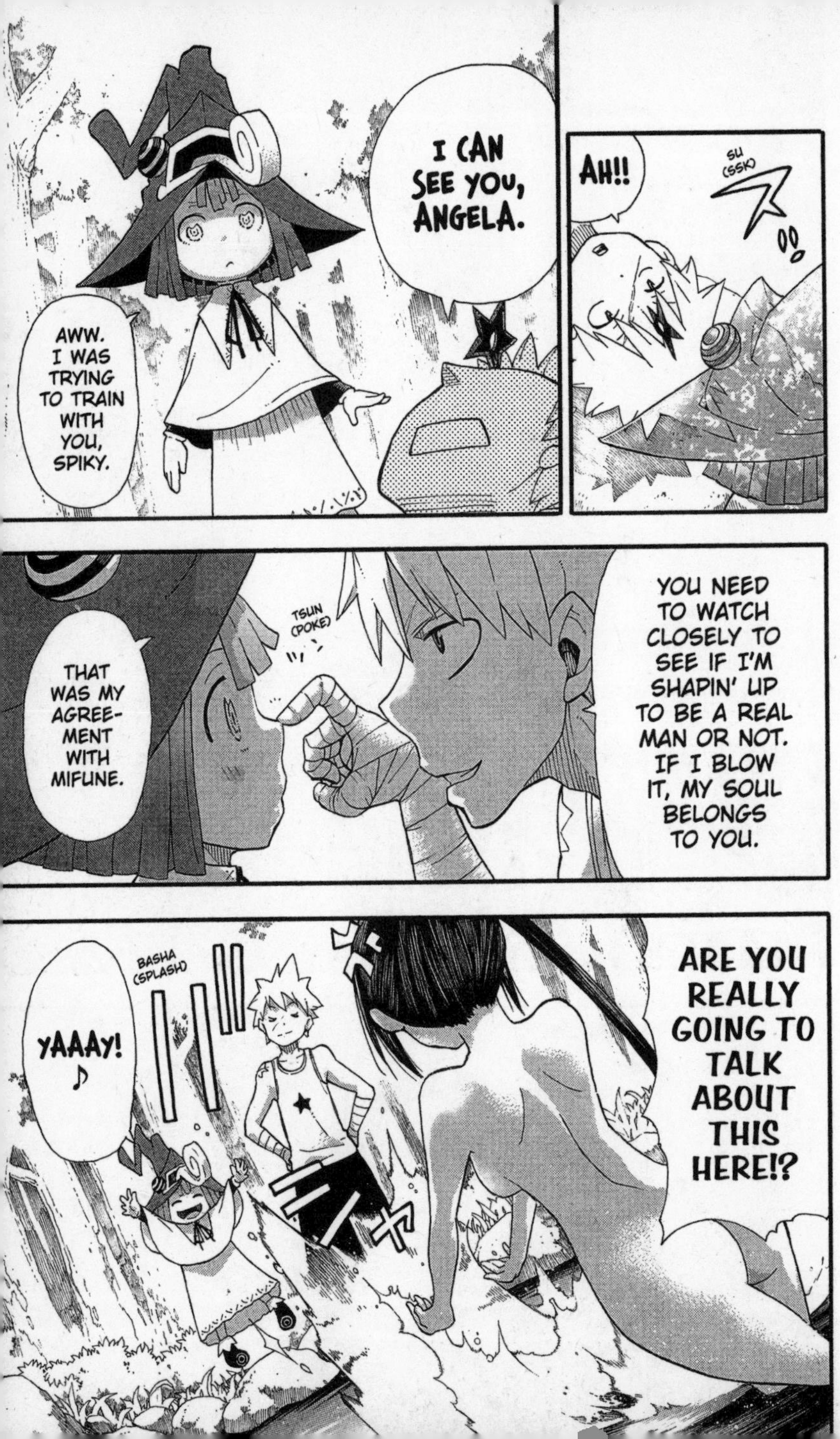
AH!!
SU (SSK)
I CAN SEE YOU, ANGELA.
AWW. I WAS TRYING TO TRAIN WITH YOU, SPIKY.
YOU NEED TO WATCH CLOSELY TO SEE IF I'M SHAPIN' UP TO BE A REAL MAN OR NOT. IF I BLOW IT, MY SOUL BELONGS TO YOU.
TSUN (POKE)
THAT WAS MY AGREE-MENT WITH MIFUNE.
ARE YOU REALLY GOING TO TALK ABOUT THIS HERE!?
BASHA (SPLASH)
YAAAY! ♪

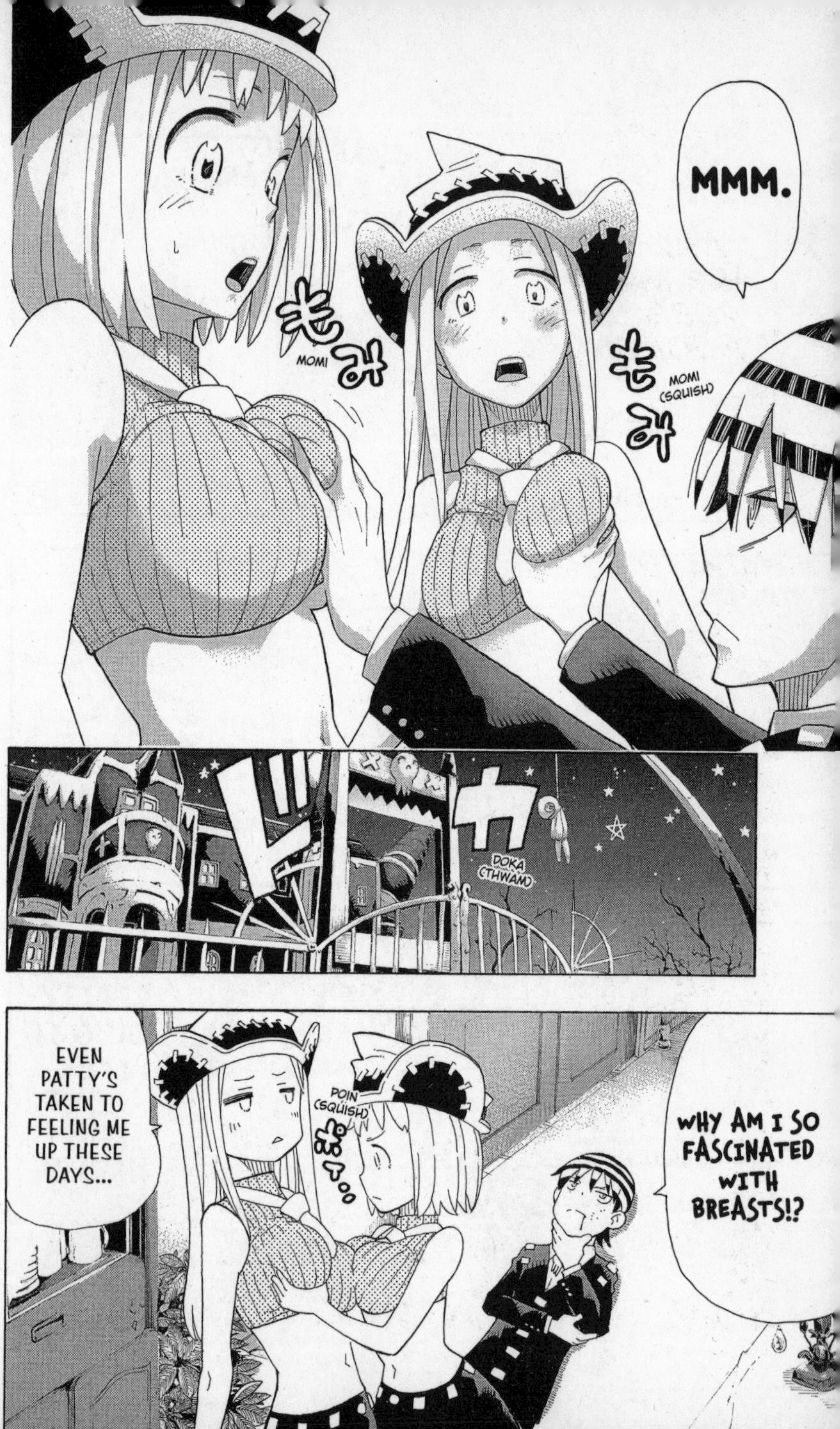
MMM.
もみ
MOMI (SQUISH)
もみ
MOMI
ドカ
DOKA (THWAM)
WHY AM I SO FASCINATED WITH BREASTS!?
POIN (SQUISH)
EVEN PATTY'S TAKEN TO FEELING ME UP THESE DAYS...

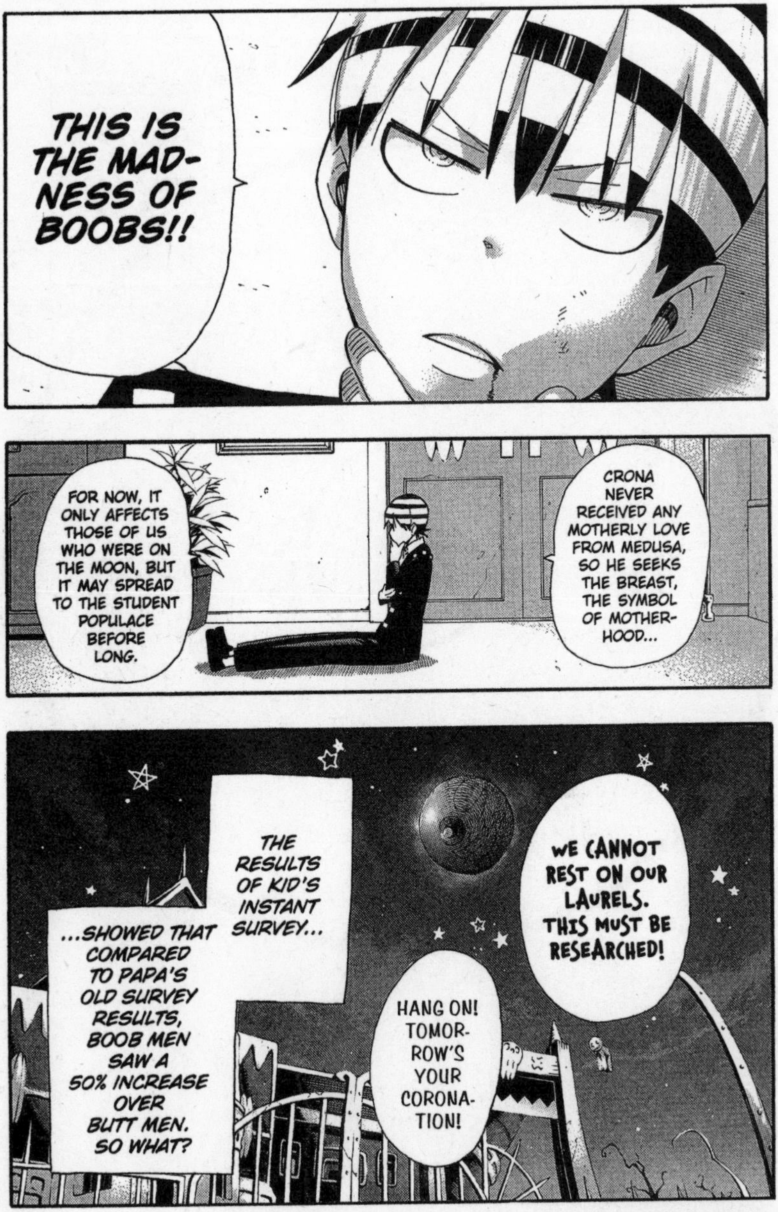
THIS IS THE MAD- NESS OF BOOBS!!
CRONA NEVER RECEIVED ANY MOTHERLY LOVE FROM MEDUSA, SO HE SEEKS THE BREAST, THE SYMBOL OF MOTHER- HOOD...
FOR NOW, IT ONLY AFFECTS THOSE OF US WHO WERE ON THE MOON, BUT IT MAY SPREAD TO THE STUDENT POPULACE BEFORE LONG.
WE CANNOT REST ON OUR LAURELS. THIS MUST BE RESEARCHED!
HANG ON! TOMOR- ROW'S YOUR CORONA- TION!
THE RESULTS OF KID'S INSTANT SURVEY...
...SHOWED THAT COMPARED TO PAPA'S OLD SURVEY RESULTS, BOOB MEN SAW A 50% INCREASE OVER BUTT MEN. SO WHAT?

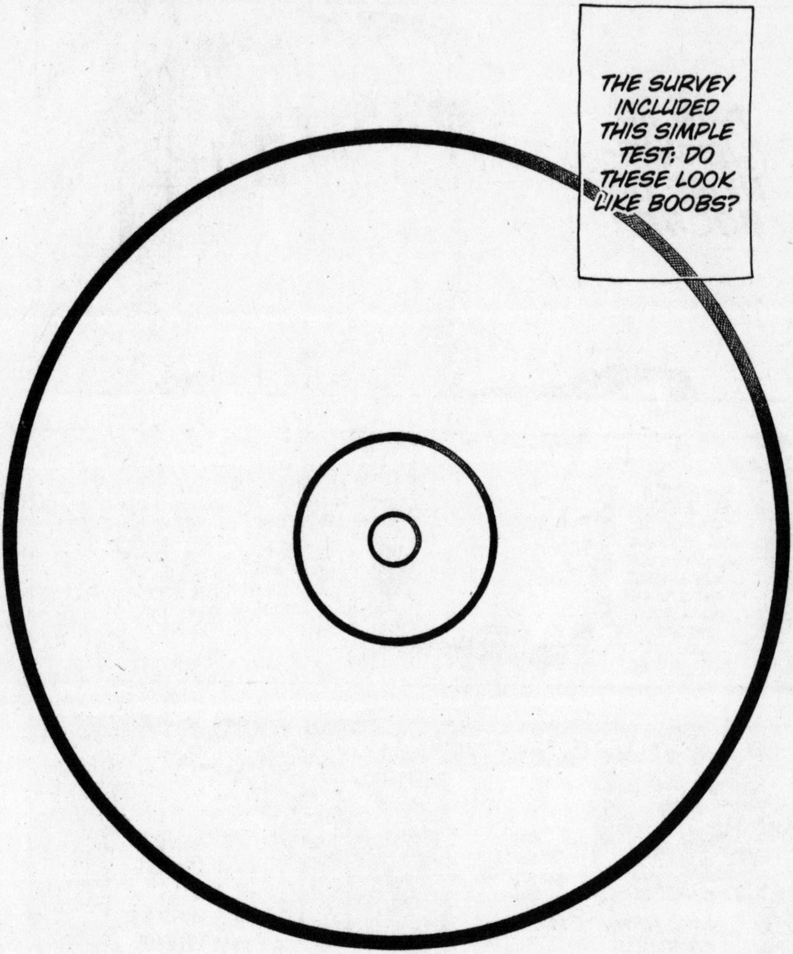
THE SURVEY INCLUDED THIS SIMPLE TEST: DO THESE LOOK LIKE BOOBS?

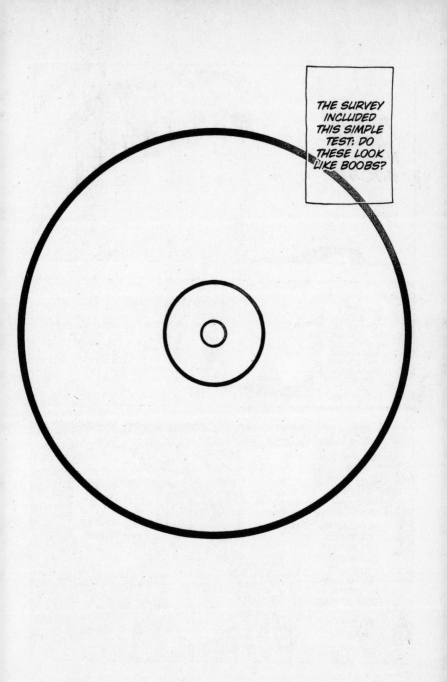

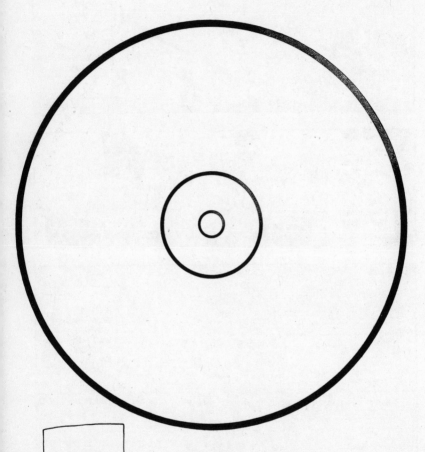

MY ANSWER WAS "YES," OF COURSE.

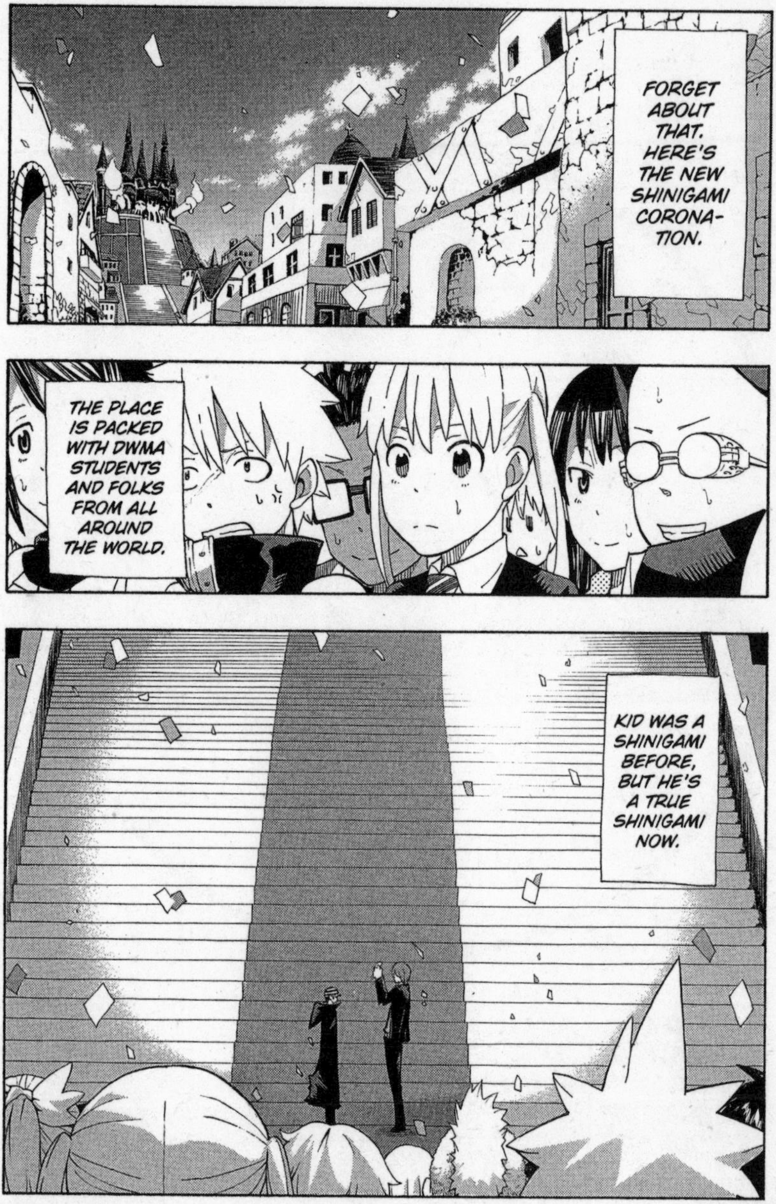
FORGET ABOUT THAT. HERE'S THE NEW SHINIGAMI CORONATION.
THE PLACE IS PACKED WITH DWMA STUDENTS AND FOLKS FROM ALL AROUND THE WORLD.
KID WAS A SHINIGAMI BEFORE, BUT HE'S A TRUE SHINIGAMI NOW.

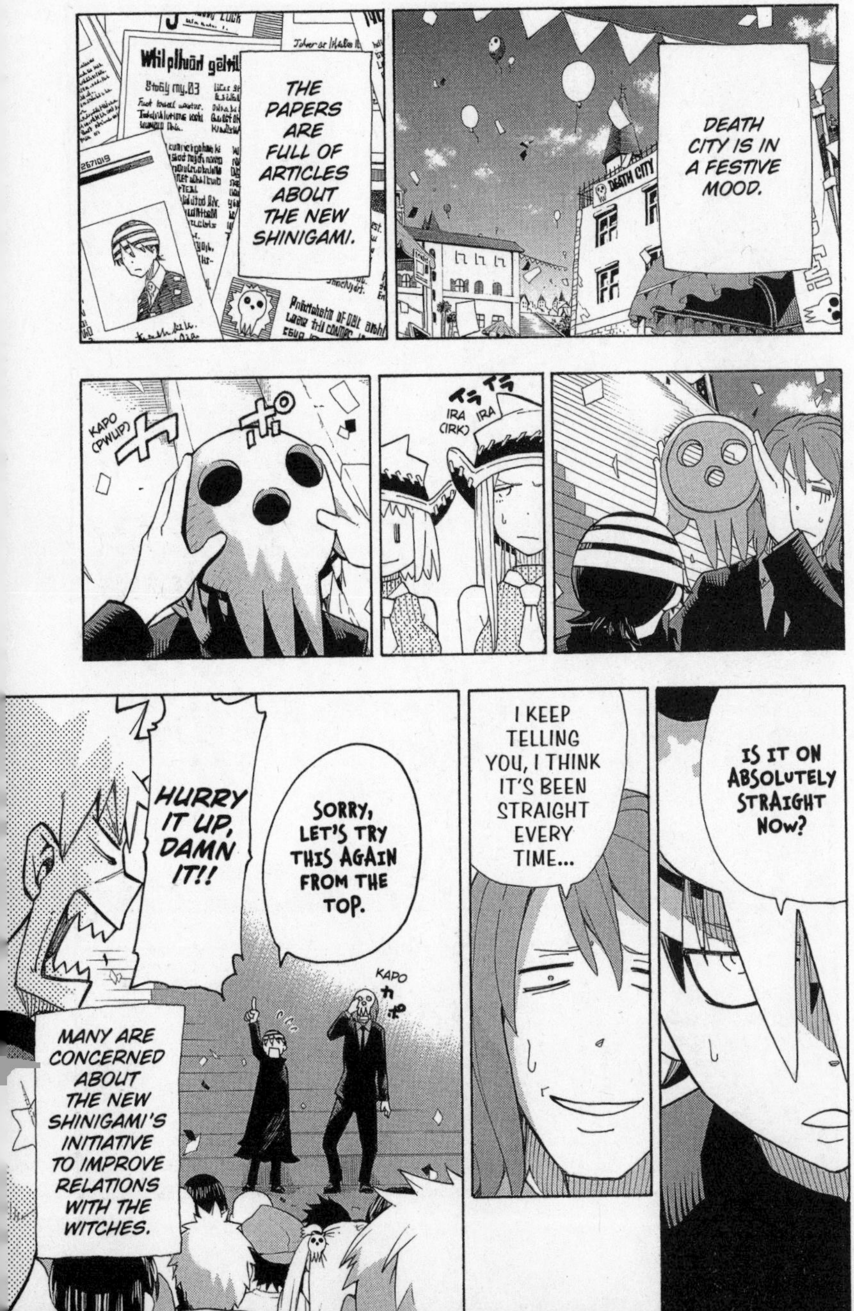
DEATH CITY IS IN A FESTIVE MOOD.
DEATH CITY
THE PAPERS ARE FULL OF ARTICLES ABOUT THE NEW SHINIGAMI.
IRA (IRK) IRA
KAPO (PWUP)
IS IT ON ABSOLUTELY STRAIGHT NOW?
I KEEP TELLING YOU, I THINK IT'S BEEN STRAIGHT EVERY TIME...
SORRY, LET'S TRY THIS AGAIN FROM THE TOP.
HURRY IT UP, DAMN IT!!
KAPO
MANY ARE CONCERNED ABOUT THE NEW SHINIGAMI'S INITIATIVE TO IMPROVE RELATIONS WITH THE WITCHES.

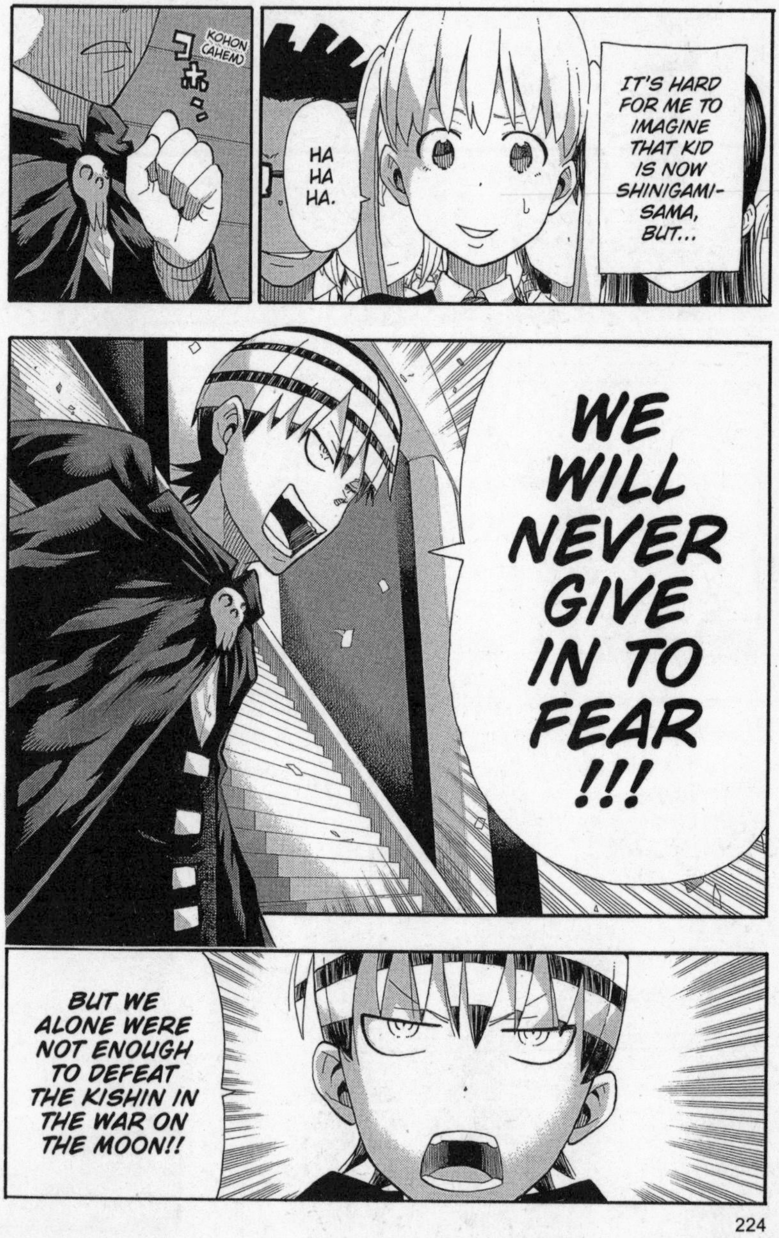
IT'S HARD FOR ME TO IMAGINE THAT KID IS NOW SHINIGAMI-SAMA, BUT...
HA HA HA.
KOHON (AHEM)
WE WILL NEVER GIVE IN TO FEAR!!!
BUT WE ALONE WERE NOT ENOUGH TO DEFEAT THE KISHIN IN THE WAR ON THE MOON!!

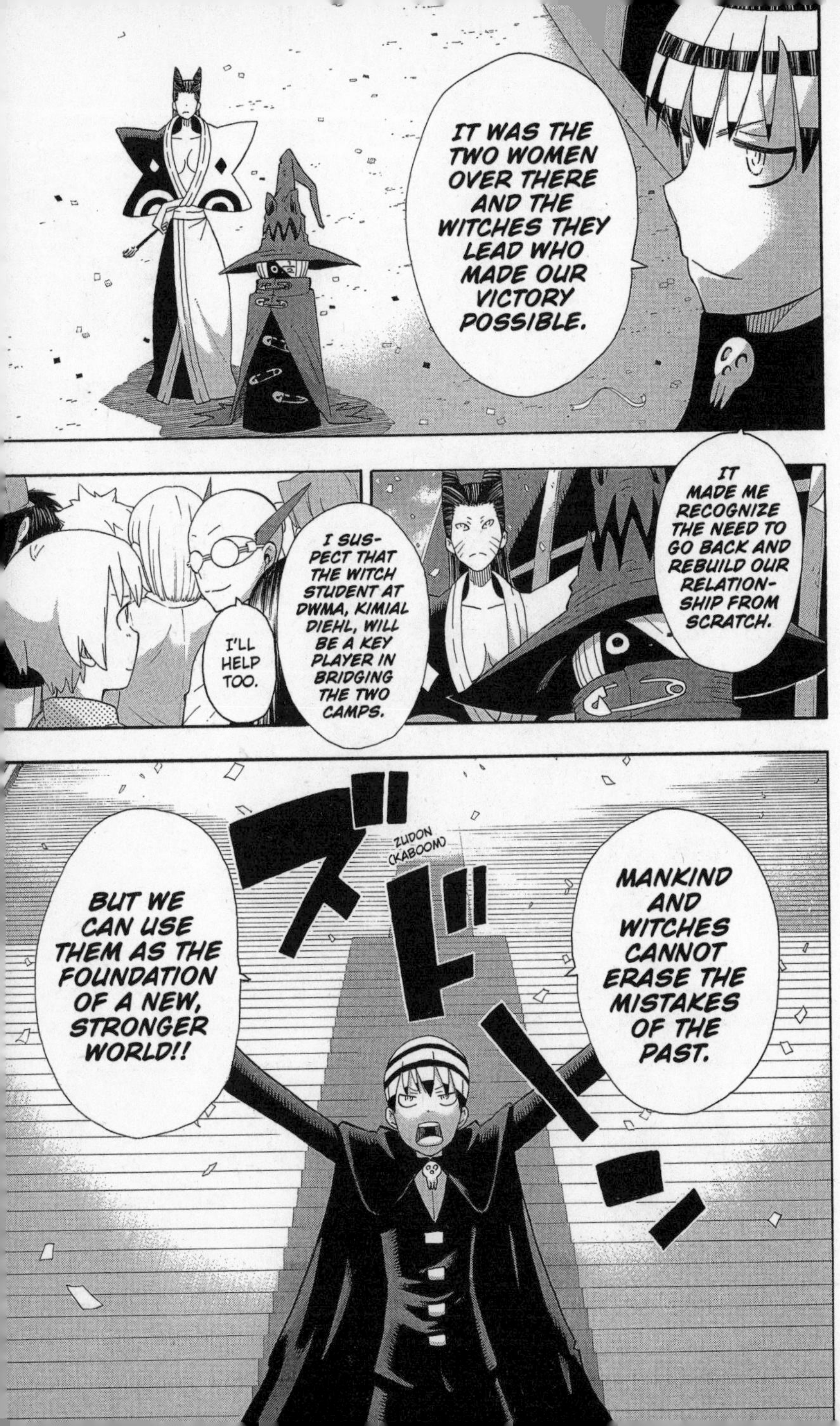
IT WAS THE TWO WOMEN OVER THERE AND THE WITCHES THEY LEAD WHO MADE OUR VICTORY POSSIBLE.
IT MADE ME RECOGNIZE THE NEED TO GO BACK AND REBUILD OUR RELATION-SHIP FROM SCRATCH.
I SUS-PECT THAT THE WITCH STUDENT AT DWMA, KIMIAL DIEHL, WILL BE A KEY PLAYER IN BRIDGING THE TWO CAMPS.
I'LL HELP TOO.
MANKIND AND WITCHES CANNOT ERASE THE MISTAKES OF THE PAST.
ZUDON (KABOOM)
BUT WE CAN USE THEM AS THE FOUNDATION OF A NEW, STRONGER WORLD!!

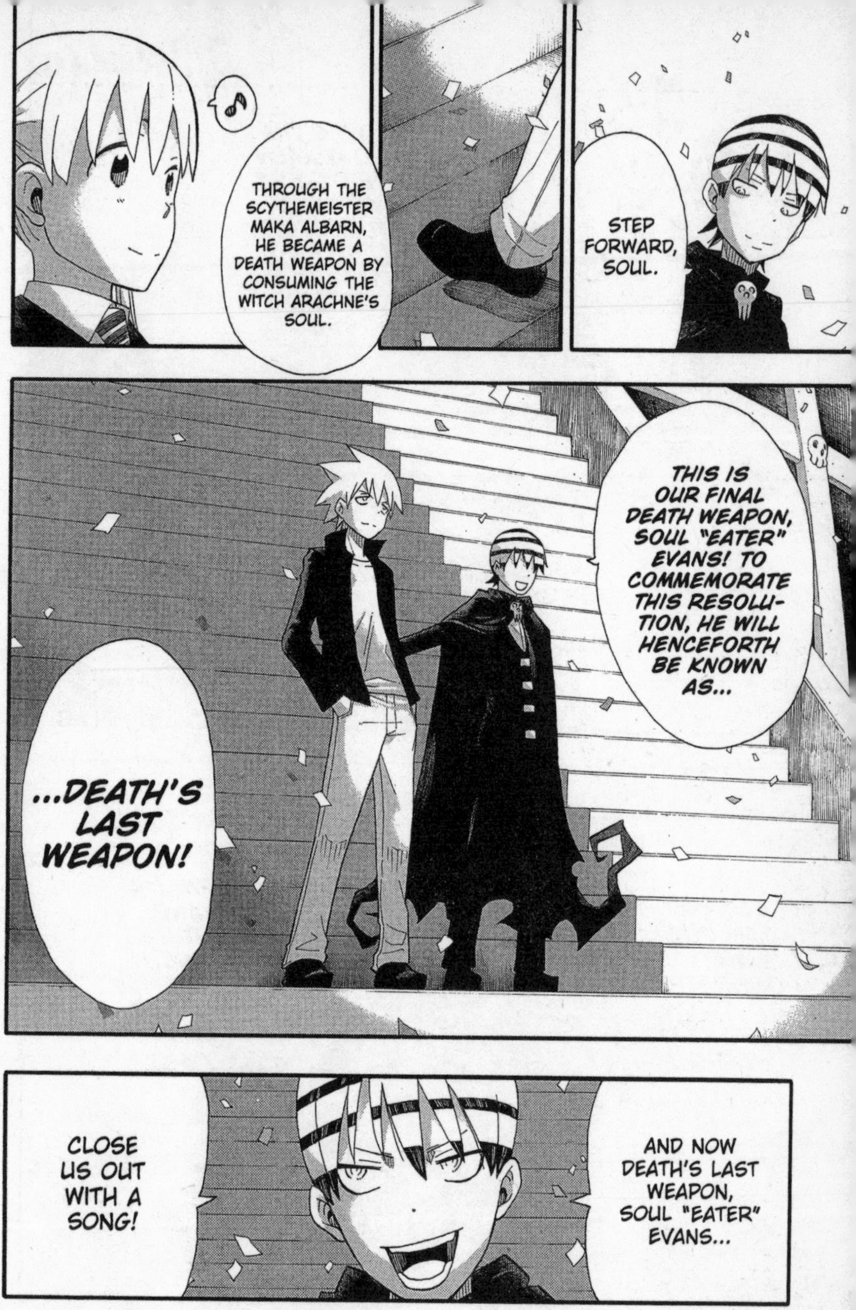
STEP FORWARD, SOUL.
THROUGH THE SCYTHEMEISTER MAKA ALBARN, HE BECAME A DEATH WEAPON BY CONSUMING THE WITCH ARACHNE'S SOUL.
THIS IS OUR FINAL DEATH WEAPON, SOUL "EATER" EVANS! TO COMMEMORATE THIS RESOLUTION, HE WILL HENCEFORTH BE KNOWN AS...
...DEATH'S LAST WEAPON!
AND NOW DEATH'S LAST WEAPON, SOUL "EATER" EVANS...
CLOSE US OUT WITH A SONG!

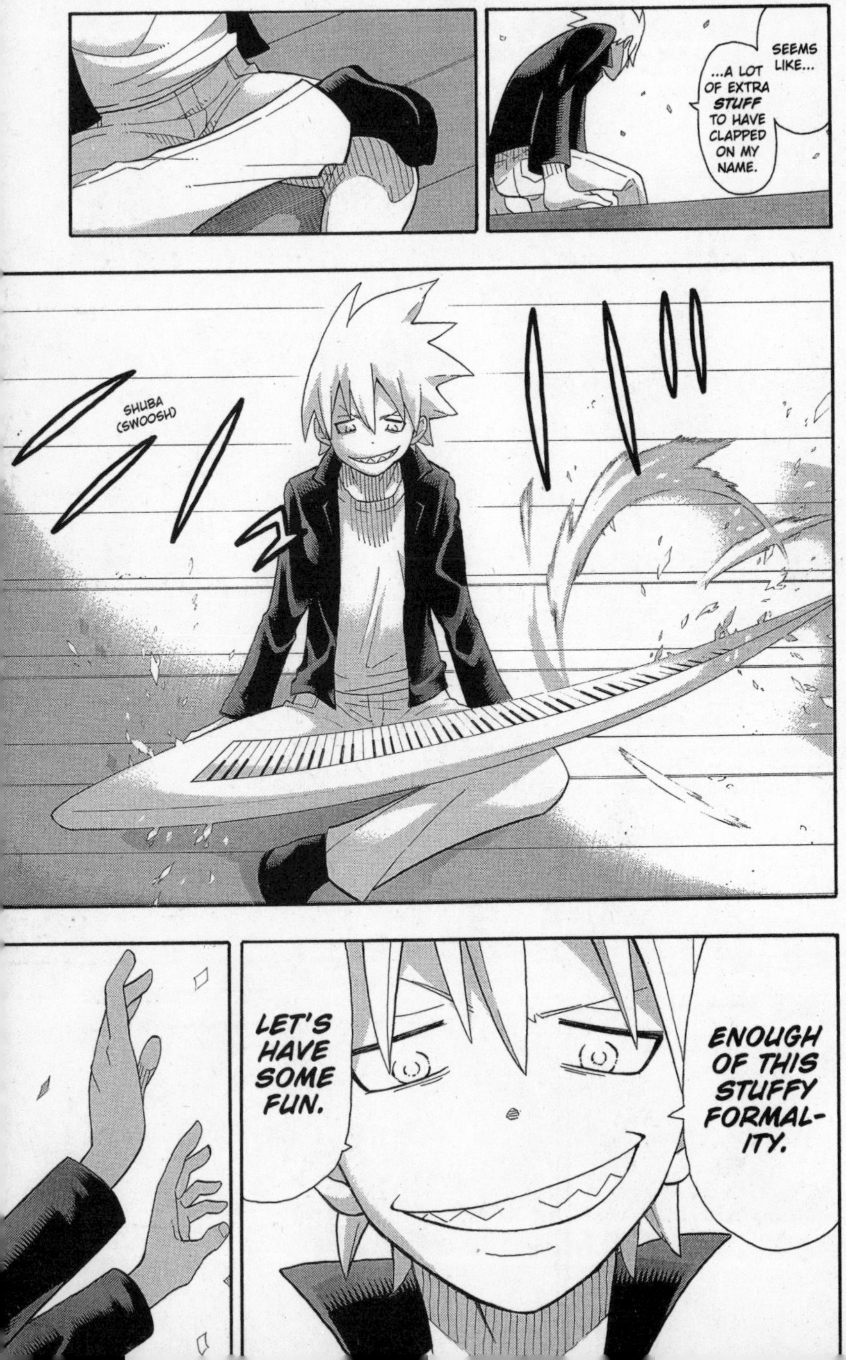
SEEMS LIKE...
...A LOT OF EXTRA STUFF TO HAVE CLAPPED ON MY NAME.
SHUBA (SWOOSH)
ENOUGH OF THIS STUFFY FORMAL-ITY.
LET'S HAVE SOME FUN.

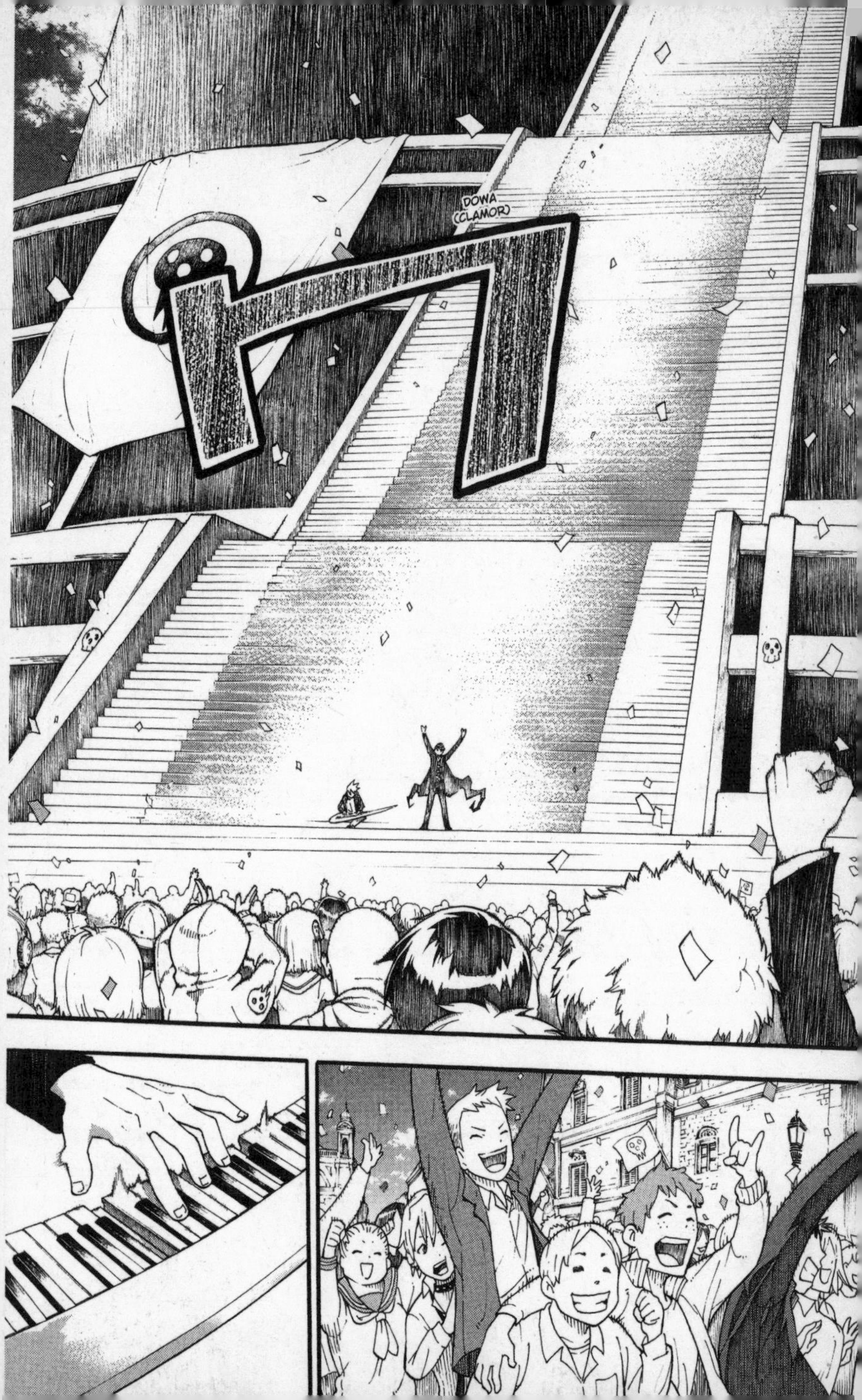
DOWA
(CLAMOR)

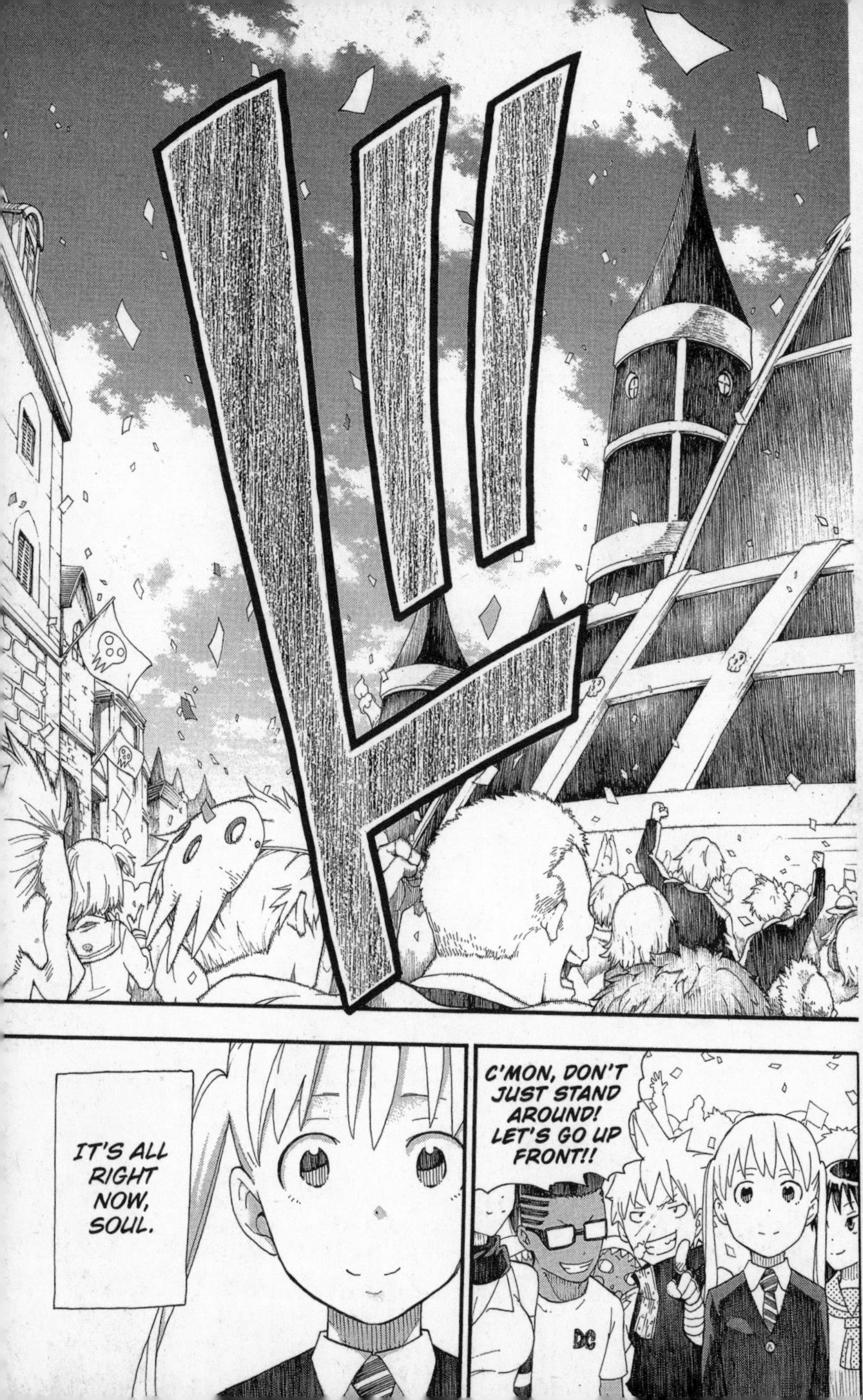
C'MON, DON'T JUST STAND AROUND! LET'S GO UP FRONT!!
IT'S ALL RIGHT NOW, SOUL.

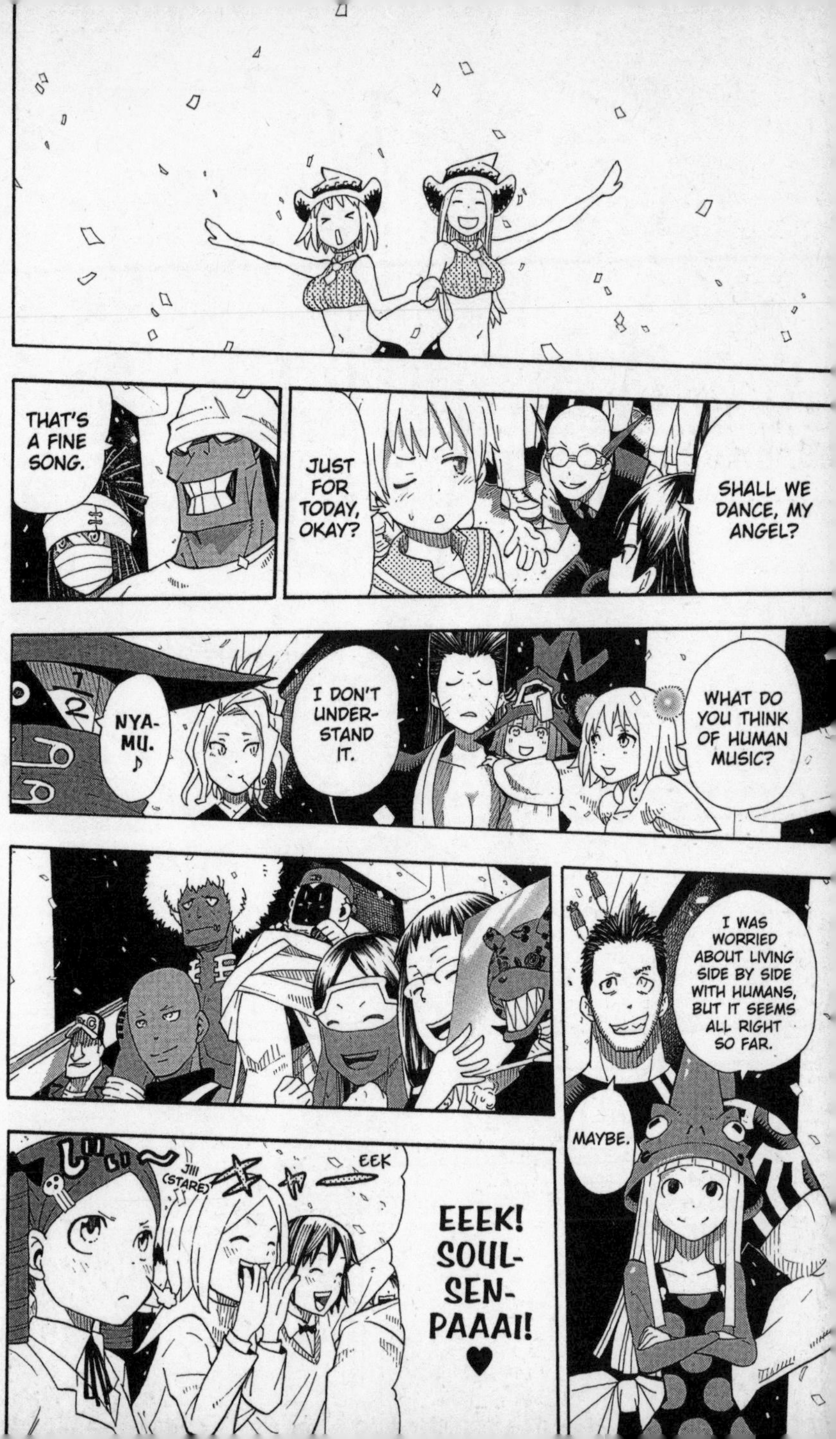
SHALL WE DANCE, MY ANGEL?
JUST FOR TODAY, OKAY?
THAT'S A FINE SONG.
WHAT DO YOU THINK OF HUMAN MUSIC?
I DON'T UNDERSTAND IT.
NYAMU. ♪
I WAS WORRIED ABOUT LIVING SIDE BY SIDE WITH HUMANS, BUT IT SEEMS ALL RIGHT SO FAR.
MAYBE.
JIII (STARE)
EEK
EEEK! SOUL-SENPAAAI! ♥

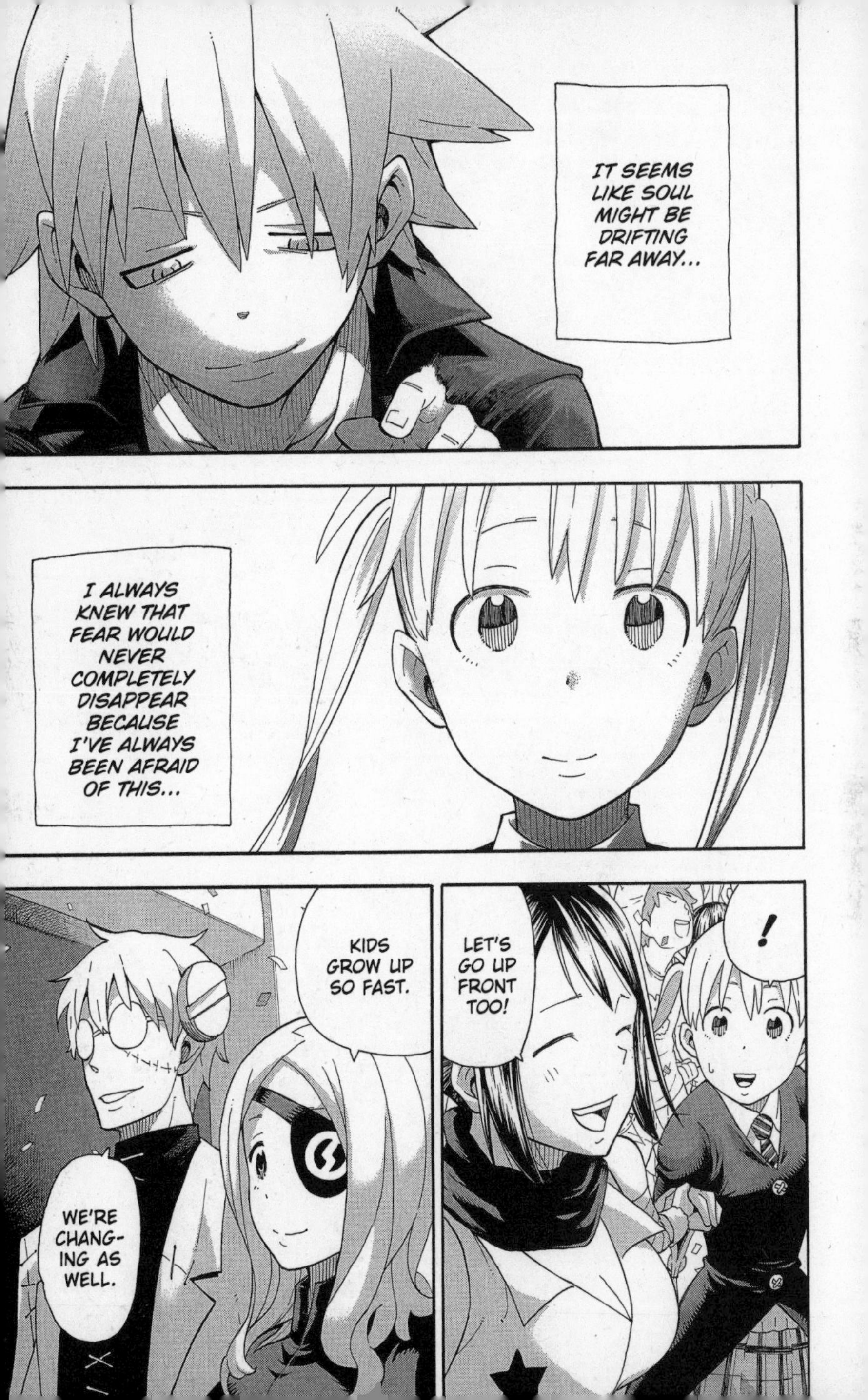
IT SEEMS LIKE SOUL MIGHT BE DRIFTING FAR AWAY...
I ALWAYS KNEW THAT FEAR WOULD NEVER COMPLETELY DISAPPEAR BECAUSE I'VE ALWAYS BEEN AFRAID OF THIS...
!
LET'S GO UP FRONT TOO!
KIDS GROW UP SO FAST.
WE'RE CHANGING AS WELL.

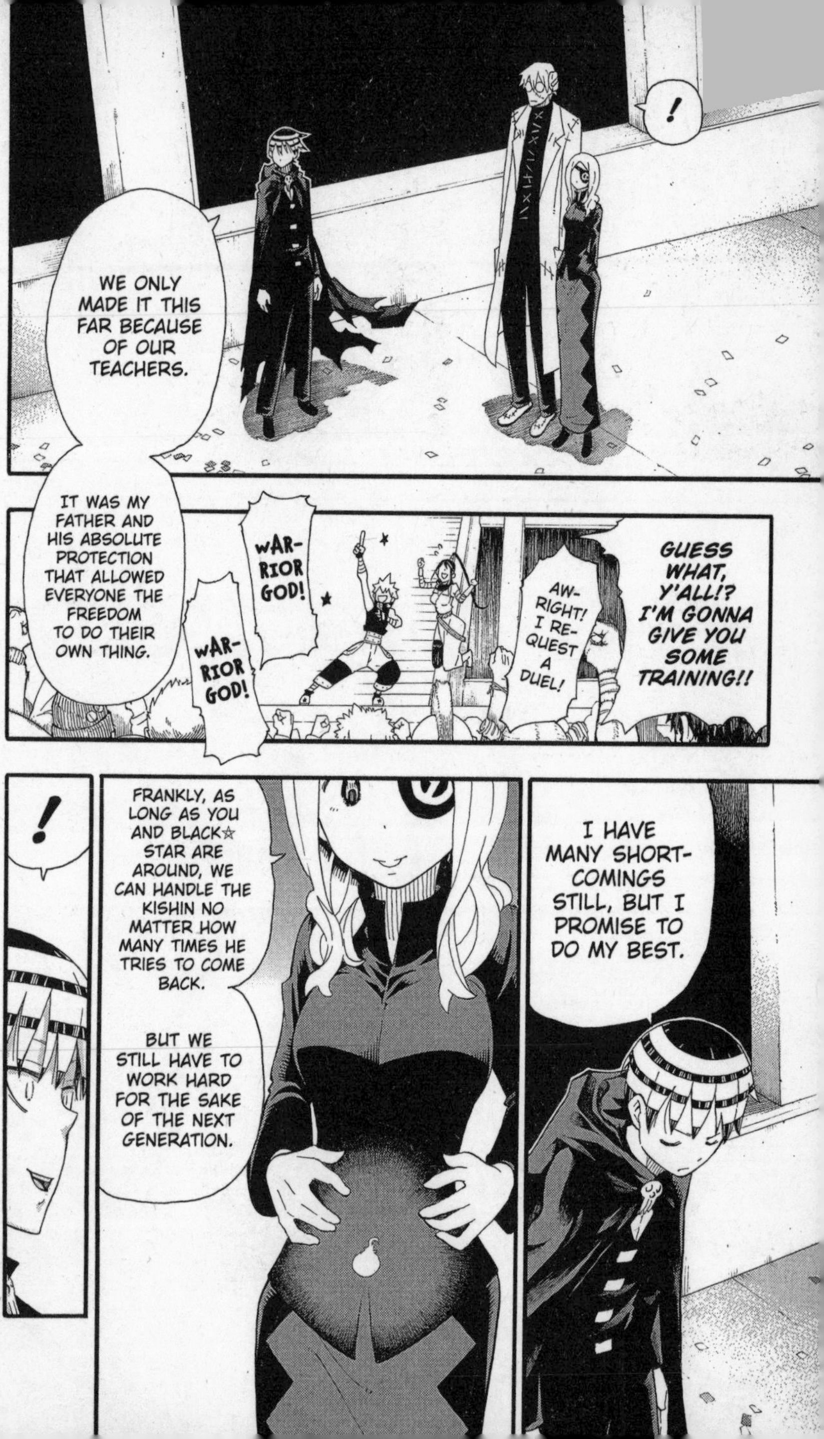
!
WE ONLY MADE IT THIS FAR BECAUSE OF OUR TEACHERS.
GUESS WHAT, Y'ALL!? I'M GONNA GIVE YOU SOME TRAINING!!
AW-RIGHT! I RE-QUEST A DUEL!
WAR-RIOR GOD!
WAR-RIOR GOD!
IT WAS MY FATHER AND HIS ABSOLUTE PROTECTION THAT ALLOWED EVERYONE THE FREEDOM TO DO THEIR OWN THING.
I HAVE MANY SHORT-COMINGS STILL, BUT I PROMISE TO DO MY BEST.
FRANKLY, AS LONG AS YOU AND BLACK☆STAR ARE AROUND, WE CAN HANDLE THE KISHIN NO MATTER HOW MANY TIMES HE TRIES TO COME BACK.
BUT WE STILL HAVE TO WORK HARD FOR THE SAKE OF THE NEXT GENERATION.
!

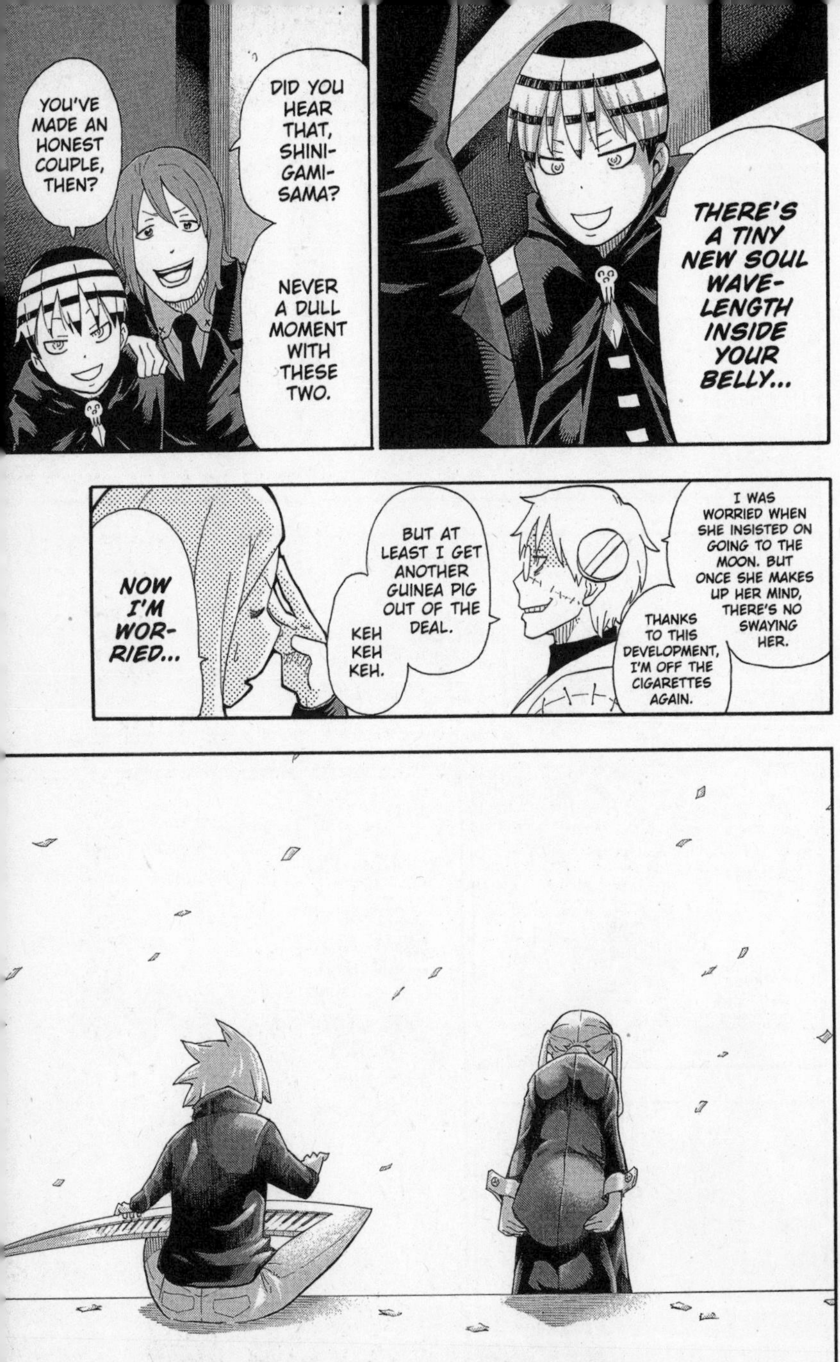
THERE'S A TINY NEW SOUL WAVE-LENGTH INSIDE YOUR BELLY...
DID YOU HEAR THAT, SHINI-GAMI-SAMA?
NEVER A DULL MOMENT WITH THESE TWO.
YOU'VE MADE AN HONEST COUPLE, THEN?
I WAS WORRIED WHEN SHE INSISTED ON GOING TO THE MOON. BUT ONCE SHE MAKES UP HER MIND, THERE'S NO SWAYING HER.
THANKS TO THIS DEVELOPMENT, I'M OFF THE CIGARETTES AGAIN.
BUT AT LEAST I GET ANOTHER GUINEA PIG OUT OF THE DEAL.
KEH KEH KEH.
NOW I'M WOR-RIED...

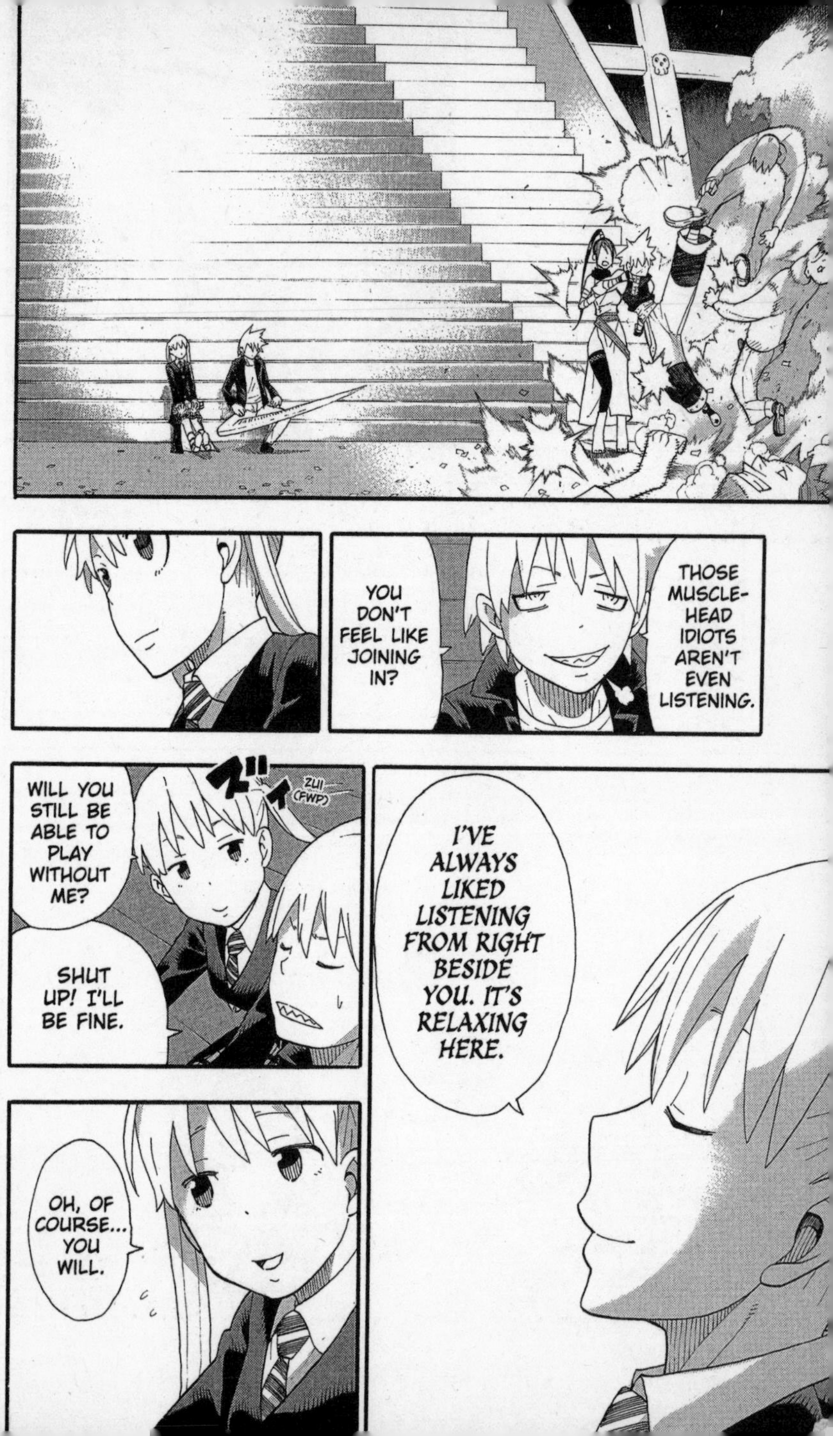
THOSE MUSCLE-HEAD IDIOTS AREN'T EVEN LISTENING.
YOU DON'T FEEL LIKE JOINING IN?
I'VE ALWAYS LIKED LISTENING FROM RIGHT BESIDE YOU. IT'S RELAXING HERE.
ZUI (FWP)
WILL YOU STILL BE ABLE TO PLAY WITHOUT ME?
SHUT UP! I'LL BE FINE.
OH, OF COURSE... YOU WILL.

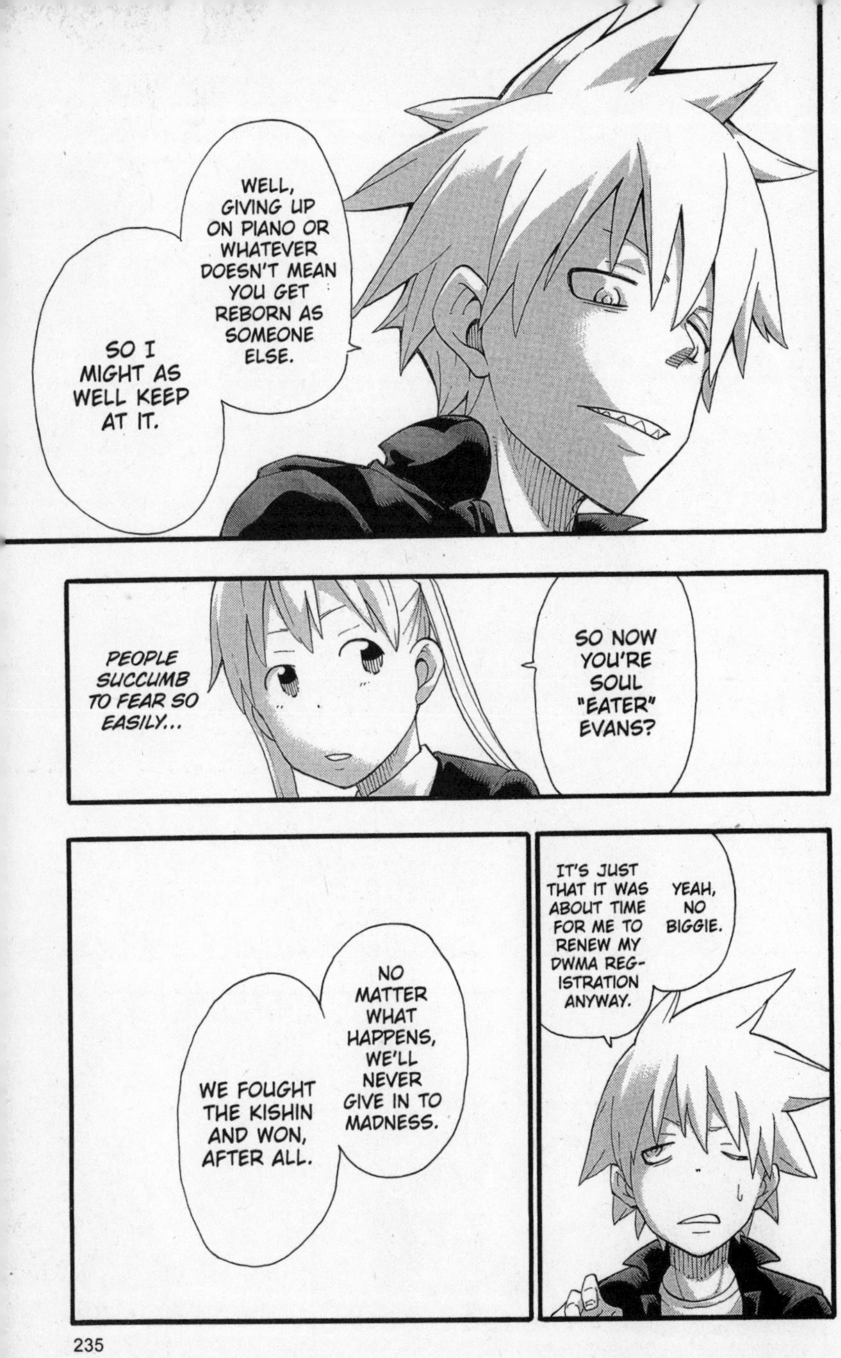
WELL, GIVING UP ON PIANO OR WHATEVER DOESN'T MEAN YOU GET REBORN AS SOMEONE ELSE.
SO I MIGHT AS WELL KEEP AT IT.
SO NOW YOU'RE SOUL "EATER" EVANS?
PEOPLE SUCCUMB TO FEAR SO EASILY...
YEAH, NO BIGGIE.
IT'S JUST THAT IT WAS ABOUT TIME FOR ME TO RENEW MY DWMA REG-ISTRATION ANYWAY.
NO MATTER WHAT HAPPENS, WE'LL NEVER GIVE IN TO MADNESS.
WE FOUGHT THE KISHIN AND WON, AFTER ALL.

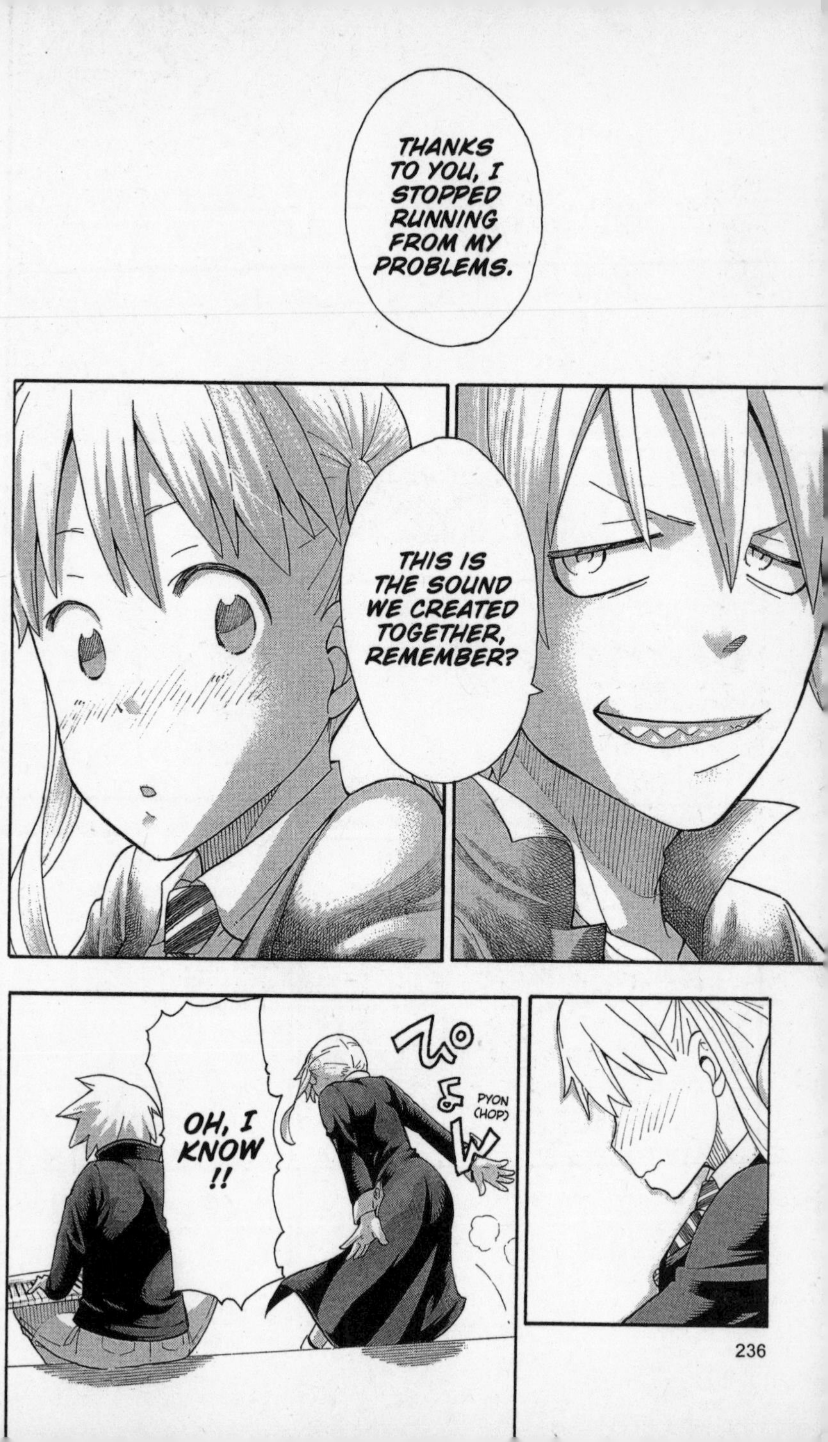
THANKS TO YOU, I STOPPED RUNNING FROM MY PROBLEMS.
THIS IS THE SOUND WE CREATED TOGETHER, REMEMBER?
PYON (HOP)
OH, I KNOW!!

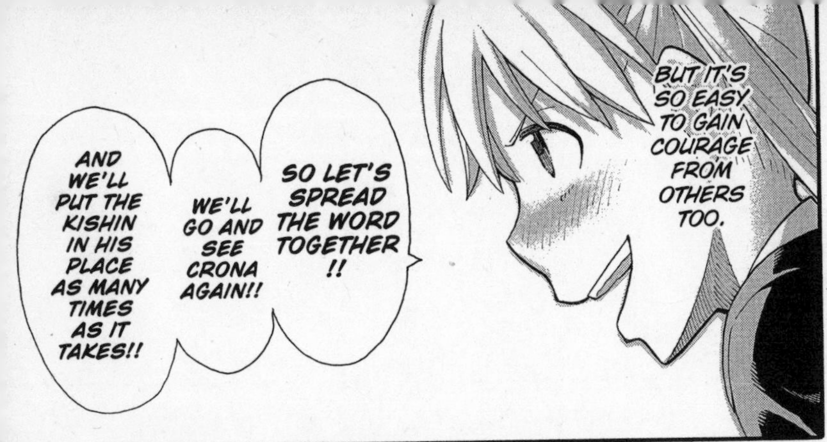
BUT IT'S SO EASY TO GAIN COURAGE FROM OTHERS TOO.
SO LET'S SPREAD THE WORD TOGETHER !!
WE'LL GO AND SEE CRONA AGAIN!!
AND WE'LL PUT THE KISHIN IN HIS PLACE AS MANY TIMES AS IT TAKES!!

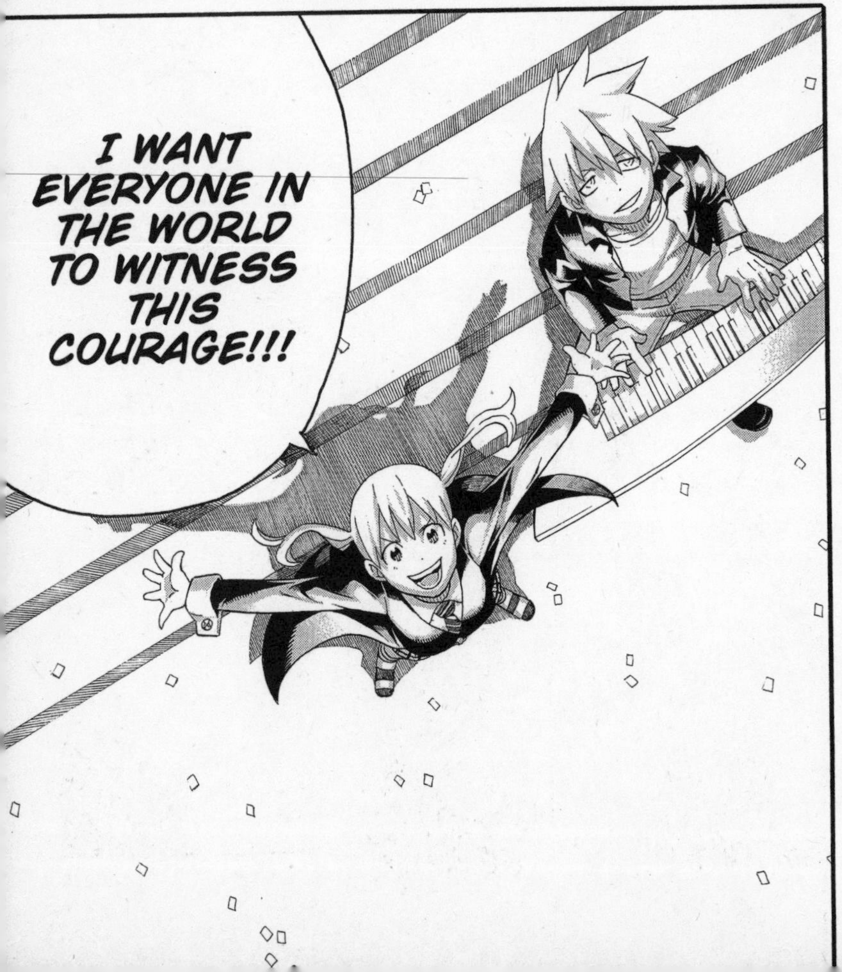
I WANT EVERYONE IN THE WORLD TO WITNESS THIS COURAGE!!!

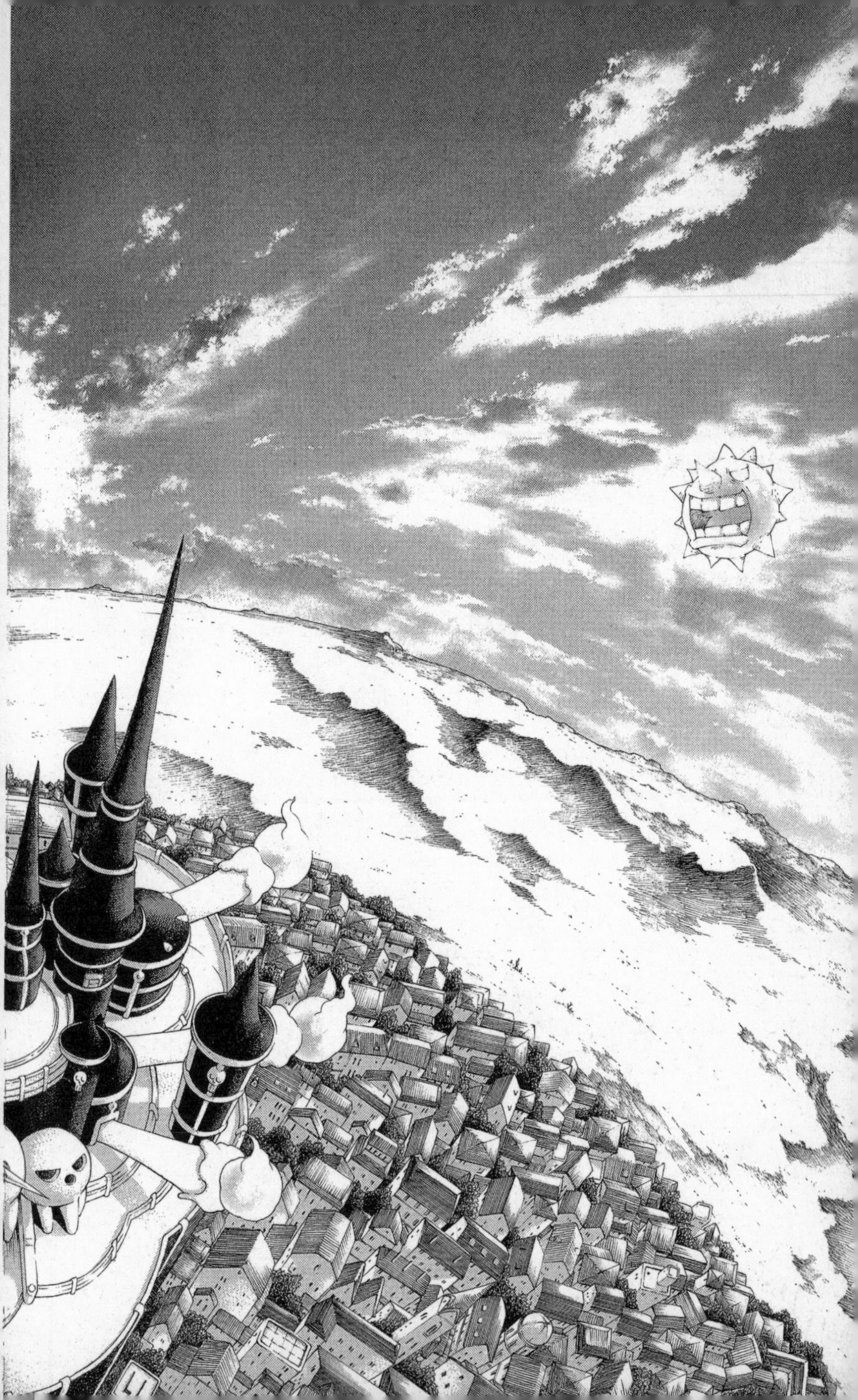

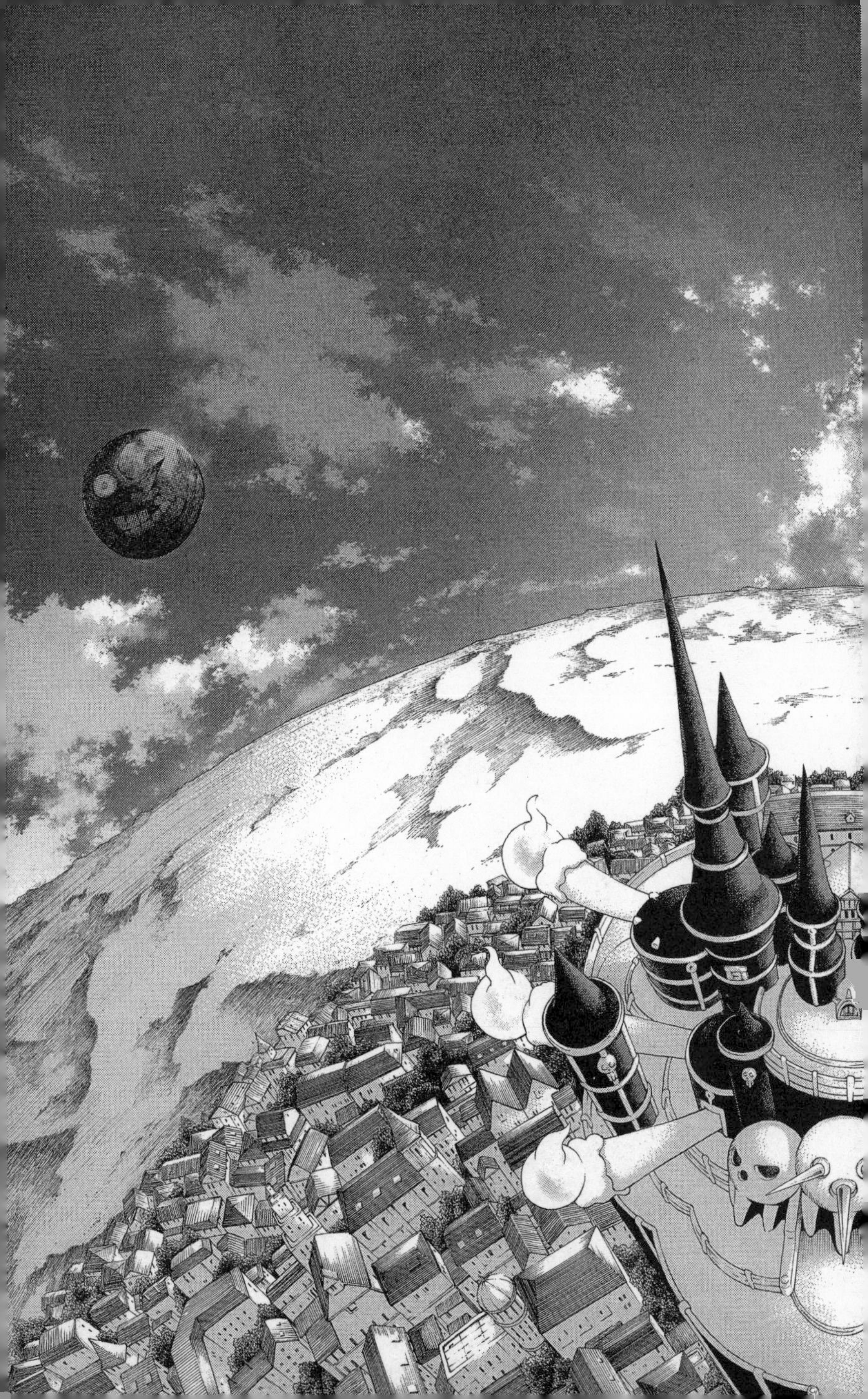

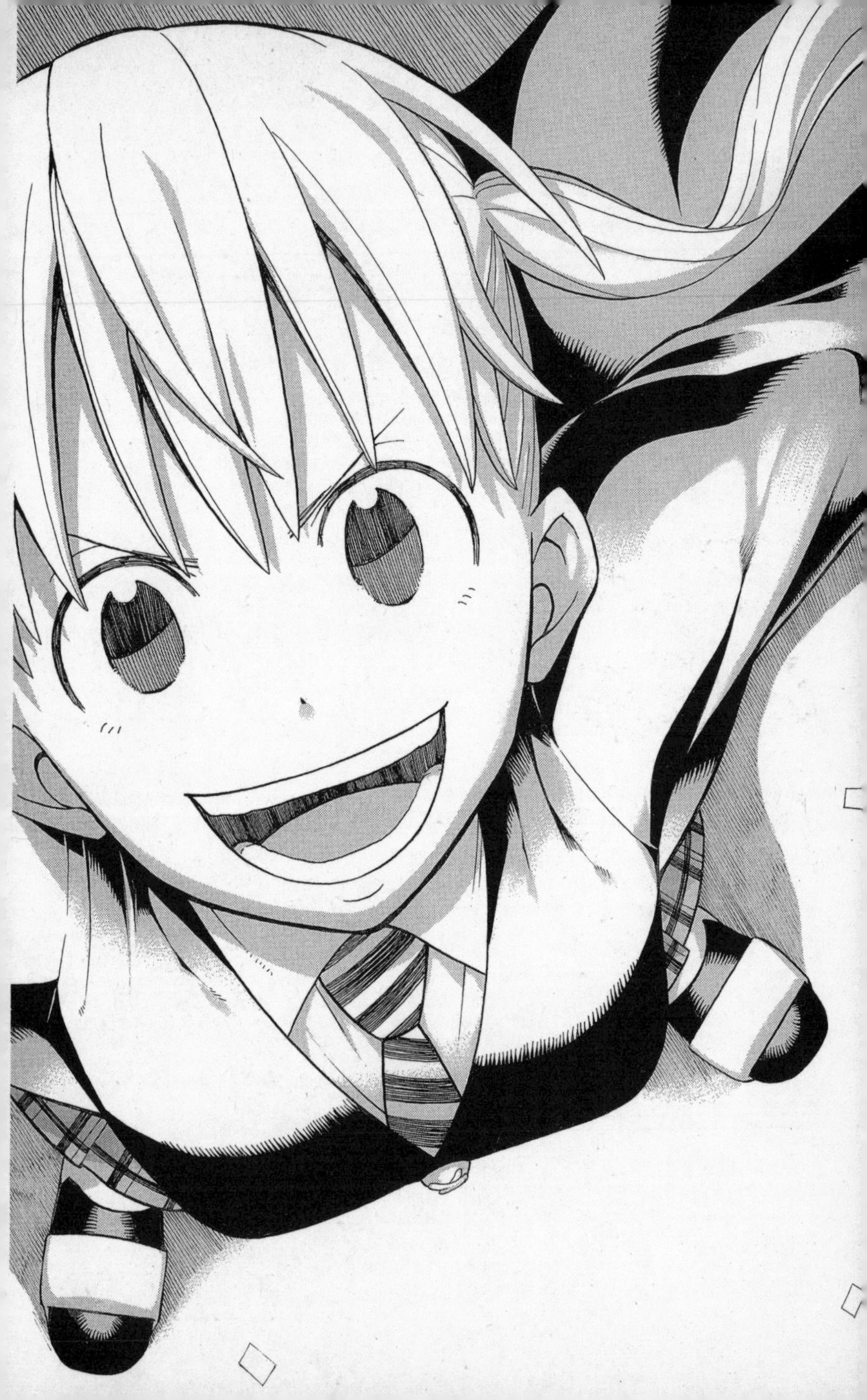

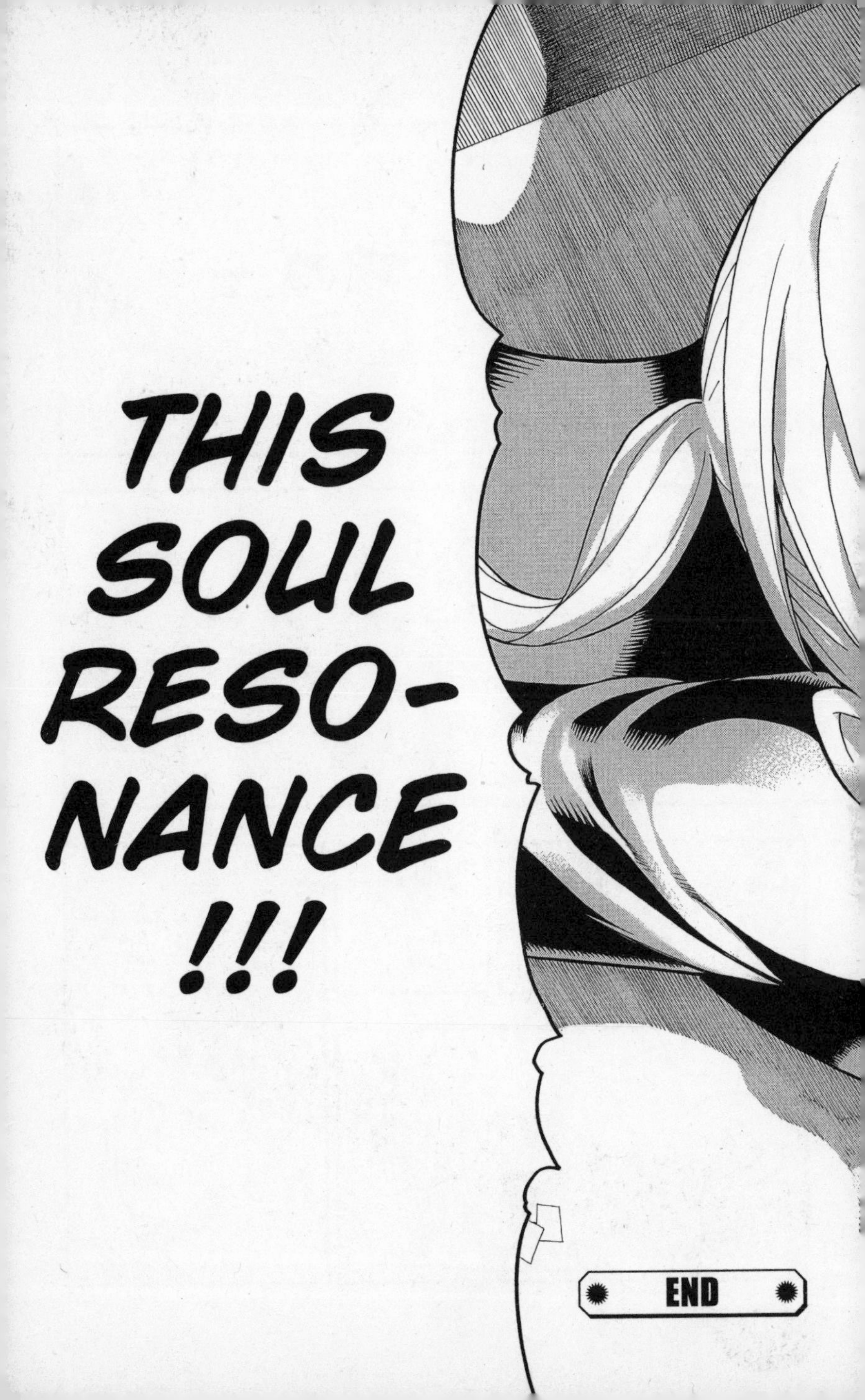
THIS SOUL RESO-NANCE !!!
END

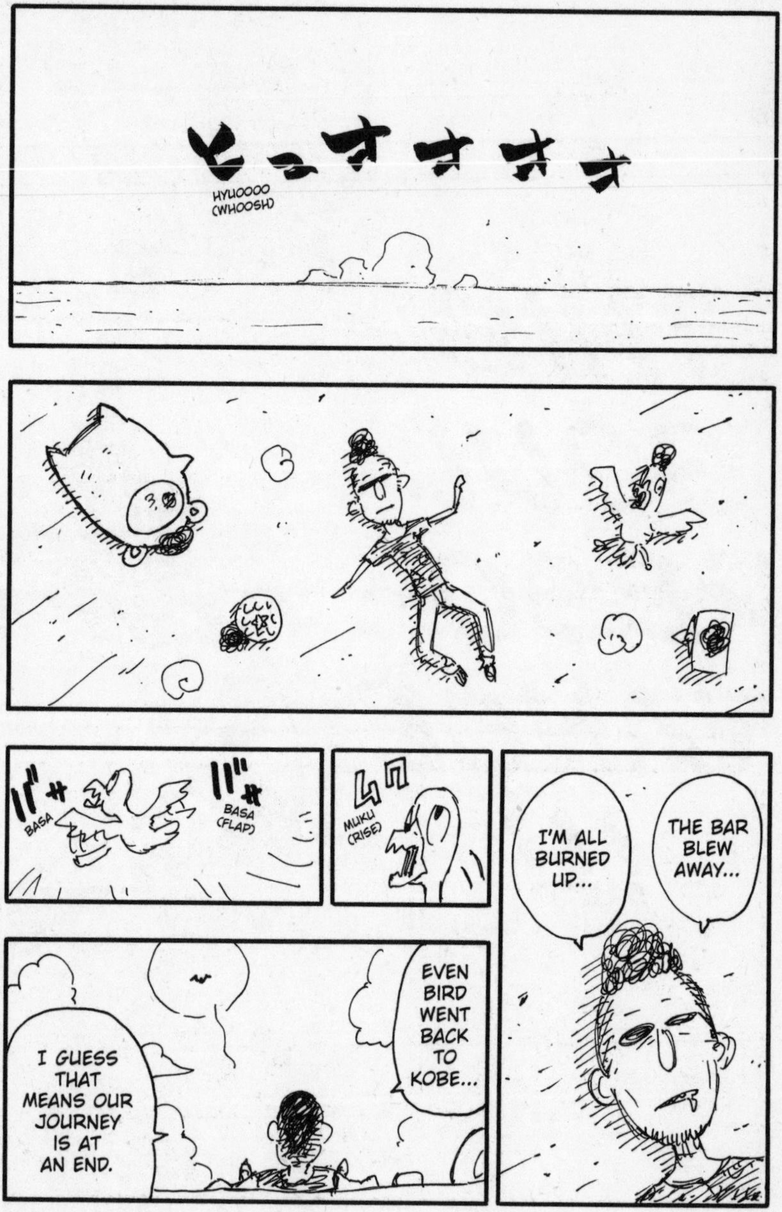

ヒュオオオオ
HYUOOOO (WHOOSH)
THE BAR BLEW AWAY...
I'M ALL BURNED UP...
ムク
MUKU (RISE)
バサ
BASA (FLAP)
バサ
BASA
EVEN BIRD WENT BACK TO KOBE...
I GUESS THAT MEANS OUR JOURNEY IS AT AN END.

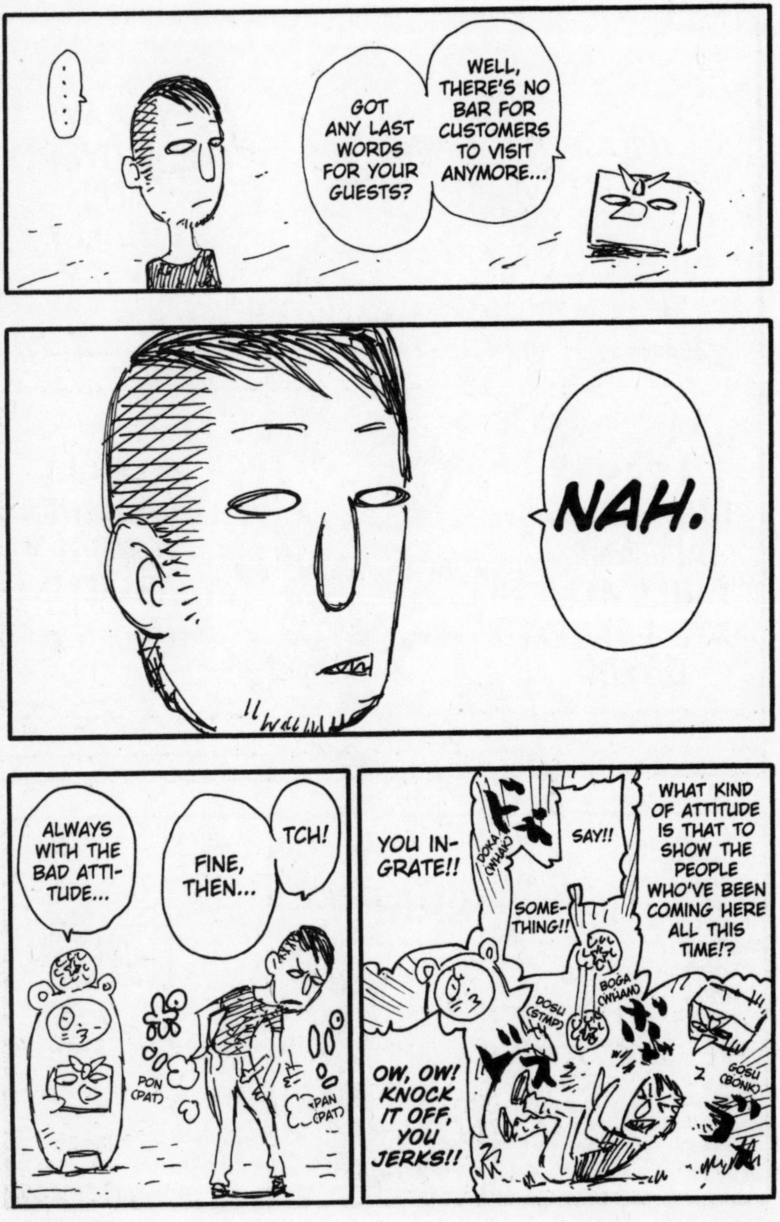
WELL, THERE'S NO BAR FOR CUSTOMERS TO VISIT ANYMORE...
GOT ANY LAST WORDS FOR YOUR GUESTS?
......
NAH.
WHAT KIND OF ATTITUDE IS THAT TO SHOW THE PEOPLE WHO'VE BEEN COMING HERE ALL THIS TIME!?
SAY!!
SOMETHING!!
YOU INGRATE!!
DOKA (WHAK)
BOGA (WHAM)
DOSU (STMP)
GOSU (BONK)
OW, OW! KNOCK IT OFF, YOU JERKS!!
TCH!
FINE, THEN...
ALWAYS WITH THE BAD ATTITUDE...
PON (PAT)
PAN (PAT)

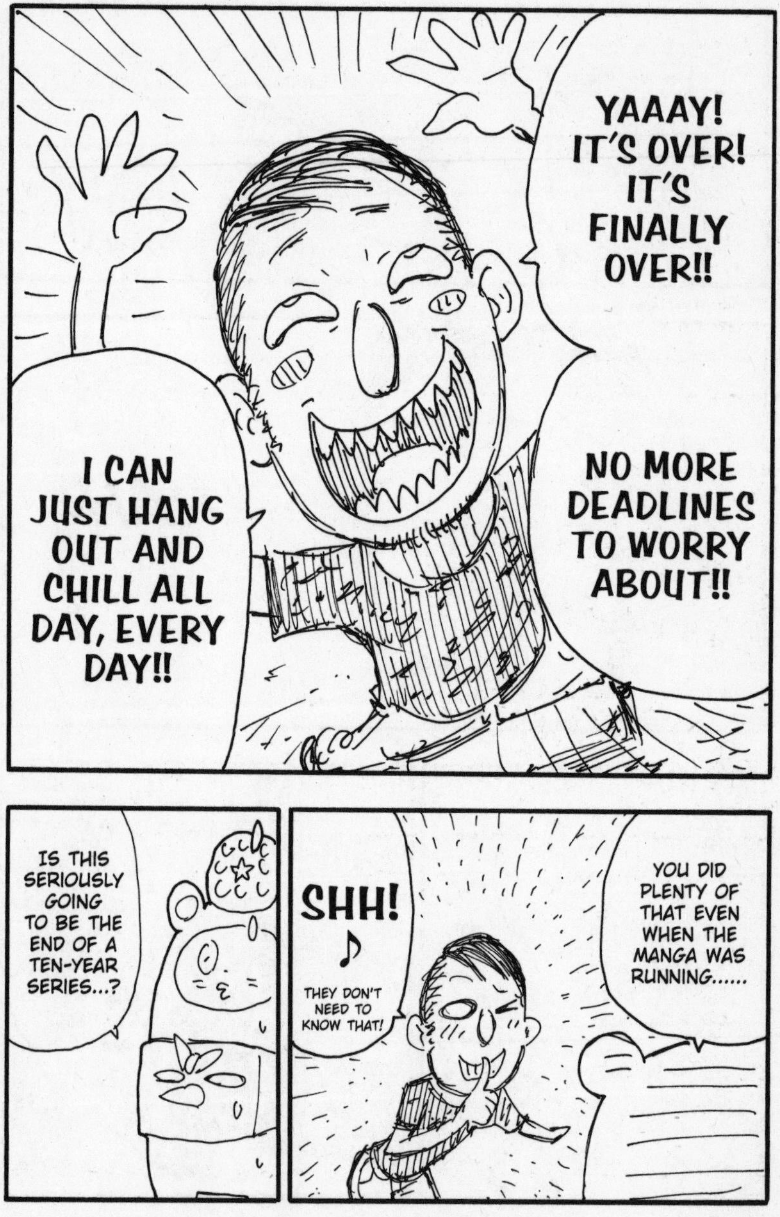
YAAAY! IT'S OVER! IT'S FINALLY OVER!!
NO MORE DEADLINES TO WORRY ABOUT!!
I CAN JUST HANG OUT AND CHILL ALL DAY, EVERY DAY!!
YOU DID PLENTY OF THAT EVEN WHEN THE MANGA WAS RUNNING......
SHH! ♪
THEY DON'T NEED TO KNOW THAT!
IS THIS SERIOUSLY GOING TO BE THE END OF A TEN-YEAR SERIES...?

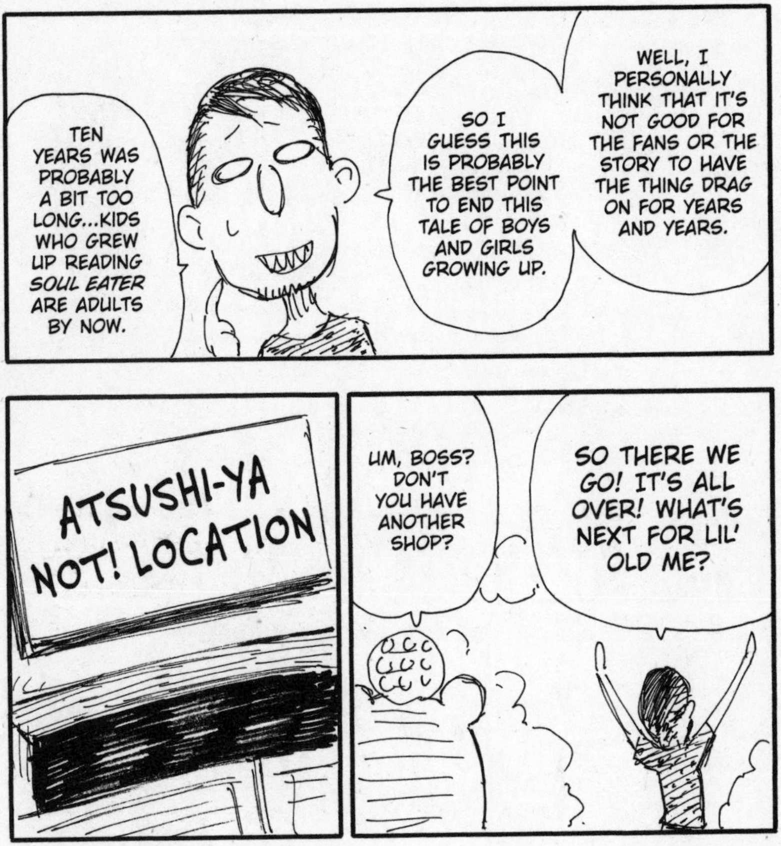
WELL, I PERSONALLY THINK THAT IT'S NOT GOOD FOR THE FANS OR THE STORY TO HAVE THE THING DRAG ON FOR YEARS AND YEARS.
SO I GUESS THIS IS PROBABLY THE BEST POINT TO END THIS TALE OF BOYS AND GIRLS GROWING UP.
TEN YEARS WAS PROBABLY A BIT TOO LONG...KIDS WHO GREW UP READING *SOUL EATER* ARE ADULTS BY NOW.
SO THERE WE GO! IT'S ALL OVER! WHAT'S NEXT FOR LIL' OLD ME?
UM, BOSS? DON'T YOU HAVE ANOTHER SHOP?
ATSUSHI-YA NOT! LOCATION
WHAT!?
ATSUSHI-YA NOT! LOCATION
SOUL EATER'S STILL GOING...

THE END

STAFF

◆ ART STAFF ◆

TAKATOSHI SHIOZAWA

YOSHIKI TONOGAI

TAKUJI KATOU

TOMOYUKI MARU

KAMOME MUKOJIMA

MIKOTO YAMAGUCHI

TOMOO YOKOYAMA

MEIDAI KAWASAKI

YUUSUKE SHIRATO

RYOUSUKE ASAKURA

YOSHITSUNE SASAKI

KANNA

◆ SPECIAL THANKS ◆

HIROSHI TAKATSU

KEIJI ASAKAWA

EDITING

YOSHIAKI YUMURA
(SQUARE ENIX)

AUTHOR

ATSUSHI OHKUBO

PUBLISHER

SQUARE ENIX

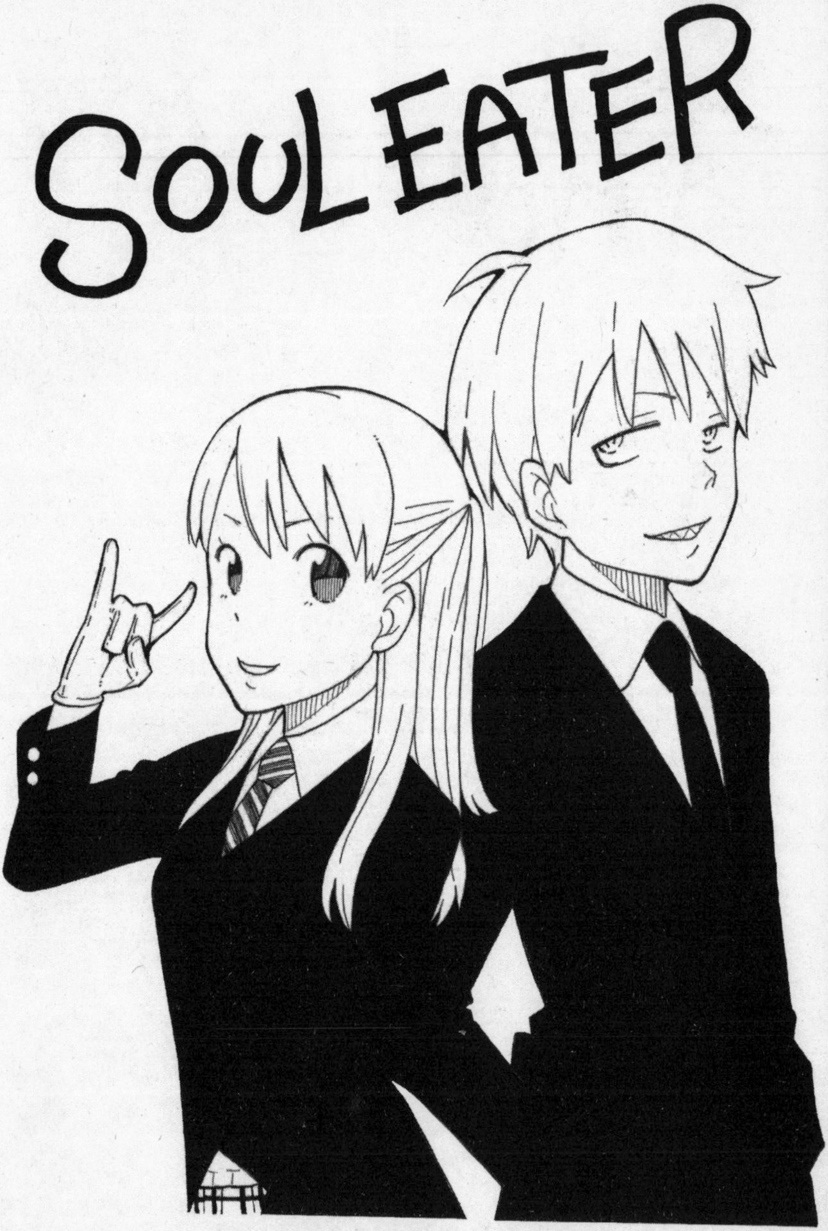
SOUL EATER